Univision, Telemundo, and the Rise of Spanish-Language Television in the United States

Reframing Media, Technology, and Culture in Latin/o America

UNIVISION, TELEMUNDO,
AND THE RISE OF SPANISH-LANGUAGE TELEVISION IN THE UNITED STATES

CRAIG ALLEN

University of Florida Press
Gainesville

Publication of this paperback edition made possible by a Sustaining the Humanities through the American Rescue Plan grant from the National Endowment for the Humanities.

Copyright 2020 by Craig Allen
All rights reserved
Published in the United States of America

First cloth printing, 2020
First paperback printing, 2023

28 27 26 25 24 23   6 5 4 3 2 1

Library of Congress Cataloging-in-Publication Data
Names: Allen, Craig (Craig Mitchell), author.
Title: Univision, Telemundo, and the rise of Spanish-language television in the United States / Craig Allen.
Other titles: Reframing Media, Technology, and Culture in Latin/o America.
Description: Gainesville : University of Florida Press, 2020. | Series: Reframing media, technology, and culture in Latin/o America | Includes bibliographical references and index.
Identifiers: LCCN 2020017646 (print) | LCCN 2020017647 (ebook) | ISBN 9781683401643 (hardback) | ISBN 9781683401919 (pdf) | ISBN 9781683403746 (pbk.)
Subjects: LCSH: Telemundo Group, Inc.—History. | Univisión (Television network)—History. | Spanish television broadcasting—United States—History. | Ethnic television broadcasting—United States—History.
Classification: LCC PN1992.8.E84 A45 2020 (print) | LCC PN1992.8.E84 (ebook) | DDC 384.5506/573—dc23
LC record available at https://lccn.loc.gov/2020017646
LC ebook record available at https://lccn.loc.gov/2020017647

UF PRESS

UNIVERSITY
OF FLORIDA

University of Florida Press
2046 NE Waldo Road
Suite 2100
Gainesville, FL 32609
http://upress.ufl.edu

CONTENTS

List of Figures vii
Acknowledgments. ix
Introduction 1
1. Lone Star Dawn, Mexican Light 15
2. MEX, UHF, and NFL 44
3. Breakout of Spanish International 67
4. The Wages of SIN 88
5. The Golden Age. 106
6. Armageddon 131
7. Univision and Telemundo 153
8. The Perenchio Era 182
9. Final Fight 214
   Conclusion 248
   Appendix 1. Univision Timeline 269
   Appendix 2. Telemundo Timeline 275
   Notes 279
   Bibliography 321
   Index 327

FIGURES

1. Don Emilio Azcárraga Vidaurreta   28
2. Raoul Cortez with Bob Hope in 1946   34
3. Rene Anselmo in 1962   46
4. Emilio Azcárraga Milmo and Emilio Nicolás   64
5. Emilio Nicolás at the opening of the Televisa teleport in 1976   103
6. Emilio Nicolás, Rene Anselmo, and Danny Villanueva in 1983   116
7. Rene Anselmo, SIN chief engineer Robert Porter, and WLTV manager Joaquín Blaya at the Miami Grand Prix in 1986   144
8. Carlos Barba   151
9. The Telemundo studios in Hialeah, Florida   166
10. Univision's studios in Doral, Florida   172
11. Venevisión owner Gustavo Cisneros greets Ray Rodríguez and Mario Rodríguez on their first visit to Caracas in February 1993   191
12. Telemundo founder Saul Steinberg welcomes former Univision president Joaquín Blaya as Telemundo's president in 1992   193
13. First broadcast of *Despierta América*, April 14, 1997   203
14. Cristina Saralegui in 1999   208
15. Mario Kreutzberger with the cast of *Sábado gigante* in Univision's 1999 commemorative photo shoot   209
16. Mario Kreutzberger hosts Emilio Azcárraga Jean at the annual dinner of the Organización Internacional de Teletones in 2012   244
17. Lili Estefan, Mario Rodríguez, and Raúl De Molina at Univision's fiftieth-anniversary festivities in 2012   250

ACKNOWLEDGMENTS

A twelve-year journey through the history of Spanish-language television brought many challenging moments. Yet the most daunting passage is acknowledging the nearly 200 people who in some way helped with the project. The largest number were past and present network and station professionals whose associations with Univision and Telemundo—and frequently with both—steered Spanish-language television through its first fifty years. Their insights during interviews and informal sessions were superseded by their often emphatic encouragement that a scholarly history of Spanish-language television was needed. They made the trek not only possible but enjoyable.

My first gratitude goes to two individuals who are prominent in the account but are no longer with us: Danny Villanueva and Emilio Nicolás. Villanueva was the very first individual I approached. It was he who inspired the transformation of what began as a series of biographical essays into a sustained book-length history. Still friends with colleagues who were major figures in Spanish-language television, Villanueva promised that "we will tee it up." From a former star kicker in the NFL, the wording meant a lot, and he kept his promise.

Not enough acknowledgment can honor the contribution of Emilio Nicolás. I made half a dozen visits to his home in San Antonio and had uncounted follow-up conversations with him. There never was a source on television history whose immense authority was matched by equally vast kindliness and grace. My gratitude extends to his wife Irma Cortez Nicolás, herself a significant historical figure; and to his son Guillermo Nicolás, whose arrangement of historical materials was unsurpassed.

No individual provided more sustaining encouragement and assistance than Mario Rodríguez. Without his steel-trap memory of every significant event during his tenure at Univision and his trove of never-before-researched historical materials, the book could not have been completed.

Several others of historical consequence played roles in bringing the story of Spanish-language television to fruition. Joaquín Blaya generously and often personally shared his many ups and downs as the head of both Univision and Telemundo. Ray Rodríguez, who took time to read parts of the manuscript, was instrumental in sharpening its themes and portrayals. Carlos Barba, who shared knowledge dating to his early days at Channel 47 in New York, affirmed his reputation as Spanish-language television's most entertaining insider.

Other professionals who helped with the project and who are to be particularly thanked include Gustavo Godoy, Ramiro Peña, Carlos Flys, Anita Luera, Fernando López, Jorge Ramos, María Elena Salinas, Alina Falcón, Hector Orcí, Ceril Shagrin, and Doug Darfield.

An inordinate debt is owed to the distinguished scholars who reviewed and directed the manuscript. They included Hector Fernández L'Hoeste and Juan Carlos Rodríguez. I had no greater blessing than to have worked with Felix F. Gutiérrez, who for almost half a century was the foremost authority on Spanish-language mass communication.

I owe a further debt of gratitude to decision makers, colleagues, and friends at Arizona State University. Funding for the project came from a succession of research grants that ASU generously provided. Chris Callahan, dean of the Walter Cronkite School of Journalism and Mass Communication, receives special recognition. Dean Callahan was the first to propose that a history of Spanish-language television be undertaken, and from start to finish, no one more vigorously championed the project.

No part of the project was more enjoyable than working with Stephanye Hunter and the staff at the University of Florida Press.

In addition to those at the press who directly contributed, thank-yous go to the many who helped administer the project. They include Margarita Liply of the National Archives and Records Administration; John Shipley, manager of the Muir Florida Collection at the Miami Library; Karen M. Lugo Ramirez, Isabel López-Machado, and Marcos Avila in Miami; Joan Greenwood and Maria Gutiérrez in Los Angeles; Mónica Talán in New York; and Victoria Eugenia Velez in Phoenix.

Finally, I thank my family, especially Austin Allen, who grew up during the twelve years the book was in progress, for their tolerance, inspiration, and ceaseless kind words.

INTRODUCTION

On the morning of November 13, 2013, a dozen Latino activists converged at a site south of downtown San Antonio. Leaping over a seven-foot steel restraining fence and penetrating a restricted area, they joined hands in a sit-down demonstration. Their issue was not immigration, profiling, or employment discrimination. Kneeling before bulldozers, they were blocking demolition of that which they considered a shrine to Latinos' contribution to the American experience and heritage. They came to fight its conversion to condominiums.

The site was the building that housed the former studios and offices of TV station KWEX. Nearly sixty years old, the structure was aging, unlovely, and recently vacated. But whether they were young or old, Latino or non-Latino, San Antonians who drove by knew it as a cradle of U.S. Spanish-language television. They told stories of risk-takers and pathbreakers who had worked there. "If only the walls could speak," lead protestor Antonia Castañeda said at weeks of public hearings, "they would tell an amazing story."[1]

The walls bore the legacy of an immigrant street peddler-turned-radio proprietor named Raoul Cortez. Imagining Latinos' participation in the new miracle of television, he had built the building in 1955. It was from there that Americans in the United States first saw Spanish-language television. In 1961, his son-in-law Emilio Nicolás helped launch an enterprise that became SIN (Spanish International Network). Fifty years later, it was a cornerstone of U.S. mass communication: the Univision network.

More haunted the protestors. In 1963, President John F. Kennedy passed the TV station the day before his assassination. In 1976, its technicians had relayed the first television programs broadcast by satellite across the United States. It was through the station's control of the network that foreign programs, notably prime-time soap operas called telenovelas, or soap opera–like serials, were telecast across the United States and united immigrants who came to the country after World War II.

By mid-morning on that November day in 2013, throngs of onlookers had congregated. They hung crepe and carried protest signs. Police gathered at the perimeter. The news media arrived. TV reporters readied live shots for the noon news. Everyone knew what the lead would be: A judge had lifted a restraining order, and it was only a matter of time before the police would move inside and order the protestors away.

The noon newscasts commenced. The protestors who were interviewed continued a refrain heard during weeks of public hearings, that their proof of the building's historical significance had fallen on deaf ears. There was no written record of the building's people and events. At the hearings, when Castañeda and others had shown city officials press clippings and faded photographs, the officials had shrugged.

One of the protestors was Andrés Ricardo Morín, who for forty years had been a KWEX weathercaster. He was frustrated that decision-makers regarded the past with "benign neglect." They understood Spanish-language television in the here and now and saw it as significant only because it reached a booming Spanish-speaking population. But Morín saw the station's history as important. "Back in the '60s," he said, a time when people think "there was only CBS, NBC, and ABC," they were "broadcasting from Los Angeles to New York. Immigrants were arriving with Univision on the air to greet to them."[2]

Another protestor who was interviewed, Victor Landa, a longtime KWEX photographer, agreed that "Latino media go back to the founding of the country. But you wouldn't know that, because it's been forgotten, erased from the history books." He added, "There was a time, before Univision became cool, when KWEX was the flagship of Spanish broadcasters across the country, when the Nielsen ratings hardly knew we existed, the sales team would count antennae in the San Antonio barrios [and] the only reason a family had to buy the antennae was to watch Spanish TV. . . . We had huge odds stacked against our success."[3]

Finally, at 2:00 P.M., police told the protestors that they had fifteen minutes to disperse. When eight protestors refused and clashed with officers, they were arrested, handcuffed, and taken away. The bulldozers rolled. By the end of the day, the former building was a pile of rubble.

The protestors were released the next day. But in San Antonio jail cells that night, those dubbed the "Univision 8" reflected on what might have saved the building. According to Morín, it came down to "how much, or how little, officials knew, whether it was just ignorance or indifference to history."[4]

* * *

Not often does passion for the past lead to civil disobedience, arrests, and jailings. But the history of Spanish-language television is not buried in ruins. In San Antonio and other locales, historical records had accumulated. Around the country, living pioneers were awaiting the opportunity to share their memories. The information I have brought together in this book, which includes dusty records and personal testimonies, corroborates the protestors' claim that if it could be collected, the history of Spanish-language television would yield an "amazing story."

What follows is one attempt to piece together the story. It is a standard historical interpretation derived from archive materials, interviews, records, and reportage. It argues that the fact that Spanish-language television rose as "big television" is a unique achievement. The account spans the first fifty years of network Spanish-language television, the period 1961 to 2012. The book explores the founders and pioneers of several enterprises and the events that linked them. One key event was the birth of the second Spanish-language network, Telemundo, which took place midway through the history in 1986. Most of the history traces the emergence of Univision, which began in San Antonio in 1961.

While to many people, Spanish-language television is of limited importance, its history is valuable for enlarging if not changing the concept of how U.S. television developed. For example, few are aware that by the 2000s Univision was equal to ABC, CBS, NBC, and Fox in the number of stations and properties, and sometimes it surpassed all four in the Nielsen ratings. Univision is often the most-viewed source of television in the United States. Fewer are aware that Univision emerged without any of the ingredients historians believe were essential to a national television network, let alone a network destined to frequently have the largest audience. It had no preceding radio network, as did ABC, CBS, and NBC; it had no financing or direction from New York; and it had no studios in Hollywood. Spanish-language television emerged from a different primordial ooze.

One aspect of Spanish-language television that is widely known but that historians have never pondered provides a further illustration: the network operated on an alternative band of television channels known as UHF (for "ultra-high frequency"). Because these channels initially could not be received on all TVs, English-language broadcasters avoided them. Almost all English-language television broadcast on channels 2–13, which were known as "very-high frequency" (VHF). Largely because English-language broadcasters had rejected UHF channels, Spanish-language broadcasters seized on channels 14–83, the UHF channels. Although it is not often acknowledged, UHF underpinned the development of television in the United States. The founders of Spanish-language television grasped that UHF stations, which were available in every U.S. city, could be used to construct a fourth national TV network.

The means of delivering Spanish-language television programs was also a departure, one that was eventually ground-breaking. Lacking the finances to electronically interconnect far-flung UHF stations, SIN perfected one of the marvels of early U.S. television: a system for physically delivering recorded programming from its San Antonio hub to stations as distant as Los Angeles and New York. But the procedure lasted only a few years before Spanish-language television embraced a new technology that was to shape all of U.S. television. In 1976, SIN was the first U.S. broadcaster to deliver programs by satellite.

Spanish-language television's dealings with the Federal Communications Commission had no parallels in the U.S. television experience. The emergence of Spanish-language television brought dealings with the Federal Communications Commission that marked turning points in U.S. broadcast regulation. With a further technical achievement—the design and demonstration of miniature TV transmitters in 1980—parties in Spanish-language television persuaded the FCC to loosen policies and permit "low-power" TV broadcasting. This was the beginning of the FCC's deregulation of television. However, before 1986, the FCC sought to police U.S. broadcasters. In fact, it found that the SIN network had violated rules limiting foreign ownership and revoked its licenses. Only in Spanish-language television did the government put the operators of a television network out of business.

Spanish-language television adds to our knowledge of the development of U.S. television in two other significant ways. First, Spanish-language television internationalized U.S. television. Standard accounts of the history of television do not mention this achievement. Historians' devotion to portraying television as an American invention that transmitted U.S. culture and values all over the world continued to weigh as an international concern. During the UNESCO debates of the 1980s, when representatives of numerous countries assailed the United States for promoting cultural imperialism, among the chief concerns was the spread of U.S. television programming into almost all other countries while Americans did not have the opportunity to watch television programming from other countries. However, it was never true that people in the United States didn't have access to programming from abroad. From the beginning of the television era, programming from other countries was a fixture on Spanish-language television broadcast in the United States.

Spanish-language television's second distinguishing contribution was its proof that television had the power to influence and shape the lives of the families and individuals who watched it. A primary consequence of Spanish-language television was that it persuaded tens of millions of U.S. Latinos to reidentify as different individuals. The United States never had a "Hispanic" population. Latinos living across the United States constitute a tapestry of diverse societies and cultures whose peoples characteristically identify themselves by their country of origin. National Spanish-language television would have been impossible without programming, advertising, and initiatives that merged a multiplicity of nationalities into a single U.S. Latino population.

Spanish-language television created a "Pan Latinidad" on U.S. soil. América Rodríguez first proposed in 1999 the idea of Latinidad as fundamental to the emergence of Univision and Telemundo.[5] Scholars argue that Latinidad congealed when the networks discovered that broadcasting foreign programs that were popular in diverse Spanish-speaking countries abroad could help construct a single Latino population in the United States.[6] As the conclusion to this book details, Pan Latinidad became a primary misgiving among critics of Spanish-language television, who accused Univision and Telemundo of subjugating Latinos' natural identities in favor of a one-size-fits-all "Latino market" that unlocked billions of dollars in profits.

Spanish-language television's reconfiguring of the Latino population clearly is significant. Arguably, it was television's most profound audience effect. As América Rodríguez observes, Latinos "understand themselves as racially and culturally diverse peoples whose primary self-identification is their Latin American nationality, e.g., 'I'm Mexican,' 'I'm Peruvian,' 'I'm Puerto Rican.'"[7] She notes that tens of millions of individuals, notably immigrants who came to the United States directly from their ancestral counties, organized much of their lives around Spanish-language television and argues that Spanish-language television "created" what the United States came to (falsely) know as a "'Hispanic' population."[8]

* * *

The coming of Spanish-language television was complex. Telemundo underwent several iterations after it was founded in 1986 and before it became a sister network to NBC and part of the modern Comcast group. The Univision network is particularly interesting. Founded in 1961, it was the first Spanish-language network and the dominant source of Spanish-language television for fifty years.

Univision did not begin with that name. It was not identified as Univision until 1987. From its inception in 1961 until 1986, it was known as the Spanish International Network (SIN), the only Spanish-language network for twenty-five years. However, SIN was not the only founding entity. There were two others.

One was an organization known as the Spanish International Broadcasting Corporation (SIBC), the corporate overseer of the Spanish International Network. While for the most part SIN and SIBC are treated in the literature on television history as one and the same, there are times when it is important to distinguish between the network and the corporation that owned and administered it. SIBC was the entity that held the network's TV station licenses and was responsible for its dealings with the FCC.

A second important entity in the origins of Univision was the Mexican corporation Televisa. Although little is said about it in U.S. media scholarship, Televisa was and remains a media colossus. It is the largest single television enterprise in the Western Hemisphere. It is identified with Mexico's Azcárraga dynasty; it was founded in 1930 by Don Emilio Azcárraga

Vidaurreta, and his son and grandson have owned and directed it ever since.

Televisa has always been the world's largest producer of Spanish-language television programming. Propelled by telenovelas, a program genre it invented in 1952, Televisa's productions instantly were popular all over the world. Azcárraga Vidaurreta was the first to envision a Spanish-language television network in the United States. He foresaw a network of U.S. television stations that could extend the Televisa network north of the border and imbue U.S. airwaves with his globally popular Spanish-language shows. He was the founder of the "Spanish International" venture that constituted SIN and SIBC.

Like the formation of SIN and SIBC in the United States, Televisa's origins in Mexico were complicated. Televisa was not known by that name until 1973; originally, it was known as Telesistema Méxicano. The network had many founders. The San Antonio protestors celebrated Raoul Cortez (1905–1971) and Emilio Nicolás (1930–2019). Before he founded the first full-time Spanish-language television station, KCOR, in San Antonio in 1955, Cortez founded the first Spanish-language radio station, also KCOR, in 1946. Nicolás, his son-in-law, began as a scientist. He assisted Albert Sabin in the development of a polio vaccine approved in 1955 and became one of the first authorities on arteriosclerosis. In 1961, he agreed to manage his father-in-law's television station and became the central figure in the events that brought about the launch of SIN.

Don Emilio Azcárraga Vidaurreta (1890–1972) was the patriarch of Mexican radio and television and one of Mexico's most revered historical figures. In 1930, in Mexico City, Azcárraga Vidaurreta founded and presided over the broadcast empire that was known as Telesistema Méxicano during his time. Soon after entering television in 1951, he imported the first "TV novelas," or telenovelas, from radio. This genre became a focal point of SIN's and later Univision's development. Azcárraga Vidaurreta partnered with a U.S. Latino entertainment entrepreneur to incorporate SIBC with a charter in Delaware. With additional U.S. partners, Azcárraga Vidaurreta negotiated the purchase of Cortez's San Antonio television station and birthed the Spanish International Network. SIN and SIBC began as subsidiaries of Azcárraga's Telesistema Méxicano.[9]

Frank Fouce Sr. (1900–1962) was the U.S. entrepreneur Azcárraga Vidaurreta partnered with. Fouce was the original chair of SIBC and the first head of SIN. His chief contribution was his licensing of KMEX in Los

Angeles, where he lived. KMEX reached one million Latinos. Its contribution not only legitimized SIN but also eventually provided two-thirds of SIN's revenues. It shored up the network during years of troubled financial affairs. Fouce Sr. died one month after SIN's inception and before KMEX signed on in September 1962.

Reynold "Rene" Anselmo (1926–1995) was raised in Boston and educated at the University of Chicago. In 1952, Anselmo moved to Mexico. He joined Telesistema, where he became a protégé of Azcárraga Vidaurreta. When Fouce Sr. died in 1962, Anselmo became the president of SIN. Eclectic, provocative, and flamboyant, Anselmo guided SIN through numerous crises. He expanded SIN to the New York market in 1968, then to its eventual hub of Miami in 1971, in effect nationalizing Spanish-language television. He headed Spanish International throughout its twenty-five-year duration; he left when it reorganized as Univision in 1986.

Emilio Azcárraga Milmo (1930–1997), the elder Azcárraga's son, succeeded his father as head of Telesistema when Don Emilio passed in 1972. Like his father a much-recalled Mexican personage, he was active in the inception, ownership, and direction of his father's U.S. TV venture. He had close ties with Anselmo and, after 1972, the figure in Mexico City Anselmo answered to. Azcárraga Milmo is best known for a merger in 1972 with a Monterrey, Mexico, firm that was at the forefront of satellite technology. The merger led to his reorganization in 1973 of Telesistema as Televisa (Television Via Satellite) and groundbreaking initiatives in global satellite communication.

Frank Fouce Jr. (1927–2013) inherited part ownership of Spanish International when his father died in 1962. He objected when Azcárraga Vidaurreta named Anselmo as president. When Fouce, a lawyer, voiced questions about Anselmo's flamboyancy and fitness as president, the two became locked in a feud. Fouce Jr. remained both the lead U.S. owner and the official chair of Spanish International. Yet because the elder Azcárraga enforced Anselmo's authority, Fouce Jr. withdrew into an absentee role, over the years tormenting Anselmo nevertheless. Their feud, which continued for twenty-five years, culminated in a lawsuit Fouce Jr. filed in 1976 that led to SIN's reorganization as Univision and the end of Anselmo's reign.

Many others shaped Spanish-language television and became important figures in U.S. television. One was Danny Villanueva (1937–2015), one of the first Latino players in the National Football League. After performing in the NFL's famed Ice Bowl in 1967, Villanueva retired from sports. Eventually he became the head of KMEX, a post he held for many years. He was an originator of Spanish-language television news, which later was a key element of SIN's expansion.

Another athlete, Carlos Barba (b. 1935), a former New York Yankees recruit who became a broadcaster, foresaw and helped accomplish the launch of Telemundo in 1987. At the time Barba became a founder of Telemundo, Joaquín Blaya (b. 1946) was seeking to change the course of Spanish-language television. As president of Univision, Blaya championed the network's independence from Televisa by initiating the first major U.S.-produced Spanish-language network programs. Blaya was the founding parent of what came to be known as "domestic production" in Spanish-language television.

There was no larger figure in Spanish-language television than "the most important person in Hollywood no one ever knew"—A. Jerrold "Jerry" Perenchio (1930–2017), a protégé of Hollywood agent Lew Wasserman.[10] Perenchio, who was known for his refusal to appear in public or talk to the press, owned Univision from 1992 to 2007. Before 1992, he was one of the most influential figures in English-language television, although his role was known only to insiders and he kept his name off the credits. In the 1970s, Perenchio developed a progression of programs that changed TV and U.S. society, including *All in the Family*.

Aware he could out-deal anyone in television, Perenchio was determined to bring Spanish-language television into TV's major leagues. Out-dealing Azcárraga Milmo in a sweetheart programming agreement in 1992, he prevailed in his quest to make Spanish-language television "big television." In a culminating stride, Perenchio brought Univision to parity with ABC, CBS, NBC, and Fox in terms of approximate number of viewers, advertising revenue, number of stations, and amount of infrastructure.

* * *

Some of the literature on the history of U.S. television tells part of the history of Spanish-language television. The authors of those works noted both of the two effects—the globalization of U.S. television and the binding of Latinos of diverse nationalities—that were chief consequences of Spanish-language television. For example, América Rodríguez's reconstruction of

Spanish-language broadcasters' evolving concept of U.S. Latinos as a single marketable audience is what led her to propose the idea of "Pan Latinidad" in 1999.[11]

In 1979, Félix Gutiérrez's essay "México's Television Network in the United States: The Case of Spanish International Network" was the first work to call attention to SIN's rise as the fourth coast-to-coast television network in the United States. It was also the first work to show that from the time SIN premiered in 1961, U.S. viewers had seen programming that consisted almost entirely of foreign content. Thus, contrary to experts' perception of a one-way flow of U.S. content to other countries, U.S. television in fact had been shaped by a flow of non-U.S. content from Mexico and Latin America into the United States.

Gutiérrez noted that by 1979, far ahead of the English-language U.S. networks, Televisa had not only embraced satellite communication but was using its Mexico City uplinks to feed programs to SIN and reach audiences across the United States. Through Televisa's satellite linkages, U.S. viewers witnessed broadcasts that originated in countries all over the world. Foreshadowing eventual confrontation, Gutiérrez questioned whether Televisa's control of SIN might run afoul of FCC regulations.[12]

Other histories appeared in book chapters written by Frederic Subervi-Vélez and John Sinclair in the 1990s. They told more of the history of the origin of SIN. They established that Azcárraga Vidaurreta had founded and financed SIN as an instrument Telesistema Méxicano could use to facilitate program distribution in the United States. Additionally, these authors were the first to introduce some of the founders and spearheads of U.S. Spanish-language television.[13]

But the full history of SIN was not known until 2006, when archivists at the National Archives and Records Administration opened several boxes of previously unseen records of the lawsuit Frank Fouce Jr. filed in 1976. Known as the "SIN Case," it concluded in 1986. The ten-year legal proceeding was the event that ended Spanish International, dispatched Anselmo, and marked the advent of Univision under new owner, Hallmark Cards. As part of the case, lawyers and FCC personnel reconstructed much of the early history of Spanish-language television.

The SIN materials provided a history through 1986. But there the trail stopped. Telemundo began the next year. The more recent period of that history began with the tenure of U.S. TV giant Jerry Perenchio, who became the owner of Univision in 1992. It was Perenchio who made Spanish-language television big television.

Perenchio's presence at Univision posed an insurmountable obstacle. He enforced secrecy about all of his dealings. Many researchers had gone to Univision requesting cooperation in historical studies but were denied. In fact, Perenchio fired Univision employees who spoke to reporters, writers, and authors.

In 2006, the trail reopened. That year, Perenchio sold the network to Haim Saban. In 2008, Saban ended Perenchio's restrictions. Chief Executive Officer Joe Uva and President Cesar Conde permitted access to Univision's materials. For the first time, the historical record included interviews with long-silenced Univision personnel. Among them were two authorities on the Perenchio years who were also Spanish-language television's greatest celebrities, Mario Kreutzberger, who for fifty-three years hosted a program called *Sábado gigante,* and his protégé, talk-show host Cristina Saralegui. The trail soon led to Mario Rodríguez, who had been a Univision president during the Perenchio years. Rodríguez not only kept records, but he knew where the Perenchio-era skeletons were buried.

Today, the trail is well open to researchers. The Guillermo Nicolás Collection in San Antonio holds papers and effects of Raoul Cortez, Guillermo Nicolás's grandfather, and Emilio Nicolás, his father. In the home of the late Danny Villanueva in Camarillo, California, are records that uncover one of the story's key episodes: the police killing of KMEX news director Rubén Salazar. Papers kept by Carlos Barba in Miami trace Barba's direction of New York station WNJU and how this led to the founding of Telemundo, which had begun much earlier in Puerto Rico.

* * *

A cornerstone of modern mass communication, Univision began as an outlaw firm on U.S. turf in 1961 because Azcárraga Vidaurreta faced a nightmare scenario in Mexico. As is recounted in chapter 1, responding to public contempt of his monopolization and Americanization of Mexican mass media, the government considered nationalizing Azcárraga's properties. The threat ended when Azcárraga announced a Mexican network in the United States.

Chapter 1 pieces together a scheme by which the elder Azcárraga had Anselmo, a U.S. citizen, falsely pose as majority owner of Spanish International. The elder Azcárraga introduced into the United States the Mexican custom of *presta nombre*, by which individuals anonymously conduct business under someone else's identity. U.S. firms had long used the practice to disguise their ownership of businesses chartered in Mexico. Anselmo, who was an Azcárraga employee, lent the elder Azcárraga his name.

For the twenty-five years it was known as Spanish International, the venture violated America's foreign ownership rule. Chapter 6 relates the first full account of the "SIN Case," in which the FCC acted after twenty-five years, during which a Mexican broadcaster had controlled part of U.S. broadcasting. While the commission had known of the irregularity since 1978, it declined to respond until a legal challenge was filed. The result was a landmark in media regulation. The FCC revoked the licenses of Spanish International's stations, and, in an event witnessed neither before nor since, a TV network was handed the "death penalty." A company that owned a television network was stripped of its licenses and owners.

But creating a national network in the years before cable TV required tremendous financial resources. Stations and infrastructure cost tens of millions of dollars. In the 1960s, Latino endeavors in U.S. had nothing approaching that level of resources. There would have been no Univision were it not for a scheme that developed in 1966. As chapter 3 recounts, the billionaire elder Azcárraga, who was aghast when his son and associates wanted to terminate SIN, secreted some of his personal fortune into the United States and laundered it to ensure that the U.S. network would survive. Chapters 2, 3, and 4 recount Anselmo's maneuvers to free SIN of millions of dollars of programming fees it owed Televisa.

Historians of early television are aware that money alone was not enough to establish a network. In the 1950s, in most cities, the FCC had made available only three commercial TV channels on the VHF band, licensing them to broadcasters whose stations were affiliated with ABC, CBS, or NBC. Historians recall the collapse of the DuMont network in 1955 because it demonstrated that a fourth network was impossible in the 1950s because ABC, CBS, and NBC had captured seemingly the only available channels. Despite the FCC's opening of UHF channels after the television freeze and expectations that a fourth network would flourish, DuMont failed largely because the predominance of UHF stations in that network could not compete against the VHF stations ABC, CBS, and NBC had already claimed.[14]

However, this was not the case. Despite Dumont's failure, there was means for a fourth network in 1961: the many channels that were available on the UHF band. As chapters 1 and 2 show, although UHF had impediments, Spanish-language television was significant for figures who were the only early broadcasters who actively confronted and surmounted them.

Thus, while early UHF is perceived to have failed, it didn't. Spanish-language television burgeoned on UHF. These chapters shed new light on 1960s FCC chair Newton Minow. His true accomplishment was his early vision of a multi-channel television universe on UHF, one that would permit a pursuit such as Spanish-language television. Minow's successful 1962 campaign for a congressional act that made UHF available to all viewers who purchased new TVs laid the groundwork for Univision's eventual rise as a TV network that was the equal of ABC, CBS, and NBC.

How could there have been nationwide Spanish-language television in the United States where Spanish-speaking individuals there are so diverse? Opportunity beckoned from the source of the Azcárragas' might: abundant TV programming tailored for global distribution. Televisa's programs had long captivated viewers in every Spanish-speaking country. It became evident to many that once they were released north of the border, these programs would enthrall Spanish speakers from diverse origins who resided in the United States.

Chapter 3 recounts a make-or-break episode in the history of Univision. In 1968, the Spanish International Network ventured beyond its home in the U.S. Southwest and entered New York. Against many warnings of failure, Anselmo was preparing to a reach a Caribbean-descended audience with the Azcárragas' variety, music, and sports programs. Yet an assistant, Carole Bird, proposed a seemingly absurd solution: abandon the varied programs and show only Televisa's telenovelas during prime time. She knew that the Azcárragas' telenovelas were wildly popular in Caribbean locales and in every Spanish-speaking country.

The rest is history. The telenovela not only went on to define U.S. Spanish-language television. Broadcasts of epic telenovelas such as *María la del barrio*, *El privilegio de amar*, and *Betty la fea* attracted tens of millions of viewers as chapters 8 and 9 recount.

* * *

Volumes have been written on the history of television. One more here may seem to have come at an awkward time. As will be shown in the conclusion, Spanish-language television and all of U.S. television encountered the juggernaut of digital communication that ended the age of big TV.

Yet there may be no better time to test the four-part thesis television historians propose (or assume) about the history of U.S. television: that it reached from New York to Middle America; that it had two founding parents, David Sarnoff and William Paley; that it had three founding institutions, ABC, CBS, and NBC, whose classic and memorable programs were epochal; and that its news programs were significant in public affairs because of two people, Edward R. Murrow and Walter Cronkite, who personified the ideal that journalists engage in a universal quest for truth and objectivity. Another part of this narrative is the belief that U.S. television drew strength from its harmonious relationship with the FCC.

The new post–TV age history of television raises questions about whether this thesis was ever correct and complete. Was U.S. television really a fortress of U.S. enterprise and Middle American values? Did the FCC really safeguard such a fortress? Were there really three original networks? Was television journalism really founded on one standard of objectivity? Were the effects of U.S. television really only the ones that Marshall McLuhan conjured?[15] Is the story of U.S. television really only the story of English-language television?

The story of Spanish-language television affirms that by amassing the largest sectors of the U.S. population, making them eyewitnesses to national and world events for the first time, and providing both a source of entertainment and an anchor to popular culture, television did change the United States in the last half of the twentieth century. But in their San Antonio jail cells, the Univision 8 were not pondering revisionist television history. They were grieving the loss of a symbol of big television that stood for Latino pride, empowerment, and accomplishment. They posed a question that transcends television and mass communication: in an English-speaking country, how could a Spanish-language institution have emerged and prevailed against all odds? This book offers some answers to their question.

1

LONE STAR DAWN, MEXICAN LIGHT

Don Emilio Azcárraga Vidaurreta grew up believing that the Mexican-U.S. border was not a barrier but an imaginary line on a map. Born in 1895, he was raised in an extended family whose members settled and thrived in northeast Mexico. Helped by its customs occupations and businesses, the region boomed. Its main city of Monterrey was the gateway for U.S. companies seeking opportunities in Latin America. Azcárraga's father was a customs agent, and Don Emilio had watched the first exchange of commerce and fortune between the two nations: at his boyhood home of Piedras Negras, east of the river's big bend, where the terrain split at Eagle Pass, the Mexican and the U.S. railroad systems joined at the Rio Grande.

At the age of twelve, Azcárraga became a U.S. resident, attending middle school in San Antonio. After he completed high school in Austin in 1912, he worked in a shoe store during the day and attended classes at St. Edwards College at night. However, within a year he abandoned college and returned to Mexico: inspired by his success in his day job, his sights were set on forming his first business.

His start came when his sales receipts multiplied from pitching customers a line of Boston-made shoes. Toying with a plan that would allow him to return to Mexico, the eighteen-year-old traveled to Boston to meet the manufacturer. He praised the firm's shoes and insisted that it could expand its clientele by selling them throughout Mexico, a project he was eager to undertake. A warehouse in Monterrey was available. He knew customs protocols and where the railroads led. But he asked for one condition: that the Boston firm not sell shoes in Mexico through any other distributor. The young Azcárraga succeeded and won the exclusive rights to sell the shoes in Mexico.[1]

Azcárraga's first enterprise led to his first tenet of successful entrepreneurship: do business without competition. Settling in Monterrey in 1913, he founded a nationwide shoe distributorship. Its several years of profits prompted a second venture. This time, Azcárraga approached the Ford Motor Company. In 1922, Ford licensed him as its exclusive northeast Mexico dealer.[2] Azcárraga formed ninety-five businesses during his career. Except for one—television—they all had a common feature: they all began as monopolies.[3]

His next venture took him into broadcasting. In 1924, the Victor Corporation awarded Azcárraga the exclusive right to sell its Victor Talking Machine in Mexico. He moved to Mexico City. There, he contracted with almost all of Mexico's prominent singers and entertainers and founded a recording company called Mexico Music. Aware that Azcárraga's artists could boost phonograph sales, Victor executive and pioneer record producer Ralph Peer proposed that Victor and Mexico Music merge.[4]

But Azcárraga's interest had shifted from automobiles and phonographs to a different invention. The radio age had begun, and his brother had launched Monterrey's first radio station. Azcárraga was fascinated. A fortuitous event took him back to the United States. U.S. broadcast pioneer David Sarnoff recently had founded the Radio Corporation of America (RCA). In 1926, Sarnoff and RCA formed the National Broadcasting Company (NBC). At nearly the same time, Sarnoff arranged for RCA to acquire Victor. RCA Victor needed Azcárraga's Mexico Music.

In 1928, Sarnoff invited Azcárraga to New York. Sarnoff admired his fluent English, genial personality, and entrepreneurial promise. Sarnoff convinced Azcárraga to sell Mexico Music to RCA. Pledging to give Azcárraga good prices on RCA's transmitting and studio apparatus, Sarnoff partnered with him to launch a nationwide radio system in Mexico.[5]

Azcárraga had another backer: his wife. Mexico was suffering economically. Its five million homes were scattered in a poor country in an area one-third the size of the United States. There were no telephone lines that could feed programs to radio stations. In many cities, there were no radio stations. The expense of building the infrastructure that a national network required was more than Azcárraga could handle on his own.

He had married Laura Milmo in 1920. She had been born into an affluent family that owned banks, railroads, and mines. However, during the 1920s, the family's holdings were at risk. Mexico was reeling from the years of bloodshed and assassinations that followed its 1910 revolution. After insurgents who had plunged Mexico into civil war had forced a new constitution in 1917 calling for reforms and General Alvaro Obregón consolidated control, Obregón asserted his authority to confiscate farms and businesses and redistribute wealth. In these circumstances, a business that was so new that it was safe from nationalization may have seemed like a good bet, and Azcárraga was able to persuade the Milmos to redirect their fortune into radio.[6]

* * *

In early 1930, Azcárraga acquired two radio stations, one in Monterrey, the other in Mexico City. That summer, he assembled a large group of musicians, entertainers, and announcers. On September 19, he launched Mexico's first national broadcast network from an art deco structure that resembled Sarnoff's Radio City.[7] He named it XEW. Azcárraga convinced the government to permit it to transmit at 200,000 watts, which made it four times more powerful than the strongest stations in the United States. Its vast reach overcame the absence of interconnecting telephone lines. Affiliates rebroadcast the XEW signal from Hermosillo in the distant northwest to Mérida on the Yucatan Peninsula. XEW reached far beyond Mexico's southern border, and artists from throughout Latin America gravitated to it. Azcárraga soon had a corner on the Latin American entertainment market.

But Azcárraga realized that his success would depend on the Mexican government, which licensed XEW and all other stations. He wasted little time commencing a lifelong pursuit, courting government officials. His timing could not have been better. Mexico's first national political party, the Partido Revolucionario Institucional (PRI), had formed in 1929. Vowing to bring about democratic reforms and end years of political discord, the PRI claimed sole control of the Mexican government.

Azcárraga did more than fraternize with the new party's founders; he became a founding member.[8] He offered party leaders an instrument for consolidating one-party rule and received virtually every radio license.[9] As his biographer Alexander Olmos observed, Azcárraga placed "the foundations of a rising Mexico on his vision . . . of modern mass media." Because PRI officials believed Azcárraga's claim that mass communication was a key to unlocking economic and social development, Azcárraga rose as a "key personage of Mexico during this period."[10]

His newest monopoly was destined to be an empire. Hastening to add stations in every city and town, he completed the XEW network in 1935. By then, he had realized that his fortune was tied to his relationship with Sarnoff. Sarnoff partnered with Azcárraga knowing that a Mexican network would be an ideal stage for U.S. firms that wanted to sell their products in Latin America. Brokering deals and sharing the proceeds with Azcárraga, Sarnoff and NBC delivered a bounty of U.S. advertising to XEW.

Sarnoff's rival, CBS chair William Paley, was also studying opportunities south of the border. After the government granted Azcárraga a second powerful Mexico City station, XEQ, he met with Paley. The result was a second partnership, this time with CBS. Azcárraga launched a second network, XEQ, in 1938.

Azcárraga became a billionaire. Each year, NBC and CBS directed tens then hundreds of millions of dollars in U.S. advertising into Mexico and into Azcárraga's coffers.[11] In 1944, he bought out Mexico's scattered film producers one by one and founded one of the world's largest film-making companies, Churubusco Studios.[12]

His only son, Emilio Azcárraga Milmo, who had been born in 1930, watched Azcárraga build this media juggernaut. Unlike his self-made and affable father, the son was "a character full of contradictions" who was "obsessed with control."[13] His mother pampered him. But his father, dismayed by Emilio's fondness for horses, cars, and movie stars, did not extend a loving embrace. To toughen him up, Azcárraga sent Emilio to the Culver Military Academy in Indiana. After dropping out, the son grudgingly accepted his father's offer of a trainee sales post.[14] On the eve of Azcárraga's move into television, the two came together because the son needed a job and the father needed an heir to a billion-dollar corporation.

* * *

U.S. Spanish-language television was sown from the seeds of Azcárraga's only defeat. In 1946, he submitted a plan for Mexican television. It called for the construction of three national networks from three key stations in Mexico City he would own. But the year ended with a transforming election. Incoming president Miguel Alemán Valdés reorganized Mexico's

Department of Communication and named a commission to consider Azcárraga's plan. The commission ordered a delay so it could plan how TV would expand.¹⁵ Azcárraga was not deterred. In 1949, confident that the government would consent to his control of television in Mexico, he broke ground on a television facility that he named Televicentro. By 1955, it had become one of the largest TV facilities housed in one location in the world.¹⁶

A year later, Azcárraga was stunned when President Alemán Valdés awarded the first TV license to industrialist Rómulo O'Farrill, one of his associates. It was O'Farrill, not Azcárraga, who founded Mexican television. Television was seen there for the first time in 1950, when O'Farrill launched Channel 4. Azcárraga did not even get the second license; Alemán Valdés gave Channel 5 to inventor and party loyalist Guillermo González Camarena. It launched in 1952. The president kept a controlling interest in Channel 5 for himself. Azcárraga did receive the third license, and he launched XEW Channel 2 on March 15, 1951. He was facing competition for the first time.¹⁷

Azcárraga's setback was not unforeseen. O'Farrill was popular with PRI officials because he had begun automobile production in Mexico and had backed the construction of the Pan-American Highway both politically and financially. He had recently founded an independent radio station, XEX, and had acquired the newspaper *Novedades*. While Azcárraga and O'Farrill lobbied Alemán Valdés for the TV licenses, the third figure, González Camarena, a noted pioneer in television technology, headed the presidential committee that studied the arrangement and allocation of TV licenses and made the final recommendations.

González Camarena was the inventor of color television. In 1934, at age seventeen, González Camarena invented color TV, using mechanical disks that spun behind a TV screen to render black-and-white pictures in color. He obtained the world's first patent for color TV in 1942. Four years later, in a Mexico City, he staged the first experiment in continuous color transmission in a broadcast from his lab. NASA later used González Camarena's system to transmit color telecasts of Apollo moon landings and from probes in deep space that traveled beyond Pluto.¹⁸

In 1947, Alemán Valdés named González Camarena to the commission that was charged with recommending a plan for initiating Mexican television. González Camarena did not want a single owner to control Mexican television and argued that the new media would best be facilitated by adoption of a competitive system like that in the United States. Largely on the word of the esteemed inventor, Alemán Valdés agreed to a competitive system.[19]

Another thing worked against Azcárraga. Alemán Valdés was the first Mexican president who did not wear a military uniform. He was a populist who had awakened the PRI to distresses the party had not addressed. Even under the new government, Mexico remained 70 percent poor, 60 percent subsistent on family farms, 40 percent illiterate, and 20 percent unemployed.[20] He proposed that the PRI shift its priorities from land reform to industrialization. Two parts of the plan discomforted the party and the public. Industrialization meant a fortification of big business, and that meant that it was likely that U.S. companies would make inroads in the Mexican economy.

While Azcárraga was a hero for providing radio to a poor country, his accumulation of wealth and his control of Mexican mass media had left him vulnerable to allegations that he was not in touch with the needs of the Mexican people and was content to have Mexico overrun by U.S. corporations. He was partnered with NBC and CBS, and radio ads on his stations promoted the products of U.S. firms.

Azcárraga reacted. In a series of speeches and appearances, he portrayed himself as the loyal Mexican that changing policies and politics demanded. He emphasized that the new medium, a "great patriotic endeavor," would put "Mexico at the vanguard of television."[21] In 1950, he wrote an article for Mexico's largest magazine about the opening of Televicentro that said that he and the facility were "at the service of the people of Mexico."[22]

He backed the claim. Televicentro became a factory dedicated to the production and distribution of Mexican programs. It housed ten studios. A warehouse dubbed "the vault" stored every production. Similar to XEW radio, XEW Channel 2 teemed with native Mexican producers, creators, actors, and crew.

In 1952, viewers flocked to Channel 2 to watch *Ángeles de la calle* (Angels of the Street), the first telenovela. The show's producers had adapted a popular prime-time radio soap opera for television. However, the first TV novela and those that followed were not about Mexico. Azcárraga conceived the genre as one of generic settings and universal themes. He instructed writers and actors to develop a "standard Mexican Spanish" devoid of dialect.[23] A star-studded variety show, *La Hora de Paco Malgesto*, and its host, Paco Malgesto, became the first fixtures of Mexican TV. XEW quickly fit its moniker of Canal de las Estrellas (Channel of the Stars).

Although it was trivial at the time, another development revealed Azcárraga's attention to his public image. In January 1952, a brash 26-year-old who was between jobs arrived at his office unannounced. The U.S. expatriate actor was a comedic ex-marine with a Boston accent and a college degree. Azcárraga agreed to see him. As the intruder often later said, "This legendary man showed me in" and "treated me like a son." Azcárraga told the guest he, Azcárraga, would win admiration "if he did business in the United States." Noting that no Mexican TV producer had entered the U.S. market, he said that his idea was "syndicating [his] shows on American television." To do this, "he felt he needed an American he could trust."[24] Azcárraga hired the visitor, who was named Reynold V. "Rene" Anselmo. Anselmo was of Italian, not Latino, origin. He had not worked in television and barely spoke Spanish. But he agreed to start as a production trainee.

The competition between Azcárraga, O'Farrill, and Camarena lasted four years. Azcárraga bested them in an essential yet politically dangerous pursuit. He instituted U.S. advertising, enlarging his pipeline of U.S. revenue from radio to TV. His rivals lacked such a pipeline. Camarena's Channel 5 and, more conspicuously, O'Farrill's Channel 4 resorted to broadcasting cheaply obtained U.S. shows dubbed in Spanish. In contrast, Azcárraga's Channel 2 was prized for its many hours of native programming, and few objected to his U.S. sponsorships.

At an opportune moment, Azcárraga became a hero again. Alemán Valdés's term as president came to an end in December 1952. The new president, Adolfo Ruíz Cortines, continued Alemán Valdés's policies of promoting big business in order to shore up Mexico's middle class. Ruíz Cortines set a new national priority: that television broadcasts would be available in every Mexican home. He was convinced that only Azcárraga had the financing and expertise to construct television stations in cities across the country and interconnect them so they could provide nationwide delivery of television programs. Just two years after XEW signed on in 1951, his TV network was broadcasting to half of the Mexican population.[25]

On June 7, 1955, Ruíz Cortines announced that the rival networks had merged to form a new corporation called Telesistema Méxicano.[26] Ruíz Cortines declared a national holiday, "Freedom of the Press Day." At a public ceremony, Ruíz Cortines introduced Azcárraga as president and

O'Farrill as vice president. Azcárraga again presented his vision of television as "our definitive enterprise."[27]

Although he was president of the new corporation, Azcárraga had not fully restored his monopoly. While the PRI permitted the merger, it invoked a state charter that required Telesistema to stimulate domestic development and to promote a reversal of U.S. influence. Accordingly, Telesistema was to complete all three Mexican TV networks, Channels 2, 4, and 5, by 1963 and to initiate a phaseout of U.S. programs and advertising. At any time, Mexico's Department of Communication could conduct a review. If Telesistema was found unfit, the government could revoke the charter and nationalize the company.

Azcárraga was frustrated by the contradictory conditions of the charter: he could not build out three networks while sustaining the loss of U.S. revenue. Advertising from Mexico's small business sector might support one network, but not three. However, Azcárraga had a plan. He knew that television was about to explode throughout Latin America and in Spain and other countries with Spanish-speaking populations. He knew that owners of television stations in these countries were struggling to pay for infrastructure and could not afford to produce original programming. This was why he had recorded and stockpiled the programs Telesistema aired. He had looked ahead to a project devoted to international sales and distribution and, in turn, to Telesistema's rise as a global corporation.

Because Azcárraga now needed the revenue, that project's time had come. Just weeks after the merger, in September 1955, he launched a Telesistema export subsidiary under the name Teleprogramas de Mexico. Azcárraga had handpicked two people to lead the operation: his son as the president and Rene Anselmo as the company's director.

Anselmo had been born in 1926 to a working-class family in Medford, Massachusetts; his father was the postmaster of Bedford, Massachusetts. While his teachers recalled his high marks in school, Anselmo remembered the pranks he had pulled. In one particularly significant prank, an under-aged Anselmo, determined to fight in World War II rather than finish school, "forgot" his birth certificate and fooled marine recruiters. Later, he rarely spoke of his forty missions as a marine corps aerial gunner and the decorations he received. Many believed that his later affection for disrupting authority could be traced to a confidence from having survived combat forty times.

Anselmo believed that his formative experience came after the war while he was an English major at the University of Chicago. Struggling to become an actor, he invented a way to get himself on stage: he founded the forerunner of Chicago's Second City theatre group. He had mixed success as an improvisational comedian, but he found that he excelled at running the theatre's front office. At an early age, he became an accomplished entertainment entrepreneur.

Then, suddenly, he quit. In 1951, inspired by Jack Kerouac's book *On the Road,* Anselmo drifted to Mexico. As he later told the story, he was in the southwest Mexico city of Taxco when he found himself in a bar with a former classmate who worked at XEW. Over drinks, his friend shared the Azcárraga legend. It was then that Anselmo decided to go unannounced to Azcárraga's office.[28]

Anselmo fascinated Azcárraga, who frequently conversed with him. Anselmo suspected that he was being positioned to help groom Azcárraga's pampered son Emilio. They were nearly the same age, but Anselmo's résumé had shown initiative and wit, while Emilio Azcárraga's had not.

Only months after joining as a production trainee, Anselmo had an inkling that he was marked for a long career at Telesistema. The elder Azcárraga transferred Anselmo to the sales department, where he worked alongside Emilio. Anselmo settled in Mexico City. He married Mary Morton, an actress he had met while guest directing at the famed Pasadena Playhouse in California. Their son Reverge was destined to become a decorated marine.[29]

Now working directly under both Azcárragas as the director of Teleprogramas, Anselmo encountered Telesistema's catch-22: it needed to finance the final construction of three networks and at the same time curtail U.S. revenue. The elder Azcárraga had two reasons for fearing a government review. To avoid the appearance of a monopoly, the charter permitted O'Farrill to separately own Channel 4, and Azcárraga could not stop O'Farrill from broadcasting U.S. programs. Second, Azcárraga had continued U.S. advertising. The first projected revenue of Teleprogramas would not provide the $100 million Azcárraga needed to meet the deadline of 1963 for building out three networks. He needed to step up the contribution Teleprogramas was making. In 1955, Azcárraga "got serious about selling programs to the U.S. networks," Anselmo later recalled. While he was planning to make Teleprogramas a fully international operation, Azcárraga made clear that its immediate destination was the United States.[30]

* * *

The launch of Teleprogramas initiated the rise of Azcárraga's Mexican conglomerate as a foremost presence in international mass communication. His film warehouse had thousands of hours of television recordings for global distribution. Workers constructed suites where these recordings could be duplicated and loading docks to facilitate their shipment all over the world. Around 500 of Telesistema's 10,000 employees—film editors, translators, shippers, and couriers—were transferred to the new firm.[31]

As director of the company, Anselmo had a relatively easy task. He and his staff took orders from numerous startup TV systems in Latin American countries. In 1957, Teleprogramas turned a profit on two-year revenue of $10 million.[32]

But Anselmo failed in the United States. In New York, ABC, CBS, and NBC ridiculed his requests that they schedule Spanish-language Mexican shows. Giving up on the networks, he started calling local stations. While most were affiliates of ABC, CBS, or NBC, all had many hours of airtime for syndicated programming. All of them but one brushed Anselmo away. The exception was KCOR in San Antonio. Launched in 1955 by Raoul Cortez, KCOR was the first U.S. TV station to broadcast full time in Spanish. It was also one of the first to broadcast channels few in the United States had seen.

Prospects for a vast and diverse TV landscape had begun three years earlier, when the FCC had approved seventy channels on the ultra-high-frequency, or UHF, broadcasting band. Originally, U.S. television was to operate on the very-high-frequency, or VHF, band. The twelve VHF channels, Channels 2 through 13, were not enough to accommodate an expansion of television. In 1948, the FCC halted station licensing. The "TV freeze" ended in 1952, when the FCC opened seventy UHF channels, Channels 14 to 83.[33] Cortez's UHF station broadcast on Channel 41.

When Anselmo called on KCOR in late 1955, Cortez rebuffed him, saying KCOR could not afford the programming that featured the star performers and sophisticated production elements that distinguished the programming that came from Telesistema's vast Mexico City studios. KCOR had a limited budget, and it mixed locally produced programs with inexpensive films and syndicated material. However, in 1958 Cortez relented, scraped together funds, and introduced Azcárraga's programs on KCOR.

By the time the programs premiered in San Antonio in 1958, a new development hinted that Azcárraga might have more opportunities in the United States. Two years earlier, a Los Angeles Latino entertainment entrepreneur named Frank Fouce had asked Azcárraga to form a partnership. The two had first met in 1939, shortly before Azcárraga had consolidated Mexico's Churubusco film studios. Fouce enlarged Azcárraga's film empire by screening his motion pictures at theatres he owned in Los Angeles and around the Southwest.[34] Both profited from the arrangement.

Fouce now proposed that they join forces to build a Spanish-language UHF television station in Los Angeles with himself as director of the company and Azcárraga as the financial backer.[35] He told Azcárraga that a UHF license was available. While a Los Angeles station would guarantee a U.S. audience, Azcárraga passed on Fouce's idea in 1956. He was absorbed in other matters, including the cost of the three networks he needed to complete in Mexico.

But in 1958, Fouce returned, and word spread that he and Azcárraga had spoken of more than a single station. Emilio Azcárraga later testified that his father had "discussed a group of stations in large cities like Los Angeles, New York, and Chicago [that] would serve Hispanic minorities."[36] Fouce's son, Frank Fouce Jr., attended a meeting at which "my father told Azcárraga that UHF stations were available all over the United States" and that "if you had the money, you could start a network right now."[37] Fouce was reported to have said at the time that he held the U.S. television rights to the Mexican films he screened in theatres.[38]

Azcárraga listened. He agreed that having his own U.S. network would be the best way to enter the U.S. market. He noted advantages that Fouce had not considered: a U.S. network would attract U.S. advertisers and demonstrating his prowess for conducting business in the United States to Mexican leaders would garner political rewards for a Mexican venture on U.S. soil. Again, though, he backed away, fearing the high cost of a U.S. network when he still had not completed three in Mexico.

There was an additional constraint. The 1934 Federal Communications Act specified that only U.S. citizens could own U.S. radio and television stations; in Title 47, Section 310 of the U.S. Code outlined this requirement. The foreign ownership rule sought to safeguard U.S. broadcasting from individuals like Azcárraga whose enterprises courted foreign governments.

Section 310 allowed non-citizens to own up to 20 percent of a licensed

U.S. broadcast property, but Fouce had turned to Azcárraga with the intention that the billionaire Mexican would provide 100 percent of the financing for his company.[39] To do this, Fouce and Azcárraga used the Mexican custom of *presta nombres* (lending one's name). This enabled Azcárraga to circumvent ownership laws. Anonymously, Azcárraga would found a business above the 20 percent foreign ownership limit by using someone else's name.

As Fouce continued to urge a partnership, Azcárraga learned that Raoul Cortez was likely to sell his San Antonio station. In addition, the PRI had selected Adolfo López Mateos, the first self-declared left-wing politician to rise since the party had been founded in 1929, as the next president. Popular with Mexicans, López Mateos took office after a record turnout in the December 1958 elections.

After twelve years of the conservative and pro-business policies of Alemán Valdés and Ruíz Cortines, López Mateos returned the party to social reform. As the secretary of labor, López Mateos had backed workers during strikes and unrest. As president, he promised to reduce corporate power, redistribute wealth, and slap the intruding hand of the United States. He fulfilled the latter promise by aligning Mexico with Cuba's Communist leader, Fidel Castro. In 1959, he nationalized U.S.-owned utilities and banks.

While López Mateos did not target Telesistema, his reform movement affected the monopoly. Independent print and radio proprietors complained that Telesistema was intent on running them out of business. These included the owners of several recently licensed independent radio stations in Mexico City who were seeking to enlarge two independent national radio networks, La Cadena de Radio Independiente and RED Mexico. In January 1960, López Mateos enacted a revised Ley Federale de Telecomunicaciones y Radiodifusión (Federal Law on Radio and Television). The government still could review and break up Telesistema, but provisions of the new law, which encouraged expansion of private ownerships, had reduced the prospect that the government would seize and nationalize Azcárraga's firm. Instead, the government would oversee the transfer of Telesistema's units to different private owners, making dissolution more likely.[40]

In late 1960, many believed that the dissolution of Telesistema had begun. *Variety* reported a push for "government action against a top heavy 'monopoly.'"[41] After the new law passed, independent radio station owners complained that the government was not renewing their licenses or approving applications for new licenses. In statements in November, the Department of Communication denied "that it is partial to the Azcárraga interests" but said that it would study the allegations.⁴² It appeared that the government was about to conduct a review for the first time since Azcárraga and O'Farrill had merged their companies in 1955.

Although Azcárraga did not comment, he knew he would not survive unless he found a way to stop the review. He had not complied with the merger's provision that Telesistema not act as a monopoly, and he had not phased out U.S. content. The independent Mexican magazine *NACLA* called Telesistema "a huge ad for the United States,"⁴³ and *Variety* reported that Telesistema "is now using more than 500 American-produced [commercial] shorts."⁴⁴ Noting a gamut of series that included *Father Knows Best* and *Highway Patrol*, the *New York Times* commented that "virtually all of Mexican television shows the deep and not always benign influence of the U.S."⁴⁵

There was something else Azcárraga did not want explored. At Tijuana's XETV, Azcárraga had removed Mexican programming, redirected the transmitter northward, and relaunched the station as the ABC affiliate for San Diego.⁴⁶ If this were exposed, it would prove Azcárraga's unwillingness to resist U.S. influence.

Frank Fouce Jr., who at the time was a young attorney, would later testify that during or around November 1960, the same time the government was questioning Telesistema's monopoly, he accompanied his father on a hasty trip to Mexico City, where they learned that Azcárraga "was interested in [acquiring] stations in the U.S." As soon as they arrived, Azcárraga signed the partnership that the elder Fouce had long sought. Azcárraga told them that "a person named Anselmo" would leave Teleprogramas and represent Telesistema in the U.S. venture.⁴⁷ Anselmo later testified that he had known little of the proposed U.S. network, let alone that he would head it, until late 1960.⁴⁸

With the partnership, Azcárraga committed to a Mexican venture on U.S. soil. However, he refrained from announcing it. Instead, he had his press chief, Juan Durán y Casahonda, deny rumors that Azcárraga had agreed to sever Channels 2, 4, and 5 from the Telesistema Mexicano structure. The denials convinced observers that a breakup was indeed under way. They were more convinced when they heard rumors that Azcárraga and O'Farrill were arguing about terms.⁴⁹ The rumors forced the

Figure 1. Don Emilio Azcárraga Vidaurreta was the patriarch of Mexican radio and television and principal founder of Univision. Here he is seen in one of his final photographs, taken while he vacationed shortly before his passing in 1972. He built and controlled one of the world's largest media empires. He launched the U.S. Spanish International Network, Univision's predecessor, in 1961. Photo courtesy of Guillermo Nicolás.

government to consider whether, in fact, it wanted to remove Azcárraga as the only government-sanctioned and publicly recognized leader of Mexican broadcasting.

In January 1961, Mexico City buzzed with reports that Telesistema was close to demise. On January 18, *Variety* reported that "the Telesistema Méxicano framework in this city will be completely overhauled" and "that Telesistema will be disbanded." A least one report also said that Azcárraga was resigned to the breakup of Telesistema and that "Channels 2, 4 and 5 will be operated by independent entities." While "deny[ing] that there was truth to the rumors," sources at Televicentro confirmed that Azcárraga had requested a meeting with López Mateos to outline the "major change [that] is to take place."[50]

On February 20, 1961, Azcárraga did meet with López Mateos, but the change was not what observers had expected. Instead, Azcárraga told the president that he had finalized plans for a U.S. television network. That night, Emilio Azcárraga notified the rest of the country. Appearing on XEW, the younger Azcárraga informed the nation of an "invasion of the United States." He used the figure of speech to publicly disclose a "first of its kind" project by which "our programs will be [broadcast in] New York, Chicago, Los Angeles, San Antonio, and Miami" and eventually across the United States. The U.S. XEW was to be on the air by the end of the year. He did not refer to a network or to ownerships of U.S. stations and thus did not draw the attention of the FCC. He spoke only of "an exchange" that will "reach [a] wide Spanish-language audience [in the United States]" and that "opens a very great future to Mexico."[51]

The extent to which the elder Azcárraga felt that his monopoly was threatened by the government never was known. In his biography of Azcárraga, Olmos contended that although many were uncomfortable with the monopoly, Azcárraga's announcement of a plan "to extend into the United States" had sealed the "definitive concession": Telesistema's protection under the new radio-TV law.[52] The government believed that Azcárraga was acting in the best interests of Mexico and that the new law should allow him to move forward.

Only days after the younger Azcárraga had spoken on February 20, the Department of Communication canceled the review. Commissioners were satisfied that the "Telesistema combine should be continued."[53] On March 15, 1961, López Mateos and Azcárraga embraced each other at a ceremony to commemorate the tenth anniversary of XEW-TV.[54]

* * *

Azcárraga did not have a plan for the U.S. television network. There were misunderstandings. Fouce's first priority was the station in Los Angeles. When Fouce applied for a license to operate Los Angeles's UHF Channel 34 on his own in April 1961, Azcárraga raised concerns. He had told Fouce that San Antonio would be the network's headquarters, that a condition of their partnership was their purchase of Raoul Cortez's KCOR-TV.

Azcárraga was more disturbed about a miscommunication that had happened two months earlier, in February 1961, when he contacted Cortez. Hoping to quickly acquire KCOR, he had offered him $85,000. Again and again, both Fouce and Anselmo had told Azcárraga that KCOR was insolvent and that Cortez would welcome Azcárraga's rescue. But Cortez rejected Azcárraga's offer.

Nor did the parties understand Section 310 of the 1934 Communications Act, the foreign ownership rule, which required U.S. ownership of U.S. radio and TV licenses. Ownership was defined as a property obtained by sale or inheritance or, as was Azcárraga's case, original investment in a new property. When parties pooled resources in an original investment, ownership was defined by the percentage each party had invested. The law permitted 20 percent foreign ownership.

For Azcárraga, this left a problem that had to be addressed: where would the remaining 80 percent come from? It had to be negotiated as coming from U.S. citizens. The issue came up at the meeting in November 1960 when Azcárraga and Fouce agreed to form a partnership. Fouce explained to Azcárraga that papers submitted to the FCC needed to show that Azcárraga owned no more than 20 percent of the company. To comply with Section 310, for every dollar that Azcárraga invested, Fouce had to invest four dollars more. However, Fouce was not wealthy, and he had envisioned that Azcárraga would be the sole investor.

According to Frank Fouce Jr., soon (perhaps days) after the November 1960 meeting, Azcárraga met again with Fouce to propose that they list a capitalization of $167,000 in the partnership documents. He set an arbitrary figure that was double the amount he had offered Cortez for the purchase of KCOR. Azcárraga would provide $34,000, or 20 percent of the total. He told Fouce that in order to begin, Fouce had to raise the remaining $133,000. He could use Azcárraga's wealth as collateral when he approached banks for the loan.[55]

Fouce found that U.S. banks were unwilling to invest in Mexican television. However, he located two U.S. investors: Ed Noble, who had done business with Azcárraga in Mexico and was the nephew of Edward Noble, the founder of the ABC network; and Julian Kaufman, the head of Azcárraga's ABC-affiliated Tijuana station.[56] Azcárraga and Fouce abandoned the partnership they presumably had formed after meeting in November 1960. At the second meeting, instead of enlarging their partnership by adding Noble and Kaufman to it, they chose to incorporate. Incorporation provided a mechanism by which Azcárraga could claim a majority ownership and, thus, control of the firm. Azcárraga incorporated the venture as the Spanish International Broadcasting Corporation (SIBC). However, Fouce, Noble, and Kaufman raised only $58,000, 35 percent of the $167,000 total. This was not enough to show 80 percent U.S. ownership. For the remaining 45 percent, another $75,000 was needed, and it had to come from a U.S. citizen.[57]

Anselmo later detailed the breakthrough that enabled the new corporation, SIBC, and its U.S. TV network to proceed. In early 1961, "I was called into Azcárraga Senior's office [and] was asked [to swear] I was an American citizen." Azcárraga then asked, "Would you like to invest in a television station in San Antonio?" Anselmo had little money, but when Azcárraga told him that "I would be loaned the rest, 'I said yes.'" Azcárraga then gave

Anselmo $75,000. At that point, "I was informed about SIBC" and that "I was to return to the United States." In exchange for accepting the $75,000 and posing as a 45 percent owner, Azcárraga named Anselmo president of the firm.[58]

In the Azcárragas' only recorded account, a sworn affidavit from 1979, Emilio Azcárraga said that "Anselmo was authorized to finance a company in the United States which was the Spanish International Broadcast Corporation." The purpose was to "execute a legal and viable strategy for selling our programs in the American market." The younger Azcárraga maintained that he had not known that his father had contributed the missing 45 percent, which gave him 65 percent ownership of a U.S. broadcast company. When no one questioned Anselmo on how "he got the money," there was "acceptance of Anselmo's presidency" on the part of the Azcárragas, Fouce, Kaufman, and Noble. They agreed that Fouce would return to the United States and that Telesistema "would support the Americans."[59]

The problem solved, Fouce took charge. By mid-1961, he had established a Los Angeles headquarters office, contacted broadcasters in other cities about possible affiliations with SIBC, shepherded the Channel 34 license through the application process, and was awaiting word on Azcárraga's buyout of Cortez. As chair, Fouce was to direct all phases of the enterprise. Despite his title of president and the fact that he owned 45 percent of the company, Anselmo was to function as Fouce's aide. Fouce, like Azcárraga, liked Anselmo, and the two men formed a promising relationship. Fouce incorporated the SIBC firm. He filed in Delaware, where corporations were most likely to escape prying eyes.

* * *

Different predicaments engaged Raoul Cortez, who had founded U.S. Spanish-language broadcasting using both radio and television. He was proud of his properties, but he was bankrupt. Azcárraga needed Cortez's TV station to meet his goal of extending Mexican TV into the United States. The purchase of KCOR was essential because of San Antonio's location: it was directly north of and only 900 miles from Mexico City. There were no video transmission lines from Mexico to the United States, so Telesistema would need to physically deliver films and videotapes. San Antonio thrived as a distribution hub. While a station in much larger Los Angeles was forthcoming, San Antonio was a more vital geographic location.

Only ten years younger than Azcárraga, Cortez had nearly identical roots. Born in 1905, Cortez was raised in a professional family in Nuevo Laredo, Mexico. Like Azcárraga's, Cortez's family pioneered early radio. In 1923, Cortez's uncles established an experimental station in Nuevo Laredo that is believed to have been the first radio station in northern Mexico. Later christened XEBK, it was still in operation and owned by members of the Cortez family 100 years after its first experimental broadcasts.[60]

However, while Azcárraga moved south and became rich, Cortez was among a half-million immigrants, most professionals and entrepreneurs, who left Mexico for the United States after the 1910 revolution. He arrived in San Antonio at age eighteen and supported himself as a street vendor. But he noticed the factor that would make the city a cradle of U.S. Spanish-language broadcasting: its large and largely affluent Spanish-speaking population.[61]

Cortez remained in San Antonio and, except for a job he took in 1928, was self-employed until his death in 1971. He entered broadcasting from his job as a sales distributor for the Pearl Brewery: he persuaded the brewery to sponsor a Saturday-night variety show he hosted. *La Cerveceria Perla* (The Pearl Brewery), which English-language station KMAC carried starting in 1929, was one of the first Spanish-language programs on U.S. radio.

In 1934, Cortez met Fouce. Their friendship began when Fouce backed an enterprise that made Cortez wealthy, a booking agency that brought Fouce's live shows and motion pictures to San Antonio. Cortez returned to radio as the impresario of several variety shows. San Antonio's KMAC and KABC snapped up his fully sponsored Spanish-language programs. By 1938, Cortez had saved money for a new enterprise: a radio station that offered all-Spanish programming.

Cortez hesitated to establish his station in 1938, however, fearing a new government agency, the FCC, which had been created in 1934. As Irma Nicolás, his daughter, later recounted, "He did not want to go to the FCC because he would have to tell them the station would all be in Spanish." The Communications Act of 1934 did not prohibit full-time Spanish-language broadcasting, but Cortez felt his station might provoke such a rule. "He was afraid the FCC would reject him and stop Spanish broadcasting for good," his daughter explained.[62]

Finally, in January 1942, Cortez applied for San Antonio's 1350 AM frequency and the call letters KCOR. His application was denied. It was one month after Pearl Harbor and World War II had begun. As a security measure, the FCC had suspended all licensing. When he reapplied in 1943, commissioners informed Cortez that as radio was obliged to serve the public interest and as no public interest superseded that of winning the war, a "foreign language station" was "inappropriate."[63]

When he applied for a third time in 1944, Cortez submitted figures showing that local bond sales, blood donations, and enlistments were falling short of goals. Those goals could be achieved, he said, if programs were provided in all of the languages people spoke.[64] The FCC agreed and gave Cortez the only radio license it approved during World War II. However, Cortez was denied radio parts because the War Board had rationed them, and he could not begin broadcasting until after the war was over.

Finally, on February 15, 1946, the U.S.'s first full-time Spanish-language radio station signed on. Cortez emceed the inaugural broadcast, a gala first edition of KCOR's breakfast program, *Tiovivo* (Merry-Go-Round).[65] Newspaper ads promised "entertainment that fulfills the desires of those who enjoy programs that are different, varied, and new!"[66] The station's prime-time programs included *Under the Spanish Sky, Memories of Mexican Yesterday, Fifteen Minutes in Cuba, Beautiful Brazil,* and *Down in Argentina.*[67]

Cortez and station manager Nathan Safir arranged forty-seven programs and, notably, thirty-one sponsors.[68] An estimated 40 percent of San Antonio's half-million residents were of Mexican descent. Sponsorships increased, and KCOR was turning a profit in just two years.[69] In 1949, the FCC boosted KCOR's power from 1,000 to 5,000 watts. KCOR became a regional station that was heard throughout southern Texas.

The most welcome salute came from Dr. Sydney Roslow and his Pulse Corporation. Roslow had pioneered audience ratings in radio. In every sizable city, Pulse conducted scientific surveys to determine each radio station's number of listeners. The ratings were vital to broadcasters. Advertisers trusted scientific surveys and contracted with stations based on their numbers. The higher the ratings, the more a sponsor would pay.

Initially, Cortez was handicapped. Pulse's surveys were limited to English-language listeners. Cortez was certain that the city's only Spanish-language station had a huge audience. But because KCOR did not appear in the ratings, there was no proof of that. Cortez pitched to potential sponsors by showing them letters listeners had written and telling them what people said about the station. However, if they advertised on KCOR at all, sponsors paid token amounts.

Figure 2. Raoul Cortez (*left*) pioneered Spanish-language broadcasting in the United States. Cortez founded the U.S.'s first full-time Spanish-language radio station, KCOR, in San Antonio in 1946. Here, famed U.S. comedian Bob Hope joins Cortez in one of the first KCOR radio broadcasts. Cortez's sale of KCOR-TV to Azcárraga Vidaurreta led to the 1961 launch of the Spanish International Network. Photo courtesy of Guillermo Nicolás.

In 1952, Pulse enlarged San Antonio's survey to include its 50,000 Spanish-speaking homes. Overnight, KCOR shot to the top of the ratings, and the station's revenue soared. Regional and national businesses signed on, and Cortez made a profit of $100,000 in 1953.[70] He invested the radio money in what he hoped would be his capstone enterprise, KCOR-TV. In June 1954, the FCC awarded Cortez Channel 41 on the UHF band.

Cortez had his eye on a street address that would become well known in Spanish-language television: 411 East Durango Boulevard, located south of the city's downtown. The site was a vacant ten-acre property that overlooked the San Antonio River and was close to the city's freight and rail lines. Cortez purchased the property, and in 1955 he completed a radio-TV building with an auditorium studio. The *San Antonio Express* noted that the "601-foot tower" was "the tallest structure in San Antonio."[71]

Yet hiring setbacks slowed Cortez. Personnel at KCOR Radio chose not to transfer to TV. They had prospered at the radio station and were dubious about the duties they would have at the TV station. Safir, the manager of the radio station, agreed to run the TV station temporarily. Needing a permanent TV manager and finding no one, Cortez turned to his family. His daughter Irma had married a doctor-to-be named Emilio Nicolás. He had worked part-time at KCOR, sweeping floors and cleaning equipment, but he had little affinity for broadcasting. Although he was rapidly rising as a medical research specialist, he reluctantly agreed to take the manager's post.

Born in 1930 and raised in Frontera, Mexico, Nicolás moved to the United States at age eighteen in order to support his family back home. Toiling in menial jobs, he applied to San Antonio's St. Mary's University and was granted a one-year conditional enrollment. He ranked at the top of the 1948 freshman class. Pushed by professors dazzled by his aptitude for science, Nicolás graduated in 1951 with degrees in chemistry and biology. San Antonio's Southwest Research Institute, which at the time was assisting Albert Sabin as he searched for a cure for polio, awarded him a research associate position. While collaborating with Sabin, Nicolás published some of the first research on the disease that came to be known as arteriosclerosis.

Nicolás agreed to manage KCOR-TV out of loyalty to the family. His father-in-law had him apprentice as a trainee and assist Safir as he directed the launch of KCOR. He did not end his other career. "I left the Southwest

Institute with a leave of absence on the condition I would return when KCOR was on its feet. I never expected to stay in television," he later recalled.[72] In 1955, Harvard Medical School awarded him admission.[73] He considered the offer only briefly. Rather than relocate his young family and abandon his commitment to KCOR-TV, he chose to stay in San Antonio.

U.S. Spanish-language television began on Friday, June 10, 1955. That night, after an introduction and a prelude of mariachi music, Cortez walked to center stage. A camera cut to a close-up. "Hola San Antonio y América," he said, smiling broadly.[74] He was joined by Mayor Ed Kuykendall and other dignitaries.

Cortez brought together the largest troupe of entertainers he ever had assembled for a weekend extravaganza billed as the "KCOR-TV International Cavalcade of Stars." Some of the fifty acts appeared from the Channel 41 studios, while, oddly, most appeared at an event at the downtown Municipal Auditorium that was not televised. Local celebrities, well-wishers, and TV technicians greeted audiences at both sites.[75]

Writing in the *San Antonio Express*, Gerald Ashford hailed what he had seen on TV. The "big, colorful variety show presents a wide variety of first-rate talent. Most of it would be highly acceptable in any language or country." The programs introduced "Spanish-language television [on] Channel 41 in the ultra-high frequency band" with "a showcase for the type of talent that will be seen on the screens of TV sets."[76]

An article in *La Prensa San Antonio* observed, "In the midst of an atmosphere of popular enthusiasm, last Friday the new and only television station in Spanish in the United States was inaugurated, KCOR-TV. Mr. Raul Cortez, who, deeply moved, talked about the realization of a dream for long years cherished, said the scale of its triumph owes to the wide cooperation of the public."[77]

Regular television programs began the following Monday with four hours of broadcasting from 7:00 to 11:00 P.M. Cortez hired local performers for live variety, music, and talk programs and hosted some of the shows himself. Viewers saw *Rebeca Ríos, Mariachi Feminino, Los Cantabros,* and *Trío Gypsy.* Fouce contributed films he had shown in theatres that became a series called *Hora deportes,* an anthology of filmed sports coverage from past years. There was a stir the first week when viewers witnessed a bullfight that, according to the *San Antonio News*, was broadcast in "Latin fashion" with "blood, gore, and all."[78]

The auditorium event on opening night illustrated the difficulties of UHF broadcasting in the 1950s. As June 10th approached, Cortez discovered that he could not launch UHF television on television. The public could not view UHF channels on regular home TVs without a converter box, a device about the size of a shoebox that resembled small tabletop console radios sold in the 1950s. A UHF antenna was wired into and fed the device. Inside, the device contained tubes and a UHF-to-VHF converter. A second wire attached to a TV set's VHF antenna enabled reception of UHF channels. The TV technicians had appeared on opening night to explain how the boxes were to be connected. Although he had devoted time to preparing the first programs and rehearsing the many stars, Cortez had neglected to ensure that the converters would be available in stores. He resorted to the best possible solution, a TV station launch where there was no TV.

Cortez had several advantages that kept the station from going dark. His radio station was flush with sponsors, and many were willing to advertise on TV. Sponsors were encouraged when newspapers and word of mouth testified that one of Cortez's TV programs, *Teatro KCOR*, was a hit. It was a variety show hosted by rising Tejano singer and entertainer Lalo Astol. Cortez's live programming also helped. Businesses did not need to produce recorded advertisements in Spanish because Cortez, Astol, and others pitched the sponsors while hosting their shows, which were similar to early Spanish-language radio shows.

The arrival of Nicolás at KCOR that September was also beneficial. In his first duty as station manager, he had gone to local stores and asked them to order large stocks of UHF converters. Nicolás convinced store owners that people were fascinated by the novelty of a new TV station. Converters soon were flying off shelves. A business named Hopps TV touted it itself as "UHF Headquarters," and Sears Roebuck rushed into its San Antonio stores a "2-tube UHF converter" with a "plastic mahogany-colored cabinet" that gave "perfect reception of UHF Channel 41 (KCOR-TV)."[79] By 1956, 20,000 converters had been sold in San Antonio.

Nicolás foresaw another necessity that had escaped Cortez: audience ratings. It was only a matter of time before sponsors would demand the scientific surveys that could demonstrate how many viewers the TV station had. KCOR Radio had boomed when the Pulse ratings included Spanish-speaking homes. But Cortez had not approached either of the two firms that conducted local TV ratings, ARB and Hooper. After contacting both in 1955, Nicolás recognized that the station needed to broadcast for more than a few hours each night and that it needed more than local studio shows. ARB and Hooper told Nicolás that KCOR was experimental TV and chose not to survey homes in Spanish-speaking areas because of the added expense.

KCOR needed Spanish-language programming comparable in quality and duration to those on English-language stations if it wanted to be rated alongside them. In late 1955, Nicolás learned where such programming could be obtained when Rene Anselmo traveled to the United States as the new director of Teleprogramas de Mexico. However, when they met, Cortez refused to purchase Anselmo's Telesistema programs. Cortez balked at the exorbitant fees and was "offended that Azcárraga thinks we can't do our own shows," Nicolás later recalled.[80]

Nicolás and Anselmo continued to meet and talk. They were both in their twenties and were both under the thumb of forceful employers. They quickly became friends.

Nicolás did find additional programming. In 1956, KCOR originated the first Spanish-language TV newscasts. He also grabbed Spanish-language films from every known source. Syndicator Frederick Ziv donated prints of the reruns of *The Cisco Kid*, *The Big Picture*, and *Highway Patrol* overdubbed in Spanish. From the vaults of the defunct Dumont network, Nicolás found a professional wrestling series, *Lucha Libre Chicago* (Chicago Wrestling).[81] Nicolás also broadcasted free instructional films in Spanish from the Defense Department and the Social Security Administration.[82] By 1957, KCOR was broadcasting eight hours every day.[83]

Nicolás was pleased when Cortez relented and agreed to purchase Azcárraga's programs the next year. But he was not exuberant; he knew that Cortez had purchased only a few Mexican programs and that if he could not coax businesses to sponsor them the station might close. Cortez turned to Azcárraga because in 1958, unable to pay performers, he had canceled the studio shows. He signed a $50,000 one-year contract with Teleprogramas de Mexico for enough content to fill prime time. He hoped for a turnaround that could reinstate at least Astol's show.[84]

The $50,000 was a potentially crippling cost. However, Cortez was fortunate. Azcárraga paid for the cost of shipping fifty half-hour reels of film to San Antonio every week. He also built a warehouse at KCOR where films were stored before they were shipped back to Mexico City. But in

1958, Azcárraga was envisioning delivering them to other stations in the United States.[85] Azcárraga needed to test the delivery system. Because there were no network lines, it was the linchpin of the U.S. network he and Fouce were planning.

The first TV shows from Mexico premiered in May 1958. For a year and a half, they enlivened the airwaves of the Lone Star State. It was the zenith of KCOR-TV. Nicolás replaced the reruns with a lead hit show on Mexico's Channel 2, a weekly variety hosted by Pedro Vargas, one of the period's greatest Latino actor-singers. KCOR carried the drama *Charrito*, the playhouse series *Teatro*, and near-first-run Mexican movies. That year, San Antonio viewers also saw the first telenovela, *Ángeles de la calle*, which began airing in Mexico in 1952.[86] According to Irma Nicolás, during the time the Mexican programs were broadcast, viewers remarked that KCOR "looked like a network station."[87]

It did not fare as well at the bank. The station's best year was 1959, when advertising sales reached $200,000. Earnings that year were only slightly more than they had been the year before and were one-tenth the total amount that the local English-language stations, WOAI, KENS, and KONO, had billed collectively. Earlier that year, Cortez had told Anselmo that he was not renewing the Telesistema contract in 1960. As Nicolás had feared he would, Cortez lapsed into airing a prime-time schedule of hand-out films.[88]

Nicolás and his sales staff approached potential advertisers more times than ever before. They found proprietors cordial and willing to talk, but the lack of audience ratings presented a challenge in proving KCOR's reach. ARB and Hooper still refused to include KCOR in their audience ratings, citing the expense of surveying Spanish-speaking homes. To demonstrate the reach of the station, Nicolás and his staff resorted to creative methods. KCOR broadcast messages asking viewers to send box tops, labels, and sales receipts from stores and businesses that advertised on KCOR. Tens of thousands poured in, and Nicolás and his staff took crates full of these box tops when they approached potential advertisers. Without ratings, KCOR had no better means of proving that it had viewers.[89]

By early 1960, Cortez realized that bankruptcy loomed. A new issue had emerged when he scuttled programs and laid off all but six staff. His wife, Genoveva, rose in vehement opposition. She insisted that KCOR continue.[90] Caught in the middle, Nicolás believed that the time had come for him to exit. He regretted the situation, yet he wanted to return to medicine.

Nicolás prepared his resignation, but in early 1960, Cortez suffered a heart attack.

Nicolás remained at KCOR through Cortez's convalescence. But sensing that the station was bankrupt and that he would be free to depart, he approached former associates in the medical field. When Cortez recovered, a surprise development convinced Nicolás that the TV station's days were numbered: Cortez sold the KCOR radio station. He had not consulted the family, and they were incensed. Cortez's private dealings had legal implications because it was the family that owned the KCOR properties. The family dispute intensified, and, again, Nicolás felt obliged to stay. But in April 1961, in private dealings of his own, Nicolás won an offer to return to the Southwest Institute.

* * *

That April, two months after Cortez and Azcárraga had first conferred and Cortez had rejected Azcárraga's $85,000 bid for KCOR-TV, they met again. Azcárraga flew Cortez to Mexico City and over three days courted him with tours of Mexico City and Televicentro. Azcárraga told Cortez he would increase his offer to $100,000 and pay Cortez's debts. Cortez warmed to what he considered to be generous terms, and he did not object to Azcárraga's stipulation that he have no further role at KCOR. But again he refused to sell. He was forced to confess his predicament: he could not agree to sell because his family would retaliate.

Soon after the April visit, a confrontation did occur. Cortez's wife learned about her husband's meetings with Azcárraga. As Irma Nicolás later recounted, "We had a suspicion Azcárraga wanted KCOR. We got [my father] aside and told him: 'Don't you dare sell the station out from under us.'" They particularly objected to the idea that the station would be sold to a distant Mexican mogul and to the likelihood he would move Anselmo to San Antonio to head KCOR. They had not been comfortable with their impression that Anselmo had shown a lack of respect for Cortez. The family emphatically insisted that "you won't sell to that man Azcárraga."[91] Cortez told them that the station was insolvent and had to be sold.

Solutions materialized in the fall of 1961. In Mexico City, Azcárraga scheduled a meeting at which the heads of the new Spanish International Broadcasting Corporation would finalize plans for the launch of the U.S. network. In San Antonio, Cortez and the family reached a compromise. The family consented to sell the station to Azcárraga on the condition that Nicolás continue as manager. They were united in their position that Anselmo should not run KCOR. The family did not inform Nicolás, however, unaware of his plans to resign. "I just assumed the sale had not gone through" and that "the time had come to tell everyone I was leaving," Nicolás later said.[92]

In November 1961, Cortez telephoned Azcárraga to conditionally accept a $150,000 purchase effective on December 15 and set forth the condition: if Azcárraga did not hire Nicolás by December 15, the station would remain with the family. Without asking for Nicolás's résumé, Azcárraga agreed to hire him. According to Irma Nicolás, Cortez warned Azcárraga that he might be unable to coax Nicolás to take the job, in which case the deal would be off. Amused, Azcárraga thanked Cortez for the information. It was the last time they spoke.[93]

Azcárraga convened the Mexico City meeting on December 1, 1961. He and his U.S. associates, the heads of SIBC, were eager for the session. Their purpose was to coordinate assignments for the first network broadcasts. Fouce brought the news that the FCC had approved SIBC's Los Angeles license. Azcárraga decided that on December 15, his son Emilio Azcárraga would join the others in San Antonio for the sale of the station and the public announcement of the network. When Azcárraga revealed that the deal actually was incomplete, that he must hire Nicolás or the family would cancel the sale, Anselmo objected. He said that while Nicolás was qualified for the job, he was a scientist who was about to join a San Antonio research institute. Azcárraga assured the group that Nicolás would stay.[94]

The following Monday, Azcárraga had Anselmo contact Nicolás. Anselmo proposed that he fly Nicolás to Mexico City for an impromptu vacation at the end of the week. Nicolás thought the call was one of Anselmo's practical jokes. When Anselmo affirmed that the invitation was genuine, that they had gone too long without contact, Nicolás agreed to the trip.

Nicolás was no match for Mexico's master of persuasion. He later recalled December 9, 1961, as the most memorable day of his TV career. "I flew down on a Saturday dressed in casual clothes." At the Mexico City airport, Anselmo greeted him in a business suit. They motored in an eighteen-passenger Lincoln Continental limousine down streets that police had cleared. When they arrived at the landmark Camino Real Hotel, Anselmo escorted Nicolás into a banquet room that was deserted except for an older man who was sixty-six years old at the time. Tall and stocky, he had a mildly rugged square face, dark hair, thick eyebrows, and peering brown eyes. He spoke with a deep and commanding yet friendly voice. It was Azcárraga. Smiling, Azcárraga approached and hugged Nicolás. "I was overwhelmed and just about fell off my feet," Nicolás remembered.[95]

They dined at the hotel. Nicolás was amazed at Azcárraga's knowledge of polio and arteriosclerosis. Although Azcárraga had studied up on those topics to impress the visitor, he made it clear that he had wanted Nicolás to continue his TV career. "He said TV was just as important as medicine [for it] reached immigrants like [I had been] who barely had jobs, didn't know English, and were trying to survive."[96] Nicolás again was amazed when Azcárraga motioned him into the front seat of the Lincoln Continental. Azcárraga drove. They spent the rest of the day touring art galleries and, then, Televicentro.

That night, Nicolás accepted Azcárraga's offer to manage the San Antonio station. Azcárraga promised more, a future as a network executive who would direct program operations in San Antonio and rise in a corporation that spanned the globe.

Anselmo was elated. Not only had his friend joined the SIBC team, but his future role at the company had changed. Until then, Anselmo had been headed to San Antonio, a location he did not prefer, to initiate the network. After he hired Nicolás, Azcárraga reassigned Anselmo to Los Angeles to work next to Fouce. Anselmo begged to go to New York to open a sales office instead, but Azcárraga refused.

Yet Anselmo did prevail in a practical joke. The directors of the Spanish International Broadcasting Corporation assumed their network would be "SIBC." Presumably to obtain a flashier three-letter name, Anselmo campaigned for "Spanish International Network." The others did not catch on to the joke, that Anselmo had wanted to see the acronym "SIN" in press accounts and TV listings.

At KCOR, Cortez cleared his belongings. He and the parties had agreed to a final purchase price of $200,000. The sale left him wealthy, yet "he was crestfallen," Nicolás recalled.[97]

Cortez returned the following Friday. It was the day Azcárraga had designated, December 15, 1961. From Los Angeles, Fouce and Noble flew to San Antonio to join Emilio Azcárraga and Anselmo, who had arrived from Mexico City. They gathered long enough to sign papers, pay Cortez, and, in a brief office ceremony, mark the beginning of network Spanish-language television in the United States.

Cortez circulated a news release written by Emilio Azcárraga, but both parties were disappointed when the wire services and national press ignored it. Only in San Antonio was the founding reported. The *San Antonio Light* headlined Cortez's sale to a syndicate headed by "Don Emilio Azcárraga, Mexican radio and television magnate." The *Light* noted that the nation's "only Spanish-language channel" would soon feed programs from San Antonio coast to coast.[98] The *San Antonio Express and News* elaborated on Azcárraga's plans to base a national Spanish-language "TV chain" in San Antonio: "calling itself the 'Spanish International Network,'" the group "proposes in the near future to bring . . . the most current of Spanish-language programming from Mexico and Latin America."[99]

2

MEX, UHF, AND NFL

Four weeks after convening in San Antonio and founding the Spanish International Broadcasting Corporation, the principals met again. They gathered in Los Angeles to pay respects to Frank Fouce. On January 11, 1962, at the age of sixty-two, Fouce had died of a heart attack. Don Emilio Azcárraga Vidaurreta flew to Los Angeles for the funeral. Scores of well-wishers attended, many of whom were Hollywood celebrities who dated to Fouce's career as an actor in silent films.[1]

Fouce lived long enough to learn of the launch of the Spanish International Network. Azcárraga switched Telesistema Méxicano stations to SIN affiliations in five cities on the Mexican side of the border. Rene Anselmo remained for a short while in San Antonio after the December 15 signing, when Azcárraga's group acquired Raoul Cortez's TV station. By then, a small shipment of programs had left the loading dock of Televicentro, Azcárraga's studio complex in Mexico City. During the holidays, the broadcast of the programs in San Antonio and then their delivery to and broadcast in the five other cities constituted a semblance of a network launch.[2]

The first program, *Teatro fantástico,* was a nightly motion picture that aired at 6:15 P.M. During station breaks, studio cameras showed a placard with a "SIN" logo. Announcers delivered SIN network identifications. In January, Telesistema's stepped-up shipments permitted a four-hour-per-night schedule seven days a week. Viewers saw variety shows, musical series including *Guitarras,* and a drama anthology that featured star Mexican actor Ángel Garasa.[3]

Fouce had been in good health. Widely reported in trade publications, his sudden passing accomplished what Emilio Azcárraga's December news release had not. Fouce's obituaries announced the birth of SIN. Eulogizing a figure who had been a broadcaster for less than a month, *Broadcasting* magazine reported on Fouce's "startup of a chain of Spanish-language television stations." An article in *Variety* described Fouce's Spanish International Network as a "Spanish lingo group" that had "won a license for the first UHF station in Los Angeles." The article reported Channel 34 had been scheduled to begin in 1963, although because of Fouce's untimely death, "plans for the station are unclear."[4]

Nevertheless, meeting at the funeral, the group was aware that the first issue had already been resolved. Azcárraga would not pass the reins to someone he could not direct. The two surviving partners, Edward Noble and Julian Kaufman, were candidates, but neither was keen to take on the job. Everyone knew that Anselmo would be Fouce's successor.

While he was Anselmo's staunchest supporter, even Azcárraga doubted his protégé's capabilities. At age thirty-five, Anselmo was young and unseasoned. Fouce was to have been the architect of SIN; Anselmo was involved only because Azcárraga needed a U.S. citizen who was willing to pose as the owner of the network.[5] Yet Azcárraga was willing to take a chance that Anselmo would succeed. Anselmo still was an employee of Telesistema, and Azcárraga was still his boss. Azcárraga neither announced Anselmo's new position nor gave him Fouce's title of chair. If Anselmo underperformed, Azcárraga could keep him as president and name someone else as chair.[6]

However, with Fouce gone and Noble and Kaufman unavailable, Emilio Azcárraga used the occasion to advocate for delaying forthcoming steps to enlarge the small network, rethink its viability, and consider whether the project should proceed. He was skeptical about whether SIN would succeed. All along, he had warned about high costs and complications. He also did not share his father's delight with Anselmo. The younger Azcárraga complained that while Anselmo was smart and persuasive, he was a showoff who was prone to carelessness, covering up mistakes, and back talk.

Figure 3. Rene Anselmo was Azcárraga Vidaurreta's choice to head the Spanish International Network after the sudden death of Frank Fouce Sr. in 1962. He is seen here soon after becoming SIN's president, a post he would hold for twenty-five years. Anselmo quickly signaled he was not Azcárraga's puppet and emerged as a forceful and effective, albeit scheming and uncanny, leader. Photo courtesy of Guillermo Nicolás.

Emilio's opinions had weight. In 1961, Telesistema's directors elected him to the board. After his father and Rómulo O'Farrill, Emilio became third-in-command at Telesistema.

Another detractor was Fouce's son. Unlike Emilio Azcárraga, Frank Fouce Jr. did not know Anselmo. Forty-year-old Fouce Jr. had an MBA from Loyola University and a law degree from Pepperdine. While he had counseled his father on the incorporation of SIBC and had accompanied him on trips to Mexico City, the younger Fouce had no passion for Spanish-language television.

But Fouce quickly focused on a piece of his inheritance, the Los Angeles television station. Fouce knew that a TV station in Los Angeles was valuable. He also was privy to the secret that Anselmo did not own or control the largest share of SIBC. The first crisis in Spanish-language television erupted at Fouce's funeral. It was the beginning of a 25-year feud.

It began with a dispute over where Anselmo would be sent. Anselmo learned of Fouce's passing while on a temporary assignment in San Antonio. The plan called for Anselmo to leave San Antonio after he and Emilio Nicolás had organized the network distribution system. Although Anselmo had asked to go to New York and open a sales office on Madison Avenue, Azcárraga told him that likely in early 1963, after Fouce had the station in Los Angeles up and running, he would move to that city.

At the funeral in Los Angeles, Fouce discovered that Azcárraga had instructed Anselmo not to return to San Antonio. Anselmo was to assume the fallen Fouce's duties immediately. Suspecting that Anselmo and Azcárraga were taking over his inherited holdings, Fouce Jr. confronted them.[7] Fouce insisted that Anselmo stay clear of the offices where his father had managed his theater and booking businesses and where he had begun directing SIN. While Azcárraga tried to mediate, Anselmo erupted. He claimed that Fouce had no authority to impede his activities as head of SIN.

In what seemed like a resolution of the conflict, Fouce withdrew his demand that Anselmo remain in San Antonio; he needed Anselmo to build the new station. But he voiced concern that because Azcárraga was not a U.S. citizen, his ownership of the parent company SIBC was illegal under Section 310 of the U.S. Communications Act of 1934. Fouce had been with his father at the meetings with Azcárraga in late 1960 and early 1961, when the partners had needed to raise $167,000 and Anselmo's surprise $75,000 had saved the day. Fouce warned that the Los Angeles license would be revoked if the FCC raised questions and Anselmo could not prove that the $75,000 was his.[8]

Fouce's fears stemmed from the percentages of $167,000 that each of the partners had contributed. The filed documents showed that Azcárraga invested and thus owned 20 percent, Fouce 20 percent, Noble 10 percent, Kaufman 5 percent, and Anselmo 45 percent.[9] Anselmo had made no secret of the fact that his assets had totaled $7,500 at the time he had produced ten times more. An investigation was certain to uncover the fact that Azcárraga had given Anselmo the money, which meant that Azcárraga owned 65 percent of SIBC.

Fouce implemented a plan to protect the Los Angeles station. That February, he, Noble, and Kaufman agreed to pool their resources, form a new company, and sever the station from SIBC. But they found that they needed to raise $600,000 to finance the start-up of Channel 34, an amount Azcárraga was ready to pay.[10] As had his father, the son failed to find investors. When Fouce realized that he could not break the SIBC ownership arrangement, he lost interest in the Los Angeles station. He moved on to the many other enterprises his father had left, all of which were legal and lucrative.

Fouce's maneuvering infuriated Anselmo. He fumed to both Azcárragas that while he shouldered the responsibility for building the Los Angeles station, Fouce's only contribution was his attempt to steal it. Unaware of Fouce's waning interest, Anselmo warned that Fouce was bent on seizing SIBC and could do so because of his inheritance.[11] But Anselmo had a plan.

That April, the Azcárragas acted on Anselmo's idea of forming a separate corporation for SIN's network operation.[12] Anselmo outlined the same plan that Fouce had attempted, only with a network, not a station. The formation of a SIN network company had an advantage: U.S. law did not prohibit foreign ownership of networks. Not only could Azcárraga fully own SIN, but, if needed, he could use it to shelter SIBC assets. Fascinated, the Azcárragas consented to Anselmo's request that the new company headquarter in New York, where Anselmo as head would spearhead national advertising sales. The new company had a second advantage: removed from the network's revenue, Fouce's hands would be tied. He could not effectively question Anselmo's leadership if Anselmo controlled the company's purse strings.

Except for the addition of a New York office, nothing changed. Spanish International remained a single operation within the original SIBC structure with Anselmo as head. For the first time, Anselmo had impressed Emilio Azcárraga. The son congratulated him on his brilliant scheme. He okayed Anselmo's move to New York, with the caveat that he wait to move until he had put the Los Angeles station on the air.[13]

Fouce became very frustrated because Anselmo refused to learn what he could and could not do. At an April 1962 board meeting, he embarrassed Anselmo when the latter announced the breakaway of SIN. Fouce insisted that the plan was illegal. Under the FCC's anti-trust regulations, network companies were not to provide advertising to local stations or represent stations in advertising negotiations. In front of the partners, Fouce exposed Anselmo's shallow knowledge of FCC law. Although he was pointing out that Anselmo had perpetrated two illegal acts, Fouce wearied. Even though it was illegal for the SIN Sales unit to serve as the representative for local stations SICC owned in advertising negotiations, "I went along" because the company needed advertising revenue, he later said.[14]

Then Fouce abandoned active involvement in SIN and SIBC. He embarked on the sale of his father's theatre holdings in order to invest in new projects outside Los Angeles. He became wealthy after relocating Fouce Amusement Enterprises to Las Vegas in 1964. Although Fouce did not sell his 20 percent ownership of SIBC and later acquired more shares and kept his inherited title of chair, he did not attend another board meeting for eleven years. He let Anselmo, who for the time being remained in Los Angeles, convene the board and run the network. Anselmo agreed to the arrangement even though he knew that Fouce "wanted me out."[15]

* * *

Another conflict affected the embryonic SIN. The stations in both Los Angeles and San Antonio needed official FCC call letters. Both chose "KMEX." No four letters could better identify a Spanish-language television station in locales where virtually the entire audience was of Mexican descent.

When Azcárraga had purchased Raoul Cortez's TV station and the KCOR call letters stayed with the radio station, he had approved Nicolás's selection of "KMEX" for the television station. Azcárraga then encouraged Fouce Sr. to use the same call letters in his application for Los Angeles's Channel 34. He did not anticipate a problem; in Mexico, all of the stations on his main network were known as XEW.

The issue arose when Anselmo remained in Los Angeles after the funeral. Supporting his friend Nicolás and maintaining that Nicolás's station had been the first to air, Anselmo told Nicolás he could keep the KMEX call letters. Fouce Jr. countered that the Los Angeles station was larger and thus should have the prized name.

In characteristic fashion, Azcárraga ended the squabble with both sides pleased. He upheld Fouce's claim. The Los Angeles station became KMEX. Then he contacted Nicolás to thank him for his hard work in battling the complexities of the San Antonio distribution system. After that, Nicolás withdrew his request to keep the call letters. But Azcárraga offered a consolation prize: he gave Nicolás permission to use the call letters XEW. Nicolás was pleased that his station was about to become KXEW. Then he discovered that a radio station in Tucson had already taken Azcárraga's call sign. He decided to retain the letters XEW but spell them in reverse. The new name of KWEX almost looked like KMEX, Nicolás said, "if you held it up to a mirror."[16]

In early 1962, Azcárraga set September 15, the eve of Mexican Independence Day, as the target date. Anselmo protested that KMEX could not be built that soon. That March, the project's prospects improved when Julian Kaufman came to Anselmo's aid. Kaufman took a leave of absence from his post as head of Azcárraga's ABC affiliate in Tijuana. On the condition he be able to return there, Kaufman agreed to serve under Anselmo as interim manager of KMEX.[17] Anselmo's confidence swelled under Kaufman, one of the lions of the young TV field. He had produced the first TV programs at KSTP in the Twin Cities in 1948, had risen in the sales department at ABC-owned KGO in San Francisco, and had directed the first TV station in Phoenix, KPHO.

Kaufman soon presented Anselmo with two gifts. He located KMEX just off Melrose Avenue on Bronson Avenue in front of the entrance to the Paramount Studios. He acquired vacant studios originally built for KTLA, the city's first television station, which Paramount had owned. Then he suggested to KTLA and the other Los Angeles stations that their support of a Spanish-language station would impress the FCC. The stations agreed that KMEX could build a tower at their jointly owned 6,000-foot Mt. Wilson transmitting site.[18] From there, KMEX would reach almost halfway to Mexico.[19]

Yet by summer, the momentum had stalled. The transmitter from Mexico was waylaid at the border. Studio cameras, controls, and video machines either had not cleared customs or had arrived in pieces. Anselmo and Kaufman sat idle during most of June and July.

As activity slowed, Anselmo became preoccupied with Nicolás's distribution system in San Antonio. There was no guarantee about which Telesistema programs, if any, San Antonio would provide. By the spring of 1962, SIN had not yet reliably programmed its six original stations: KWEX, the San Antonio flagship, and the five Mexican border stations Azcárraga had given to SIN. These were XEFE in Nuevo Laredo; XHJ in Juarez, which carried into El Paso; XHFA in Nogales, which extended into Tucson; XEM in Mexicali, which broadcast into Yuma, Arizona, and El Centro, California; and XEWT in Tijuana, which brought SIN to San Diego.[20]

Azcárraga did not exaggerate when he told Emilio Nicolás that the network's future depended on whether Nicolás could master one of the marvels of early U.S. television, the "bicycle network" system of distribution. There were no network lines from Mexico City to San Antonio or from San Antonio to the outlying SIN stations. Trucks from Mexico City transported filmed programs to the San Antonio hub, a warehouse on the Durango Boulevard property that Cortez had purchased years earlier. From there, trucks delivered the films to XEFE in Nuevo Laredo, then to

SIN's other stations. As soon as one station had broadcast the program, a bus would take it to the next station in the network. This required reliable transportation and intricate programming schedules.

While this system was commonly used in the United States to deliver non-network syndicated programs, it had never been used to continuously feed network stations. It was essential in Mexico, where telephone lines did not permit video transmission. Azcárraga had long relied on this distribution system to link his three Mexican networks.

Nicolás's experience as a scientist paid off. The procedure required a specialist able to devise a system with intricate variables and calculations. He hired Pedro Majul, a like-minded individual who had a special talent for devising efficiency measures, to direct the KWEX station. They perfected the SIN distribution network, not only getting programs to the first five stations but also eventually to twenty more.

But the system was slow to take shape and slower to promise dependability. At first, Nicolás received Telesistema programs sporadically and had to juggle the schedules of SIN's affiliates. Finally that May, progress came, and Nicolás and Majul began to relax as reel upon reel of recorded Mexican programs reached the warehouse on truck after truck.[21]

On June 3, 1962, Nicolás announced SIN's first fully coordinated primetime schedule.[22] It included the first U.S. telecast of Mexico's popular *Programa Paco Malgesto*, a variety show, and the novelas *Elena* and *Estafa de amor* (Love Scam).[23] Majul staggered the programs so episodes were seen in different cities on the same nights but in successive weeks. Still, many films that left San Antonio wound up damaged, out of sequence, or lost. Anselmo was anxious because he was not sure of the condition of films or which ones he would receive after they had hopscotched five times between San Antonio and Tijuana before they reached Los Angeles. Nicolás notified him that problems might not be solved until close to KMEX's premiere.[24]

* * *

Azcárraga had unrealistic expectations about when the SIN network could launch. He believed that KMEX could be built in eight months, in time for Mexican Independence Day. More unlikely was his premise for committing to SIN: he believed Fouce's characterization of UHF as untapped magic. Azcárraga overlooked the lesson learned in San Antonio on the opening night of Raoul Cortez's Channel 41, that home televisions were equipped to receive only the twelve original VHF channels. Few households could view the seventy UHF channels the FCC had made available in 1952.

Los Angeles awaited the arrival of Spanish-language television during an eventful period. It was the second year of the presidency of John F. Kennedy. That spring and summer, the Azcárragas, Anselmo, and others involved in the Spanish International Network became fans of JFK's New Frontier. Kennedy's initiatives included a policy that expanded the audiences that could be reached on UHF channels. They also brought a technological stride in satellite communications that excited Anselmo because it would eliminate the bicycle network and use satellites to interconnect SIN's stations.

Early in 1962, SIN found its first ally on U.S. turf. Kennedy's FCC chair, Newton Minow, took on UHF as a crusade. A year earlier, he had gained fame for a speech scorning television as a "vast wasteland." He blamed the "wasteland" on a small number of powerful broadcasters who controlled the twelve VHF channels. He went to Congress to demand legislation that would give all U.S. residents access to the seventy channels on UHF.

Although television manufacturers opposed him, Minow fought a fierce battle and prevailed. On May 18, 1962, Congress approved his All-Channel Receiver Act, which required that all TVs manufactured after April 1964 have UHF tuners.[25] "The public interest entails a television system . . . which will increase the diversity of commercial program choices," the law said.[26]

However, the UHF-equipped televisions would not arrive for two years. Publicity for Minow's push for new stations included an article in *Variety* that chose as an example "Los Angeles' new ultra-high frequency channel, KMEX-TV, [which] begins operations here on Sept. 15." This reminded Anselmo that trouble might lie ahead.[27]

However, Kennedy's signing of the All-Channel Receiver Act enthralled Anselmo. On July 23, 1962, the White House broadcast the ceremony to audiences in the United States and Europe via Telstar, the first communication satellite. Anselmo, who was frustrated with the problems with SIN's "bicycle" distribution system, foresaw that Telstar could be a way to deliver SIN's programs. He ordered pamphlets and materials from NASA. After he settled in New York, he traveled to Andover, Maine, to observe NASA's Telstar control and uplink center.[28]

One month earlier, Anselmo had gone to San Antonio to produce SIN's first telecasting feat. He had worked up the plans with his former associates at Telesistema. All were ready on June 30, 1962, when the president and Mrs. Kennedy visited Mexico City. Massive crowds gathered to see them. Telesistema broadcast the events using forty cameras. That night, a Mexican Air Force jet fighter flew the recordings to San Antonio. The next day, viewers of KWEX witnessed all fourteen hours of the coverage. "It's the public service world's record," Anselmo exclaimed.[29]

His elation was short lived. That year, Anselmo, who had recently relocated to the United States from Mexico, was in San Antonio for his first U.S. Fourth of July in ten years. On July 4, Anselmo picked up the phone and heard a frantic voice. It was Kaufman. "There was a crisis," Anselmo later related, and "I went [to Los Angeles] the same day, the Fourth of July, and had a long discussion with Kaufman."[30] Because they had been focused on equipment delays and the distribution network, neither had confronted the problem of UHF.[31]

It was the same issue that had escaped Raoul Cortez in 1955. To view KMEX on VHF-only TVs, viewers needed to install UHF converters. While Anselmo was away, Kaufman had turned to the task of publicizing KMEX's September 15 sign-on. But then he realized that the station also needed to tell viewers that they needed to purchase converters. He called Anselmo after driving through Los Angeles and finding no converters in stores.[32]

Kaufman advised Anselmo to inform Azcárraga that the September 15 premiere was off. But instead, Anselmo went to Los Angeles with a list of converter manufacturers Nicolás had contracted with seven years earlier. After one of the smaller firms, Hoffman Electronics, said it could attempt a rush production, Anselmo devised a plan to salvage KMEX's opening night. In exchange for free advertising, he signed the local Thrifty Drug Store chain on as California's "official UHF distributor." Thrifty contacted Hoffman and ordered 100,000 units. The size of the largest-ever UHF converter order lowered the cost of the units. Thrifty sold the converters in its 200 neighborhood stores for $21.97.[33]

Anselmo went ahead and initiated publicity. This freed Kaufman to concentrate on the technical snarls. Both were relieved when the last of the missing equipment arrived in early August. On August 8, newspapers reported the first test of the transmitter. The KMEX test pattern could be seen fifty miles in every direction.[34]

Three weeks later, Anselmo's drugstore campaign brought SIN its first sizable national notice. On August 27, *Broadcasting* featured the campaign in a section called "Fanfare." The magazine credited KMEX with "the most sophisticated UHF rollout to date." It noted "four-color, 24-sheet billboards in Mexican American neighborhoods, inside and outside bus cards, display material in all Thrifty stores," and "a contest offering five new Chevrolet Corvair sedans and 10 round-trip vacations for two in Mexico."[35]

Not all of the promotion went as planned. Anselmo believed that the best way to attract viewers to Spanish-language television was through Spanish-language radio. He approached KALI and KWKW, the city's two Spanish-language radio stations. Not only did both refuse to meet with him, announcers on KALI attacked KMEX on air for lying to advertisers. KALI told listeners that UHF could not reach nearly the audience that KMEX claimed. The radio stations recognized a rival that threatened to steal their audiences and sponsors.[36]

Anselmo persisted despite the brush fires that flared up. In the last weeks, one more problem emerged. After program schedules for September 15 were published, Thrifty sold all of the first 50,000 converters Hoffman had delivered. Told that truckloads with more converters would arrive within days, Kaufman delayed the launch until September 30.[37] When programming commenced at 3:00 P.M. that day, a Sunday, nearly 100,000 converters had found their way to Los Angeles homes. Anselmo changed the date on billboards and flyers. He surmised that one of the forthcoming programs had compelled more than Spanish-speaking viewers to buy the converters. It was *Corrida de toros,* recorded live coverage of bullfights from the Plaza de Toros in Mexico City.[38]

The launch of KMEX was the first triumph of U.S. Spanish-language television. Academy Award–winning actress Rita Moreno glowed as emcee. That afternoon, KMEX preceded a nighttime gala with the taped broadcast of President and Mrs. Kennedy's June visit to Mexico City. Through the evening, between samplings of weeknight programs, Mayor Sam Yorty, Governor Pat Brown, and former vice president Richard Nixon appeared. (Brown and Nixon were running against each other in the California gubernatorial race that fall.) At 9:00 P.M., the festivities climaxed with a two-hour broadcast of *Corrida de toros.*[39]

In the *Los Angeles Times,* Pepe Arciga, describing a "fantastic demonstration," wrote that the first broadcast of the new television station was a "phenomenal success."⁴⁰ He and *Times* reporter Rubén Salazar went on to publish weekly columns on the Spanish-language viewing experience. In an October 18 article, Arciga highlighted sports broadcasts. He was gripped by up-close camera angles of boxers and soccer players that had never been seen on English-language television. Later he complimented the drama *Hombres de Mexico* as a "well-acted" portrayal "of Mexican patriots." But he criticized *Humoroso musical* as "buffoonery" with "beauteous Mexican fashion models." He did not like the first Los Angeles broadcast of telenovelas. Because novelas exhibited "absurdity" and "over saturation," Arciga predicted that "this kind of fare" would cause viewers to "click back to regular channels."⁴¹

Corrida de toros touched off a tempest. Kaufman and Anselmo ensured a sizable audience by translating the audio portion into English and broadcasting it on radio. English-speaking viewers were able to watch the broadcast on TV while listening to an English-language account on the radio. The simulcast was promoted in English-language print ads. *Times* columnist Cecil Smith winced at the spectacle. "The bull was a very stalwart fellow who clung tenaciously to life and endured a great deal of killing. A third sword thrust—a coup de gras [sic]—finally got him."⁴² Hundreds wrote protest letters. The Society for the Prevention of Cruelty to Animals complained to the FCC.

The controversy amused Azcárraga. From Mexico City, he sent the U.S. an open letter to newspapers and magazines. "We respect your right to express your sentiments against bullfighting. However, it has been our experience here and in Spain that spectators from the United States attend bullfights with a feeling of superior benevolence." Azcárraga pointed out that "the good clean sport of American football accounted for some 65 deaths last year."⁴³

* * *

The debut of KMEX solidified SIN. Demographers had determined that upward of one million Mexican Americans lived in the Los Angeles area, three times more than in San Antonio. Those numbers promised large audiences and receptive sponsors.

Even so, red flags waved. Azcárraga's rush to launch KMEX and the crisis-ridden prelude to its ultimately riveting premiere revealed complexities of U.S. television that the Telesistema leader did not grasp. Although

Kaufman was pleased that Azcárraga could boast that he had taken Mexican television to a world media mecca, he remarked that never had a TV station been so poorly planned and so successfully launched.[44] It was a sign that the dream of a rich and visionary Mexican patriarch would not be fulfilled without ingenuity and effort.

No sooner had the station debuted than one of the first audience studies of the U.S. Spanish-speaking population suggested that more had escaped Azcárraga. The Pulse Corporation conducted a national field survey to determine the feasibility of expanding its Spanish-language marketing research. The findings raised questions for SIN. While Azcárraga claimed that "millions of Mexicans" lived in the United States, Pulse estimated that the total U.S. Spanish-speaking population was no more than five million. Notably, not all hailed from Mexico. Of the five million, one million lived in Los Angeles. But nearly as many, around 800,000, lived in New York. While San Antonio was the third-largest Spanish-speaking locale with 300,000, Miami followed closely with 250,000. New York and Miami were essential to a U.S. TV network. Yet they were far from Mexico. "Cultures vary," the study stressed, "Mexican in the Southwest" but "Cuban in Florida, and mostly Puerto Rican in New York."[45]

In addition, Anselmo's leadership had not shaped up exactly to the Azcárragas' liking. Anselmo had made two decisions that rankled the father and son. In late 1962, Anselmo introduced a nightly newscast at KMEX. Several weeks earlier, he had approved the hiring of a permanent newscaster and weathercaster. These hirings upgraded KWEX's long-running fifteen-minute nightly newscast. Anselmo had a passion for Spanish-language news. "A station should be like a crusading newspaper [and] a beacon where the Spanish can look for help," he maintained.[46]

When he learned of the newscasts, the elder Azcárraga contacted Anselmo to affirm that he understood that SIN was not to produce programs. He reiterated that the purpose of SIN was to broadcast Mexican shows. The cameras and studios he provided were to be used only for commercials. Azcárraga relented and agreed to the newscasts, and he also consented to the production of any local program. However, he strictly prohibited SIN's production of network programs. Anselmo was to observe the restriction as a cardinal rule.

Emilio Azcárraga instructed Anselmo on the other issue, payment for access to Telesistema programming. It came up late that fall when Anselmo was preparing to relocate to New York. He had not paid Telesistema for the programs SIN had televised in 1962. As Telesistema's chief financial officer, the younger Azcárraga was accountable for revenue. When Anselmo explained that SIN had not earned enough in sales to make the payment, Emilio postponed collection until Anselmo had gone to New York and gathered cash from national advertisers. But he repeated that "the programs are not free" and that SIN had to pay all of its fees. This was the younger Azcárraga's cardinal rule.[47]

Because cash flow had made the need for Anselmo's move to New York more urgent, another complication arose. With Anselmo bound for New York and Kaufman returning to San Diego, KMEX had no station manager. Anselmo and Kaufman had hired advertising executive Bert Avedon before they left Los Angeles. Avedon, who was not a broadcaster, took the post reluctantly. Anselmo hoped to bide his time until he could recruit a permanent manager in Los Angeles, one he could trust to radiate SIN's identity and service to Latinos in its largest locale.

Anselmo arrived in New York in January 1963. He immediately incorporated the venture he had proposed, naming it SIN Sales. This delighted the Azcárragas. Although SIN Sales had no operational identity and was phantom within the structure of SIN and SIBC, the unit officially and legally was a separately chartered firm. Officially, it not only generated network sales but also owned the programs and facilities used to deliver SIN to its affiliate stations. But its importance was as an official and legal entity that the Azcárragas owned. Because it was created to officiate over network programming and network delivery—not station broadcasting—SIN Sales could not be licensed by the FCC. Also, the Azcárragas, who were allowed only 20 percent ownership of the stations, owned 100 percent of SIN Sales. Looking ahead to his incorporation of SIN Sales and his direction of all of the company's functions from New York, on January 1, 1963, he hosted a swank holiday press party to inaugurate SIN's Park Avenue headquarters.

In addition to a newfound craving for opulence, Anselmo shed his appearance as Azcárraga's stooge. He signaled that new persona when he revealed that he had not forgotten radio station KALI's bashing of KMEX on air. He filed a $1.2 million libel suit in Los Angeles County Superior Court. The suit alleged that KALI had known that tens of thousands of Los Angeles homes were equipped to receive UHF, yet its personnel had persisted in telling listeners that KMEX had lied to advertisers and the public about the large numbers of viewers it could reach. Anselmo's attorneys withdrew the suit when KALI agreed to suspend further incriminating reports about KMEX.[48]

Soon after the lawsuit concluded in January 1963, the press in Los Angeles turned to a brighter story. Nashville radio broadcasters Calvin Young and Jerry Glaser had come to Los Angeles to initiate the city's second UHF station. The station, KIIX, was one of the first to specialize in African American programming. After they launched the station that March, they made headlines by announcing that KIIX would be the flagship of KIX, the first African American television network. The partners had begun making arrangements for affiliate stations in New York, Philadelphia, Detroit, and St. Louis. Observers lauded a breakthrough in media diversity. The *Los Angeles Times* compared KIX to SIN. Young and Glaser told the *Times* that "like KMEX," the key station, KIIX-TV, "is a UHF facility operating on Channel 22." Like SIN, they intended to feed minority programs to "UHF stations all over the United States."[49]

Six months later, KIX was bankrupt. *Times* columnist Cecil Smith puzzled over the ruin of African American network television. It was curious, he said, that the African American network "quickly ran out of money [while] Spanish TV has prospered."[50] It was puzzling only because observers did not know about SIN's rich Mexican benefactor. The difference was SIN's vast supply of programs, its startup financing from experienced media personnel, and language differences between Spanish- and English-speaking audiences that gave KMEX a unique advantage. Had Smith and others dug deeper, they would have discovered that a year after the startup, SIN was faring no better than KIX at its fundamental and life-sustaining task: attracting advertisers.

Anselmo started off well. Settling in as head of SIN Sales, he formed a capable staff. In late 1963, they landed a contract with Quaker Oats. Quaker was the first major corporation to advertise on television in Spanish.[51] But total sales sputtered, and revenue fell far below Anselmo's projections.

Anselmo's attention was divided between sales and grander initiatives. He was eager to assume the duty that the late Frank Fouce was to have performed: expanding the network. Anselmo blamed the slow sales on SIN's lack of a TV station in New York. Major ad agencies were located there. In mid-1963, Anselmo applied for a New York license and traveled to other cities in search of additional stations and affiliates.

He routinely visited Los Angeles and San Antonio. He continued to oversee and sometimes contribute to the local news operations he pushed at KMEX and KWEX. In April 1963, he attended the premiere of KMEX's upgraded nightly newscast, *Actualides y personalidades* (News and Personalities). While virtually all English-language stations broadcast fifteen minutes of news, the KMEX newscast was half an hour long. Its presenters consisted of a permanent news anchor and a permanent weathercaster.[52]

At the end of 1963, Anselmo returned to San Antonio to orchestrate another news spectacular. As he had the year before, he tapped the resources of Telesistema. On November 21, 1963, with Telesistema cameras and crews in San Antonio, KWEX originated live coverage of a visit by President Kennedy and the First Lady. On KWEX, viewers saw the only extended TV coverage of Kennedy's San Antonio motorcade and his speech at Brooks Air Force Base. That night, recordings were flown to Telesistema for broadcast in Mexico. Mexican viewers saw the San Antonio events the following afternoon, at the same moment when Kennedy was assassinated in Dallas.[53]

Financial concerns multiplied. After losing $100,000 in 1963, Anselmo notified Emilio Azcárraga that, again, SIN could not pay its programming fees. It was another violation of the son's cardinal rule. But the elder Azcárraga intervened. Over the son's objections, the father delayed the 1963 payment. In 1964, despite the fact that Anselmo had signed Pepsi, Colgate, Schick, and Miller Brewing Company as advertising clients, SIN's $350,000 in revenue did not approach its $500,000 in expenses. After salaries, programming fees of $100,000 remained the largest expense. For the third year, SIN had not paid them.[54] When the father again delayed payment, the son urged that they cut their losses and shut down SIN. The father scolded him. He did not want to hear the topic of terminating SIN again.[55]

Knowing none of this, the press continued to publicize SIN's success. The flagship journal of the broadcast advertising industry, *Sponsor*, twice showcased the "power" and increasing "importance [of the] Spanish International Network (SIN)."[56] In 1967, the popular magazine *Television* featured SIN on its cover. It observed that Anselmo "is geared for what promises to be a bullish future." Ethnic TV "can be done," it said, and "Spanish International Broadcasting did it."[57]

Anselmo manufactured much of the fanfare. He treated each sponsor signing and affiliate acquisition as a media event, including his 1966 addition of Chicago's Channel 26, WCIU .[58] He had a knack for holding court with reporters. They liked a figure they could portray as a TV crusader with a talent for colorful quotes. When a reporter asked about his language proficiency, Anselmo replied, "I can speak Spanish better than most militants."[59] Asked about the devices viewers needed for switching to UHF, Anselmo said there were "so many conversions that Billy Graham never had it so good."[60]

However, the moment Anselmo first approached potential advertisers, he struggled against a familiar obstacle. The industry excluded Spanish-language television in its reports of TV viewing. Ethnic discrimination was rife within the TV industry, and writers and reporters did not want to cover that story. In 1965, an event in San Antonio illustrated the handicap. Emilio Nicolás and the KWEX sales staff were close to landing an advertising contract with a Ford dealership in San Antonio. Yet at the last moment, owner Red McCombs, eventually one of Texas's most famed billionaires, pulled out. Years later, McCombs recalled the episode. "I adored Emilio Nicolás and wanted to help SIN, but you couldn't do it," he said. "You couldn't advertise if you didn't know how many people were watching."[61] McCombs did place a small order, and his support did help SIN.

At first Anselmo believed that the two providers of TV ratings, Nielsen and ARB, gave lists of programs to viewers. In fact, the ratings were calculated from diaries in which viewers were free to write in any programs they viewed. It was apparent that SIN was absent in the ratings because the ratings companies excluded Spanish-speaking viewers. While convinced of discrimination, Anselmo was not ready to amplify his conclusions by making public a case that discrimination existed.

But he did raise the issue with humor. At the 1965 convention of the National Association of Broadcasters, Anselmo made light of the industry's bias at a reception while treating attendees to tacos and margaritas. They came because he had papered the convention with a flyer made to look like an FBI all-points bulletin. It read: "WARNING! We've got our eyes on you slick banditos. . . . A bunch of audience thieves showing all those sexy Latin women . . . gory bullfights . . . and those serials full of disgusting emotion. . . . Advertisers are getting lots of results . . . so lay off." The warning was issued by the "SPMMMS," the "Society for the Preservation of Monoglothic Marketing and Media Strategy."[62]

* * *

On the afternoon in 1962 that KMEX signed on from its Melrose Avenue studio, sports history was made five miles away at the Los Angeles Coliseum. That September 30, a 24-year-old Los Angeles Rams athlete named Danny Villanueva kicked a 51-yard field goal. At the time, it was the longest kick in the annals of the National Football League.

For Villanueva, the day did not end well. His team lost to the Dallas Cowboys. The Rams finished the season at 1-13. Yet during postgame TV interviews, Villanueva made every defeat seem like a victory. KMEX manager Bert Avedon noticed his cool and articulate demeanor. Anselmo watched him on TV for the first time in 1964, around the time Avedon departed.[63] Still looking for a leader for SIN's largest property, Anselmo had a notion of who it might be.

Born in 1938 in Tucumcari, New Mexico, Villanueva was the ninth of twelve children of parents who were Protestant ministers. The family lost its home in Calexico, California, moved to Phoenix, and returned to Calexico. Villanueva excelled in high school. At New Mexico State University, he acted, edited the school newspaper, and quarterbacked the Aggies football team. He also was the team's kicker. In 1960, he graduated with a degree in literature. He applied for jobs as a teacher. But then former Rams star and then executive Elroy Hirsch flew to Las Cruces to audition him. Instead of testing him as a quarterback, Hirsch asked Villanueva to kick the ball. Hirsch signed him up, and Villanueva joined the Rams that fall.[64]

After Tom Fears, who had starred for the Rams in the 1940s and 1950s, Villanueva was the NFL's second Latino player. For three years, Villanueva held the league's best punting average. He set another NFL record by kicking sixty-six consecutive points after touchdown. He was "bronze, bull shouldered, and square jawed," sports writer John Hall wrote, and "brimming with charisma."[65] Nicknamed El Kickador, he was a hero in the Los Angeles Latino community and in all of Los Angeles.[66]

Not all of his battles were on the field. His family struggled against racial prejudice. Immediately after joining the Rams, that is what he encountered. During his rookie season, star running back and future KIIX sportscaster Dick Bass stood up and joked, "All you whites get on that bus, all you blacks on the other—and you, Villanueva, you catch a cab."[67] Villanueva appreciated Bass's humor, but he was changed by the episode. "I knew I was different," he later said. "Crystal clear to me was to use my position for good as a role model." After games, he said, "Instead of going out for beer, I went out to speak."[68]

In 1964, Villanueva joined KMEX as a high-profile sportscaster on its enlarged nightly news. He continued to play for the Rams. After KMEX "sent me out in public to sign autographs and mingle with advertisers" and after securing numerous sponsors, Villanueva took on a larger role. He gravitated to KMEX's business side. When Avedon left, Joseph Rank, an associate of the late Fouce Sr. who was nearing retirement, agreed to head KMEX. Immediately, Rank began preparing Villanueva to be his successor.

The grooming hit a bump. On the eve of the 1965 season, the Rams traded Villanueva to the Dallas team.[69] "I was still a player and I knew I had to go to Dallas," Villanueva later recounted. The Dallas coach, Tom Landry, had assembled numerous future Hall of Fame players, including Don Meredith, Bob Lilly, and Mel Renfro, for a team that was certain to contend for the NFL championship.

However, Villanueva could not bring himself to resign from KMEX. He proposed to Rank that he continue some of his duties while commuting from Dallas, but Rank answered that the Cowboys management had to approve. Villanueva approached Landry and explained his passion for staying at KMEX. "I decided I would quit [football] if the Cowboys showed no understanding."[70] Landry understood.

For three seasons, Villanueva continued to work in Los Angeles while shuttling to Dallas and to other cities when the Cowboys were on the road.[71] On December 31, 1967, the Cowboys played for the NFL championship in subzero temperatures in Green Bay, Wisconsin. Villanueva kicked a field goal that appeared to provide the winning points. However, thirteen seconds before the game ended, Green Bay Packers quarterback Bart Starr called a sneak play and won the game. Remarkably, Villanueva flew back to Los Angeles and reported what many would consider one of the greatest football games ever played on KMEX's late news.[72]

That day's game, known as the Ice Bowl, was Villanueva's last. It was so devastating, Villanueva would relate, "that I went back to Dallas and cleaned out my locker. I didn't speak to Landry for ten years."[73] By this time, Rank had promoted Villanueva to an executive post as program manager.

Villanueva later recalled that he first met Anselmo when the SIN president visited KMEX in the summer of 1966. Rank introduced him as the new program manager.[74] Villanueva remembered the meeting because he was attending the Cowboys' summer training camp in nearby Thousand Oaks, California, and because Anselmo barely acknowledged the introduction. "He looked like he'd seen a ghost," Villanueva thought. After the session, Rank explained to Villanueva that Anselmo had been "going around to banks trying to find a loan" and "was upset about money that involved our partners in Mexico."[75]

* * *

During an unpleasant year at Telesistema, new questions about the future of SIN had precipitated a confrontation between the two Azcárragas. Early in 1966, Anselmo submitted his report on SIN's performance the previous year. In 1965, the network had earned $550,000, spent $750,000, and finished with a $200,000 deficit.[76] In events later reconstructed in court, Emilio Azcárraga finally pressed Anselmo about four years of Telesistema program fees that SIN had not paid. Anselmo had not paid the latest fee of $150,000 owed for 1965. Nor had he paid any of the $400,000 that was due from 1964, 1963, and 1962. "I would have taken anything" merely so "we'd know [he knew] we were not giving him the programs for free," Emilio Azcárraga later said.[77]

When Anselmo brushed off the issue of the growing debt, the son went to the father. Complaining that SIN owed half a million dollars for programming, more than Anselmo ever could repay, Emilio Azcárraga demanded that the father abandon SIN. The son wanted to sell the stations SIBC owned and use the proceeds to recover the loss. The elder Azcárraga was furious. He reminded the son that he wanted no further discussion on ending the U.S. venture.

Emilio Azcárraga revolted. In the summer of 1966, he turned to the seven other members of the Telesistema board. All of them shared his concerns. That August, he summoned Anselmo to Mexico City to appear before the board. An insurrection ensued. "Isn't it about time those stations paid for the programming?" the younger Azcárraga clamored. Anselmo flailed about. He later recalled that no matter what he said, "someone would let out a remark, 'When are they going to pay for the programs?'"[78]

The session ended with the board's decision to terminate SIN. Eight members voted in favor. Only the elder Azcárraga dissented. Members gave Anselmo one last chance: SIN could immediately pay all of the money that was owed. Emilio Azcárraga later explained that two factors sealed the

Figure 4. Emilio Azcárraga Milmo (*left*) is seen with Emilio Nicolás at a 1987 reunion that brought together founders of the Spanish International Network. Although eventually a champion of SIN, in 1966 Azcárraga Milmo advocated that his father, Azcárraga Vidaurreta, abandon the U.S. network. Milmo was heir to his father's firm, Telesistema Méxicano, which Milmo reorganized as Televisa in 1973. He played a major role in the growth of SIN in the 1960s and 1970s and in its conversion to Univision in 1986. Photo courtesy of Guillermo Nicolás.

decision to end SIN. First, the Telesistema directors agreed that their network could not continue providing "free" programs. They had approved of the U.S. network because of the elder Azcárraga's promise that Telesistema would earn income from programs broadcast in the United States. Second, the prevailing sentiment was that SIN could not overcome losses and turn a profit unless Telesistema sent its own executives to the United States.[79] They suspected that Anselmo was extravagant.

Anselmo confessed that he had gone to Los Angeles with no prospect of raising $500,000 dollars. As he later recounted, "Don Emilio was pressured by his partners . . . to insist on payment of long overdue programming expenses."[80]

But instead of closing the book on SIN, the episode turned a page. Before or soon after the revolt, the elder Azcárraga had assigned an associate to investigate which foreign countries were friendly to offshore corporations. The associate recommended an ideal locale: Panama. Its government had no restrictions that prohibited non-Panamanians from chartering corporations there. Many foreign enterprises had chartered in Panama because owners were not required to identify investors and say where funds were spent. Because part of Panama was a U.S. territory and the country's currency was the U.S. dollar, a case could be made that funds transacted in Panama were from the United States.[81]

The elder Azcárraga sent an emissary to Panama who brought back approved papers from Panama's Department of Commerce for a sole-proprietor TV program corporation called VT Latin. Azcárraga then told the Telesistema board that SIN had enlisted VT Latin as a partner and that its revenue was now contributing to SIN's cash flow. That fall, Azcárraga presented a promissory note produced by SIN that acknowledged the debts SIN owed Telesistema. The directors were satisfied. Without objection, they agreed to continue the U.S. network.[82]

VT Latin later became a program distributor. But at the time it was a dummy corporation with one asset: Azcárraga's bank account.[83] With VT Latin, Azcárraga had created a mechanism for using his personal money to save SIN. No doubt suspecting the ruse, Telesistema's directors did not pry. They were delighted by the windfall of cash. Azcárraga's scheme deepened his violation of the U.S. foreign ownership rule. Yet only through an intricate investigation could the U.S. government trace money laundered in Panama that wound up as income on SIN's books back to Mexico. Azcárraga did not invent the device as a temporary measure to resolve the 1966 crisis. The arrangement was permanent. Azcárraga's gesture and largesse had rebirthed SIN as an enterprise that was not without challenges but that would now pay its bills.[84]

A development in San Antonio underscored Spanish International's brightened fortunes. In late 1966, Emilio Nicolás negotiated a $1.6 million loan from San Antonio's Frost National Bank. Nicolás's achievement brought SIBC its first significant U.S. financing. When he heard of the loan, Anselmo persuaded a second investor, real estate tycoon Herbert Scheftel, to allow SIBC to build and operate a forthcoming New York station. Scheftel's company, Trans-Tel, had a TV license in New York.[85]

Encouraged by Nicolás's initiative, Azcárraga gave Anselmo new orders. With money in hand, he was to begin building the New York station at once. It was assigned Channel 41.[86]

At the end of the year, Anselmo gathered reporters to announce an achievement: SIN's first profit. He did not acknowledge VT Latin or say that without it, SIN would have reported record loses. *Variety* featured the story under an inch-high headline: "Spanish U's Move Into the Black."[87]

It is said that in late 1966 the elder Azcárraga, complaining of his son's excessive investment of Telesistema resources in projects for Mexico City's forthcoming Olympic Games, first publicly uttered a characterization he would repeat. While the remark did not refer to SIN, the elder Azcárraga had occasion to express his feelings about the person who had nearly destroyed it: "My son the idiot."[88]

3

BREAKOUT OF SPANISH INTERNATIONAL

In 1964, the two Azcárragas again felt political heat. Back in 1960, newly elected president Adolfo López Mateos and his Department of Communication had listened to concerns expressed by independent radio station owners and small film producers that they could not do business and enlarge and diversify Mexican mass media in an environment in which the Azcárragas and their massive Telesistema Méxicano controlled audiences, advertising, infrastructure, production, and distribution. The Azcárragas' fears that the government would initiate the breakup of Telesistema had contributed to their decision to launch a television network, the Spanish International Network, in the United States. In 1961, pleased when the Azcárragas announced their venture to extend Mexican television into the United States and to reverse a decades-long course in which U.S. firms had entered Mexico and controlled much of the country's economy, Mateos and the government backed off. In 1961, they left the Azcárragas monopoly intact. But in 1964, the Mexican government's restlessness resurfaced when Gustavo Díaz Ordaz was elected president. Strict and uncompromising, he had initiated whirlwind economic reforms that had brought Mexico its first glimmer of prosperity. But he administered his "Mexican miracle" with an iron fist. He told Azcárraga to use his fortune for the betterment of Mexico or face massive taxation and government oversight.

Heeding Díaz Ordaz, Azcárraga joined Telesistema with another monopoly that was under pressure, Teléfonos de Mexico, in one of Mexico's boldest modernization projects: a nationwide microwave communications system that carried Mexico into the telecommunications age.[1] The initiative fulfilled a primary objective of modernization: sophistication of Mexico's creaking telephone system. For the first time, Mexicans could direct dial all telephone calls. They no longer needed to place calls by first calling operators. This meant that Telesistema no longer had to rely on the bicycle network to get programs from Mexico City to stations in outlying regions. The new system made it possible for Telesistema's three networks to electronically feed programs directly to viewers throughout the country, from Mexico's northern tier to the Yucatan peninsula.[2] But the government forced Azcárraga to pay for a share of the $100 million it cost to construct the new infrastructure.

Díaz Ordaz pushed another expensive project intended to showcase his "Mexican miracle." The International Olympic Committee had chosen Mexico City as the site for the 1968 Olympic Games. Azcárraga was aware that Díaz Ordaz expected him to contribute and freed his son Emilio to work with the organizing committee. By late 1966, Emilio Azcárraga was spending lavishly on arrangements for the games. He was directing the construction of Mexico's largest structure, the 80,000-seat Azteca Stadium in Mexico City, which Telesistema paid for. The stadium was where the games were to be played. For several years, Emilio's attention was focused on the Olympics.

Despite Azcárraga's measures to assist Díaz Ordaz, the government dealt him a hammering blow when it ended his monopoly on Mexican television in 1967. After accepting bids for the construction of a fourth TV network, it gave the licenses for the new network to billionaire industrialist Eugenio Garza Sada of Monterrey.[3]

In 1967, when Garza Sada launched Televisión Independiente de México from Mexico City and financed a studio there, Azcárraga's Telesistema felt distress on two fronts. Garza Sada's network was producing programs that vied for Azcárraga's viewers. In addition, he was the founder and head of the progressive Instituto Tecnológico de Monterrey, whose engineers were working with NASA on the design of parts for communication satellites. While Telesistema was touting the microwave system, Garza Sada was focused on delivering his network from outer space, perhaps internationally.[4]

The elder Azcárraga had yet another concern. U.S. companies were eating into Telesistema's largest source of revenue, international program sales. One of the Hollywood studios, Columbia Pictures, was finding fortune south of the border. The threat materialized in the form of a Columbia Pictures subsidiary called Screen Gems. Under John H. Mitchell, Screen Gems had become a dominant producer of popular series seen on the U.S. networks. In the early 1960s, Screen Gems released its hit shows with Spanish-overdubbed soundtracks and sold them abroad. Latin American viewers saw dramas that included *Naked City,* comedies such as *I Dream of Jeannie* and *The Flying Nun,* and the popular cartoon series *The Flintstones* and *The Jetsons.*[5]

At age seventy-two, the elder Azcárraga had entered his last years. Anselmo believed that the patriarch was salving his anxieties in Mexico by contemplating the possibilities of his venture in the United States. Since the passing of Frank Fouce Sr., Azcárraga had spoken little of the vision that had joined the two in the founding of SIN. But since Anselmo had obtained a license in New York, Azcárraga's zeal had resumed; he knew that it would mean broadcasts in the United States from coast to coast.[6]

However, times had changed. Economic constraints were making it difficult to acquire UHF stations. Telesistema's heavy spending on public works had coincided with its board's assault on SIN in August 1966. Telesistema could no longer finance U.S. stations and infrastructure, and Azcárraga could no longer subsidize the network as a secret financier. He continued his VT Latin funding scheme but covered no more than SIN's programming debts and operating losses. Expansion depended on whether Anselmo and his U.S. associates at SIBC could attract investors.

Slowly, SIN and SIBC did expand. In 1966, it acquired its third station, KFTV on Fresno's Channel 21. That year SIN signed Weigel Broadcasting's WCIU, Channel 26, in Chicago, and KPAZ on Channel 21 in Phoenix. These stations plus KWEX in San Antonio, KMEX in Los Angeles, and the five border stations in Mexico brought the number of stations in the SIN network to ten.[7]

The $1.6 million loan that Emilio Nicolás negotiated with the Frost National Bank in San Antonio had taken Anselmo to the starting line in New York. The job of constructing a new station was shaping up as a repeat of his triumph at KMEX. However, by the time Anselmo began work on New York's Channel 41, rumors were circulating about a new experience in Spanish-language television: competition.

* * *

WNJU had studios in the historic Mosque Theatre Building in downtown Newark, New Jersey, and a full power transmitter on New York's Empire State Building. Nothing on television was like it. In 1963, six company directors had raised a million dollars for a license to operate on Channel 47. They envisioned a form of public television that they felt the official U.S. public network, NET, the predecessor of PBS, was ignoring. WNJU's founder, Edwin Cooperstein, was a former NET executive. He hoped to "out public" public TV and to prove that it could be done with sponsors. He courted his fellow directors with an inventive business plan: programming aimed at every conceivable sector of New York's diverse population.

Cooperstein launched WNJU on May 16, 1965. Promoting it as TV's "most innovative channel," he combed New York's ethnic communities for producers and talent. Cooperstein and his WNJU programming staff assembled a schedule of programs in multiple languages. The first night the channel broadcast, viewers saw *Noticias Italia* (Italy News; in Italian), *Señorita española* (Spanish Lady; in Spanish), and *Jewish Caravan* and *Negro Builders of America* (both in English).[8] Other programs were broadcast in German, Polish, Greek, and Yiddish.[9] "This is not like Channel X where the viewer sits down and watches 'I Love Lucy,'" Cooperstein told the *New York Times*. "We're reaching for diverse programming. We're reaching for diverse performers. And we're reaching, of course, for a diverse audience."[10]

The station attracted viewers and launched to rave reviews. Its wealthy investors subsidized a formidable technical operation; WNJU was the first New York station to fully broadcast in color. Cooperstein showed foresight by addressing the problem that had hamstrung Anselmo in New York. He hired a research firm, Med-Mark, to record the number of viewers in ethnic neighborhoods. The first ethnic audience ratings brought advertisers. The chief asset was WNJU's full-power Empire State Building transmitter, which provided a clear color signal across three states.[11]

But by 1967, the novelty had faded and ratings were in decline. The investors reduced the endowment. Cooperstein acknowledged that the station was $1 million in debt. Although sponsors were still supportive of WNJU, they complained that programs that changed languages every half-hour repelled viewers. Cooperstein responded by populating prime time with exclusively Spanish-language variety shows. Latino artists were available, and Spanish-speaking individuals constituted New York's largest ethnic concentration. When Cooperstein introduced programs hosted by entertainers Gaspar Pumarejo and Bobby Capó in the spring of 1967, ratings increased.¹²

That spring, Anselmo began construction of Channel 41. By the summer, he was obsessively watching the programming on WNJU. He was not troubled by its local Spanish-language variety shows, but he noticed that WNJU's lineup included a few Hollywood shows. All were popular U.S. series that had been overdubbed in Spanish, and all of them ended with the animated logo of the woman holding the torch that people saw on Screen Gems and Columbia Pictures films.

Anselmo's concern grew on September 16, 1967. That day, WNJU changed its programming. "With the start of our third Fall Season," ads announced, "almost all of our programs . . . are completely in Spanish." Now as the "Number One Spanish-language TV station in the Western Hemisphere," WNJU claimed, "more than 1,500,000 Spanish-speaking residents of the N.Y.,-N.J.-Conn. area believe in and depend on Channel 47."¹³

What alarmed Anselmo was WNJU's adoption of programs from Columbia Pictures, an enterprise with a large stock of Spanish-language content that rivaled Telesistema in international sales. But the *New York Times* did notice that WNJU, which once had been known for "opening its studios [to] wrestling and boxing matches," had turned to "taped programs." Cooperstein conceded that in previous years, "the prime reason we lost money is that we decided on the heavy live programming."¹⁴ WNJU viewers now saw *Ruta 66* with Martin Milner and George Maharis, *La ruta del sol* (Follow the Sun) with Gary Lockwood, and *Hechizada* (Bewitched) with Elizabeth Montgomery.¹⁵

In 1965, Columbia president Abe Schneider reorganized Screen Gems as a unit that was engaged in broadcasting, not just in producing programs. That year, Screen Gems acquired stations in New Orleans and Salt Lake City. For the first time since the government had forced Paramount Pictures to exit from television, a move that had killed the early Dumont network, a Hollywood studio owned TV properties.

The acquisitions brought attention because Columbia Pictures was one of six major motion picture studios. Long the weakest studio, Columbia benefited from two developments at the onset of television. One was its creation of Screen Gems. The other was the Justice Department's breakup of its rival, Paramount, in 1948. The landmark antitrust ruling effectively prohibited the studios from forming and owning outright a television network that could compete with ABC, CBS, and NBC and had forced Paramount to sell the theatres it owned and withdraw from motion picture exhibition. The Justice Department believed that the studios that controlled exhibition through network television would constitute a restraint of trade. However, motion picture studios remained interested in forming a television network.

Not long after its programs appeared on WNJU, Columbia Pictures disclosed another acquisition. Its latest purchase suggested a plan by which the studio might own a network and not compete with ABC, CBS, and NBC: it bought out WAPA, a television system in Puerto Rico in San Juan. The Puerto Rico network was a producer and exporter of telenovelas. In early 1968, Hollywood learned of another move. Screen Gems announced an agreement by which it would provide a combination of movies overdubbed in Spanish and TV series and WAPA's novelas to independent stations WCIX in Miami, KSCI in Los Angeles, and WSNS in Chicago.[16]

There was no doubt that Columbia Pictures was embarked on the launch of a Spanish-language network. Columbia Pictures had reason to believe its venture would succeed.

Pending FCC approval of its acquisitions, Screen Gems refused to discuss the emerging network. However, reports from New York supported the rumors that the studio was committed to a venture in Spanish-language television. All along, Cooperstein had denied rumors that his eclectic TV station was about to succumb to Hollywood interests. Yet in 1968 others on the WNJU board who shared ownership of the station began quarreling with Cooperstein and then fired him. The next move identified the flagship of a network in the making. On September 15, 1968, paying $8 million, Columbia Pictures acquired WNJU.[17]

* * *

At Spanish International, Anselmo sized up a situation that, in his words, "comes upon us like a breath of fresh mustard gas."[18] He was preparing to celebrate SIN's arrival on New York's Channel 41, which he named WXTV. He had acquired a building in Paterson, New Jersey, for WXTV's studios and tower. He had hired technicians and recruited a sales staff. Personnel had rehearsed arrangements with San Antonio for delivering Telesistema's programs via the bicycle network. He had circulated advance materials to ad agencies that promoted WXTV's "wealth of talent."[19] He announced that the channel would debut in February 1968.

But Anselmo called off the February launch. He was prepared to compete against Screen Gems, but he delayed because of a problem that was certain to sink WXTV. Broadcasting from the roof of the Paterson building, WXTV could not match WNJU's transmitting signal. While WNJU could be seen in three states, WXTV would not have reached all of New York City.

In October 1967, Anselmo applied for an installation on the Empire State Building. He was shaken when New York City commissioners did not respond right away. WNJU's engineers claimed that because of interference, Channels 41 and 47 could not use the same transmitting site. The commissioners leaned toward siding with WNJU. But when they agreed to study Anselmo's claim that side-by-side UHF towers would not cause interference, the decision was delayed. Anselmo pushed the premiere to July 1.[20]

In the midst of the transmitter dispute, Anselmo and his staff realized that they were facing a second problem. WXTV was intending to compete for WNJU's Puerto Rican- and Caribbean-descended audiences with Azcárraga's Mexican shows. When Anselmo consulted Danny Villanueva, the program director of Los Angeles's KMEX, he and Anselmo "argued ceaselessly about showing the [Mexican] programs in New York." Anselmo pressed Villanueva about what programs might appeal to Puerto Rican and Caribbean viewers. Villanueva recommended that Anselmo confer with his New York staff.[21]

Anselmo did so. But rather than consulting with senior executives, he turned to a 22-year-old sales trainee named Carole Bird. Anselmo chose her because she had grown up in New York and Miami, had traveled to Spain and Latin America, and had knowledge of different Spanish-speaking nationalities and cultures. Anselmo asked Bird to view the recordings he had obtained from Villanueva.

The recordings, known as air checks, enabled Bird to screen programs exactly as viewers in Los Angeles had seen them. On a typical night, KMEX and SIN carried a variety of programs similar to those seen in Mexico on Azcárraga's Channel 2. Prime time usually began with comedies, then moved to music and variety shows, and finished with a sports broadcast. Bird rejected them as too Mexican. However, Bird, who was aware of other programs Telesistema produced, told Anselmo what WXTV might do instead. She proposed that the station schedule novelas back to back in prime time. Bird explained that "the *novelas* [in other Spanish-speaking countries] were not about Mexico." She told Anselmo that the music, locations, and actors were not Mexican and that "the speaking had no [Mexican] dialects." Moreover, the "*novelas* were so captivating that you were going to watch regardless of your nationality," Bird said.[22]

Anselmo pondered Bird's radical idea. Network television had never attempted a prime-time schedule of programs of one genre. However, Bird spoke to highly informed ears. Years before, Anselmo had peddled novelas as the director of Teleprogramas de México. He remembered the strategies Azcárraga had used to universalize the novelas and how rapidly they had sold in all Latin American countries.

Anselmo followed up by sending WXTV projects director Loraine Ramer to Los Angeles to study the occasional novelas KMEX aired. Villanueva objected to the banality of the programs. He questioned the plan to request more novelas so that WXTV could break away from SIN's regular schedule. Yet in his first network-level assignment, Villanueva agreed to team with Emilio Nicolás in San Antonio to procure the novelas from Telesistema and get them to New York.[23] "When I went to Los Angeles to learn about the programming," Ramer later recounted, "I came back convinced that if we did this, we would do very well."[24]

The transmitter battle came to an impasse. The WXTV transmitter was in boxes one week before the July 1 sign on. Blaming "ludicrous" WNJU petitions and New York City commissioners biased against a new Latino channel, Anselmo gave up on the 102-story Empire State Building. The commissioners offered a compromise. They approved a tower on top of the sixty-seven story Cities Services Building. Yet when WXTV engineers tested the transmitter, all of the building's elevators and air conditioners shut down. For the time being, Anselmo gave up on daytime programming. Only at night when the building was empty was there enough electricity.[25]

The waiting ended on August 4, 1968, a Sunday night. Interested merely in "getting the damn thing on the air," Anselmo staged a simple premiere. There was no opening gala like the one in Los Angeles. The first broadcast was a Catholic Mass. The *New York Times* reported that "a staff announcer briefly welcomed viewers to the new outlet." Then, "Channel 41 made its programming debut with tape recordings of bull fights from Tijuana,

Mexico, and then [broadcast] only filmed or taped material."[26] Anselmo did not order billboards and ads until three weeks later.

Yet by October, the station, as Bird recalled, had "caught fire."[27] The first of the novelas began their episodic runs. According to Ramer, "enthusiastic telephone calls" poured in.[28] Sponsors placed orders. Sales executives heard talk of WXTV on the street. Med-Mark's ratings of the New York City area estimated the total number of viewers who tuned in to WXTV and WNJU, then reported the percentages of the total viewers the two stations reached. Surveyed for the first time that November, the new station achieved 40 percent of New York's Spanish-speaking audience. Seven months later, in June 1969, WXTV was the top Spanish-language channel with 56 percent of the Spanish-speaking audience; WNJU was second with 44 percent. The ratings were close, but they defied expectations that WNJU would trounce WXTV.[29]

WXTV did more than schedule novelas back to back. Each one was extended across WXTV's Monday–Friday schedule. Six half-hour novelas were shown every night of the week. WXTV claimed first place when it carried *Alma de mi alma* (Soul of My Soul), *El dolor de amar* (The Pain of Loving), and *La leona* (The Lioness).[30] The station anticipated high ratings when *La leona* began; it already had been televised in several countries and was a hit everywhere. It featured a typical novela plot: a destitute woman falsely jailed for kidnapping a child is arrested. Abandoning the child, she flees to Las Vegas. Growing up angry, the child then learns that the parents she knows have been killed but that the mother who abandoned her has actually saved her and loves her.[31]

The outcome in New York turned heads. The foreign novelas from Mexico exposed the Spanish-overdubbed Hollywood series of Screen Gems and Columbia Pictures as weak. Bird's idea became a defining characteristic of Spanish-language television in the United States. Later Valeria Palazio, a company program director, recalled that the "*novelas* appealed to everybody" and employed a "universal Spanish [with] no inflections." She explained that "people in Central America, Colombia, Peru, Puerto Rico, and Spain, were glued to the telenovelas of Mexico," that they "cherished Mexico's actors and actresses," and that "our partnership [with Telesistema] was an incalculable asset."[32]

Later, a company president, Mario Rodríguez, recalled the impact of the first nightly soap operas in New York. He had arrived in New York as a child with his family during the Cuban Airlift of 1967. Having gone "from serene Cuba to the scary world of New York," Rodríguez had "fallen in love" with *Route 66, Bewitched,* and other shows on Channel 47. But his parents "were typical immigrants who each held two jobs while raising kids." To them, the novelas "were nirvana." Because of the novelas' "fantastic themes" and "reminders of home," the adults flocked to WXTV.

Rodríguez also recalled that WNJU attempted to break the spell of the novelas. As its ratings declined, WNJU canceled some of the Hollywood series and reinstated its original live programs. Although the local programs increased the station's ratings, their stars outright begged viewers to return. "They came on and shouted, 'Come to back to us. Don't watch Channel 41. They're fake. We're reality. Everything on 41 comes from a [film] can.'" They would finish the routine by tearing apart and battering film cans.[33]

WXTV's first-place ratings coincided with a series of financial setbacks at Columbia Pictures' motion picture division. SIN moved far ahead as the enterprise that would establish Spanish-language television. While Columbia Pictures was stalled, it did not abandon the Spanish-language project. Screen Gems still owned the WAPA studios in Puerto Rico. In addition, structurally and financially, WNJU rivaled SIN's KMEX as the strongest Spanish-language station.

In 1970, Columbia Pictures hired a promising executive named Carlos Barba to head and rejuvenate WNJU as the planned network's flagship station. Barba joined WNJU and WAPA into a partnership that led to an exchange of the two stations' programs. By 1972, he had begun syndicating the programs to the Chicago, Los Angeles, and Miami stations that Screen Gems still had agreements with. In addition, Barba prepared several WNJU local programs for national distribution.[34] That a network might rise from WNJU was indicated when Barba introduced a logo that the small system's outlets carried as a network identification. Eye-catching and original, the logo showed an animated drum-playing cat.[35]

The 1970 census was another watershed. For the first time, the Census Bureau estimated the populations of the nation's ethnic groups. This was the census that used the term "Hispanic" for the first time. However, instead of estimating the populations of U.S. residents descended from Mexican, Puerto Rican, Caribbean, Cuban, and South American immigrants, the Census Bureau lumped them into a single group.

At 23 million, African Americans constituted the largest ethnic population. Yet observers also noted a boom in the Hispanic population. It had doubled in size in one decade; it numbered 10 million in 1970. Most observers expected a larger Hispanic population: immigration was continuing and the number of families with five children suggested a high birth rate.[36]

* * *

Soon after he had assisted WXTV with the telenovelas, Danny Villanueva finished his training at KMEX. While apprenticing as a program director, he had also excelled as a news director. In 1969, Anselmo announced that Joseph Rank was retiring and that Villanueva had been promoted to station manager at KMEX. By that time, Anselmo had promoted Emilio Nicolás to vice president of SIBC. Soon Villanueva would be named as a second vice president and the company's third-in-command. While Nicolás continued to supervise network operations at the San Antonio hub, Anselmo wanted Villanueva on the road. Expansion was still a priority, and Villanueva's duty to SIN was to work in tandem with Anselmo to add stations and affiliates.

Villanueva's promotion required him to recruit a new news director. He prized the post he was vacating. Through his good relationships with Rank and Anselmo, Villanueva had obtained resources in 1968 and 1969 that made KMEX the first prominent entity in Spanish-language television; it was able to air two half-hour editions of *Noticias 34* (News 34). Villanueva had assembled a news staff of thirty people. KMEX was the first station in the United States to use portable video cameras and videotape in what became known as "electronic newsgathering." Villanueva spoke of building *Noticias 34* into a national news program for SIN. He was grooming KMEX news anchor Guillermo Restrepo to become the future Spanish-language Walter Cronkite.[37]

Villanueva's dissatisfaction with the telenovelas grew from his feeling that SIN should be broadcasting news instead. In 1968, unrest spread through a low-income area of East Los Angeles where most of the city's 1.2 million Mexican Americans lived. The unrest was part of the city's growing Chicano movement. Activists organized boycotts and demonstrations to protest the government's indifference to dilapidated housing, inferior schools, and disease. Local newspapers, notably the *Los Angeles Times*, reported on the protests of conditions in the *barrio*, but few Mexican Americans read newspapers. "Spanish-speaking people don't have a *Time* or *Newsweek* or *Los Angeles Times*. We [in television] have a tremendous social obligation," Villanueva told Los Angeles news reporter Maury Green in 1972.[38]

Villanueva recalled that in late 1969 or early 1970 he had seen Green broadcast a news segment on a newscast called *The Big News*. Carried on English-language station KNXT, it was the most viewed news program in the Los Angeles area. Green had interviewed a senior *Los Angeles Times* correspondent who headed the newspaper's award-winning coverage of the Mexican American community. As he watched the interview, Villanueva winced. Observing the *Times* reporter as he spoke in generalities to please Green and KNXT's English-language audience, Villanueva had seen an individual torn "by what he was saying" who knew "he was making no difference."[39]

The speaker was Rubén Salazar. He had joined the *Times* in 1959, where he started as a reporter and then became a foreign correspondent. In 1965, he covered the war in Vietnam. From 1966 to 1968, he headed the *Times* bureau in Mexico City. There, he filed reports on Mexico's worst civil disturbance, the Tlatelolco Massacre, in which the military confronted demonstrators who demanded that the government address poverty and unequal opportunities instead of promoting the 1968 Olympic Games.

When he returned to Los Angeles later that year, Salazar focused his reports on the Mexican American community and the Chicano movement. Salazar's discomfort as a secure upper-middle-class professional who commuted from a home in Orange County was evident. Telling associates that he was tired of explaining Chicanos to Anglos, he complained in an interview, "I was frustrated. I wanted to really communicate with the people about whom I had been writing for so long."[40]

In April 1970, Villanueva gave Salazar the opportunity to do that when he gave Salazar the job of news director of KMEX. Salazar's role at the *Times* shifted; he began writing weekly columns instead of working as a reporter. In one column, Salazar wrote about his newspaper colleagues' disbelief when he joined Villanueva's station. "KM . . . what?" they asked. Yet at age forty-two, Salazar was eager for a "new career."[41]

Villanueva told Salazar that at KMEX the rules of objective journalism did not apply. As news director, Villanueva encouraged editors and reporters to break from the traditional Anglo news agenda and determine what was news based on "what's good for our community." "If we can effect change," he told them, "that's our journalism." He called the concept "advocacy journalism."[42]

Salazar advanced Villanueva's concept of news. His reports encouraged both citizens and noncitizens to approach authorities and decision-makers and publicly demonstrate their distress about their conditions and their dissatisfaction with those responsible for inaction. He did not merely provide facts; he also identified agencies such as housing authorities, public health agencies, and school districts and displayed contact information. In April 1970, he began investigating the underfunding of Chicano neighborhood schools. In May, he reported on discriminatory hiring. By June, he had reported on alleged racial profiling and brutality by Los Angeles city and county police. He had sometimes appeared on camera in stories videotaped in the field. The man who had been obscure to most Latinos as a newspaper reporter became a TV celebrity. Viewer and activist Alicia Escalante noted that Salazar created "the kind of reporting experiences . . . that made [him] a household word."[43]

In July, Salazar explored another issue, the military's disproportionate drafting of Chicanos during the Vietnam War and the numbers of deaths of those soldiers. Antiwar activists had drawn attention to the subject when they organized a public demonstration they called the "Chicano Moratorium." Reports on KMEX advertised a protest march through East Los Angeles that was to take place on August 29, 1970. It became the largest mass gathering of Mexican Americans at the time. "We have really been covering it," Salazar told a friend. "We have to show the Anglo what we can do."[44]

Most observers estimated that between 20,000 and 30,000 marchers paraded down Whittier Boulevard and peacefully converged on Laguna Park. As they gathered there, participants soon heard the sirens of arriving police. Their cordoning of the area and their attacks on marchers touched off hours of rioting. Sixty were injured and three were killed. That evening, Salazar and his video crew retreated to a cafe. Police in riot gear approached, and a deputy sheriff fired a tear-gas projectile through the door. It ripped through Salazar's head.[45]

This was the first time a TV news director had been killed by police. Villanueva never overcame his outrage. Through an informant, he had learned that police and the FBI had Salazar under surveillance, and he had warned him. Villanueva later testified that police had wanted Salazar silenced.

Villanueva privately shared with associates that KMEX opted for calm, to the disgust of numerous activists. The following week it broadcast the programs "Peace on Our Time " and "The Death of Rubén Salazar" on succeeding nights.[46]

But disorder ensued at an inquest that September and October. After sixteen days of shouting, scuffling, and ejections, a seven-person jury returned a confused verdict. Three jurors ruled that Salazar had died by accident. Four jurors ruled the death had come "at the hands of another person."[47] District Attorney Evelle Younger did not file charges, maintaining that the deputy involved had not acted with malice.[48] No one was sanctioned. Rioting and violence resumed.

At succeeding anniversaries of Salazar's killing, observers debated what his legacy was. Many believed that Salazar was a martyr who had given his life in sacrifice to the concerns of ethnic minorities. Others disagreed. Reporter Frank del Olmo had joined the *Times* as a summer intern in 1970, shortly after Salazar had left the paper for KMEX, but had continued as a *Times* columnist, then was hired as a full-time staff member. He eventually became an associate editor; in 1984 he won a Pulitzer Prize for his reporting on the Latino community. Del Olmo maintained that Salazar was "a professional newsman . . . enjoying immensely the independence and authority [his] new job [at KMEX] gave him."[49] Another associate, Rosa Martínez, felt that "Rubén's legacy [was] his livelihood, journalism." He "left an example for other Latinos to pursue his trade," mindful that there "[would] be a struggle for them also."[50]

Inspired by the growth of the U.S. Spanish-speaking population as reported in the 1970 census, new studies confirmed the impact of Spanish-language television news. A 1971 study by the Economic Research Service at Texas A&M showed that while virtually all Latinos used radio and television, only 20 to 30 percent were exposed to print media. In another study that year, Belden Associates reported that 28 percent of Latinos reported that they had never read a newspaper. Sixty-one percent had never read a magazine. "Spanish-culture people are not readers," the study reported. "They don't read newspapers, even the Spanish-language papers." This finding was "consistent regardless of where they came from originally."[51]

Anselmo was stunned by Salazar's killing. He was appalled by Villanueva's claim that he had evidence that police and the FBI had planned it. But he was infuriated by the virtual absence of coverage of the story on ABC, CBS, and NBC. The silence of the major networks crystallized Anselmo's contempt of, and willingness to fight, the establishment. He began writing letters to the FCC urging a "bust up of the networks" and recommending that they be "kicked out of New York."⁵² But a signal development forced Anselmo to listen to Villanueva's indictment of SIN as a telenovela fantasyland.

In 1970, KMEX won a Peabody Award, television's equivalent of the Pulitzer Prize, for its programs "Peace on Our Time" and "The Death of Rubén Salazar." In April 1971, Villanueva traveled to New York to receive the award. While there, he told Anselmo about a plan for a network news division based at KMEX. According to Villanueva, Anselmo agreed and said, "We must do this."⁵³ Although they could not act immediately because SIN was still constrained by the absence of the live interconnection a nightly news program would require, Anselmo took one step toward enacting the plan. He instructed that a newscast begin on New York's WXTV.

Villanueva left New York pleased with the thought that Salazar's legacy would be a nightly network newscast in Spanish. But Anselmo had not told him of the elder Azcárraga's cardinal rule: the network was not to produce network programs.

* * *

In Mexico, Emilio Azcárraga was preparing to inherit a corporation whose financial and political problems he had not solved. The Tlatelolco Massacre in Mexico City had stained the reputation of Telesistema. Ten days before the 1968 Olympics commenced, on October 2, tens of thousands of students and civilians had converged in a plaza to demand social, educational, and political reforms. Decrying the opulence of the forthcoming Olympic Games, protestors denounced the promoters, including Telesistema, for providing luxurious accommodations for elite athletes and rich attendees. When President Díaz Ordaz brought in the military, hundreds were killed and injured.

At Telesistema, turbulence continued after the Olympic Games. The firm's finances were suffering from contributing to the costs of constructing Azteca Stadium and from Emilio Azcárraga's overspending. Difficulties deepened when Díaz Ordaz, reeling from public rebuke of his actions during the Tlatelolco Massacre, attempted to restore goodwill. The measures he took to weaken the grip of corporate monopolies and to redistribute wealth stung Telesistema, which was hit with a 25 percent tax to redistribute wealth.⁵⁴

Fearing that further moves might escalate into a breakup of Telesistema, the father and son made some decisions designed to shore up their position with both the government and the public. In April 1970, Telesistema initiated Mexico's first important national newscast and the first to broadcast in prime time, *24 horas*. They took the advice of the PRI and of the new president, Luis Echevarría Álvarez, when they named reporter-editor Jacobo Zabludovsky, a PRI functionary and loyalist, as the director of the program and the anchor of the program. On a newscast the government controlled, Zabludovsky was to become the best-known figure in Mexico.[55]

The debut of Zabludovsky improved relations between Telesistema, the government, and the PRI. Telesistema further benefited from Emilio Azcárraga's newer endeavors. In the first distinguishing venture of his career, he negotiated the rights to originate and televise the 1970 World Cup soccer tournament, which Mexico would host.[56]

Emilio had also taken the lead in a vital initiative that he feared his father, who was in decline, had neglected. By 1970, Eugenio Garza Sada's Instituto Tecnológico de Monterrey was one of several universities contributing to a U.S. consortium led by Hughes Aircraft. At their Monterrey laboratories, engineers were testing miniature components that could lower satellite costs, which could help Hughes reach its goal of launching the first commercial satellites by 1974.

Aware that Garza Sada's Televisión Independiente de Mexico was in line to begin delivering its programming by satellite, Emilio Azcárraga made overtures to Hughes while conferring with his engineers on what would be required to convert Telesistema's three networks from microwave to satellite transmission. He reportedly told the firm's directors that "a lot of financing," initially more than $50 million, would be needed.[57] Sharing Emilio's concern that the firm needed to move to the forefront of newer technologies, the company directors backed his expenditures.

Emilio Azcárraga had not interacted with Anselmo since the Olympics projects. Emilio later testified that he did not know that it was his father who had continued to fund SIN after 1966. Because SIN had paid all of its program fees and reported profits, the younger Azcárraga was convinced that Anselmo "had turned [SIN] around."[58] However, his opinion of Anselmo was about to change.

Soon after his success at WXTV in New York, Anselmo braced for a sensitive but inevitable next step: SIN's entry into Miami. Anselmo knew that the elder Azcárraga would not approve a Miami station until he had obtained loans and financing. But there was more behind Azcárraga's resistance. The Florida city was small then, and it was home to very few Mexicans. Its Spanish-speaking population largely consisted of people who had fled Cuba after its takeover by Fidel Castro. Anti-Castro factions railed against Mexico for its support of the Castro regime. Even in the face of these divisions, Anselmo insisted that SIN needed to include Miami. He emphasized that Miami had the fourth largest Spanish-speaking population in the United States and argued that, without it, Azcárraga would not have a genuine U.S. network.

Even though he had not raised the money or won the elder Azcárraga's approval, Anselmo went ahead and arranged for SIBC to purchase WAJA, a struggling Miami channel that was owned by the International House of Pancakes. The only asset of Channel 23 was its right to televise the games of the Floridians, an American Basketball Association team. Anselmo agreed to pay $1.4 million for the channel and to pay IHOP founder Al Lapin's $1 million dollars' worth of debts. In October 1970, the aging Azcárraga agreed to Anselmo's request that Telesistema pay Lapin.[59]

Emilio Azcárraga did not know of the purchase. Not until January 1971, when the FCC approved the transfer, did he discover that Telesistema was required to pay Lapin $2.4 million. He was dumbfounded, and he ordered Anselmo to cancel the sale. Anselmo ignored the order, knowing that the license had been transferred and that Don Emilio Azcárraga had approved the deal. In March, the son summoned Anselmo to a meeting in Mexico City. During their confrontation, Anselmo stood firm on keeping the Miami station. Citing insubordination, Emilio Azcárraga fired him with a display befitting his nickname of El Tigre (The Tiger).[60] He demeaned Anselmo for not fully grasping the extent of the alleged anti-Mexican sentiment in Miami. He claimed that because of Anselmo's ineptitude he had to explain to the Mexican government why Telesistema had invested its resources in a city that was believed to hate Mexico. Emilio Azcárraga hated Miami. He refused to set foot in a place that he felt was an unsophisticated small town.[61]

The $2.4 million was enough to justify Anselmo's dismissal. Emilio Azcárraga later testified that because of the money Telesistema was spending on satellite technology in Mexico, the timing of the Miami purchase was not good.[62] He was troubled when he saw pictures of Anselmo's acquisition. It was in a strip mall on North 199th Street, twenty miles from downtown Miami. Emilio Azcárraga fumed that while Telesistema needed money for a satellite, Anselmo used it to purchase a dive.[63]

Anselmo was unemployed for two weeks. Emilio Azcárraga had named Emilio Nicolás as Anselmo's successor, and Nicolás mediated his friend's reinstatement. Conceding that Anselmo had maneuvered behind the Azcárragas' backs, Nicolás maintained that Anselmo should be the one to address the problems the new station introduced. The son softened when Nicolás calmly explained that, in fact, Miami was "an important city in the United States and you cannot have an American network on your idea [that] it does not exist."[64]

It was evident that another factor was responsible for Anselmo's return. Despite twenty years of Anselmo's bluster, antics, and irritation, Emilio Azcárraga was attached to the SIN leader. He was not ready to end their relationship. Nevertheless, Anselmo understood that a new day had come at Telesistema. The days of dealing with the supportive and benevolent elder Azcárraga were over; the son was now the boss. Anselmo returned to the firm on the condition that he would comply with the father's original instructions. He was not to acquire any more new stations until he had located investors, approached banks, and secured loans.[65]

Miami's first full-time Spanish-language television station premiered on March 5, 1971. WAJA relaunched as WLTV; the call letters were for its slogan, "Watch Latin Television."[66] However, although Anselmo had beaten the odds with successful launches in Los Angeles and New York, his good fortune ended in Miami.

Many Miami viewers quickly connected WLTV to Mexico, to its government's support of Havana, and, thus, to Fidel Castro. They denounced Channel 23 as a Communist front and picketed the station, although for the moment, protests were peaceful.[67] Anselmo filled key positions with figures who were respected in the Cuban community. As station manager, Humberto Estévez screened Telesistema's programs to make sure that the themes were not Mexican. When he spotted political content, he substituted local WLTV shows. He was especially careful to ensure that programs showing Zabludovsky, Telesistema's Mexican news anchor, were not seen.

Tensions dissipated when Estévez managed to premiere a nightly news program, *Reportador 23*, on a small budget. He teamed well-known Cuban-identified news anchor Esteban Lamela with María Elena Prío, the daughter of Cuba's last democratically elected president.[68]

As in New York, the novelas were popular in Miami. Yet advertising revenue lagged. Unlike New York, Miami lacked audience ratings. Potential sponsors balked for another reason. While the programs appealed to the throngs of Cubans, Chileans, Venezuelans, Dominicans, Nicaraguans, and Panamanians who lived in Miami, the commercials, whose messages tended to slant toward Cubans, did not. WLTV could attract a multinational audience, but it did not yet have the means for marketing to it.[69] For the first time, SIN had inaugurated a foundering station.

During the first year, WLTV earned $200,000 from advertising. The station barely could afford to pay its utility bill. Estévez relinquished the manager's post and took a lower-paying position. Even Anselmo was prepared to admit that Emilio's Azcárraga's misgivings might be correct. He considered selling WLTV.[70] In June 1972, at the SIN sales office in New York, Anselmo stood on a desk and announced that anyone who was willing to move to Miami and head WLTV would receive a promotion. Joaquín Blaya, a 25-year-old Chilean immigrant who worked in sales, volunteered. He was the only one.[71]

* * *

On September 23, 1972, Mexican television and radio programming was interrupted by a voice that advised people to stand by for an urgent announcement. Zabludovsky then appeared and read a proclamation he had received from President Luis Echeverría Álvarez. A national period of mourning had begun. Don Emilio Azcárraga Vidaurreta was dead.

He had suffered a heart attack the day before. The family had contacted famed Houston cardiologist Michael DeBakey, and President Echeverría had flown a Mexican Air Force plane to Houston to collect him. DeBakey had performed emergency surgery that had gotten Azcárraga through the night, but Azcárraga had died the next morning.[72]

While Azcárraga's passing was a major event in Mexico, it was relegated to back-page obituaries in scattered newspapers and magazines in the United States. Anselmo was affected not just because the "old man" had been a friend. The moment was touched with irony: the day before the heart attack, Anselmo had fulfilled what the elder Azcárraga would have considered his protégé's greatest achievement. He had gone to a bank in New York and secured a $12.3 million loan.[73]

Anselmo's day at Marine Midland National Bank in New York began when he joined his two vice presidents, Nicolás and Villanueva, at the bank's Broadway tower. Anselmo asked for funds for stations SIBC owned in San Francisco and Phoenix; funding for advertising compensation that could encourage independent stations in Dallas, Houston, and Washington to affiliate with SIN; a microwave system to connect stations in California; and the network newsroom that Villanueva wanted.[74] He presented the 1970 census figures and projections of the growth of the Spanish-speaking population and of advertising revenue.[75]

Although they behaved like sedate businessmen throughout the meeting, even when the bank approved the loan, when they got outside the bank, they jumped up and down and howled like children. They celebrated on the sidewalk for half an hour. People who dodged them or "stopped to look ... thought we were nuts," Villanueva later recalled.[76] Nicolás recalled it as "the most exciting event of the entire company."[77]

The loan warranted celebration. The bank had not questioned Anselmo's annual statements for the period 1966–1971, which showed the income provided by the late Azcárraga but did not give details about the source. One outcome of the loan was an overture by New York paperback books magnate James Jacobson. The owner of Pocket Books, Jacobson now owned the firm Trans-Tel, which had invested in SIBC five years before and held the license for WXTV. Jacobson offered to merge Trans-Tel with SIBC in exchange for a reorganization of SIBC that would give him 8 percent ownership. Anselmo was delighted because he knew that SIBC would gain 100 percent ownership of the New York station and rushed to complete the merger.

During the rest of 1972, Anselmo focused on reorganizing the Spanish International Broadcasting Corporation. On December 12, 1972, Anselmo chartered its successor, the Spanish International Communications Corporation (SICC). Jacobson joined the board, which reallocated SICC's stock.[78] The process rewarded Nicolás and Villanueva, who, with a combined 15 percent, became part owners. They, too, joined the board.[79]

Anselmo named himself as president of SICC and de facto chair of the new company's board. Frank Fouce Jr., still absent and silent but unwilling to relinquish his part ownership, was the official chair. After feuding with Anselmo and moving to Las Vegas ten years before, Fouce had remained the largest shareholder. Even though the new distribution of stock decreased his 30 percent ownership to 26 percent, Fouce voted for the reorganized SICC by proxy. His 26 percent was still more than Anselmo's 22 percent. The firm emerged much stronger.

Most U.S. observers were surprised when word came in 1972 that Emilio Azcárraga had negotiated a merger with Eugenio Garza Sada. Their rivalry was over. Garza Sada abandoned television; his Televisión Independiente de Mexico could not compete with the three networks Azcárraga controlled. Azcárraga acquired Garza Sada's chief TV assets: his Mexico City studio and his key station there, Channel 8. [80]

Garza Sada's departure from television paved the way for Azcárraga's dealings with the Hughes satellite consortium, which had been named Intelsat. Azcárraga was first in line to pioneer television satellite delivery. Hughes's expected customers were the U.S. commercial TV networks. But ABC, CBS, and NBC were content to deliver programs through AT&T's Long Lines system in which telephone lines and eventually a network of microwave relays facilitated long-distance delivery of television transmissions, as they had since 1948, and chose not to participate. The engineers Garza Sada had assembled in Monterrey would now team up with Azcárraga to fulfill his aspirations.[81] Garza Sada returned to his primary enterprise, a family of corporations known as the Alfa Group. He was killed two years later in an aborted kidnapping.

Three months after succeeding his father, Emilio Azcárraga Milmo was enjoying the feeling of success that comes from a defining accomplishment. The government had approved the merger, which reinstated the Azcárraga monopoly. Azcárraga pledged that the new corporation would be devoted to a "synergy of television and technology." Accordingly, he ended the eighteen-year reign of Telesistema Méxicano and named the new corporation Television Via Satellite. It was to be known by its acronym, Televisa.[82]

Anselmo later maintained that although he was feeling very low because of the elder Azcárraga's passing, Emilio Azcárraga's initiative inspired him. Anselmo had been fascinated by satellites since he had seen the Telstar satellite in 1962. SIN was certain to benefit from Televisa's role in outer space. However, the ascension of The Tiger posed a problem for Anselmo on the ground. It was only a matter of time before Emilio would discover that his father had paid SIN's bills.

4

THE WAGES OF SIN

Accounts differ about when Emilio Azcárraga learned that although the Spanish International Network had posted a profit every year since 1966, it never had earned a dime. Azcárraga told associates that he learned of the anomaly soon after his father died in September 1972. Executors informed him of bank withdrawals made out to VT Latin, Azcárraga Vidaurreta's phantom corporation in Panama.[1] The elder Azcárraga had transferred his personal funds to VT Latin and converted it to U.S. currency that had wound up as income on SIN's books. His money had paid for SIN's years of debts and losses.

Rene Anselmo later guessed that the discovery came several weeks later, probably in December 1972, a memorable time. That was when the younger Azcárraga had founded Televisa, Anselmo had reorganized SIN's parent firm as the Spanish International Communications Corporation, and Azcárraga had summoned Anselmo to Mexico City.

The meeting was likely to be a repeat of the inquisition in August 1966, when Azcárraga had wanted to shut down SIN. Now he had the authority to do it. And he had a reason to do it. Anselmo had kept not one but two secrets. Not only had he falsely reported profits in 1966, 1967, 1968, 1969, 1970, and 1971, but he had also pretended to rectify the issue of unpaid programming fees. After eleven years, SIN had paid nothing for the vast majority of programs it had carried; it was the senior Azcárraga's money that had covered those costs.[2]

But Anselmo relaxed when he got to Mexico City. Azcárraga did not fire him, and he did not terminate SIN. When Anselmo confessed about the arrangement the elder Azcárraga had made with him, Emilio laid down an ultimatum: either SIN would pay for the programs or Televisa would cancel them, sell its SIN holdings, and leave the network to its fate. SIN's benefactor was in his grave. There would be no more subsidies. Then he backed away from his hardline approach. He canceled SIN's current unpaid fees, saying that its obligations would die with the shuttering of Telesistema Méxicano.[3]

The moment was not right for a bloodletting. Azcárraga was enjoying a pinnacle achievement, the merger that created Televisa. The new, larger firm would direct SIN. Aware that SIN was positioned to advance Televisa's prospects in the United States, he was eager to hear about Anselmo's recent successes, his $12.3 million loan from the Marine Midland Bank and his successful reorganization of SICC. Azcárraga repeated that Televisa would sever its ties with SICC if it did not pay its programming fees, but he was in a mood to wipe the slate clean.

Anselmo soon deduced another reason for Azcárraga's good mood. Azcárraga was thrilled that with his acquisition of Eugenio Garza Sada's technology-rich Televisión Independiente de Mexico, Televisa had sprung to the forefront of satellite communication. Anselmo, an outer space enthusiast, was also intensely interested in an innovation that interested no one else in U.S. television: TV delivery by satellite. Azcárraga predicted that within two years, Televisa would cover Mexico and SICC would cover the United States with television delivered by satellite.[4]

On January 8, 1973, Azcárraga chartered Televisa.[5] It was the largest corporation in Latin America at the time.

* * *

As soon as he returned from Mexico City, Anselmo faced another potentially contentious encounter in Los Angeles. The first meeting of the new SICC's board was to be held there, and Anselmo had to reveal how the late Azcárraga had propped up SIN with his own financial resources. And he could not tell that story without also telling its latest chapter: the younger Azcárraga's warning that SIN's access to Televisa's programs would cease if SIN failed to pay its programming fees. Board members were certain to ask whether SIN could actually pay them.

Anselmo knew that SIN could not. The fees were derived as a share, 18 percent, of the programs' U.S. revenue. In 1972, SIN reported revenue of $3.5 million, 80 percent of which came from advertising during Televisa programs. Eighteen percent of that revenue was $500,000, the amount the elder Azcárraga had paid every year for years.[6] In 1973, the program fees would be the same, only now SIN must pay them. It was not likely that SIN could increase its advertising revenue by $500,000 in 1973 to make the payment.

Televisa was not desperate for SIN's $500,000. After the merger, its revenue would be a hundred times greater than that. But Anselmo knew that despite the small size of the revenue in the grand scheme of Televisa's business and regardless of whether SIN could survive without programming from the giant network, Azcárraga would cancel the programs if SIN could not pay.

The board met in Los Angeles in late January 1973. Anselmo's anxiety increased when he learned that Frank Fouce would attend. Since leaving Spanish International in 1962, Fouce had remained its largest shareholder. He had allowed Anselmo to direct and unofficially chair the enterprise, but for his appearance at SICC's first board meeting, Fouce would take the gavel.

Fouce called the meeting to order. There were formalities and introductions. Anselmo then began his report. He told the board that SIN's past profits had derived from the late Azcárraga's funds. But the board members, who were new to the firm, were more interested in what was ahead. Anselmo roused them with a shining account of the new Televisa and its rock-solid promise of future programs. Fouce, though, wanted to know "what they would do if we couldn't pay." When Anselmo answered that Televisa would stop sending the programs, Fouce exploded. He asked Anselmo why he had not negotiated either a fee SIN could pay or contingencies that would preserve the programs if payment was not made. Fouce lambasted Anselmo for making a "terrible business decision."[7]

As he had eleven years before, Fouce exposed Anselmo's failure to grasp an issue that SIN's survival depended on. But Fouce did not convince the board. The members warmed to Anselmo's positive tone, notably his report of SIN's likely role in Televisa's satellite program. They were not impressed by the fact that Fouce, who had not attended a board meeting in eleven years, had appeared long enough to disrupt a happy moment. According to SIN vice president Emilio Nicolás, the board "rallied around Rene."[8]

Nevertheless, Anselmo had no choice but to increase SIN's cash flow. Caught between Azcárraga's demand for money and Fouce's veiled threat to oust him, his demeanor became rougher. His closest associates, Nicolás and fellow vice president Danny Villanueva, recoiled. The nation was in a recession, and they told Anselmo to expect flat revenue in 1973. Ignoring them, Anselmo increased the sales quota to 15 percent sales. Anselmo showed a harshness, if not a ruthlessness, that, according to Villanueva, "we had not seen before."[9]

By 1973, Anselmo realized that he was in a situation that was similar to the one Nicolás had confronted in 1955, when he had used box tops as proof of numbers of viewers when he pitched KCOR to advertisers. There were no audience ratings that reported SIN's total national viewership. Certain that SIN's programs were absent in ratings reports because ratings companies excluded Spanish-speaking viewers and now needing to prove it, Anselmo harangued impeding parties in public for the first time. He declared war on the Nielsen ratings.

His rampage began in November 1972 at the fall conference of the National Association of Broadcasters in St. Louis, where FCC commissioner Robert E. Lee criticized broadcasters for their "slavishness to the ratings."[10] Anselmo rebuked the FCC for dismissing rather than investigating the ratings. We have been "fighting for 10 years against the biased, misrepresentative ratings reports," he said. In December, he filed a complaint with the FCC alleging that Nielsen and the Broadcast Ratings Council (BRC) had conspired to create "a discriminatory barrier to any broadcaster attempting to serve a minority group." He pronounced that "the ratings system [was] the biggest con job around" and that those who relied on its biased data were "parties to sham."[11]

A controversy erupted. Anselmo insisted that the ratings companies were lying when they claimed that their random samples were valid. He alleged that without valid samples, the ratings were "a sham." Forced to reply, Nielsen said that minorities were "too costly" to survey. That remark raised eyebrows at the FCC. Lee spent a week examining Nielsen's procedures. His findings supported Anselmo's allegations. "The methodology of ratings is a 'hot issue' because . . . [the] ratings may under represent minority viewpoints," Lee said.[12]

The controversy intensified when *Television/Radio Age* devoted its February 19, 1973, edition to an "ethnic rating storm." There is "a problem," the magazine reported, and "the waves that have churned up already are beginning to rock the boat under both ARB and Nielsen." Hugh Beville, the head of the BRC, defended the company. He claimed that minority individuals "do not cooperate." Anselmo seized on Nielsen's and Beville's statements as "proof of racism." "The theory of random probability does not rest on the color of a person's skin, or the language one speaks," he declared. Accusing television ratings companies of operating a "lily white" system, he said, "You've got a lot of bigots in this business."[13]

That spring, Anselmo retained attorneys James McKenna and Norman Leventhal as counsel for SICC. McKenna's first assignment was to petition the FCC to investigate Anselmo's claims. It declined.[14] Yet that April, ARB, the main provider of local TV ratings that was soon to be known as Arbitron, announced revised procedures that would include samples of ethnic viewers.[15] Nielsen did nothing and declined further comment. The controversy raged for twenty more years. But by late 1973, the first storm had dissipated. So, too, had Anselmo's fears that Azcárraga would cancel the programs.

Anselmo finished a disturbing year. In 1973, SIN earned $4.5 million but spent $5.5 million. Anselmo reported—and Fouce noted and marked—the first annual loss since 1965. Televisa's program fees totaled $700,000. While Anselmo had paid as much he could, $200,000, SIN had once again fallen $500,000 short.[16]

But the shortfall paled in the glow of an event in Tucson, Arizona. Engineers had tested the device that would enable Televisa to become the first enterprise to broadcast radio and TV by satellite. Azcárraga was elated. By late 1973, he and Anselmo were well into a venture that would pave the way for SIN to use Televisa's satellite.

Azcárraga did not forgive the $500,000. Yet well before the December 1973 deadline, Anselmo was aware that, for the time being, there would be no collection. Azcárraga's exuberance over the satellite—and the new venture—provided another reprieve.

* * *

In early 1974, Western Union was weeks away from becoming the first private company to enter outer space. The first commercial satellite was in the final stages of construction at the Hughes Aircraft labs in Tucson. The Westar satellite was scheduled to launch from Cape Canaveral in April 1974.

By this time, Azcárraga had told Anselmo that SIN would receive a satellite relay, but not from the first device. Engineers were able to put only six relays on Westar 1. Two belonged to Televisa. Western Union had commissioned a second and larger satellite called Westar 2. With twelve relays, the newer satellite had the capacity for Televisa's remaining channels. The consortium had invited U.S. broadcasters, including ABC, CBS, and NBC, to participate. All of them had rejected the offer. Because of this, relays were available on Westar 2 that SIN could use. The launch of Westar 2 was planned for early 1975.[17]

While Anselmo was delighted to learn of decisions that he knew would transform SIN, the satellite program introduced new financial concerns. Around $5 million would be needed for a transmission facility at SIN's San Antonio hub and for dishes at SIN's affiliate stations to receive the signals from the satellite. Azcárraga agreed to shoulder much of SIN's expense. He and the consortium had much to gain by providing the first satellite network in the United States. But Azcárraga insisted that SIN pay part of the cost.[18]

Gambling on a successful launch of Westar 1 in April 1974, Televisa invested heavily in providing coverage of the quadrennial World Cup soccer tournament that West Germany would host three months later. Televisa purchased the TV rights for the Western Hemisphere. Fed by trans-Atlantic cable to Mexico City, the matches were to be relayed on Westar 1 for broadcast in Mexico and northern Latin America.[19] Aware that Westar 1 also covered most of the United States, Azcárraga saw an opportunity.

In January 1974, Azcárraga and Anselmo incorporated a firm called MagnaVerde. They set to work making plans to downlink signals from Westar 1 to portable dishes at auditoriums and theatres in cities across the United States. They calculated that they could earn huge profits by selling tickets—more than enough to pay both SIN's debt to Televisa and the amount it needed to raise to pay for satellite technology. Azcárraga was enthralled by the World Cup. He had witnessed the impact of the matches four years earlier when Mexico had hosted them. Further, by charging viewers for telecasts, he would be advancing a new concept in television that came to be known as pay per view.[20]

Although he chartered MagnaVerde as separate from SIN, Anselmo intertwined the two operations. His first priority was to ensure that revenue from MagnaVerde could pay SIN's debts. Then he withdrew temporarily from the day-to-day operation of SIN. For six months, Nicolás ran the network. Instead of moving to New York, Nicolás remained in San Antonio. There, Televisa's engineers were surveying the Durango Boulevard property and planning the construction of the network's teleport. To manage the New York office, Anselmo hired former Miami TV executive William Stiles as executive vice president.

Anselmo did not overlook SIN's other key individual. Former star player of the Dallas Cowboys and the Los Angeles Rams Danny Villanueva was ideally suited to promote soccer ticket sales. By the time he joined MagnaVerde as promotions director, Villanueva had initiated projects and ventures that would help determine the direction of SIN, many of which had come to fruition.[21] While he was Anselmo's vice president in charge of network expansion, Villanueva continued to manage SIN's Los Angeles station. It had become Spanish-language television's first profit center; of the $4.5 million SIN earned in 1973, two-thirds came from KMEX.

Villanueva had excelled in his first network-level endeavor. Because of the revenue KMEX generated, Anselmo gave Villanueva permission to begin taking the first steps toward creating a national news resource. In June 1973, Villanueva launched television's first continuous news service. Named *Newstelevision*, it was a ten-hour news block in English during KMEX's daytime hours. Villanueva, who knew of the vacant relays on Westar 2, hoped to expand the venture into a 24-hour news channel delivered by satellite.[22] Broadcaster Ted Turner succeeded with the same concept when he founded the Cable News Network (CNN) seven years later.

Villanueva did not pursue his ambition of having *Newstelevision* evolve into a multihour provider of television news delivered to a national audience. Anselmo's feud with Fouce had gotten in the way. The venture gradually attracted sponsors and showed promise, and Villanueva had hired some of Fouce's family members as anchors and reporters. In October, Anselmo traveled to Los Angeles and, infuriating Fouce, fired Fouce's son, whom Villanueva had installed as a member of the *Newstelevision* news team. Finally terminating *Newstelevision* late that October, Villanueva blamed SIN's failure to obtain bank loans needed for long-term financing. Years later, Villanueva acknowledged that tensions between Anselmo and Fouce that the venture had stirred had contributed to his decision to end it.[23]

While continuing to advocate for SIN's efforts to expand its news programming, Villanueva moved from *Newstelevision* to his more essential assignment: implementing the network's expansion. He pursued projects funded by the Marine Midland Bank loan. Part of the loan was earmarked for the launch of stations in San Francisco and Phoenix that would not be affiliates but, like the stations in Los Angeles, New York, San Antonio, Miami, and Fresno, would be those SICC would own. The FCC had approved licenses for both stations. What was more valuable to Villanueva was the bank's funding of a microwave system to interconnect KMEX with stations in California. Although Westar 2 would provide a more advanced means of delivery, Villanueva was eager to form the first interconnected Spanish-language television network.

In 1974, Villanueva introduced a fully linked "network" called SIN-WEST. The new network attracted affiliates. When he learned about SIN-WEST, independent TV owner Chester Smith affiliated his two stations, KLOC in Sacramento and KCBA in Salinas, with SIN so they could receive and broadcast blocks of programming—and advertising—that were fed from KMEX on SIN-WEST's interconnected lines.[24] As the mini network moved northward, from XEWT in San Diego to KFTV in Fresno and then to Smith's station in Sacramento, Villanueva looked ahead to extending SIN-WEST to Oregon and Washington.[25] He talked with the owner of KPTV in Portland. The independent station had recently introduced Spanish-language programming with a local variety program called *The Modesto Ríos Show*.[26]

Yet Villanueva encountered obstacles when he turned east. When it acquired the licenses for the San Francisco and Phoenix stations, SICC had reached the legal limit of the number of stations it could own. SIN programming was not seen in Houston and Dallas, both of which were vital Spanish-speaking markets. In every other city, the three commercial stations were affiliates of ABC, CBS, and NBC. In order to expand SICC, Villanueva needed to enlist more independent broadcasters like Smith. In 1974, there were few independent stations in the United States.

Shortly after Azcárraga announced that Westar 1 would deliver Televisa's main channel, XEW Channel 2, the cable TV system in Loma Linda, California, informed subscribers that it would carry Televisa's vaunted Canal de las Estrellas (Channel of the Stars). Its idea was to purchase a satellite dish, point it at the satellite, and retransmit satellite signals as if they were regular local channels.

However, because the programs on XEW and SIN were nearly identical, SIN filed a petition with the FCC requesting an injunction to prohibit Loma Linda operators from delivering the Televisa channel on their cable system. Upholding the international doctrine of free flow of information, the commission denied the petition.[27] However, in the ruling, the FCC established a new policy called retransmission consent. The cable system was free to carry XEW, but only if Televisa approved. Knowing that Televisa would not allow free delivery of XEW, the cable system dropped its plan to carry Televisa's satellite transmission of XEW.[28]

The Loma Linda innovators opened the eyes of Villanueva and the rest of the TV industry. Villanueva realized that every cable system was certain to acquire satellite dishes that carried multitudes of channels. Villanueva announced that SIN would pay ten cents per subscriber to any cable system that carried the network. Immediately, twenty systems signed; one was the system in Loma Linda.[29] Villanueva understood that while expensive for SIN, the cost was an investment that was certain to convince cable systems to add SIN to their channel lineups, which in turn would increase SIN's audience and revenue. Cable systems such as that in Loma Linda were enticed because at the time they were merely mechanisms that rebroadcast programs from local stations to give viewers better reception. They made money only from viewers who paid subscription fees. The local stations they carried paid them nothing. That SIN had committed to paying them meant that cable systems would have an additional revenue stream. According to Villanueva, SIN never considered abandoning broadcast television and becoming a cable channel. He explained that because "most of our viewers could not afford to subscribe to cable TV, we [still] had to go out and find stations."[30]

During the spring of 1974, Anselmo called Villanueva to New York. During the time in early 1974 when Villanueva first made concerted efforts to add affiliates and cable systems and enlarge the number of locales where SIN could be seen, he had seen little of Anselmo. Temporarily departed from SIN, Anselmo was headlong into arrangements for the World Cup and in booking sites for the pay-per-view telecasts he and Azcárraga had planned. Villanueva finally glimpsed the so-called MagnaVerde project that spring when, while traveling, he was summoned to New York. They met at an office near Madison Square Garden rather than at SICC headquarters. Villanueva had long known that Anselmo had founded MagnaVerde and was planning to televise the World Cup in theaters. He recalled feeling anxious because the first satellite, Westar 1, had not yet launched. Even so, within weeks of announcing the birth of MagnaVerde that February, Anselmo had booked thirty arenas and auditoriums, most with at least 1,000 seats. All of the venues were to televise all seven culminating matches.

With tickets priced as high as $50, Azcárraga and Anselmo looked forward to a $10 million gate.[31]

Although anxiety about the launch of MagnaVerde was high, when Anselmo invited Villanueva to temporarily step away from SIN and help promote ticket sales, Villanueva agreed to do it. In April, Villanueva traveled around the country to ask newspapers to publish pieces that promoted "the first team sports event continuously televised from Europe by satellite."[32]

On April 13, 1974, a Delta rocket carried Westar 1 into a perfect orbit. Hours later, technicians relayed the first test pattern at a station in Glendale, New Jersey. Anselmo drove to New Jersey to see it. The signal was crystal clear.[33]

* * *

Three months later, on July 7, West Germany claimed the World Cup with a 2–1 victory over the Netherlands. The theater-based broadcast did not work out as Anselmo had hoped. At Madison Square Garden, the Felt Forum, which had a capacity of 6,000, had 5,500 empty seats. None of the matches in any of the cities drew more than a handful of viewers. While soccer was avidly followed all over the world, it was not popular in the United States. *Sports Illustrated* reflected the dominant U.S. attitude: "On television soccer looks like a bunch of guys chasing a big balloon around."[34]

The World Cup failure ended the détente between Azcárraga and Anselmo. Accepting blame, Azcárraga agreed to absorb MagnaVerde's $1.5 million loss.[35] But he was tired of fruitless U.S. ventures. SIN was in limbo, if not in bankruptcy. It had no money for its share of the Televisa satellite. It could not pay the $500,000 in program fees left from 1973. No one expected it could pay a projected $1 million in fees for 1974. The fees had increased because of provisions in the programming contracts between SIN and Televisa that required SIN to pay a modicum of revenue based on the number of additional viewers anticipated from the addition of stations and cable systems. This allowed Televisa to be compensated for the new stations and cable systems that Villanueva had added. Anselmo waited for Azcárraga's next move.

Azcárraga kept him in suspense. Televisa had other projects. He preferred to dwell not on the U.S. fiasco but on the wild success of Televisa's World Cup broadcast in Mexico and throughout Latin America. An oversight that was soon to become significant betrayed Azcárraga's drift from SIN. He had financed MagnaVerde by placing around $5 million in a U.S. bank account that was joint with SIN. Anselmo paid expenses from and deposited gate receipts into that account. Azcárraga would notice the loss when he withdrew the funds that were left.[36] But he had yet to close the account.

In late 1974, a decision came. Azcárraga informed Anselmo that the Televisa board had agreed to waive the fees that were due on December 31, but on June 30, 1975, all programming fees had to be paid in full. The board agreed that without full payment, Televisa would not renew contracts of any of its programs. Programming would cease as each program's contract expired. The Televisa board further agreed that the firm would immediately terminate funding and technical support for SIN's satellite facilities.[37]

Anselmo rode out the rest of an uncertain and dispiriting year. Nicolás canceled delivery of the satellite dishes and the remaining equipment for the San Antonio teleport. This was heartbreaking because on October 14, 1974, ahead of schedule, the Hughes consortium celebrated the flawless launch of Westar 2 and finally signed a U.S. customer. The Time-Life publishing company had purchased a relay for a new type of television channel. But SIN was not aboard; Televisa had mothballed its U.S. satellite program.[38]

Anselmo's year-end report confirmed suspicions that SIN was in its worst crisis since the elder Azcárraga had begun bailing it out in 1966. In 1974, for the second consecutive year, it posted a loss, this time of $1 million. It also had unpaid program fees of nearly the same amount that year. With the $500,000 that carried over from 1973, SIN now owed Televisa $1.5 million.[39] The crucial amount would be what it owed on June 30, 1975. Based on the latest full-year fee of $1 million, six months of fees would likely amount to $500,000. By June 30, SIN would need to pay Televisa $2 million.[40]

When he read the report, Fouce notified the SICC board that he would be attending all regular board meetings. They were due to meet three times in 1975, in January, June, and December. As was the custom for regular meetings, all were to be held at West Coast locations.

When the board gathered on January 14, 1975, Fouce surprised Anselmo and the board. He proposed that SICC initiate a public sale of stock, arguing that the $2 million could be raised on the open market. While they were listening, the board members were concerned that if the stock was rushed onto the market, the value of their shares might tank. Consensus formed that Fouce's proposal needed more study.[41] Fouce later recalled that although "[members of the board] disagreed," he was confident that Anselmo would return with a plan for "going public."[42]

But Anselmo returned with a different plan. The SICC lawyers, McKenna and Leventhal, had noticed that MagnaVerde's $1.5 million was still on Azcárraga's books. The attorneys proposed that SICC absorb the defunct firm. That would enable SICC to raise $1.5 million by claiming the loss as a tax credit. To pay the remaining $500,000, SICC would give Televisa newly written stock. McKenna outlined the steps by which SICC would reemerge as a provider of both Spanish-language and closed-circuit sports television. The parties referred to the plan as MagnaVerde 2.[43]

When Anselmo informed Fouce about this plan in February 1975, their battle resumed. Fouce vociferously opposed MagnaVerde 2. He did not question the lawyers' wisdom on the issue of tax credits. But he protested the idea of giving more stock to Televisa, whose holdings he had long suspected exceeded the legal limit under the U.S. foreign ownership rule. He was aghast at Anselmo's willingness to invent new stock. He instructed Anselmo to "cease and desist."[44]

Anselmo ignored Fouce's order. By the time the board met that June, when it expected to vote on MagnaVerde 2, Anselmo had presented the plan to Azcárraga. Anselmo was relieved when Azcárraga agreed to delay the June 30 deadline for paying program fees on Anselmo's promise that funds were forthcoming. Anselmo explained that, after the vote, the lawyers would need time to fuse the tax credits and the promised stock into a lump-sum payment to Televisa.

Yet at the June session, SICC's directors did not make a decision about MagnaVerde 2. After hours of arguing, during which Anselmo pressed for and Fouce bashed the reorganization, the directors postponed the vote. According to Nicolás, "there was [too much] poisoned air."[45]

Although Anselmo was not victorious, he was satisfied with the postponed vote. The impasse created an interim period during which he could push ahead with the reorganization and, most important, resolve the conflict with Azcárraga.

* * *

On August 25, 1975, the crisis ended. Anselmo submitted a $1.9 million promissory note to Televisa. Azcárraga accepted Anselmo's promise to pay as tantamount to payment in full.[46] Anselmo conceded that the SICC board could still vote against the reorganization. He understood that if members rejected reorganization, he would likely have to void his promise to pay Azcárraga. But he assured Azcárraga that final approval at the December meeting was a formality. He was right; four of the nine directors supported MagnaVerde 2, and Anselmo's vote made for a majority. Azcárraga did not press Anselmo about that possibility. The Televisa leader presumed that SIN's debt would be paid.

Spanish International sprang back to life. Azcárraga resumed funding for the SIN satellite system. Nicolás restarted construction of the San Antonio teleport. Anselmo reauthorized orders for downlink dishes for New York, Los Angeles, Miami, and other cities where SIN had stations and affiliates. That September, Nicolás prepared a one-year timetable. He set September 1976 as the target date for the first satellite broadcasts.[47]

News that December dampened the excitement. While SIN's Westar 2 relay sat idle, Time-Life's relay had begun transmitting. The company offered the first U.S. TV channel to be relayed by satellite, a subscription cable channel called Home Box Office. While to finish second overall, SIN still could claim partial victory in the race to be first in providing the public a continuous transmission of television from satellites. It would be the first to deliver programs from space to a broad audience that received free television and did not have to pay for programming, as did the then small HBO audience.

After the settlement with Televisa, SIN moved forward with its new stations in San Francisco and Phoenix.[48] Anselmo transferred his New York executive, William Stiles, to San Francisco. Stiles's launch of KDTV on Channel 14 in 1975 brought the first full-time Spanish-language television to the Bay Area. By this time, Villanueva had completed the first phase of his SIN-WEST project, in which a land-based microwave system established direct transmission of programs from KMEX to SIN's stations in Fresno, San Diego, Sacramento, and Salinas. When the microwave system was extended to the new station in San Francisco, Villanueva announced that he had finished remaining work in California and that the first interconnected Spanish-language network was fully operational.[49]

The next project was the Phoenix station, KTVW on Channel 33.[50] Nicolás traveled to Phoenix in 1975 and purchased flat property located next to mountains that was ideal for satellite reception. Anselmo assigned

Villanueva the task of constructing the station. They looked forward to the completion of the first television station in the United States "built for satellites from the ground up."[51]

The most auspicious development occurred in Miami. In the closing months of 1975, Joaquín Blaya, the sales recruit who had volunteered to head the dying Miami station WLTV, reported a turnaround. Under Blaya, an influx of sales revenue poured into SIN, $1.5 million by the end of the year. Boosted by income from WLTV, SIN's 1975 revenue soared to nearly $8 million.[52] That was not enough to avert a third annual loss, this time of $750,000. Yet the trend was improving. Anselmo loudly cheered Blaya's achievement.[53]

He still needed a "yes" at the December meeting. After more exchanges with Fouce, Anselmo expanded the purpose of the meeting. Anselmo had gone ahead and resolved SIN's debt to Televisa on his presumption that the board would approve the MagnaVerde 2 reorganization and its production of the $2 million in proceeds SIN needed to resolve the debt. Yet the board had not formally approved the reorganization, leaving open the possibility the move would be rejected in which case the payment likely would be voided.

But Anselmo was not worried. On the contrary, he was convinced not only that the vote would sail through because four of the nine board members had promised to vote yes and Anselmo's own vote ensured a majority. He knew that at the December meeting he would have much good news to report, including the impending success of the satellite program. Further anticipating the meeting, he was certain that Fouce would protest the MagnaVerde fait accompli and spoil an otherwise festive occasion. Before the meeting, Anselmo conferred with Nicolás, Villanueva, and others who were weary of Fouce. He told them that he foresaw the December meeting as an opportune moment to eliminate him.

On December 15, 1975, the board gathered in Los Angeles. Fouce opened by attempting to rule the MagnaVerde 2 reorganization out of order. "It is illegal and improper," Fouce declared. Instantly, Nicolás moved for the vote. It was 7:2 in favor. Fouce launched into a tirade and walked out, as Anselmo had anticipated. After Anselmo took the gavel, Villanueva proposed a motion for a vote to oust Fouce. Nicolás seconded the motion. The board passed the motion with a vote of 5:4 and elected Anselmo as chair.[54]

* * *

On September 12, 1976, SIN's fifteen stations and affiliates across the United States commenced the first relay of network programming by satellite. It was a Sunday night. An estimated five million U.S. viewers saw the same program at the same time. SIN broadcast Televisa's six-hour weekly variety program *Siempre en domingo* (Always on Sunday). That week, the first episodes of the novelas *La hija de Ángela* (Angela's Daughter) and *Carita de primavera* (The Face of Spring) premiered, as did soccer and boxing programming.[55]

The feat was widely reported. Writers marveled about the never-before-seen presentation. In the *New York Times,* Les Brown explained that the "Spanish International Network [is] purchasing programs from Spanish-speaking countries [and] carrying direct transmissions from Mexico's network, Televisa, on a regular schedule—just like a real network."[56]

All of the programs were uplinked from the first broadcast teleport in the United States, a complex arrayed adjacent to KWEX in San Antonio on the Durango Boulevard property. Because the country was divided by four time zones, SIN had two satellite feeds, one each for the East and West Coasts.[57]

The network's transformation was swift. Independent stations KDOG in Houston, KMXN in Albuquerque, and KRIO in Brownsville became SIN affiliates. By the end of the year, more than 200 cable systems also carried SIN.[58] Advertisers responded. SIN finished 1976 with revenue of $10 million and its first genuine profit.[59] Ironically, SIN withdrew the MagnaVerde 2 plan of paying Azcárraga with newly created stock, the issue that had angered Fouce and led to his overthrow. The increased revenue enabled Anselmo to abandon the stock endowment and finish the payment to Azcárraga with cash.

For the first time, Anselmo's leadership seemed correct. The network was turning a profit. He had directed a historic technical achievement. His acuity in the boardroom had accomplished the December 1975 coup. By eliminating Fouce as chair, he had hamstrung a disruptive absentee owner. The affirmative vote at the December meeting meant that Anselmo could follow through with payment of all the money SIN owed Televisa. An era of good feeling between the two firms had begun.

But a problem arose. In April 1976, five months before the satellite premiere, the Los Angeles law firm of Balaban and Berman sent Anselmo a letter that notified him that they were representing Fouce in a complaint against SICC. Fouce claimed that he was entitled to damages dating to

Figure 5. Emilio Nicolás in 1976, at the opening of the San Antonio teleport where the Spanish International Network became the first U.S. broadcast network to transmit by satellite. Three years earlier, Azcárraga Milmo had formed Television Via Satellite, or Televisa. Nicolás worked with Televisa to bring worldwide broadcasting to SIN's U.S. audiences. Photo courtesy of Guillermo Nicolás.

1973, when the firm posted losses after seven years of profits because of Anselmo's mismanagement.

Anselmo dismissed the letter as "sour grapes." Back in January 1973, no one had complained when Anselmo had admitted that the late Azcárraga had subsidized the SIN network for seven years and that it had never actually profited. Fouce also appeared to be contending that he had suffered personally from having been forced off the board. That claim, too, was specious. The board had removed Fouce through a formal vote.

However, SICC's attorneys, McKenna and Leventhal, sensed danger. Fearing a lawsuit, they believed that a jury would side with Fouce out of sympathy for the pain he had endured as a result of being removed as chair of the board. Moreover, Fouce's attorney, Frederick Stern, likely could persuade a jury that Anselmo had mismanaged SIN merely by having Anselmo testify that he had nearly lost SIN's supply of programs. McKenna urged Anselmo to acknowledge the complaint and find out what Fouce wanted.

What Fouce wanted was the solution to every distress. In June 1976, Anselmo met with him. In a session both recalled as cordial, Fouce confessed that he was tired of fighting and that it would be best for all if he were to leave the company. He told Anselmo that he would sell out and leave if SICC paid him $2 million for the 30 percent of shares he owned. Although receptive, Anselmo questioned the figure of $2 million. Fouce admitted that because no one knew the market value of SICC, his request was arbitrary, but he insisted that $2 million was fair.[60]

It was more than fair. By asking $2 million for his 30 percent of SICC shares, Fouce was accepting a total valuation of SICC at $6.7 million. By itself, the Los Angeles station, KMEX, would have sold for more. They agreed that Anselmo would conduct an appraisal of SICC and that he would finalize SICC's $2 million buyout of Fouce before the August board meeting.[61]

That July, Anselmo and Fouce met again. According to the later testimony of both men, Anselmo agreed to the buyout. He pledged to steer the board's approval and transfer of the $2 million at the forthcoming August meeting. Their July encounter was less cordial than their meeting a month before had been. Anselmo had not conducted the appraisal. He argued that SICC should pay a lower amount. Fouce reiterated that the price was fair. Aware that buying out Fouce meant that he no longer would have to contend with him, Anselmo agreed to Fouce's amount. They departed with the understanding that Anselmo would go to the meeting and secure the buyout.[62]

When the SICC board gathered in New York on August 20, 1976, Anselmo not only did not secure the buyout, but he did not even inform the board that he and Fouce had conferred. Anselmo used the occasion to celebrate the satellite premiere. "We have earned our place as the fourth network," Anselmo crowed.[63]

The board members suspected that something was amiss. Anselmo had never called a meeting in New York; all previous board meetings had been held on the West Coast. According to Villanueva, it was apparent that Anselmo had relocated the session to ensure that "Fouce wouldn't be there." Ousted as chair but still an owner, he was entitled to attend. The board was not aware that Anselmo had reneged on an opportunity to part peacefully with Fouce.[64]

Days later in Los Angeles, Fouce and Anselmo met alone for the last time. Giving no explanation, Anselmo told Fouce that he had decided against placing the buyout before the board. He told him, "Go ahead and file a goddam lawsuit."[65]

* * *

On November 4, 1976, Fouce filed the suit in U.S. District Court in Los Angeles. His attorney, Frederick Stern, named the Spanish International Communications Corporation as the defendant. The lawsuit asked that SICC pay Fouce damages to compensate him for SICC's "self-dealing, mismanagement, waste, and breach of fiduciary duty."[66]

Four weeks later, Judge Irving Hill heard the opening arguments in *Fouce Amusement Enterprises and Metropolitan Theaters Corp. v. Spanish International Communications Corp.* When SICC's attorneys moved for dismissal, Judge Hill denied their motion; he was intrigued by testimony he had read in an affidavit Fouce had filed. SICC was stunned when the judge issued a restraining order prohibiting its current capital expenditures.[67] And both sides were surprised when Hill ordered a lengthy process of discovery instead of setting a trial date.

Anselmo's decision not to buy Fouce out has endured as the greatest mystery of Spanish International Communications. Anselmo would say only that Fouce had badgered him. Blaya speculated that Anselmo believed that "he was the cat with nine lives who always landed on his feet."[68] The fact that Anselmo had averted catastrophe with Azcárraga no doubt fortified his sense of invincibility.

It is possible that Anselmo simply forgot to inform the board. The August meeting was devoted to discussing plans for the satellite. It was more likely that Anselmo knowingly kept the plan to buy out Fouce from the board. Nearly destroyed by Azcárraga's $2 million demand, he may have concluded that he could not pay the same amount to Fouce. There was another possibility, that Anselmo was so emotionally absorbed in his feud with Fouce that he could not bring himself to end it.

Not for many years would anyone have reason to analyze what had occurred. Spanish International was in the black. Its best years, and those of U.S. Spanish-language television, were ahead.

5

THE GOLDEN AGE

On December 15, 1976, Rene Anselmo did not behave like the president of a television network who had just been named in a lawsuit and hit with a judge's restraining order. On the fifteenth anniversary of the Spanish International Network, Anselmo dedicated new headquarters in New York for the Spanish International Communications Corporation. "We are primed for a great occasion," a "golden age" when SIN "takes its place as America's fourth television network," he told attendees. Vowing to provide "pathbreaking" television, he promised the "climax" to "all that we have worked for and dreamed about. . . . It is our pleasure to begin a new era [of] helping to preserve Spanish heritage, one of America's most valuable assets," he said.[1]

Anselmo had never been more optimistic. He had presided over the first continuous satellite delivery of a U.S. broadcast network and was credited with helping open the rest of the U.S. broadcast industry to satellite interconnection. He had finished the year with SICC's first genuine profits. Although a lawsuit against him had begun, he had eliminated his rival, Frank Fouce. In addition, after purchasing New York station WNJU, Columbia Pictures, which had the potential to create a competing Spanish-language network, had suffered financial difficulties. By 1976, the network it had planned had faded away. SIN had no competition.

Emilio Azcárraga also was optimistic. Anselmo still answered to him, and Televisa was still part owner of SICC, the entity that operated the seven stations SIN owned. It was SIN's lone program provider. Most had forgotten SIN Sales, the dummy corporation Anselmo had created in 1962 and that lingered unnoticed under SICC's umbrella. On paper, Televisa could claim that it owned SIN's network operation, including the satellite system, through SIN Sales. That December, Anselmo not only paid SIN's fees for programming on time, but he also sent a dividend for Televisa's share of SIN's first profits.

At peace with Televisa, Anselmo was free to set his own course. His "golden age" was characterized by bold albeit unorthodox initiatives. The first was the new headquarters at 460 West 42nd Street. There, 200 staff, mostly sales personnel, worked in a complex they called the Atrium. Passing through ornate doors, they reached their offices through a courtyard decorated as a Mexican hacienda. Foliage hung from three floors of railings on the courtyard's four sides. They walked past paintings and sculptures. While they worked, they listened to music from a grand piano on the ground floor.[2]

But SIN had no network studios in New York, at its property in Los Angeles, or at the network hub in San Antonio. This was because of Azcárraga's second cardinal rule: SIN was not to produce its own network shows. SIN's only original content was local broadcasts, mainly newscasts, that SIN's stations produced. For hours each day, SIN relayed Televisa's Mexico City satellite feed to U.S. stations.

Most guessed that Anselmo was exaggerating when he spoke of a golden age. Television's golden age was remembered for its classic and memorable programs. But Anselmo was not exaggerating. Because of the satellite feed and Televisa's largesse, another golden age was about to unfold.

* * *

Anselmo knew that a project that had long been on Televisa's drawing board was about to launch: the first international television network. Azcárraga had founded Televisa with the intention of pioneering a satellite channel that would be relayed to broadcast networks in multiple countries and unite people regardless of nationality. He had long toyed with ideas for an identity for the international network he envisioned. He played with a phrase—"one vision"—that he used when he described a worldwide population joined by television. In 1976, he named the big network Univisión. The initiative depended on SIN.

Emilio Nicolás, SIN's senior vice president, was the first in the United States to learn of the project. In 1976, when he was working with Televisa on the teleport in San Antonio, he realized that he was not building a domestic satellite system. Azcárraga had gifted the satellite so that SIN would become the first affiliate in a network of national networks. That July, Azcárraga invited Nicolás to Mexico City. At the SICC board meeting the next month when Anselmo celebrated the satellite, much of the hoopla derived from Nicolás's report of the teleport.

Azcárraga's lieutenants had told Nicolás that Televisa was inviting networks in Spanish-speaking countries to join in a multinational alliance. Plans called for a free Spanish-language satellite service that would broadcast Televisa's programs and programs that members would contribute. Nicolás was impressed by the fact that "they wanted to instill Hispanic pride [not only] by sharing programs" but through "live telecasts of sports and special events." He was dazzled by Azcárraga's boast that the network of networks would join 350 million Spanish-speaking individuals in every country where they lived.

While network members would enjoy free programs in fringe and weekend time periods, they would pay for Televisa's premier novelas, sports telecasts, and movies. For occasional prime-time special events, members would have to sacrifice their regular programs and the local advertising the programs carried.

Azcárraga's eye was on the same prize as his father's eye had been on forty-six years earlier, when he had partnered XEW with NBC: revenue from U.S. advertising. He recognized that an international network would afford U.S. firms an economical way to advertise abroad. He also recognized that in order to attract U.S. advertisers, the network had to be seen in the United States. Thus, SIN's participation was essential. It was easily obtained. Televisa's plan had an irresistible feature, that Televisa would solicit all of the ads, embed them in the free programs, and through SICC compensate the SIN stations for carrying them. "We got money [from programs] we did not have to sell," Nicolás later explained.[3]

Azcárraga refused to actively seek participants or publicly unveil the Univisión name until he had access to a new satellite that could reach all of the countries whose networks he hoped to enlist. He planned to initiate Univisión in 1978, when Western Union was scheduled to launch the third device in its Westar fleet, Westar 3. However, Azcárraga was eager to pilot the project as soon as he could. Using the modicum of satellite relays he had available, he coordinated an exchange of programs and broadcasts between Mexico and three other countries in 1977. On the cusp of a satellite age, visionaries forecast a cornucopia of worldwide television. In the United States, satellite television could be seen on the high-numbered UHF channels.

In early 1977, Azcárraga contracted with Spain's TV Española. In the United States, the result was the first regularly scheduled live sports telecasts from abroad: soccer matches played in Europe on Saturday nights, which U.S. viewers saw at 1:00 P.M. on Saturdays.[4] By that summer, Televisa had enlarged the feed. On Saturday evenings, U.S. viewers saw TVE's dramatic series *Mujeres insólitas* (Unusual Women), a Televisa talent competition show, and a combination variety show-game show from TV Chile. The TV Chile broadcast, *Sábados especiales* (Special Saturdays), resembled and competed against *Sábado gigante* (Giant Saturday), which broadcast on its rival network, Canal Trece.

The next expansion was to prove the most notable. Anselmo yielded a half-hour of SIN's Monday–Friday nighttime programming to the Mexican national news. It was carried live at 11:00 P.M. on the East Coast, then rebroadcast by tape delay on the West Coast, also at 11:00 P.M.

Millions in the United States saw *24 horas* (24 Hours), the nightly news anchored by the immensely popular Jacobo Zabludovsky, the PRI political functionary the elder Azcárraga had hired in 1970 to resolve tensions with the government. Zabludovsky brought a new dimension to SIN, particularly to those in the United States who were of Mexican descent. Each night they saw a figure who was familiar for his stentorian voice and the earphones he wore on the news set. Zabludovsky personified Mexico.[5]

In 1978, Televisa extended the still-fledgling Univisión feed with programs broadcast in SIN's afternoon hours. Viewers saw the first telenovelas that Televisa had not produced. Venezuela's two networks, Radio Caracas Televisión, owned by Hernán Pérez Belisario; and Venevisión, owned by Gustavo and Ricardo Cisneros, had partnered to pool their resources and establish Venezuela as a telenovela producer.[6] That year, Univisión's first Venezuelan novela, *La usurpadora* (The Usurper), attracted viewers to SIN.

The next move drove networks to Univisión. Intending to launch Univisión in 1978, Azcárraga tied the event to that year's World Cup soccer tournament. As it had in 1970 and 1974, the Fédération Internationale de Football Association (FIFA) awarded Televisa the right to broadcast the 1978 matches in the Western Hemisphere. Once again, countries' networks would pay Televisa to carry them. However, to encourage them to join Univisión, Televisa announced free supplemental World Cup coverage.

Two months before the World Cup opened that June in Argentina, Azcárraga not only canceled the offer but postponed further work. Western Union had informed Azcárraga that Televisa would not immediately receive relays on Westar 3. Although engineers had worked to enlarge the satellite's relay capacity to twelve channels, they could not activate all of the twelve relays when the device was launched in August 1979.

Azcárraga did not anticipate Western Union's news that, currently, no vacant and working relays were available. In 1974, the Hughes–Western Union consortium had struggled to find customers. By 1978, TV providers, largely startup U.S. cable channels, had overwhelmed the satellite market.

Azcárraga had no choice but to continue with a small number of network participants and wait for a functioning relay on Westar 3. That wait lasted two years. In the summer of 1980, Western Union finally achieved full transmission on Westar 3 and provided Televisa with a working relay. Unlike Westar 1 and Westar 2, which orbited over U.S.-Mexico longitudes, Westar 3 was positioned farther east, over the Atlantic Ocean and South American longitudes. From there, much of South America could be reached. That helped, but it was only an intermediate step for Azcárraga. In order to reach all of South America, Azcárraga needed relays on a new and more powerful device that could cover an area the size of a continent. The solution lay at Hughes Aircraft. After severing its partnership with Western Union, Hughes began a new generation of satellites called Galaxy. Although Televisa had secured a complement of relays on Galaxy, Hughes did not expect to launch Galaxy 1 for another two years.

The international satellite bottleneck did not affect SIN's delivery of Univisión-provided programs in the United States. Because SIN was already connected to the system, regular viewers of SIN saw consequential programs and broadcasts that U.S. viewers accustomed to watching ABC, CBS, and NBC did not have access to. At a time when the English-language U.S. networks were giving viewers *Laverne and Shirley* and *Happy Days*, SIN was giving them popes, presidents, world-class entertainers, sports spectacles, and continuous live coverage of history-making events.

Azcárraga did not abandon the 1978 World Cup. At appearances in Buenos Aires during the matches, he touted his "television without borders." Univisión was "directed at the [world's] Spanish-speaking population [from] a desire to open up channels of mass expression," he proclaimed.[7]

For the first time on free broadcast television, U.S. viewers saw the World Cup on SIN.

The following year, viewers witnessed a series of programming feats. In June 1979, SIN stayed on the air for twenty-five hours to televise Pope John Paul II's visit to Communist Poland. U.S. viewers saw similar coverage of the pope's visits to Mexico in 1979, to the United States in 1980, and to the Philippines in 1981. In May 1980, SIN's Miami station, WLTV, telecast its coverage of Cuban refugees arriving during the Mariel boatlift to the United States, Europe, and South America. On May 3, the world saw WLTV's fund-raising telethon for the refugees.

* * *

In 1981, Azcárraga finally realized his vision of a multinational network of networks. Univisión was transmitting from Westar and Galaxy satellites to networks in twenty countries. In addition to SIN, TVE, TV Chile, and Venevisión, the participants included the América network in Perú, Cadena Uno in Colombia, the ABS network in the Philippines, and Canal Siete in Argentina.

However, Azcárraga needed to resolve a question: which country and which participating network to use for the event that would officially launch the Univisión network. Azcárraga chose the United States and SIN. When Anselmo and Nicolás learned that SIN would stage the event, they conducted one of the network's largest publicity campaigns. Advertising promoted Univision as the network "that unites the entire Spanish-speaking world. . . . For the first time, a live commercial television network will interconnect countries worldwide, 20 nations, 35 million TV homes, 270 million people!"[8]

SIN claimed that close to that number, around 250 million, witnessed its global gala on October 11, 1981. WXTV originated a seven-hour spectacular from the streets and stages of New York. Viewers saw *El desfile de la hispanidad,* New York's Hispanic Day Parade. Soccer great Pelé was grand marshal. After the parade, the extravaganza switched to Madison Square Garden, which was packed. A three-hour arena concert and variety show emceed by Raúl Velasco, the host of Televisa's internationally broadcast Sunday program *Siempre en domingo* (Always on Sunday), carried the festivities into the night.[9] Audiences on four continents heard ¡*Viva España! ¡Viva la Hispanidad!*[10]

More spectacular broadcasts followed. Each night for two weeks, SIN relayed a TVE docudrama from Spain on author Miguel de Cervantes.[11] U.S. viewers also watched live bullfights from Quito featuring Ecuador's famed Spanish Domecq bulls.[12] From Lima they saw an exhibition of Andean music and Peruvian ballet. In October 1982, SIN carried a week of live telecasts commemorating the 490th anniversary of the first voyage of Christopher Columbus. The following October, an estimated 250 million viewers saw a broadcast from Madrid of a joint appearance of popular singer Julio Iglesias and opera tenor Plácido Domingo. Arbitron reported that in both Los Angeles and Miami the Iglesias-Domingo telecast garnered more viewers than the programming ABC, CBS, or NBC offered in the same time slot.[13]

Univisión peaked with its coverage of the 1982 World Cup, which Spain hosted. The network amassed an audience of an estimated 300 million that stretched from New York to Cape Horn. The achievement complemented another one: Azcárraga co-chaired the committee that placed Mexico's successful bid to host the next World Cup in 1986. Televisa won worldwide rights to sell its origination of the World Cup matches to networks in other countries.

However, by 1983, Univisión's novelty had waned. Participating networks began to complain that Univisión was too broadly programmed. When Venevisión and others located plentiful alternative satellite content and withdrew and advertising revenue declined, Azcárraga discovered that he and the visionaries had been wrong about what satellite television could do. Instead of joining the world's people, the myriad channels had fragmented them. Azcárraga shifted his focus to the World Cup. He let Univisión dwindle and contemplated a niche that a successor network might fill: he planned to use the 1986 matches to announce Univisión's rebirth as a news channel called Empresa de Comunicaciones Orbitales.

Yet SIN's Univisión period was robust. Those in the United States who had not heard of SIN read of its international programs in Sunday newspaper supplements and in *People, Reader's Digest,* and *TV Guide.* SIN brought the end of the TV signoff. In the early 1980s, most U.S. television stations concluded programming at one in the morning, but SIN stations broadcast around the clock. Andrew Martinez, SIN's operations manager in San Antonio, recalled the public's fascination with the network's technical quality. Compared to the telephone-line delivery of ABC, CBS, and NBC, SIN's satellite signal was pristine. "People [who did not speak

Spanish] wrote in and told us they watched because the pictures and sound were so good," Martinez later recalled.[14]

As the 1980s began, Anselmo was confounded by two developments that had accompanied Azcárraga's pursuit of the satellite relays. After obtaining the two relays on Westar 3, Azcárraga used one to beam the first Spanish-language cable channel to the United States. Although only a small number of Latino homes subscribed, the new channel, Galavisión, competed with SIN.[15] Anselmo's larger anxiety was his discovery that Azcárraga had not included SIN when he was negotiating for access to the Galaxy satellite. This omission alarmed Anselmo because SIN had outgrown its one relay on the aging Westar 2. Anselmo did not confront Azcárraga about the issue, but he realized that unless he negotiated himself with satellite companies, SIN would be back to the bicycle delivery system when the expected life of Westar 2 ended.[16]

Some questioned the torrent of foreign programming SIN offered. In 1979, the American Federation of Radio and Television Artists (AFTRA) filed a complaint alleging that SIN denied opportunities to U.S. performers.[17] The complaint had merit. Arturo Gonzalez of California State University at Northridge found that of forty-four KMEX programs, twenty-five were from Mexico and twelve were from Puerto Rico, Colombia, Venezuela, and Brazil; only seven were from the United States. KMEX produced all seven locally, including the only U.S. program on the Univisión feed, a pro wrestling series called *Lucha libre Los Ángeles*.[18]

Anselmo refused to address the absence of domestic productions on his network. "We can do these things better in Mexico," he had said in 1969.[19]

* * *

On January 20, 1980, Anselmo sent a letter to the *New York Times* that blasted President Jimmy Carter and his administration for not including the "so-called illegal aliens in this country" in the 1980 census. He condemned the "immorality" of government decision makers. "Let's wake up," end the "scare stories and bloated rhetoric," and "come to grips" with the large population of individuals who were not documented as U.S. citizens and residents but who were living in the United States, he wrote. In 1980, it was estimated that undocumented residents numbered around eight million.[20] The letter announced a changing direction in U.S. Spanish-language television. A new Rene Anselmo had risen. (His close associates knew that this was the real Rene Anselmo.) The SIN network had begun turning a profit in 1976, and profits had grown in 1977, 1978, and 1979.[21] Although Azcárraga was still SICC's primary owner and the nearly exclusive provider of its programming, Anselmo no longer needed to court his approval or worry about the reprisals the Televisa leader threatened, such as those he had made in 1973, 1974, and 1975, if SIN should face distress in the future.

Anselmo signaled his new stance during an interview with syndicated columnist Rick DuBrow. Railing against the "injustices" that denied Spanish-language television a "fair environment," Anselmo said that "people who are mentally lazy" and "full of sanctimony" were to blame. "I envision . . . becoming the voice that strengthens Spanish-language television and Latin pride," he told DuBrow.[22] Anselmo's list of enemies now included AFTRA and the "bigots" at the Nielsen ratings. Anselmo also counted as bigots the ad agencies on Madison Avenue that spurned SIN.

Anselmo foresaw disaster from rhetoric about the issue of acculturation. According to this idea, Spanish-speaking individuals in the United States would preserve their original nationalities and cultures but would use Spanish less because they were compelled to use English in daily conversation. This model of adapting to life in the United States was a potential threat to SIN.

In 1980, acculturation became a buzz word in marketing and advertising circles. Interest was fueled by the 1980 census. In 1970, the Census Bureau merely had estimated numbers of U.S. residents by ethnicity. The bureau took an actual count for the first time in the 1980 census.[23] African Americans, who numbered 25 million, were the largest ethnic group. The "Hispanic" population had doubled since 1970; it now numbered 20 million. The census also showed that although 20 percent of Hispanic families survived on incomes of less than $10,000, which was below the government's poverty line, the average family income was $20,000. The census bureau estimated that the average Hispanic household had $10,000 of disposable income. This meant that the nation's five million Hispanic families had $50 billion in buying power.[24] Businesses rushed to tap into a Latino market. Ad agencies J. Walter Thompson, Young & Rubicam, and Ogilvy & Mather opened Spanish-language divisions. The Spanish Advertising and Marketing Service had formed in 1978.

However, data was scarce. Experts stepped forward to educate marketers and advertisers. Agencies invited them to training events. They headlined seminars and symposia. National publications quoted them. The trade magazine *Madison Avenue* devoted an entire edition in 1982 to "Hispanics: A World of Their Own."[25]

One of those experts was Dr. Peter Salinas, an urbanologist at Hunter College. Salinas urged businesses to stop advertising on Spanish-language television. Those who "program [a] campaign in Spanish are fighting a lost war," Salinas said, because his studies showed that few U.S. families "held on to Spanish." The "thrust," he said, is "toward learning English." Thus, "if advertisers begin to gear programs to Spanish-speaking people in Spanish, they may be making a mistake."[26]

Another expert was Eduardo Caballero, the head of Spanish Media, Inc., the largest national sales representative for Spanish-language radio stations. Caballero advised clients about the division of the Spanish-speaking population by nationality. This was a revelation to marketers. He named SIN as an outlet that advertisers should "rule out" because its "one size fits all" programming wasted advertising budgets. Spanish-speaking groups are "too numerous and far too varied," he said. "You cannot sell to Hispanics [on] a national medium."[27] Business and agency executives, most of whom were Anglo, listened. Alex Berger of Sibley Advertising said he had "no idea that the Spanish-language market is not blending into the great American melting pot."[28]

According to SIN vice president Danny Villanueva, Anselmo was "beside himself" when advertisers heard "the fiction of acculturation." While no advertisers withdrew, Anselmo was concerned that the vast majority of businesses that did not advertise on SIN "never would" do so. SIN had proven that a national network could reach a diverse Spanish-speaking population, and Anselmo was incensed that anyone would believe, let alone promote the idea, that Spanish would become extinct. "We always heard the lie we could not survive because young people would grow up speaking English," Villanueva recalled.[29]

In August 1980, Anselmo contacted Emilio Nicolás for assistance in arranging the first comprehensive study of Spanish-speaking individuals in the United States. Nicolás was surprised when Anselmo said he would spend $100,000, one-tenth of the previous year's profits, on the project. According to Nicolás, Anselmo said "spend money, make it public, and see if we can clear the air."[30] Anselmo hired the Dallas marketing and research

Figure 6. Emilio Nicolás (*left*), Rene Anselmo (*center*), and Danny Villanueva were the triumvirate that led the coast-to-coast expansion of the Spanish International Network in the 1970s. Villanueva was a former NFL star who publicly identified and brought credibility to the network as a vice president of SIN. Here they unwind at the 1983 National Association of Broadcasters convention in Las Vegas. Photo courtesy of Joaquín Blaya.

firm Yankelovich, Skelly & White, which sent field teams into most U.S. states. Over eight months, the firm recorded in-depth interviews in more than 1,000 homes. In July 1981, Daniel Yankelovich held a news conference in New York to announce the release of the study findings as a book entitled *Spanish USA*.[31]

The work uncovered a direction-setting finding. Spanish-speaking individuals had not just settled in New York, Miami, and near the Mexican border; they also lived in Connecticut, Kentucky, Pennsylvania, Wisconsin, Utah, and Montana. Yankelovich predicted that Latinos would live in all fifty states by 2000. Families were large; they averaged 5.5 members. Typically they were male dominated, cohesive, extended, and religious.

Yankelovich produced the findings Anselmo wanted him to report. He emphasized the "strength and endurance of the Spanish language." Ninety percent of respondents claimed some fluency in Spanish. Only 1 percent favored strictly English speech. Ninety percent of Hispanic young adults named Spanish as the first language they learned to speak as children. Two-thirds of young people preferred to speak Spanish in the home. Those of all ages "think of themselves" as "Hispanic first, American second" and "place great importance on perpetuating [Spanish] throughout succeeding generations."

Yankelovich's report debunked the notion that multiple nationalities and cultures meant that nationwide Spanish-language television would not succeed. Respondents attested to the same finding the Pulse study had identified two decades earlier: only 10 percent read newspapers. Yet after examining responses to questions about how respondents viewed television and noting that regardless of nationality they said they viewed the same programs, the researchers reported a "a blurring of differences in the way Hispanics of varying nationalities feel about each other." Moreover, Spanish-language television helped "cultivate unity." Half of the respondents said that they watched television for at least two hours a day. More than half preferred television programming in Spanish.[32]

Yankelovich's study was frequently cited in publications. It remained a resource for the business community's further pursuit of the Latino market. For many years, it was a resource advertisers relied on when they made decisions about where to spend their dollars. Pepsi credited *Spanish USA* for its decision to augment one of the most successful advertising campaigns of the 1980s, the commercial in which Michael Jackson sang "*Pepsi, para la sed de la nueva generación*" (Pepsi, for the thirst of the new generation).[33] The report was perhaps most influential as a cornerstone of one of the decade's best-selling books, *Megatrends*, published in 1982. Drawing from *Spanish USA*, author John Naisbitt predicted that language use in the United States would evolve into "English, Spanish and computerese."[34]

The release of *Spanish USA* did not put all questions to rest. Caballero attacked the book as a self-serving promotional tool that SIN had financed. Many of the findings, including confirmation that Spanish-speaking individuals and their descendants spoke English and watched English-language TV, tended to affirm the theory of acculturation. After reading *Spanish USA*, Stanford's Nicholas Valenzuela raised a question "of major concern [stemming from] the increasing immigration of Spanish-speaking people." Does "SIN smooth the transition," he asked, or "does it retard acculturalization by eliminating the incentive to learn the new language and culture[,] keeping the individual isolated from the new society?"³⁵

*   *   *

Anselmo left the debate to others. Few would remember him for commissioning *Spanish USA*. But they did remember two initiatives he directed during the time he battled the theory of acculturation. In addressing more immediate problems, Anselmo found new ways to gain attention and leave a legacy that was more effective than publishing a book.

The first problem emerged in 1979, when Columbia Pictures sold its Spanish-language TV properties, which included New York's WNJU and its alliance of stations that had tentatively agreed to become affiliates of a second Spanish-language network. The news troubled SIN, for the buyer was not a novice. The new owner was veteran Hollywood producer and executive Jerry Perenchio. In 1976, Perenchio claimed proceeds of a half-billion dollars when he sold a partnership with TV creator Norman Lear. He had used some of that money to launch Los Angeles's second Spanish-language station, KVEA.³⁶

By early 1980, Anselmo had learned that Perenchio had retained Carlos Barba as head of WNJU. Barba was the executive Columbia Pictures had hired in 1970 to build the competing network. While Perenchio craved obscurity, Barba was showy and loud. He spread word that the rival network soon would premiere under the name NetSpan and that it would be headquartered at WNJU.

Shortly after Barba leaked reports of Perenchio's plans for NetSpan, Villanueva visited Anselmo. According to Villanueva, Anselmo was "desperate" for suggestions about "what we could do to solve our problem in New York." Although SIN's WXTV fared well in the ratings, it never consistently bested Barba's station and often trailed it. Because WNJU was certain to be the headquarters of a rival network and because national advertising was traded in New York, Anselmo could no longer ignore SIN's sporadic performance in the nation's largest market.

In Anselmo's view, the problem was television's worst transmitting injustice. Twelve years earlier, the commissioners of the city of New York had refused to allow WXTV to broadcast from the 102-story Empire State Building. The commissioners instead gave WXTV a license to broadcast from the 67-story Cities Services Building. In 1979, when the commissioners finally gave WXTV permission to move its tower to the Empire State

Building, it was because they had given rival station WNJU permission to broadcast from the new 110-story World Trade Center. When Anselmo requested the same site, he was told that having two UHF towers on the same building would pose a "radiation danger."[37]

On May 9, 1980, Anselmo parked a travel trailer affixed with a banner denouncing the Port Authority's discrimination against New York's Spanish-speaking community on a street alongside the World Trade Center. He walked onto the plaza and took a chair. He then instructed a messenger to deliver a letter to Port Authority commissioners that said he would stay in the plaza and would refuse food and assistance until he heard that WXTV would be allowed a World Trade Center transmitter.

The first day, people came and went. But the next day, passersby began to notice the network president and his banner. Several telephoned the Port Authority to find out what was going on. On day three, the news media arrived. New York's local stations took viewers to the scene of Anselmo's hunger strike.[38] On day four, Mayor Ed Koch called a meeting of commissioners and community leaders.[39]

On day five, Anselmo won. The commissioners approved a WXTV installation on the trade center's north tower broadcasting mast.[40] The story finished with a twist. When transmissions began in June, the Channel 41 signal faded in the Brooklyn area almost directly underneath the tower. Ironically, although he had won a permit for increased power, Anselmo decided to keep the station at the Empire State Building.[41]

Another problem arose in December 1979. That month, a rocket went off course. Its payload, the first satellite built by RCA, a device called Satcom, was lost in space. Anselmo had succeeded in winning relays on Satcom in exchange for a multimillion-dollar contract with RCA for satellite receivers and TV transmitters. Villanueva needed the gear, but the satellite was gone.[42]

Western Union, agreed to place SIN on a waiting list for its older Westar 3. With fifty relays on its sleek Galaxy fleet, Hughes Aircraft was by far the largest of the two remaining satellite providers. Although relays on Galaxy were available, Hughes refused to assign any to SIN. Hughes Aircraft ascended to the top of Anselmo's enemies list.[43]

That June, the Satcom debacle swelled into an industry controversy. Hughes had denied all of the displaced Satcom customers, not just SIN. Anselmo had SICC attorney Norman Leventhal file a petition asking that the FCC take jurisdiction of Hughes's satellite.[44] He won a pyrrhic victory.

While it agreed to intervene, the commission, "besieged by disgruntled satellite customers," chose to "defer complaints" to a study group that would solicit filings, conduct fact-finding, and make recommendations.[45] Anselmo instructed Leventhal to work full time on a submission of briefs, records, and documents that would persuade the FCC to compel Hughes to give SIN a Galaxy relay.

By January 1981, nothing had happened. Hughes had not answered SIN's further requests for relays. RCA had not replaced Satcom. Western Union had kept SIN on its wait list. The FCC had yet to act on the filings it received. Anselmo waited.

That February, Anselmo handed a messenger a box filled with envelopes that looked like wedding announcements. Each had a handwritten address. He told the messenger to mail the envelopes without return addresses. The next day in Washington, FCC commissioners, administrators of federal offices, White House officials, judges, diplomats, and members of the news media opened envelopes to find an engraved announcement from socialite "Samantha Fairfax" that the FCC would be the "guest of honor" at a private and exclusive "Satellite Cotillion Ball the Hugheses are planning." The socialite sent another engraved invitation to a second event. She and the FCC were throwing a benefit for the needy: "Westy Union's Charity Affair." A subsequent mailing looked like a ransom demand. It was signed by Chilean revolutionary "Pedro Gonzales de la María y Gonzales." He wrote, "Who this Hughes? Explain me what this dirty word 'common carrier' mean."[46]

Anselmo got the relays. Hughes allocated two relays on Galaxy 1 to SIN.[47] None of the letters' recipients publicly admitted they had contacted Hughes and told it to comply with Anselmo's request for relays. Anselmo believed it might have been President Ronald Reagan, and stories circulated to that effect. However, there was nothing to prove Anselmo's speculation that the president was the one who intervened.[48] Anselmo later explained that "we must have [had] six feet of filings on satellite problems.... It occurred to me: Who the hell wants to read about all that?... If you want to get your point across, write a letter to the guys who are making the decisions and say, 'This is what it's all about.'"[49]

* * *

Anselmo needed the relays because of a technological innovation Villanueva had learned about. In 1980, the KMEX manager and SIN vice president was Anselmo's closest associate. Frank Fouce's lawsuit had brought them into a closer relationship. Pretending disinterest in the lawsuit, Anselmo distanced himself from the company's attorneys and the events in Los Angeles federal court. But secretly, he had Villanueva attend the proceedings and report back to him what was happening.

However, Villanueva's primary duty was still network expansion. The effort had stalled. After signing KORO in Corpus Christi, Villanueva had failed to locate other independent stations that were willing to affiliate with SIN. The lawsuit slowed the expansion. The judge's 1976 restraining order had prohibited projects that included the building of the station SIN owned in Phoenix, KTVW, which Villanueva was to supervise. However, when a new judge lifted the restraining order in December 1980, Villanueva had already traveled to Phoenix and ordered construction to begin.

In early 1979, engineers had finished testing KTVW's satellite dish when several miniature TV transmitters they ordered arrived. In Phoenix, TV stations could not reach all viewers. The region was large and was hemmed in by mountainous terrain. To compensate, the FCC allowed stations to rebroadcast signals at low power on unused UHF channels. This was accomplished by small, remotely controlled transmitters called translators.

Villanueva became very interested when he saw the robot devices. As he prepared to deploy them, he realized "that if we connected satellite dishes to translators, we could broadcast SIN any place the satellite could be received."[50] Because a satellite has a large footprint, there would be no city SIN could not reach. He urged Anselmo to spend several million dollars on dishes and translators.

Anselmo was dubious, and not because of the cost. Villanueva's idea was illegal. The FCC expressly prohibited the importing of distant signals. It permitted low-power TV channels only within the designated market areas of TV stations and only to fill gaps in the designated areas where stations could not be received. It refused to allow any TV station to operate by remote control.[51]

Villanueva pushed ahead. He contacted SIN's chief engineers, James Meek, Richard Morse, and Robert Porter. They went to Phoenix and connected one of the translators directly to the KTVW satellite dish at night. Severed from the station and wired only to the dish, the translator beamed out a perfect signal. The SIN engineers approached technicians at RCA and told them of their discovery that a translator could broadcast signals that a satellite dish received. This meant that television broadcasting could be facilitated without TV stations and at potentially little cost. Instantly, RCA prototyped a dish-translator device. When RCA agreed to manufacture it, Anselmo placed the order that won the Satcom relays.

Leventhal accomplished the crucial step. In June 1979, the SICC attorney, pleading both a viable technology and a lack of television diversity, filed applications with the FCC to broadcast distant satellite-delivered signals on low-power transmitters. Anselmo expected "years of hearings."[52] Instead, that December, the commission not only awarded SIN an experimental license for a one-year trial in Denver to determine if the broadcast of satellite signals from translators and without tv stations and personnel would be reliable, but it also indicated that new rules would be forthcoming pending the results of the Denver tests.[53]

The experiments produced a device, a robot TV station, that Villanueva dubbed the "satelator." On February 22, 1980, SIN unveiled it. That night, Spanish-language television arrived in Denver on Channel 31, a low-power "station" with no human beings on site. Beamed from 7,500-foot Lookout Mountain, the signal traveled thirty miles. *Denver Post* columnist Clark Secrest heralded "Denver's sixth television outlet." Because of a "new technology" that "picks up programs being bounced via satellite from San Antonio," Secrest noted, it "is the only [station] of its type in the nation."[54] Anselmo sent William Stiles, SIN's executive vice president, to monitor the telecast. After he heard Stiles's positive report, Anselmo reported the success to the FCC.[55]

The commissioners shared Anselmo's enthusiasm. One month later, on March 28, 1980, the FCC granted four permanent licenses to SIN. Channel 31 became a permanent station in Denver. On May 3, SIN signed on in Philadelphia on Channel 35.[56] On June 22, full-time Spanish-language television was seen for the first time in Hartford, Connecticut, on Channel 62.[57] Anselmo later recalled the sign-on of the fourth satelator in Washington, DC, as one of the pinnacles of his career.[58]

On June 29, around 750 ambassadors, diplomats, and members of the cabinet, Congress, and the FCC gathered at the Mexican Embassy in Washington. Emilio Azcárraga led a delegation from Mexico City. The embassy had installed television sets in the banquet hall. Azcárraga welcomed guests and introduced Anselmo. After Anselmo's emotional opening remarks, attendees witnessed the inaugural telecast of Washington's Channel 56. Festivities concluded when Jorge Luis Celaya Coronado, assistant secretary general of the Organization of American States, toasted "Rene Anselmo, TV pioneer."[59]

In 1981, the FCC awarded SIN forty more licenses. That year, SIN initiated satelator stations in Albuquerque, Austin, Tucson, Las Vegas, Bakersfield, Milwaukee, and Tampa. The next year, SIN brought Spanish-language television to Boston, Baltimore, Detroit, Pueblo, and Salt Lake City. It added Cleveland, Indianapolis, and Oklahoma City in 1983.[60]

The satelator project crowned Anselmo's career in Spanish-language television. While the satelators were unable to reach viewers much beyond city limits, they gave credence to Anselmo's claim that SIN was the "fourth network." By 1986, SIN claimed to reach 60 percent of the U.S. population on stations in 100 of the 210 total TV markets.[61] In 1982, on the recommendation of the FCC, Congress enacted the Low Power Television Act.[62]

The signing of the act was part of the deregulation of U.S. broadcasting. The year before, under chair Mark Fowler, the commission had endorsed a shift in direction away from broadcasters' stewardship of the airwaves: it no longer viewed broadcasters as public trustees subject to extensive government oversight but as participants in a competitive marketplace. Congress's enactment of the Low Power Television Act and the FCC's approval of direct broadcast satellite delivery initiated the deregulation of television. Representative Lionel Van Deerlin, the chair of the House Subcommittee on Communications, observed that deregulation "would have been impossible without the thunder and lightning sparked by [LPTV and direct broadcast satellite]." Anselmo and SIN had sparked both of these changes.[63]

However, the satelators brought an unanticipated development. Viewers saw a vast array of international content from Univision but no U.S. network programs. The first to notice were the owners of Spanish-language radio stations. Outraged that the FCC had changed its policy to help SIN but not the radio industry, radio station owners wanted the satelators shut down. In September 1980, they filed petitions that asked the FCC to investigate SIN's satelators with an eye toward revoking the permits it had granted the network. They alleged that SIN was foreign owned and that the FCC had thus granted permits to an illegal firm.[64]

Anselmo declined to discuss Frank Fouce's lawsuit, saying that he was not absorbed in it and had lost track of it. After four years, the case had not come to trial. Villanueva assured him it never would. However, in

December 1980, the attorneys and Villanueva informed Anselmo of a serious situation. Fouce had introduced evidence that SIN was not owned by a U.S. citizen. The court could not extract damages from an illegitimate defendant, so the presiding federal judge, Mariana Pfaelzer, had sided with the radio owners in asking for clarification about SIN's legality. She insisted the court could not proceed without the FCC's detailed conclusion on whether SIN and its parent firm, SICC, were operating within U.S. law.[65]

Out of this came both Anselmo's undoing and his final initiative: he launched the first Spanish-language network news program. For ten years, Villanueva had campaigned for a network newscast that would originate at KMEX in Los Angeles and honor Rubén Salazar. Anselmo's hands were still tied by Azcárraga's rule that SIN generate no local, U.S.-based programming, but things changed in December 1980. According to Villanueva, SIN's attorneys pointed out the difficulty of their position: although they needed to prove that SIN's owner was a U.S. citizen, the network had no U.S. shows. Anselmo responded to that concern by ordering the only network program SIN could stage in a hurry: a nightly network news program.

Villanueva recalled that while Anselmo was concerned about "crossing swords with Azcárraga," he assured the others that Azcárraga would not object "if he [Anselmo] was in charge." Moreover, Anselmo "swore we had to do it in Washington because no network news was [based] there and [this] would impress the commissioners." Anselmo scoffed at Villanueva's fears that the commission might revoke SIN's licenses and invoke its "death penalty." Anselmo maintained "the FCC would never harm a network that did a national news."[66]

Observing Anselmo's obsession with basing a newscast in Washington and launching it himself, Villanueva declined to participate. However, when word reached Miami, Joaquín Blaya, the manager of WLTV, was pleased. Blaya was elated that Anselmo was defying Azcárraga and opening domestic production on the network and saw an opportunity for his station.

By that time, Blaya was a force within SIN. When Anselmo purchased the dilapidated WLTV, Azcárraga was so angry that he had briefly fired Anselmo. But Blaya had vindicated Anselmo; he had transformed WLTV into a profit center that rivaled KMEX. He continued to rise in Anselmo's esteem.

Blaya generated profits by spending little on news. Yet in 1977, he had organized a campaign for a network news program. That year, WLTV had begun televising *24 horas*. Miami was a hotbed of sentiment directed against Cuban president Fidel Castro and his ally, Mexican president José López Portillo. Anti-Castro factions were furious at WLTV's admiration of Castro as seen on its 11:00 P.M. program, the Mexican state news. Again and again, police converged on WLTV in response to bomb threats, pickets, protests, and, in one case, a violent confrontation. Blaya urged Anselmo to remove *24 horas* and replace it with a newscast produced in the United States.[67]

Yet local hostility toward *24 horas* did not entirely explain Blaya's interest in producing news. In June 1979, Televisa engineers had contacted Blaya for advice on purchasing property in Miami. Blaya soon learned that Televisa had committed to building a satellite teleport there.[68] It was to be a sister to SIN's teleport in San Antonio. That summer he met with Anselmo and presented a plan for a network news program that WLTV would develop. Over the next year and a half, Blaya set aside funds, recruited personnel, and campaigned for the project. The teleport "changed everything," he later explained. Blaya reasoned that if a network news operation were based in Miami, SIN might move its headquarters to Florida and its direction would come under his control.[69]

Blaya's plan hinged on his hiring of Gustavo Godoy, the executive news director of WTVJ. Godoy had supervised the newscasts of prominent Miami news anchor Ralph Renick at the peak of Renick's career.[70] In late 1980, Blaya offered Godoy the post of WLTV news director, telling him the job would lead to his direction of SIN's first network news program. Although Godoy was interested, he declined the offer. He balked at leaving WTVJ and Renick because "Joaquín could not guarantee that Anselmo would put [a WLTV newscast] on the network."[71]

Blaya continued to court Godoy in 1981. Like Villanueva, Blaya believed that Anselmo "could not pull off" a national news program and that if he hired the experienced Godoy, the two could "come to [Anselmo's] rescue." However, early in 1981, Anselmo moved to Washington, where he had recruited a news staff. On April 25, he held a news conference to announce the June premiere of *Noticiero nacional SIN*. Blaya was so surprised that two days later he traveled to Washington. "I had to see it myself," he later recalled.[72]

Blaya found "a train wreck." He located the SIN president alone in a student studio at Howard University. There was no newsroom; Washington rents were too high. Anselmo had hired only ten news personnel and they were working from their apartments. The university, which had recently installed a satellite uplink, gave Anselmo access to the uplink and the student studio for free.

Anselmo remained resolute. He rejected Blaya's suggestion that he delay the premiere and hand the project to WLTV. When Anselmo insisted that the first broadcast of *Noticiero nacional SIN* would be successful, Blaya asked Anselmo's permission to bring Godoy to Washington so he could observe the broadcast.

While *Noticiero SIN* first aired on June 21, 1981, it consisted largely of video clips and news presenters who read wire service news. Nevertheless, it was a historic TV event. In words Anselmo likely had scripted, President Reagan welcomed an audience estimated at five million. "*Buenas tardes.* I want to say how happy I am to help inaugurate the first national news program carried in Spanish," the president said. Newscaster Guillermo Restrepo then anchored a newscast that had no technical flaws but was limited by the small staff and the student studio. Anselmo had managed to generate graphics, maps, theme music, and two field reports from SIN correspondents. The most polished elements were the commercials by the broadcast's numerous national sponsors.[73]

The evening's main event came after the newscast. Having Godoy on the scene worked as Blaya had planned. Godoy was the only person present who had experience in television news. He confronted Anselmo, telling him of "fifty things you are doing wrong" and saying that "your newscast is a disgrace to the Hispanic community." Anselmo, angered by Godoy's audacity, fired back. Godoy and Anselmo argued into the night.[74] Finally, Anselmo offered to name Godoy as SIN's first network news president and to move the newscast to Miami. Godoy took the job.[75]

Godoy moved the news operation to Miami six months later. Complaining that the Washington-based broadcast was "dehumanizing our reporting," Godoy did not wait for Televisa's Miami teleport to be completed. He relaunched *Noticiero SIN* at Miami's PBS station, WPBT, on the set of its PBS national newscast, the *Nightly Business Report*.[76]

When Anselmo hired him, Godoy gave Anselmo a list of newspaper, radio, and TV journalists whom he felt were the crème de la crème of Spanish-language news reporting. Godoy hired most of them. They included Josie Goytisolo, the executive producer, and José Diaz-Balart, the co-anchor. Ricardo Brown and Guillermo Descalzi joined as national correspondents. Others who were to become household names to viewers included María Elvira Salazar, Carlos Botifoll, Osvaldo Petrocino, and Armando Guzmán. In 1985, Godoy hired another Villanueva protégé, KMEX reporter Jorge Ramos.

Blaya proclaimed them "the dream team." By the end of 1983, Godoy was presiding over a news operation that he felt was equal to news programs on ABC, CBS, and NBC. He convinced Anselmo to loosen the purse strings and opened bureaus in El Salvador, Puerto Rico, Buenos Aires, Jerusalem, and London. Pushing the limits of Televisa's Miami satellite hub, SIN carried news from its own bureaus as well as Televisa's and from the newsrooms of the national networks in the Univisión exchange.[77]

Viewers saw live reports on revolutions in El Salvador and Nicaragua, Argentina's war with Great Britain, the ravaging of Colombia by drug cartels, and a 1985 earthquake that devastated Mexico City. During a wave of reforming elections from Costa Rica to Perú, SIN conducted exit polling.[78] Deposed Nicaraguan president Daniel Ortega learned of his fate from SIN's polls. SIN did not confine its coverage to Latin America. Correspondents reported on bombings in Beirut, unrest in Poland, and the Reagan-Gorbachev summits in Geneva and Reykjavik.[79] Godoy referred to the period as "the era of Camelot."[80]

* * *

In late 1985, magazine ads picturing a smiling Carlos Barba announced the forthcoming launch of NetSpan. In San Antonio and Los Angeles, Nicolás and Villanueva threatened to retaliate if Blaya's plan to move SIN to Miami worked. In Washington, observers awaited an FCC judge's ruling on the commission's investigation. In New York, Anselmo remained calm. He was expecting good news.

All along, Azcárraga had an ace up his sleeve that he could play if the FCC cited SIN for violating the foreign ownership rule. Although SIN Sales, the company Anselmo had formed in 1962, existed only on paper and was hidden within SICC's corporate structure, its charter included provisions that stated that, except for SICC's licensed stations, Televisa owned 100 percent of SIN's network operation. Although foreigners could not own licensed properties, they were not prohibited from owning U.S.

networks. Even though the "network" company was a phantom, its 1962 charter gave Televisa a legal claim to the network properties it had built for SIN in the United States.

In early 1986, Azcárraga played his card. He severed the SIN "network" company from SICC and took steps to assert Televisa's control. He facilitated the maneuver by rechartering the SIN "network" as a property of Univisa, the Televisa U.S. subsidiary directed by Jaime Dávila. This meant that under Dávila, Televisa now controlled the facilities of SIN News and that it now was the employer of Godoy and his 100-person news staff. That August, Azcárraga announced that the long-planned news channel Empresa de Comunicaciones Orbitales (ECO) would be based in the United States at SIN's Miami newsroom, which immediately would start being directed by Televisa news personnel who had been transferred from Mexico City.

Azcárraga's apparent takeover of SIN News came just weeks after a development in Mexico that had disgraced Televisa and its news director-anchor Jacobo Zabludovsky and had upset and alarmed Godoy and his journalists. Starting with Mexico's national elections in 1982, SIN's correspondents had reported on the first mass support for the Partido Acción Nacional, a political party that had been formed in 1939 and that had weakly rivaled the long-dominant Partido Revolucionario Institucional. Azcárraga depended on the PRI; it was by courting PRI's leaders that he had preserved Televisa's monopoly in Mexico. But sentiment had grown that the PRI was corrupt and unwilling to run candidates who supported the interests of the masses. In growing numbers, Mexicans voted for PAN candidates. During local elections in 1984, PAN candidates ousted scores of PRI office holders. Many foresaw the 1986 local elections as the tipping point that would enable the PAN to replace the PRI as the national leader.

In July 1986, SIN sent correspondents to the Mexican state of Chihuahua. There, the PAN was expected to sweep the state's elections. Protests erupted when the PRI, which was discovered to have rigged the elections, won the vote. Public outrage soon fixed on Zabludovsky, who had kept the protest and the PRI's vote-rigging off Televisa's news. Evidently, he had done this to prolong the PRI's control. But it was clear that Zabludovsky had suppressed news of an event that tarnished the PRI and contributed to the unraveling of Mexico's one-party rule. Critics savaged Zabludovsky's censorship and his alleged affection for Mexican dictatorship.[81]

Few could imagine that Zabludovsky's next episode would be an appearance in the democratic United States, but on September 9, that is what happened. Azcárraga summoned Godoy to a meeting in New York. Stunned to see Zabludovsky at the meeting, Godoy was outraged when Azcárraga introduced him as Godoy's new boss. Zabludovsky wasted no time in asserting command. He told Godoy that by the end of the year, he would relocate to Miami and would direct and anchor *Noticiero SIN*. He ordered Godoy to prepare the news staff for his visit to the SIN newsroom the very next day. When Godoy returned home, "there was a revolution in Miami."[82]

Zabludovsky and his entourage arrived in limousines. Godoy struggled to maintain order. Several SIN journalists jeered at Zabludovsky and impeded his tour of the facility. His stay was brief. He had stopped in Miami to tour the city and begin the process of selecting and purchasing a home. But news media widely reported Zabludovsky's tempestuous visit and the fact that he would return. On Miami radio talk shows, hundreds of callers decried Zabludovsky's commandeering of SIN News.[83] The *Los Angeles Times* news service reported that "the prospect of a shill for the Mexican government running SIN news has caused nothing short of panic in SIN news operations from Miami to Los Angeles."[84]

Again and again, Godoy confronted Dávila. "I said [that] Zabludovsky was a puppet" and that if he was not stopped "we'd have a foreign government on American soil using an American news organization for foreign propaganda," Godoy later recounted.[85] On October 20, Dávila fired him.

A mutiny began. The second-in-command, Josie Goytisolo, followed Godoy out the door. Within two weeks, a total of forty-one news personnel, including all of the senior members of the "dream team," had resigned in protest.[86] "This is a statement of what we believe is freedom of the press, of professional dignity and journalistic ethics," anchor José Díaz-Balart told Eleanor Randolph of the *Washington Post*.[87] Junior reporter Jorge Ramos was rushed in as anchor. "They went and found the only on-air male still on the premises," Ramos recalled.[88]

The resistance proved successful. On November 3, Dávila announced that "Mr. Zabludovsky would probably not come" after all.[89] This was confirmed in December, when Zabludovsky had been scheduled to begin as SIN news anchor. Instead, Ramos remained in a seat he would occupy four decades later.

While the protest against Zabludovsky was perhaps the greatest single defense of U.S. journalism, it was an anticlimax. By the time it ended, Azcárraga was out, Anselmo was gone, and SIN by that name was dead. The FCC had revoked SICC's licenses and forced the U.S. owners to vacate the properties, which had the larger effect of ending the public identity of SIN. The network continued in two respects. The arrangement of stations and their transmission of Spanish-language programming stayed intact. More important, Azcárraga/Televisa owned the unit that owned the network's infrastructure. Because the FCC has no authority over networks, Azcárraga owned 100 percent of the "network" unit. However, by the time the court and commission had sorted this out, the network had new U.S. owners who had abandoned the SIN name and relaunched the network as Univision. All of this took place in 1986. That story is the subject of the next chapter.

6

ARMAGEDDON

On January 8, 1986, Judge John H. Conlin ruled on the FCC investigation that the presiding judge in *Fouce Amusement Enterprises and Metropolitan Theaters Corp. v. Spanish International Communications Corp.* had ordered. The ruling ended the first case to cite mass violations of Section 310 of the Communications Act of 1934, the foreign ownership rule. Conlin determined that Mexicans had founded and controlled the Spanish International Communications Corporation, SIN's owner, in violation of the rule. He instructed the Federal Communications Commission to remove the principals, revoke the network's licenses, seize SICC's stations, and find and appoint new owners. The broadcasting world had never seen a more dramatic rendering of its "death penalty."

Conlin's ruling in Washington came ten years after a judge in Los Angeles had heard the first testimony. Even after the ruling, the case was not completely over; related cases occupied the courts. The FCC had yet to act on the complaints of Spanish-language radio owners, and inexplicably, Frank Fouce's original 1976 lawsuit had yet to be tried.

The death penalty, though, resounded. The FCC put the operator of television stations that were the core of a national network out of business. That action raised many issues. A first question was whether the network would stay intact. Conlin's ruling returned the question to the FCC. But the commission had no jurisdiction over networks—a fact that Emilio Azcárraga realized. He had already severed SIN's network operation, a separate U.S. entity his Mexican firm Televisa legally held, from SICC.

The FCC also lacked jurisdiction over content. The judge was mute on the big question: would Spanish-language television continue? Parts of SIN would go on. Potential new owners eyed its lucrative properties. Under the law, nothing could stop them from converting broadcasts from Spanish to English.

Yet that January, there was a possibility that nothing would change. Conlin had pinned his decision on one individual's "abuse of the law."[1] That person, SICC chair and president Rene Anselmo, refused to comply. Seeking to quash Conlin's ruling, he filed an appeal with the FCC Review Board. The FCC set no timetable for acting on the appeal. Anselmo stayed at his desk, assuring SIN's 1,000 employees that business would continue as usual. The "judge's decision is totally off the wall," Anselmo said. "Everything brought up at the hearing the FCC has known about for 25 years."[2]

The FCC should have known about who really owned SIN, but it had never asked questions about information it had. The FCC chair and staff had been given a report about the fact that the Azcárragas owned and controlled SICC in September 1978 at a meeting at FCC headquarters.

Yet the commissioners did not know about what had transpired inside SICC in 1975, when Televisa had threatened to terminate SIN's access to its programs, Fouce had opposed Anselmo's scheme for paying the $2 million SIN owed Televisa, and the SICC board had fired Fouce as chair. Nor did they know that Fouce had offered to sell his remaining shares of SICC and leave the company and that Anselmo had accepted the offer and then had not presented it to the board.

Fouce did not intend to start a legal proceeding that became so notorious. He wanted to show that he was the victim of ongoing mismanagement, but the main purpose of the lawsuit was obtaining financial remuneration. Fouce's attorney, Frederick Stern, intended to concentrate on the period after 1972, the year the elder Azcárraga's secret funding ended. The following year, for the first time in seven years, SICC reported losses. Stern asked the court to award damages based on Fouce's losses in 1973, 1974, and 1975. The filing alleged that SICC was a "self-dealing" company that was characterized by "mismanagement," "waste," and "breach of fiduciary duty."[3] It did not allege that the company's true owner was not a U.S. citizen.

A case that was to span eleven years might have ended on the first day. Anselmo expected the case to be dismissed on the grounds that Fouce, who still owned shares of SICC, had sued himself. There were two turning points that determined the course of the lawsuit. First, on November 7, the judge received a motion from Fouce's attorney for a restraining order that would stop SICC from any spending on capital expenditures, such as enlargement of its Miami satellite transmission facilities and the reoutfitting of studios at stations that were planned at the time. Stern requested this in order to stop SICC from spending funds that a shareholder, Fouce, was claiming as damages. Stern claimed that when the board fired Fouce, it severed its relationship with him. Judge Irving Hill, who was presiding over the case, persuaded that Fouce and SICC had parted, granted the restraining order. The case would go forward.[4]

The second turning point came on January 10, 1977, when Stern filed a motion to admit testimony on SICC's activities before 1972.[5] Judge Hill granted that motion too. By that time, Fouce had filed an affidavit.[6] The court was interested in "apparent improprieties" before 1972 that might void a possible award of damages because of how SICC was incorporated. During his ruling Hill quoted parts of Fouce's affidavit that stated that "Spanish International has submitted to Televisa's control." The judge ruled that the court needed to determine whether SICC had violated Section 310 of the Communications Act since its inception. He informed the attorneys that damages could not be awarded if "the corporations have unclean hands."[7]

Hill's January 1977 ruling enlarged and protracted the proceedings. Stern was certain to lead the court on an expedition through SICC's less-than-pristine past. SICC's attorneys again moved for dismissal, this time on grounds that current claims that required distant evidence could not be tried. Hill denied the motion. He also denied a motion to immediately set a trial date. He admonished the attorneys to cooperate with a "deep" and "wide ranging scope" of discovery.[8]

Stern pushed ahead. He revised the lawsuit into an eighteen-point complaint that alleged that Fouce had suffered because of the Azcárragas' "continuing pattern of coercion and interference."[9] He had Fouce compile a list of SICC board members and key figures who would be compelled to testify. He requested lists of SICC's earliest company records. He wasted little time in issuing his first subpoena. It went to the star witness. On February 2, 1977, Stern began deposing Anselmo. If SICC's attorneys had recommended tight lips, Anselmo ignored such advice. He willingly and openly responded to Stern's questions. With detail and anecdotes, he recounted his personal career, his associations with the Azcárragas, and the history of SIN. Anselmo's deposition continued for three days. It would decide the outcome of the case.

Under oath, Anselmo confirmed what Fouce and others long suspected, that in 1961 the elder Azcárraga, a Mexican citizen, had given Anselmo, a U.S. citizen, the $75,000 to purchase SIN and its licensed stations. While Anselmo said he could not testify to whether "official filings had been falsified," he recounted many times when he had carried out the Azcárragas' orders.[10] Anselmo stunned even Fouce with details about the elder Azcárraga's scheme by which he had used his own money to fund a subsidiary company he had created and chartered in Panama and then had the company transfer the money to SICC. It was during Anselmo's deposition that the Panamanian company called VT Latin, through which he had paid SIN's debts from 1966 to 1972, first became publicly known.[11]

Stern studied the subpoenaed SICC materials. Fouce believed he would win by demonstrating violation that seemed more blatant than foreign ownership. Under Section 73.658(i) of the FCC rules, companies that operated networks could not represent local stations in the stations' negotiations for national advertising. Half or more of a local station's revenues came from national advertising in the form of nationally produced commercial messages called spots. Stations needed agents who could negotiate with national ad agencies for spot sales. For this, stations were clients of companies that were independent from networks and that represented many stations to sell local spot airtime. While networks were motivated to represent their affiliates and claim commissions on local station sales, anti-trust concerns first set forth in the FCC's 1941 chain broadcasting report prohibited them from doing so.[12] Section 73 prohibited networks from skimming off the top of station revenue.[13] Anselmo denied that SICC represented local stations.[14] However, a confidential letter from company controller Ronald Rosen had asked Anselmo, "Why doesn't SICC have its own [independent] rep company? [The stations'] arrangements with SICC are not favorable." That document was proof that Anselmo had known that SICC was violating Section 73.[15]

The attorneys continued to joust. They returned to court eight times on motions to block or compel evidence. Judge Hill resolved almost every dispute in Fouce's favor. He permitted documents on the 1974 episode when Emilio Azcárraga employed SIN personnel in his closed-circuit telecasts of World Cup soccer.[16] He permitted documents about the 1971 episode when

Azcárraga fired Anselmo. Although Anselmo returned, the judge wanted to know more about the firing; if Azcárraga could fire the company's president, there was no doubt that he had authority over all of its personnel.[17]

By the end of 1977, Fouce's attorneys had produced almost all of the evidence the judge later used to sanction SICC. Hill set a trial date of May 18, 1978. However, when the attorneys informed Judge Hill that they were discussing a settlement, he granted a delay. SICC refused to settle, apparently on Anselmo's orders, and Stern insisted that the trial should begin immediately. Although Hill expected to set a trial date that fall, in November 1978, President Jimmy Carter promoted him to a senior federal judgeship.

The court transferred the case to Judge Mariana Pfaelzer, who for two decades had been a prominent criminal attorney who was also active in liberal political causes. Pfaelzer received the case on November 13, 1978. At the time, she was Carter's newest appointee to the federal bench. She called the attorneys to her court on February 16, 1979, to tell them that she would not speed up the proceedings and that they should try again to reach a settlement. This, of course, frustrated Fouce and his attorney. The judge noted a "labyrinth of issues."[18]

By summer, the judge still had not set a trial date. On August 17, 1979, concerned that the judge might dismiss the suit—and convinced that Fouce's case was conclusive—Stern moved for a "summary judgment."[19] In summary judgment, proceedings stop and a trial is avoided. Instead, a court renders an immediate judgment from evidence in hand and testimony that can be determined as fact. The procedure requires that a judge serve as factfinder. On November 19, Pfaelzer agreed to serve as factfinder and consider summary judgment, but on her extended timetable.[20]

From November 1979 to December 1980, the judge delved into Fouce's evidence pointing to SICC's foreign ownership. She reached decisions that were to change the trajectory of the case. This is when she allowed Spanish-language radio owners, who had evidence that supported Fouce's arguments, to intervene. Supported by the radio owners, Fouce seemed to be the victor. He and Stern were eager for a summary judgment.

However, the judge foresaw a complication: based on Fouce's and now the radio owners' testimony, the FCC was unclear about whether SICC was legal. Like her predecessor, she feared that if SICC had been operating illegally, damages would also be illegal. In later review by the FCC, Pfaelzer explained that "a long-lasting maze of ties and interconnections [that] became internecine in 1979" required the FCC's "administrative direction."[21] With the evidence she had, she could not determine whether SICC was legal.

On December 12, 1980, Pfaelzer denied the motion for a summary judgment, ordered that the case continue, and suspended opening arguments pending an administrative investigation she ordered the FCC to conduct. "The Court finds genuine issues of material fact in [both parties'] claims," she ruled.[22]

Pfaelzer approached the FCC as a blinded agency in the executive branch. She had seen uncontested sworn testimony that Televisa had founded and had long controlled a TV network in the United States. She was astonished that for twenty years the FCC, an agency that was mandated to safeguard U.S. airwaves from foreign control, had allowed the arrangement.

The commission had had reason to look the other way. Its policies mandated diversity. Nothing better demonstrated diversity than an enterprise that broadcast in Spanish. Yet in seeking diversity, the FCC had violated its own rules when it had approved SIN's use of robot TV stations, the satelators, in 1980. The FCC had not only changed its policy but had awarded SIN satelator licenses in fifty cities.

Spanish-language radio was new in most cities. As large English-language stations moved to FM channels, small operators purchased vacated stations on the AM band. In Denver, Ed Romero revived an early Spanish-language radio venture founded by pioneer broadcaster Francisco "Paco" Sánchez. In 1975, he launched KBNO on Denver's 1280 AM frequency. As had occurred at every initiation of Spanish-language broadcasting, Romero struggled to sign sponsors. His sponsors had limited budgets.

Fortuitously for Romero, he and other Spanish-language radio owners had caucused the year before at the annual convention of the National Association of Broadcasters in Dallas, where they had founded the Spanish Radio Broadcasters Association (SRBA). They elected Ed Gómez, the owner of Albuquerque's KABQ, as president.[23]

That February, Romero contacted Gómez, who, in turn, contacted the FCC. Expecting that the FCC would license a SIN satelator station in Albuquerque, Gómez notified the SRBA's thirty members. Unanimously, they backed Gómez's plan to petition the FCC to have the satelators removed.

On March 20, 1980, Gómez filed for the revocation of SIN's satelator permits on the ground that "SICC is unfit as a license holder. . . . [because it] is subject to the control of aliens in violation of Section 310 of the Communications Act."[24]

Gómez expected a timely response that agreed to his request. Instead, just a week later, on March 27, the FCC permanently licensed the satelators in Denver, Philadelphia, Hartford, and Washington. That April, Gómez refiled the petition. That was when Pfaelzer learned of the SRBA's complaint against SICC. Studying Fouce's motion for a summary judgment and finding violations of Section 310, the judge grew certain of the need for an FCC investigation. She also questioned why the commission had ignored the SRBA and then, without public notice, awarded SIN the satelator licenses. She and the radio owners waited for the FCC's reply.

After four months when the FCC still had not answered, the matter took a significant turn. Spanish International fell at odds with a U.S. hero, former astronaut Harrison Schmitt. Eight years before, as the pilot of Apollo 17, Schmidt and Eugene Cernan were the last individuals to walk on the moon. Now, as a U.S. senator from New Mexico, Schmitt had an interest in Gómez's Albuquerque radio station. Schmitt listened while Gómez protested the possible destruction of his radio station by agents of a foreign country.

On July 28, 1980, Schmitt summoned FCC chair Charles Ferris to Capitol Hill. Ferris was the chair who had been briefed on the Azcárragas' control of SICC and SIN in 1978. The next day, Ferris sent letters notifying SICC that the FCC had received the SRBA complaint. On September 4, Ferris followed with a statement that announced that the FCC would review SIN's satelator operations. The chair acknowledged "claims made in a suit filed three years ago in U.S. District Court in Los Angeles by an SICC stockholder alleging misconduct."[25]

Once Ferris consented to review the satelator licenses, Pfaelzer acted. She asked the FCC to enlarge its review into a full investigation of SICC. She informed Ferris that to help with that investigation, she had named the SRBA as the intervenor in Fouce's lawsuit.[26] In doing so, she opened the court's evidence to the FCC. Ferris listened. After the November 1980 election but before departing as chair of the FCC, Ferris discussed a one-year, closed-door investigation with deputy administrator Jeffrey Bauman, the head of the Mass Media Bureau. Pfaelzer was troubled when the investigation did not move forward. In December 1980, Pfaelzer stopped asking the FCC to investigate; she made it a court order.[27]

The investigation was conducted by a small staff in the FCC's Mass Media Bureau, which Bauman headed. Slowed by members' other assignments, it took two full years. The investigators examined much but not all of the courtroom testimony and interviewed Anselmo. The findings pleased Anselmo, but they surprised everyone else involved in the case.

The Mass Media Bureau did find violations of Section 310. Yet instead of punishment, the Bureau recommended a "reorganization" that would allow SICC to conform to the law. Bauman proposed, first, that parent firm SICC sell the 20 percent of shares that Azcárraga legally owned and, second, that Anselmo step down as chair of the board. The sanctions would permit Anselmo to remain as president of the company. In August 1982, midway through the Mass Media Bureau's investigation, Bauman, who as bureau head supervised the investigation, conferred with Anselmo. Anselmo agreed to implement the reorganization.[28] Six months later on March 14, 1983, the Mass Media Bureau released its report. The FCC confirmed Anselmo's "positive reaction" to the "SICC changes" and said that SICC had addressed the FCC's concerns.[29]

The radio owners were furious. In reaching agreement with Anselmo on ownership and managerial changes, the Mass Media Bureau had not acted on the SRBA's request that SICC's satelator stations be shut down. The radio owners prepared to sue the FCC. Fouce, meanwhile, was beside himself. The FCC's appeasement of Anselmo threatened his certain victory in court.

Judge Pfaelzer also was unhappy with the FCC's decision. On April 14, she convened the attorneys to assess the new stumbling blocks in the court case. Fighting ensued. SICC attorney Lawrence Dam blasted Stern. "The FCC investigation was precipitated by your client's [Fouce's] actions," Dam stated.[30] Stern was equally vehement. "Mr. Anselmo has admitted mismanagement and breach. . . . He is to blame" for the difficulty, Stern maintained.[31]

A week later on April 22, 1983, the proceedings reached a pivotal moment. In an order outlining her concerns about due process, Judge Pfaelzer asserted that her court had jurisdiction in "all matters pending against the defendant." The judge announced the appointment of a special master who would have both judicial and administrative authority. She issued a court order directing the FCC to comply with the special master's decisions. She then appointed New York federal Judge J. Roger Wollenberg as special master and charged him with "assembling magistrates [and] disposing of seven years of legal entanglements."[32]

Wollenberg requested a conference with Mark Fowler, the new FCC chair, to explain that an issue before the court was "unsettled" because of disputes stemming from the Mass Media Bureau's investigation. Wollenberg advised Fowler that after finding Section 310 violations, the FCC should have pursued license revocations as the law required. While defending the steps the Mass Media Bureau had taken, Fowler agreed that sanctioning should not have stopped at a bureau level. He agreed to a private conference between Wollenberg and FCC commissioners. Wollenberg gave him evidence that strongly suggested that SICC had a foreign owner.[33]

At a closed-door meeting on May 26, 1983, the commissioners unanimously voted to hold a hearing to determine whether SICC was a legal enterprise and thus fit as a FCC licensee. The commission's decision to convene a hearing and indicate that it would take action encouraged Pfaelzer to again focus attention on Fouce's lawsuit and resume Fouce's proceeding. At the meeting, the commissioners voted unanimously to hold a hearing regarding SICC's licenses.[34] The FCC frequently convened such hearings. As a rule, licensees who had violated FCC rules escaped sanctions by appearing and answering questions. But this was the first time the FCC had voted to investigate an organization it had favored. It is "the only way to get to the bottom of a difficult case. . . . This agency has gone on record wanting to promote program diversity. But the law's the law," an unnamed commissioner told the *Los Angeles Times*.[35]

Days later, the FCC appointed the judge who would preside at the hearing. The commissioners notified Anselmo of a formal hearing at which his company would need to bear the burden of proof.[36] In a report of the special master dated July 15, 1983, Wollenberg expressed satisfaction with the measures the FCC had taken.[37]

* * *

At age seventy-five, John H. Conlin was the FCC's senior administrative law judge. He had announced his retirement, but Fowler had asked him to come back to convene the SICC hearing. Since his appointment to the commission in 1950, Conlin had presided in more than 100 license revocation hearings. He had invoked the "death penalty" twenty times. His rulings all involved small local radio stations who had been caught bilking advertisers, favoring political candidates, or running rigged contests. In its fifty years, the FCC had revoked roughly 200 of the thousands of licenses it had granted. Virtually all were incidental cases.

The commission rarely revoked television licenses. The most recent case, resulting in the FCC's removal of three of RKO's TV licenses, had occurred ten years earlier. The commission had never sanctioned the operator of a network and revoked network-owned stations, and it had never sanctioned a primary source of diversity broadcasting. Experience and circumstance suggested that the FCC would acquit SICC. Yet only a year earlier, Conlin had revoked the license of Los Angeles radio station KROQ.[38]

Conlin conducted the formal hearing on August 17, 1983. SICC's attorneys, who were required to prove that the network deserved to keep its licenses, had witnesses parade its achievements in ethnic television. However, testimony about SIN's independence from Televisa and the extent to which SIN had control over its financial, programming, and personnel matters did not gel. The judge asked questions that forced Anselmo to tell how the elder Azcárraga had given him the money to incorporate Spanish International in 1961. "It seems you never had American owners," Conlin remarked.[39]

After the August hearing, Conlin ended the evidentiary phase. In a brief, he said that there were "stark violations" of Section 310. But mitigating factors were still at issue, notably the fact that the FCC, which in the past had investigated SICC on some alleged improprieties but never cited violations, had never found violations that merited the severity of license revocations.[40]

As she waited for Conlin's decision on whether SICC was a legal corporation, Pfaelzer scheduled pre-trial hearings for early 1984. However, two new lawsuits were in process in 1983 and would be filed in 1984 and 1985. Alleging fraud, SICC sued the SRBA. Alleging violations of antitrust laws, Eduardo Caballero, the radio executive who years earlier had angered Anselmo for urging advertisers to flee SIN, sued SICC. SICC's busy lawyers favored a continuance. Wanting to proceed, Pfaelzer again was forced to suspend Fouce's suit. Conlin told her that he would not be ready to rule any time soon.

Several factors slowed Conlin's ruling. He had committed to personal projects upon his retirement. He called and recalled witnesses to clarify testimony. Later he would observe that the case was one of his most complex, the evidence voluminous. The central evidence, that from Pfaelzer's court, included solicited testimony from seventy-five witnesses, 1,308 items from the plaintiff, and 2,020 items from the defense.[41]

In February 1985, Conlin notified Pfaelzer that although he was close to a decision, he still had not resolved several parts of his review. On February 19, Pfaelzer issued a notice that set forth "indefinite postponement of Fouce's civil action."[42] In May, when the judges again conferred, Pfaelzer realized that Fouce's case would be tried with a defunct defendant. Conlin told Pfaelzer that he had reached his decision and that his verdict would be the "death penalty."[43]

Some of the 1,000 personnel at SICC believed that the worst had passed. Most forgot the proceedings. Yet in November 1985, many voiced alarm. In Washington, reports were circulating that the FCC was about to release the findings of one of its most exhaustive investigations. At SICC, rumors spread that SIN had lost its licenses and would be ordered off the air. On November 18, 1985, Anselmo said in a letter to employees: "I have heard reports of nervousness . . . that we stand to lose our television licenses. . . . We are awaiting a decision . . . and fully expect to win." Anselmo's letter ended on a positive note. "Think how sweet our victory is going to be when [we hear] the final verdict," he said.[44]

* * *

Seven weeks later, on January 8, 1986, the verdict arrived. Conlin revoked the licenses and permits of SIN's seven full-power and fifty low-power stations. He forbade Televisa and Emilio Azcárraga from participating in any processes related to licensed stations. He recommended that the FCC seize SIN's holdings and that it or the court name a receiver. The remaining steps in dismantling SICC would be determined in later hearings. *Television/Radio Age* noted that it was one of the "most sweeping" FCC rulings ever because it involved the largest number of TV stations in a single action.[45]

In an order that spanned 151 paragraphs, Conlin maintained that SICC's violations were so severe that the "only choice" was to "remove the Licensee." He traced the "groundwork" to the late "Emilio Azcárraga Vidaurreta[, whose] brain child" was a U.S. enterprise "dependent on influence and direction from non-U.S. citizens." Subsequently, "alien influence [that] greatly exceeded that permitted by Section 310(b) had flourished under Emilio Azcárraga Milmo, Azcárraga's son and [the] current Televisa director." Their abuses were "reflected in the composition of the ownership and board of directors," the "stations' management," their "programming," and in the "personal ties between the Licensee and the Azcárraga family." Noting the elder Azcárragas' *presta nombres* arrangement with Anselmo, Conlin cited Anselmo as a figurehead who had who promulgated "Televisa's ability to coerce." "At the center of these relationships is Rene Anselmo who, realistically speaking, must be regarded as a representative of aliens," Conlin wrote.[46]

Just a few days later, Azcárraga informed Anselmo that he had severed SIN Sales from SIBC. It now was controlled by Televisa's U.S. subsidiary, Univisa, the entity directed by Jaime Dávila. In 1962, Anselmo had formed the phantom "network" company SIN Sales. This entity was legally owned by Televisa and was separate from SICC and the licensed stations. He had done this to safeguard Televisa's U.S. assets against Fouce's very first threats against him and the Azcárragas. Azcárraga's removal of the "network" company from SICC and Anselmo showed he understood Conlin's ruling.

Anselmo did not understand. He did not vacate his office at SICC headquarters, and he did not provide further communication to anxious employees. By this time, Joaquín Blaya, the successful Miami station manager who had risen as a member of the SICC board, was Anselmo's closest associate. "He carried on regular business as if nothing was going on," Blaya recalled.[47] Blaya was troubled by Anselmo's appeal to the FCC Review Board. Anselmo knew that the Review Board could not convene until after the FCC conducted the hearings on SIN's disposal that Conlin had set forth. For as long as the appeal was pending, the FCC could not forcibly remove Anselmo.

However, a stunning development stung the defiant SICC leader. In March 1986, Judge Pfaelzer again returned to Fouce's lawsuit; his damage claims were still unresolved. Instead of attempting a trial with a defunct defendant on a case that had been delayed for ten years, the judge proposed a settlement. She called on Fouce and the other SICC shareholders, those who had ousted Fouce as chair eleven years before, to work together to sell the firm. She urged them to leave the firm, certain that their joint agreement to depart would be enough to oblige Fouce to withdraw the lawsuit and that the naming of a new owner would moot the need for more hearings. Fouce agreed. So did most of the shareholders. They recognized that they could either sell or have the FCC confiscate their holdings. Soon they were eager to sell: Pfaelzer's plan for the sale, an auction for all of the holdings, promised large proceeds.

However, Anselmo vehemently opposed a sale. It would end the case and force him to leave. By April, Anselmo was threatening SICC board members who had agreed to a sale. He turned against one of his closest associates, Vice President William Stiles, who had contacted possible buyers. After suspending him, Anselmo loudly vowed to destroy Stiles's career. Associates were shaken and appalled. Reacting to the turmoil, board members contacted one another to discuss whether Anselmo should remain.[48]

Azcárraga had already reached the end of the line. His seizure of the "network" company and his installation of Jaime Dávila as its president made it clear that after thirty-five years of escapades and battles, his time with Anselmo as SIN chief was over. Even if Anselmo won his appeal, Conlin's ruling had made any future role for him impossible. Yet Anselmo was still SICC chair and president. Because he had been legally banished, Azcárraga could not fire him. The issue depended on whether the board of the fallen SICC was willing to oust Anselmo just before they, too, had to leave.

Blaya was a member of the board. He traveled from Miami to New York to try to convince Anselmo to resign. Blaya insisted that Anselmo could not reverse the dissolution of SICC. He cringed at Anselmo's resistance. "He said, 'Don't worry, it's not going to happen, it's not going to happen.' I said, 'Rene, it *is* going to happen,'" Blaya later recounted.[49]

The board members pled with Senior Vice President Emilio Nicolás to go to the resistant Anselmo and convince him to resign. On April 24, Nicolás talked to the seven other directors. The group reached three decisions. They approved the sale and Pfaelzer's recommendation that they form a sales committee. On the next issue, they hesitated briefly, then agreed unanimously to fire Anselmo. They elected Nicolás as the new chair who would finish the business of the firm.[50]

On May 2, 1986, Nicolás went to Anselmo's office and told him he was through. Hearing this from the mild-mannered associate he had befriended thirty-one years before, Anselmo agreed to resign.[51] That day, 200 stunned employees gathered in the Atrium to hear Anselmo's farewell speech. Anselmo announced he was "retiring . . . in [an] effort to help

Figure 7. Smiling at the Miami Grand Prix, Rene Anselmo (*left*) is seen one month after the January 1986 FCC ruling that led to the demise of Spanish International. Next to Anselmo is SIN chief engineer Robert Porter. On the right is Joaquín Blaya, the manager of Miami's WLTV and then Anselmo's closest associate. Scoffing at the FCC's ruling, Anselmo rejected Blaya's appeals he step aside. Photo courtesy of Joaquín Blaya.

resolve a long-standing stockholder suit [and] accommodate issues raised by the FCC."[52] He then departed for his Greenwich, Connecticut, home.

* * *

On May 15, 1986, Nicolás appeared before the FCC to confirm SICC's willingness to dissolve through sale. Delighted, the commissioners hurried through a settlement agreement. The FCC claimed SIN's holdings for ninety days, named Pfaelzer's court as the receiver, and assigned Pfaelzer as a special master whose charge was to locate a buyer.

The sales committee consisted of Nicolás, Blaya, Stiles, Danny Villanueva, Andrew Goldman, and Blair Decker. They presumed that all of the TV stations and satelator transmitters that SICC owned would be sold, but Pfaelzer could not guarantee that the stations would remain together. The committee tried to guarantee that the stations would continue broadcasting Spanish-language formats. At best, Pfaelzer could ensure this for two years, for that was what the FCC's settlement agreement stipulated. But even that might not happen. Pfaelzer explained that because the FCC had no authority over content, the buyer or buyers would be free to decide what they put on their broadcast schedules.[53]

The group raised another issue. It was not part of the settlement, but it related to the question of whether Spanish-language content would continue. Except for the network news Anselmo had introduced in 1981, SIN did not produce programming. Inevitably, a buyer or buyers would have to bargain with Televisa. The successor could legally purchase Televisa programs. In fact, to continue the network, the successor would need to rent the network facilities Televisa now controlled. However, stripped of the enterprise he and his father had founded, Azcárraga was not likely to accommodate the new owner with sweetheart deals. He might charge exorbitant fees.[54]

One outcome was certain. The sale of the Spanish-language network was about to make some people very rich. This was because Pfaelzer, moved by pleas that she try to keep the network intact, had agreed to a buyer-take-all auction. She narrowed the field of potential buyers to well-endowed applicants whose competing bids would net SICC's board members a sizable price. SIN's book value of $100 million was the starting point. Pfaelzer's process promised them a financial bonanza, how big nobody knew.

Ironically, Pfaelzer's plan ended what had started the ten-year ordeal—the 25-year feud between Anselmo and Fouce. Each owned around 25 percent of SICC. Although they were the two largest shareholders, neither was allowed on the sales committee. Now with a common interest in driving up the price of the company, Anselmo and Fouce reconciled. Both of them worked to encourage wealthy acquaintances to place bids. However, Anselmo made a mistake that cost them millions.

One of the bidders was Jerry Perenchio. Seven years before, Perenchio had purchased the TV holdings of Columbia Pictures, including SIN competitor WNJU. That May, Perenchio was close to launching NetSpan, the second Spanish-language network. The head of NetSpan, WNJU's Carlos Barba, expected the network to premiere by the end of the year. Perenchio was eager to commiserate with Anselmo when he was fired. Perenchio told Anselmo that he wanted to purchase SICC. He shared his hope of abandoning WNJU and NetSpan and taking the reins of SIN. He also told him confidentially that he would bid $360 million and was prepared to go as high as $500 million.

Before the auction began, the *Wall Street Journal* and other news media reported that Perenchio's opening bid would be $360 million.[55] Anselmo had disclosed the amount in an effort to elicit still higher bids. This was a blunder. Anselmo's disclosure touched off repercussions that would define the next phase of Spanish-language television.

Perenchio withdrew. He was outraged that Anselmo had spoken to the press. His withdrawal meant that subsequent bids would not approach the half-billion dollars he would have paid. More consequentially, the new owner would have no experience in Spanish-language television. Outside SIN, only Perenchio had such experience. In addition, Anselmo's loose tongue ensured that Perenchio left NetSpan. Embarrassed that the public knew of his desire to switch sides, Perenchio had no choice but to sell his properties and depart.

Pfaelzer had set up the process to finish within ninety days. She opened a one-month solicitation period on June 1, 1986. On June 30, five applications sat before the sales committee.[56] Hallmark Cards had offered $301 million, outbidding Sony, the Reliance Capital Corporation, and two investor groups. The committee selected Hallmark. Next were meetings to finalize the sale.

Under its new president, Irvine Hockaday, Hallmark epitomized the best in U.S. corporate enterprise. Hallmark was a progressive Fortune 500 firm that had never been the subject of restraining orders and investigations. However, it had no Latino owners. Its headquarters in Kansas City were not close to the centers of the U.S. Latino population. And it would not commit to a Spanish-language format beyond the two years stated in the FCC settlement agreement.

Although it was a greeting card company, Hallmark had long eyed a stake in television. It had produced prime-time TV programming since the 1950s. It had ventured into cable TV in the 1980s. Hockaday had explored station acquisitions toward forming a network that would challenge ABC, CBS, and NBC. Observers regarded its successful cable venture, the Hallmark Channel, as a forerunner of that network.

During discussions of the sales committee, Villanueva contended that after the sale, Hallmark would convert the SIN properties to English-language stations, then launch a Hallmark network. He insisted that they should not close the deal unless Hockaday pledged to continue

Spanish-language content beyond the two-year requirement. Villanueva continued to push for a pre-sale pledge.⁵⁷

Hockaday wound up volunteering precisely the pledge Villanueva sought. An eleventh-hour crisis forced Hallmark to preserve network Spanish-language television. On July 3, one of the rejected bidders, a consortium of Latino investors called TVL, went to the press and denounced Hallmark. Seizing on Hallmark's refusal to commit to Spanish-language content for more than two years, they demanded that the sale be governed by "a 20-year commitment." Supported by U.S. Representative Matthew Martinez of California, they vowed to block Hallmark's acquisition. On the eve of the sales committee's first meeting with Hockaday, Pfaelzer suspended the sale and asked for further review of the TVL application.⁵⁸

Mystified by but responding to a fast-moving controversy, Hockaday contacted the sales committee. Soon after that, Villanueva told the sales committee that Hallmark had amended its application. Hockaday changed the passage that indicated that Hallmark would comply with the provision that it broadcast Spanish-language programming for only two years. It now read, "Hallmark's commitment to [a Spanish-language format] is long-term."⁵⁹

The sales committee decided to stay with Hallmark. Pfaelzer approved. TVL finished with a low bid of $260 million. Pfaelzer staged-managed the notification that SICC would pass to the Kansas City firm. To head off more controversy, Pfaelzer scheduled the final negotiating session on a Friday night. Just minutes before midnight on July 17, 1986, the parties signed the agreement and circulated a news release.⁶⁰ The announcement and TVL's angry response were buried in the weekend news.⁶¹

The following Monday, Hockaday held a news conference in Kansas City. By then, the press was interested less in the dispute and more in a Fortune 500 company about to own a TV network. "Hallmark is dedicated to servicing the Hispanic community," Hockaday said. He promised details after the court reviewed and approved Hallmark's reorganization of SICC.⁶²

* * *

The decade-long case of *Fouce Amusement Enterprises and Metropolitan Theaters Corp. v. Spanish International Communications Corp.* continued. After the FCC transferred the licenses to Hallmark on September 26, 1986, TVL sued the FCC. As *Coalition for the Preservation of Hispanic*

Broadcasting v. Federal Communications Commission, the suit reached the Ninth Circuit Court of Appeals in San Francisco, where judges ruled in favor of the FCC and denied a request for a rehearing. In January 1988, the Supreme Court dismissed a request to rehear. On a technicality, the suit was resubmitted to the U.S. Court of Appeals in the District of Columbia. The epic proceedings—more than thirteen years in duration—finally ended on January 12, 1990, when the DC court again ruled in favor of the FCC.[63]

Two months before the Supreme Court's decision, the FCC Review Board completed the review of Anselmo's appeal. Its November 1987 report gave the complex affair a humorous conclusion. A passage read: "Until 1979, therefore, the Azcárragas, Anselmo, and the FCC seemed dreamily docked in a dory of delight, a delta of devolutionary desiderate. From the depths of the derma, however, drifted the dree descent of the dearly disaffected, denouncing the deal and demanding the deliquescence of the deceased Don's dynastic duumvirate."[64] The Review Board found that except for one issue, the actions of the court and the FCC were correct.

In the end, Fouce did not collect damages. The radio owners received no relief. The satelators remained; the FCC determined that the radio owners had not proven their allegation that SICC's satelators had harmed the livelihood and prospects of Spanish-language radio and TV broadcasters. The commission also rejected as untrue the radio owners' allegation that Anselmo had lied to it when he sought the satelator permits. Anselmo had never concealed the fact that the satelators would be used to give U.S. viewers content from non-U.S. sources. The FCC ruled as legal the illegality that Fouce saw as his "smoking gun," that SICC controlled local station advertising. For those involved, the scene of Anselmo and Fouce shaking hands underscored that the unfathomable eleven-year experience could possibly have been avoided.

There was another postscript. In December 1980, when Pfaelzer had refused to conclude the lawsuit and enjoined the FCC, Anselmo had initiated SICC's nightly network newscast. Not once did the FCC comment on the newscast. The commission also did not comment on SICC's reliance on foreign programming. The commissioners strictly limited their considerations to the violations of Section 310 of the Communications Act.

Anselmo did not retire. The FCC Review Board reversed the part of Conlin's ruling that found Anselmo categorically at fault. Anselmo contended that he had chartered Phoenix station KTVW separately from

SICC.⁶⁵ The commission permitted Anselmo to remain its owner.⁶⁶ His attorney proclaimed that this was "essentially a vindication of Anselmo" and "a tribute to [his] three-decade effort to provide Spanish-language television throughout the United States."⁶⁷

By this time, Anselmo was far along in a more ambitious enterprise. After witnessing the birth of Telstar in 1962, Anselmo believed that he could operate a communication satellite in competition with the NASA-conscripted, government-run Intelsat monopoly. In 1984, financed in part by Azcárraga, Anselmo formed a company called PanAmSat. Azcárraga also agreed to contribute Televisa's technical support. Working with engineers at Televisa's Monterrey complex, Anselmo won patents on small-diameter receiving dishes. He intended to best Intelsat by offering TV networks and syndicators cheap satellite service.

Battling factions that sought to protect Intelsat, Anselmo used the same tactics he had used to win satellite relays for SIN: he sent letters and created publicity. He adopted a mascot called "Dog Spot." Comedically in newspaper and magazine ads, he pictured the dog defecating on Intelsat's proponents. The venture hinged on a gamble in 1988. Without funds to insure the device, he launched his first satellite on a European Ariane rocket that had previously blown up. The launch was perfect. Anselmo succeeded in ending Intelsat's control of satellite communication. The deposed leader of SICC rose again, becoming a multibillionaire.

At Hallmark, a firm in the glare of FCC scrutiny, a top priority was following the letter of the law. Hockaday did not announce the court-mandated reorganization until after the September 26, 1986, relicensing.⁶⁸ The reorganization required few firings. Many SICC executives had resigned, including Stiles, but Hallmark retained the vast majority of SICC staff. Hockaday retained Nicolás as president and returned Villanueva and Blaya to their original posts as station managers in Los Angeles and Miami; he needed their counsel.

In September, the three SICC veterans faced the issue that had concerned the sales committee. To meet the "long-term" commitment to Spanish-language content, Hallmark might go to Hollywood for English-language material overdubbed in Spanish, or it could turn to Azcárraga for the Spanish-language programming that had drawn millions of viewers to SICC.

Hockaday heard different opinions. All were aware that Hallmark had to negotiate with Azcárraga, and all agreed that Azcárraga would set high fees. Villanueva was adamant that Hallmark should pay whatever he asked. He insisted that the network would lose viewers if it failed to continue broadcasting Televisa's novelas. Blaya, though, urged that such money would be better spent on Hallmark's own Spanish-language television productions. While he listened to Villanueva and was aware that Hallmark would need to purchase some Televisa programs, Hockaday preferred Blaya's idea of U.S.-made programs. It conformed to the wishes of the FCC.

Hockaday initiated negotiations with Jaime Dávila. He benefited from Azcárraga's selection of Dávila as president of the severed "network" company. Before joining Azcárraga, Dávila had had a long association with SICC as a director of Procter & Gamble, a principal advertiser whose sponsorships had supported both SIN and Televisa. By the time Hockaday began the transition, Dávila had created a legal structure for distributing Televisa's programming that Hallmark could use.

However, Hockaday did not fare well when his dealings moved from Dávila to Azcárraga. He first met Azcárraga in late September 1986, when Miami was waging an insurrection against Jacobo Zabludovsky's proposed takeover of SIN News. The heated objections of the Miami staff chased Azcárraga from Miami. Instead, Azcárraga purchased a vacant satellite facility in Laguna Niguel, California, from Scripps Howard. Because of the FCC ruling, both the Miami facility and the network hub in San Antonio would close. In the midst of the transition, Hockaday also had to contend with relocating staff to the West Coast. Azcárraga's further news, that he would expunge the name "SIN" and rename the network, added to Hockaday's uncertainties.[69]

Then on October 27, news came from New York that the second Spanish-language network was about to launch. In an anticipated yet spectacular announcement, the Reliance Capital Corporation disclosed that it had bought out Perenchio. Reliance executives Saul Steinberg and Harry Silverman announced that they had purchased WNJU and that the long-planned NetSpan network would premiere on January 1. The new owners had deep pockets. WNJU's Carlos Barba would head the network, which Reliance renamed Telemundo. Silverman saluted SICC and said, "We will be helping each other."[70]

It was not the help Hallmark needed. That October, Hockaday and Azcárraga were far apart in their negotiations on a contract for Hallmark's use of Televisa's programs. Balking at Azcárraga's crippling terms and still listening to Blaya, Hockaday hoped to minimize Televisa's fees by having

Figure 8. While courts and the FCC deliberated the future of the Spanish International Network in 1986, Carlos Barba, head of WNJU in New York, was concluding sixteen years of plans for a second Spanish-language network. Here he appears in 1985 in a promotional photo for the network's predecessor, NetSpan. Telemundo, the new network, was announced in October 1986. Photo courtesy of Joaquín Blaya.

SICC produce its own shows. However, when Reliance announced the birth of Telemundo, Hockaday had no choice but to comply with Azcárraga's call for an exclusive contract. To do otherwise was to risk that Azcárraga would sell his programs to the new network.

With competition just two months away, Hockaday agreed to pay Azcárraga 40 percent of Hallmark's revenue on Televisa content.[71] Hockaday later would recall his uneasiness about this deal. Because almost all of Hallmark's programming would come from Televisa, the contract meant that Hallmark could keep only three of every five dollars it earned. Anselmo had never paid more than 20 percent.

On December 7, 1986, Hallmark informed employees and notified the press that the reorganization and transfer were complete. Hockaday announced that the switchover to Laguna Niguel would occur the following week. During the holidays, stations and affiliates would introduce a new logo, a version of Televisa's cross-hatched TV "eye," and new promotions that affirmed that the network would continue to broadcast Televisa's shows. On December 31, SICC would cease. The following day it would reemerge as Univision.[72] Because Televisa continued to legally own the network's facilities and infrastructure, Azcárraga had authority and was eager to rename it. Univision was the term that he had coined for Televisa's multinational satellite exchange years before.

Although much happened that summer and fall, Hockaday most vividly remembered a single event. "It was about the time when we had won the bidding that I received a telephone call from a fellow who said his name was Jerry Perenchio," Hockaday later recounted. He hesitated. "I couldn't place him." After "he told me who he was, he said that 'I had no idea of what I had gotten into,' that 'Spanish television is not what you think,' and 'If you're not careful you'll be bankrupt.'"

Although at the time, he bristled at Perenchio's audacity, Hockaday later looked back on the call in a different light. "Every red flag he waved in front of us came true," he said.[73]

7

UNIVISION AND TELEMUNDO

On January 1, 1987, Hallmark Cards broadcast a spectacle to premiere Univision that featured Pasadena's Tournament of Roses Parade. The Reliance Capital Corporation set up cameras alongside those of Univisión, which was launching Telemundo. It was a TV first. Two networks launched on the same day, at the same hour, and with the same program.[1]

That day, neither network genuinely launched. Telemundo's first scheduled programs were planned for January 12. During the parade, Telemundo's hosts and dignitaries presented a preview of coming attractions. And at the "new" Univision, only the trappings—a new name and a new logo that resembled Televisa's golden eye—had changed. Tuning in, viewers saw the same programming they had seen the day before and for years before that on the Spanish International Network. All of Univision's network entertainment programs still came from Televisa, including its popular telenovelas. Hockaday hoped that continuing with the proven formulae of SIN would put Univision in a strong position in its competition with Telemundo.

The FCC's dismantling of the Spanish International Communications Corporation fostered one sizable change. The previous year, Televisa had asserted legal control over the SIN "network," including its delivery system. At the end of the year, Azcárraga had moved the network's base of operations, including its control center, to a vacant teleport in the posh Los Angeles suburb of Laguna Niguel. Azcárraga could pursue the relocation because the 1986 dissolution and sale of the Spanish International Communications Corporation had affected only local stations and properties licensed by the FCC. Azcárraga continued to own 100 percent of the unlicensed "network" operation, which consisted of programming and the satellite system that delivered the programming to local stations. Technically, Hallmark did not have a network; instead, it had an alliance of stations and affiliates linked by infrastructure that Televisa still owned.

The TV industry and the general public tended to ignore this development. Both Univision and Telemundo did extensive publicity. Reliance touted "the power of Telemundo."[2] Hallmark touted Univision as a "spanking new TV network with a 25-year-old history."[3] But the press saw little that was groundbreaking. The truly new network, Telemundo, got a mention at most. Its rollout was limited to prime-time hours and to stations in only twenty of the nation's 210 television markets. The press paid much more attention to a third new entity, the English-language Fox network, which had launched in October 1986.

However, a few observers noted a watershed in the development of the nation's Latino mass media. Richard Mahler of *Electronic Media* heralded the twin New Year's Day broadcasts as the dawn of a "new era in minority television," which he believed had reached "a critical mass." In the *Wall Street Journal*, José de Córdoba touted the "emergence of a second network [as] the starkest evidence yet of the appeal of Spanish media." He predicted that Univision and Telemundo would thrive on "advertising in the U.S. Hispanic television market [that] has more than doubled to an estimated $184.3 million [in 1986] from $69 million in 1982."[4]

Nevertheless, Greg Crister of *Channels* magazine and Steve Beale of *Hispanic Business* were dubious. Both questioned whether revenues of $184 million, or double or triple that amount, were enough to sustain two Spanish-language networks. Crister observed that "success rests on the eagerness of advertisers" to increase spending on ethnic programs that did not have Nielsen ratings to measure audiences. Another issue, Crister noted, is "tailoring shows to attract subcultures. . . . New York's [Telemundo station] WNJU programs for Puerto Ricans, while Miami's WSCV targets Cubans." Because rivalry "create[d] pressure to sign long-term contracts [and] cut costs," Crister foresaw "embattled competitors" and "a tight window of opportunity." Beale maintained that the rivalry would provoke a battle for advertisers that was likely to impede the immediate growth of both networks.[5]

* * *

Telemundo was born as an investment property of a 150-year-old insurance firm during the insurgency on Wall Street in the 1980s. A young generation of thrill seekers in business suits were heroes of an upwardly mobile popular culture. They risked fortunes during the longest stock market boom of the century.

Saul Steinberg and Harry Silverman were among the insurgents. Both of them were in their forties and both were graduates of the University of Pennsylvania when they became known to one another through mutual investment ventures. Steinberg, who had finished his studies at the Wharton School in 1959, entered the computer field but sought a career as a financier. Eyeing the Reliance Insurance Company and its reservoir of funds, Steinberg used his fast-rising computer leasing venture to leverage its takeover.

In 1982, Steinberg hired Silverman, a graduate of the Penn School of Law who had risen as a Wall Street trader. Steinberg hoped to transform the staid insurance firm. Using its income from premiums to buy properties weakened by that year's recession, Silverman went on a tear. He invested in real estate, computers, airlines, and hotels. By 1985, Reliance was a capital corporation that had $6 billion in assets.[6]

Silverman had no experience in broadcasting. Shunning a volatile business, he had passed on deals for numerous television properties on the market, including ABC, CBS, and NBC. In late 1984, he saw something that shaped his future. "I was sitting at my desk when I happened to read a report on the Hispanic population [indicating that] television would be a good investment."[7] In April 1985, he purchased a small stake in Estrella Communications. The tiny firm owned KVEA, which at the time was struggling as an independent Spanish-language station in Los Angeles. At first, he was not charmed by KVEA, but an experience there turned his head.

In early 1985, the general manager of KVEA, Joe Wallach, invested in a new lineup of top motion pictures and serials from foreign countries to improve KVEA's audience ratings. The ratings, which were conducted by Arbitron, showed that KVEA had a 10 percent share of the Spanish-speaking audience. The other Spanish-language station in Los Angeles, KMEX, had 90 percent. Such numbers had become important in Spanish-language television. The ratings spelled success or failure now that competition had begun.

At the end of 1985, the numbers changed. KMEX's share of the Spanish-speaking viewing audience dropped to 60 percent, and KVEA's share rose to 40 percent. While KVEA's new programs explained the change, Silverman was more intrigued by the fact that KMEX continued to broadcast the programs whose ratings had decreased. Learning that KMEX was locked into carrying Televisa's programs, Silverman took action. He realized that while Televisa's programs were popular, they were constraining KMEX and all of the stations in the Spanish International Network, the one network that existed at the time. A second network would have access to everything else. The Reliance board approved a $300 million capitalization after Silverman assured them that the competition was winnable. "It's us against the Mexicans," he said.[8]

He and Steinberg moved rapidly. In early 1986, Steinberg filed license applications for full-power stations and low-power satelator stations in twenty cities.[9] In May, Reliance paid $110 million to acquire John Blair and Company; Blair owned several UHF stations. including WSCV in Miami. In June, after finishing second to Hallmark in the bidding for SIN, Silverman began negotiating the purchase of Perenchio's WNJU and the framework of stations Perenchio intended for his NetSpan network. By September, Silverman had held discussions with WNJU technicians on installing satellites. NetSpan had progressed as a program syndicator that physically delivered, or "bicycled," program recordings from one station to the next through a system SIN had used until 1976, when it converted to satellite interconnection. But NetSpan lacked the facilities for an interconnected satellite system similar to the one SIN introduced in 1976.

By that time, Steinberg had informed Carlos Barba, the head of WNJU, that Barba would direct the network and become a Reliance vice president.[10] Barba recalled that after sixteen years of leading WNJU and seeing the network project start and sputter, "My dream came true." Silverman, Steinberg, and Reliance's third-in-command, Donald Raider, did not speak Spanish. They promised to "let [Barba] run the show."[11]

Silverman's buyout of Blair gave Telemundo the largest television network in the Caribbean, WKAQ, which was based in San Juan, Puerto Rico. Its ten studios generated programming that NetSpan had syndicated. Through WKAQ, NetSpan contracted for programs from Venezuela's Venevisión, Brazil's Globo, and other South American networks.[12] Although the network was licensed with U.S. call letters, Puerto Ricans had always known WKAQ as Telemundo. At Barba's suggestion, Silverman christened the network with the Puerto Rican name.[13]

Barba, too, moved rapidly. When Silverman announced the birth of Telemundo in October 1986, he set January 12, 1987, as the date of the network's debut. Barba told Latinos that there would be a "thread running throughout our shows . . . they [will] address our feelings, our problems and our goals." The first programs he scheduled were entertainment shows.[14] However, an event that October that coincided with Silverman's announcement changed Barba's thinking about how the debut would unfold.

That month, Miami was simmering over Televisa's attempted takeover of *Noticiero SIN* and the entire SIN network news operation. This was the fracas in which SIN's Gustavo Godoy confronted Televisa's Jacobo Zabludovsky and was fired for doing so and forty frontline anchors, correspondents, and producers resigned. Although the protest had succeeded in that it had forced Televisa to retreat, *Noticiero SIN* (SIN News), now *Noticiero Univision* (Univision News), had lost its most prominent people.

Barba learned that the episode had continued. Miami business figure Amancio Suárez had approached Godoy. Sympathizing with the journalists who had resigned from SIN, Suárez had given Godoy $10 million to form an independent national news organization. Suárez erected a satellite installation at a building he donated, a former shoe warehouse located in an industrial district on Eighth Avenue in the Miami suburb of Hialeah. After Barba and Godoy conferred, Barba seized on Godoy's offer to have the Hialeah newsroom become Telemundo's network news division. Godoy reassembled the journalists and staff who had resigned from SIN.[15]

Thus, on January 12, Telemundo's maiden broadcast was a nightly newscast. On the first night that *Noticiero Telemundo* (Telemundo News) aired, the public witnessed the reappearance of the "dream team." The best-known and most trusted news anchors and reporters in Spanish-language television welcomed the Telemundo audience. Familiar anchors Jorge Gestoso and Lana Montalbán joined correspondents José Diaz-Balart, María Elvira Salazar, and others who for years had informed, comforted, and bonded with Latino viewers on SIN.[16]

Telemundo's first regular program dramatized the new network's fitness to compete. Barba later recalled the newscast as his most unforgettable experience in network TV. In the first ratings of the two networks, Arbitron ratings of the local New York area that February, Univision's WXTV garnered a 30 percent share and Telemundo's WNJU garnered 70 percent.[17]

Barba designed and scheduled programs that played to Telemundo's strength, a culture that had prioritized its own production of programs. That culture encouraged Spanish-language programs that were both domestically produced and flexible in concepts and content. Telemundo did broadcast some foreign telenovelas, but Barba broke from the other network's long-standing practice of showing one novela after another during prime time. Barba's strategy borrowed from Baughman's success at KVEA: he identified Telemundo as "the movie channel." Its first hit series was *Cine millonario* (Millionaire Cinema), which presented top Spanish-language motion pictures at 9:00 on alternating nights.[18]

Six months after its debut, Telemundo expanded into daytime and late-night hours. In May 1987, Barba introduced *Mapy y Papi*, a Puerto Rican sitcom based on CBS hit *I Love Lucy*. He initiated cooking shows, a shopping show, talk shows, and an astrology show. That summer, Barba brought popular Dominican singer and film star Charytín Goyco to the United States. From the Hialeah facility, which was now outfitted for studio production, Goyco hosted *El regreso de Charytín* (The Return of Charytín), the first U.S.-produced Spanish-language network variety program. At the end of the year, Barba announced that Telemundo had begun taping *Angélica mi vida* (Angelica My Life), the first U.S.-produced telenovela.[19]

However, Barba resorted to a strategy that some observers criticized: Telemundo copied the formats of English-language TV. Again taking talent from Univision, this time sports personality Tony Tirado, Barba premiered *Telemundo centro deportes* (Telemundo Sports Center), a segment-by-segment "clone" of the popular *Sports Center* on ESPN. Telemundo next duplicated *Wheel of Fortune*. After Barba partnered with Viacom, Barba launched *Telemundo MTV*. Its host was a popular WNJU personality, 20-year-old weathercaster Daisy Fuentes.[20]

Telemundo canceled many of the first programs, including *Mapi y Papi*, because of low ratings. Others, including Goyco's program, became fixtures. Most of Barba's concepts reflected his many years of developing the original programming that had distinguished WNJU. It was an idea Univision could ignore no longer.

* * *

Just before it launched Univision, Hallmark sent the network's managers a greeting. Inside, a member of the transition team had written: "1987—Make wine, not war." The message acknowledged Hallmark's awareness that war had raged at SIN throughout the preceding year. One manager's battle was not over, however. Only four days after the New Year's Day launch, his fight resumed. Joaquín Blaya flew to Kansas City to meet with Hockaday. He wanted to discuss domestic production.

"Domestic production," a phrase that referred to the networks' production of their own network shows, loomed large after the events of 1986, when the FCC had dissolved SICC to end foreign control of Televisa. When Hallmark took over the network, it was freed of the Azcárragas' quarter-century dictum that it was not to produce network programs. Blaya, the manager of Miami's WLTV and one of the three holdover executives Hockaday retained, recognized a crossroads. He was fervent about domestic production. Six years before, it had been Blaya who had moved SIN's one domestic production, its newscast, to Miami.

Hockaday was drawn to Blaya's idea. Domestic production would reduce the exorbitant fees that Azcárraga had imposed—40 percent of revenue on every Televisa title. Yet in the end, Hockaday sided against Blaya. The two other holdover leaders from SIN, Emilio Nicolás of San Antonio, who remained president of the defunct SICC during the transition; and Danny Villanueva, who continued as head of KMEX in Los Angeles, argued that Hallmark should retain the Televisa novelas and sports and variety shows because they were so popular. On the day the SIN network was dismantled, December 31, 1986, sales director John Pero reported profits of $10 million on record revenue of $100 million.[21] Hockaday felt he had no choice but to reject Blaya's campaign for more domestic production and continue with Televisa's programs. In the context of a competing Spanish-language network, new content risked more than ratings and losses: Telemundo was certain to claim any Televisa program Univision let go.

Thus, when Blaya flew to Kansas City on January 4, 1987, Hockaday expected him to bemoan the defeat of his idea. Blaya, though, did not believe he had lost. He sized up a situation that was identical to that in 1981, when he had lost the network newscast, plotted new steps, and gotten it back. He went to Kansas City to grieve an episode that had been obscured by the calamities of the previous year. He hoped to win Hockaday's approval of just one U.S.-produced show.

Back in February 1986, with Rene Anselmo's permission, Blaya's WLTV had carried SIN's network programs on only six nights. On Saturdays, WLTV broadcast a four-hour local variety show. For twenty-four years, the show had been a hit in Chile. Anselmo had taken note of the program's high ratings on WLTV. In April, in his final decision as head of SIN, Anselmo had put the show on the full network. The national audience saw only four episodes. Blaya was furious when SIN's directors ordered the program off the air in May, after they fired Anselmo. When Blaya asked that the program be reinstated, Hockaday refused. "I did not really know what this was about," he later said. "I appreciated Joaquín's passion for the show," but there was "too much going on to worry about that one thing."[22]

But Blaya persisted. His timing was good. In January 1987, Hockaday was worried about whether Univision would survive given his 40 percent concession to Azcárraga. Back in Miami, Blaya telephoned Hockaday. He reiterated that not only was the Miami program cheap to produce because it was live but also that its four hours would span an entire night's schedule, eliminating numerous Televisa programs with a single program that would ensure that Univision could keep 100 percent of the revenue. Moreover, Televisa's contract with Hallmark for the use of the network allowed Hallmark to feed some programs it might stage. Around January 20, Hockaday not only gave in but told Blaya to speed up preparations to get the show back on the air.

The next available Saturday was January 31, 1987. The master weekly program log had already been printed and signed by Program Director Rosita Perú. Someone kept it as a memento because its Saturday column bore dried white-out where Perú had covered up the listings for Televisa's programs *Yesenia, Super cine,* and *Boxeo desde México.* That change altered Hallmark's future in Spanish-language TV.[23]

The program that replaced the three Televisa shows was *Sábado gigante.* The host of the show, Mario Kreutzberger, was a former tailor whose family had moved to Chile to escape Nazi death camps during World War II. Using the stage name "Don Francisco," he had started *Sábado gigante* on Chile's Canal Trece in 1962. A commemorative publication included its original 1962 concept statement. The four-hour broadcast would "revolve around 'Don Francisco' [and is] a very special type of entertainment." *Sábado gigante* was to feature "interviews, music, contests and games, and lots of comedy . . . before a live studio audience." The "audience will have lively interaction."[24]

The format never changed. Kreutzberger later regarded Blaya as "his hero" for securing a home for the program in the United States. He remarked that "while in Chile I had dreamed of doing television in America. Blaya made the dream come true."[25] Kreutzberger continued to live in Santiago, where he was a wine maker. Each week, he commuted to Miami. Eventually, Univision fed *Sábado gigante* to networks in thirty countries. In 1993, *Sábado gigante* entered the *Guinness Book of World Records* as the longest-running entertainment television program in the Americas. Ten years later, Guinness named it as the world's longest-running variety show.[26] It was a world record the program never relinquished.

At first, the program languished. While the only authoritative ratings were the local ratings Arbitron conducted, a less established firm, Strategy Research Corporation (SRC), conducted Spanish-language ratings on a national basis. SRC's spring 1987 survey showed that while Telemundo had drawn 60 percent of a total Spanish-speaking audience that was estimated at around 10 million, *Sábado gigante* had attracted 40 percent.

That April, Kreutzberger invited a special guest to appear on the show, Cristina Saralegui, the editor of the Latin edition of *Cosmopolitan*. She hailed from Cuba. Viewers were delighted. The show went so well that Kreutzberger invited her back each week. Saralegui changed the program's chemistry. She pushed the clownish "Don Francisco" out of character. Audiences tuned in to witness their debates about divorce, domestic violence, and other topics that were taboo in most Latino homes. The ratings soared. *Sábado gigante* drew 70 percent of Spanish-speaking viewers in SRC's November 1987 ratings. It was number one, ahead of every Televisa and Telemundo program.[27]

* * *

Although Univision had produced only one hit program, major initiatives followed from the success of *Sábado gigante*. Although Univision finished its first year with a $20 million loss, Hockaday was not worried. He disregarded the arguments of Nicolás and Villanueva that one Saturday night program did not prove that the network could flourish with a preponderance of more domestic programs. They insisted that foreign programs were essential. Hockaday listened to Blaya's promise of more triumphs like

Kreutzberger's show. He prepared to promote Blaya and, in 1988, begin implementing plans to "dedicate Univision to domestic production."[28]

Through 1987, Azcárraga and Televisa had continued to own and control the Univision network operation. Through its U.S. subsidiary, Univisa, Televisa had both programmed the network and, through its satellite system, fed programs to Univision's stations and affiliates. Yet in late 1987, less than a year after establishing the Univision network operation at the facility in Laguna Niguel, Azcárraga sold the "network" to Hallmark.[29]

The deal marked a notable turn. Univision became an enterprise that was fully owned by U.S. citizens. But the move was a surprise; no one had anticipated that Televisa would withdraw so quickly. Hallmark was quiet about the purchase. The story broke in Mexico, where reports indicated that Azcárraga and Hockaday had privately negotiated a purchase price of $50 million.[30]

When Hallmark absorbed the network in early 1988, Hockaday stepped aside. He passed control to Univision's first management team. That August, he introduced William Grimes as Univision's corporate president and CEO. Grimes had been sales director of ESPN. He had won acclaim for saving the sports channel when it nearly folded in 1979. Grimes admitted that his knowledge of Spanish-language television was "virtually non-existent." Yet he was confident about his abilities; he said that "I didn't know anything about sports when I went to ESPN."[31]

Three weeks later, Grimes presented Blaya as the first official Univision network president, and Blaya named Rosita Perú as vice president and program director. Journalists heralded Univision's emergence from the shackles of its predecessor SIN. Grimes established headquarters in New York. He agreed to Blaya's request that Blaya run the network from Miami. That August, Blaya was silent about Univision's fall 1988 programs, virtually all of which were from Televisa. He looked ahead to a rollout of original productions the following spring. "We are really concentrating on the development of new programming," he told the *New York Times*.[32]

On January 22, 1989, Grimes and Blaya held a press conference to announce the rollout and more. Circulating pictures and materials about a dozen new programs, Blaya proclaimed a "historic" redirection of Spanish-language television. For the first time, he said, a Spanish-language network has made a "major commitment to domestic production." At a "moment when Hispanics are taking their place in American society," television would reflect "their American experience." He said that in three years, 50 percent of Univision's programs would be produced in the United States.[33] Grimes and Blaya unveiled a new logo, an artistic four-colored U, and they previewed the network's new slogan: "Univision: The Vision for America."

They also announced that Univision would leave Laguna Niguel. Grimes had announced that the network would build a $50 million complex in Miami. Blaya could not conceal his elation about the fact that the network would move to Miami with him in charge. He had envisioned precisely this when he took the newscast to the Florida city in 1981. His aspiration fulfilled, Blaya purchased property in the west Miami suburb of Doral. He planned to open "television city" in early 1991.[34]

Blaya again hit the jackpot with one of Univision's first new shows. He premiered a daily afternoon talk show hosted by Cristina Saralegui. On April 17, 1989, viewers saw the first broadcast of *Cristina*.[35] It debuted with a share of 60 percent. Although it was a daytime program, it joined *Sábado gigante* at the top of the ratings.[36] "We were successful," Saralegui later said, "because we broke a path. We were therapy for Hispanics with subjects like drugs, sexuality, hate groups, [and] runaway children that you could not discuss in Hispanic homes."[37]

Univision followed with *El jue* (The Judge), *Cita con el amor* (The Dating Game), *Desde Hollywood* (patterned after *Entertainment Tonight*), and *El Show de Paul Rodríguez,* a Friday-night comedy that resembled NBC's *Saturday Night Live*. A news magazine called *Portada* (Cover Page) resembled ABC's *20/20*. That May, Univision preempted regular programs to carry the Grammy Awards.[38]

In a 1989 special report on Spanish-language television, *Broadcasting* highlighted the "resolve" of the "eldest and largest player in Hispanic television, Univision." The magazine headlined the network's "Coming of Age."[39] Conspicuously, as each new U.S. program appeared, a novela, musical, variety, or sports event from Televisa disappeared.

* * *

All along, many had wondered whether Univision and Telemundo were as secure as their publicity made it seem. The grapevine in the television community told of frictions at Telemundo. Even though Godoy was soundly besting Univision's news program in the ratings, he resigned. His surprise exit accompanied rumors that financial concerns might force the news division to close. More than a few had heard Barba fume about Silverman's tightened budget. Meanwhile, at Univision, a crisis hinted that the network hadn't come of age yet.

In March 1989, two months after Grimes and Blaya celebrated Univision's new direction, Danny Villanueva resigned. Emilio Nicolás had already left. Villanueva's exit was not unanticipated. While he had contributed twenty-five years to the network, his influence had diminished when Hallmark committed to domestic production. He did not leave quietly. When the newspaper *La Opinión* interviewed him, Villanueva complained that while KMEX profits had kept the network afloat, Hallmark had refused to build studios, originate programs, or recognize employees in Los Angeles.[40] He questioned both Hallmark's removal of Televisa's programs and the "television city" planned for Miami. His implication was clear: he felt that Hallmark turned its back on the 60 percent of Latinos who were of Mexican origin and was instead catering to those in Miami, who mostly were of Cuban descent.

The national media soon reported an uprising. Half of the KMEX's 150 employees signed a petition that protested "production operations in Miami, a city whose cultural and economic life is dominated by former Cuban refugees." They criticized Hallmark's "lack of meaningful Mexican-American representation," and they condemned the "cloroxification" of Univision, which had hired white executives.[41] Hockaday went to Los Angeles to meet with employees and respond to their complaints. For the time being, the dispute subsided.

But the departures and tensions fueled speculation that Univision and Telemundo were hiding a larger story, that one or both was broke. Hallmark and Reliance were privately held corporations. They allowed only a trickle of financial information to reach the public. Almost from the beginning of their competition, insiders suspected that both were in trouble at the bank.

In July 1987, the New York Academy of Television Arts and Sciences invited Donald Raider, the Reliance executive who was number three to Steinberg and Silverman and who was helping Barba direct the new network, to enlarge on reports of Telemundo's rapid progress. *Broadcasting* magazine covered Raider's speech. Instead of affirming Telemundo's sizzling success, Raider used the occasion to decry the handicap that had maddened Rene Anselmo years before: there were no Spanish-language

Nielsen ratings. "Half of [our] advertising inventory [is] going unsold," Raider said, adding that Telemundo had "turned into a challenge."[42]

One month later, Silverman turned to Wall Street for cash. Reliance offered a small public sale of Telemundo's stock, an odd move for a privately held company that had $6 billion in assets and had lavished a $300 million capitalization on Telemundo.[43] Silverman raised $165 million.[44] He referred to the sale as "a bump in the road." But the move suggested a scare. The $165 million was almost exactly the amount Reliance needed to pay the $70 million it owed Perenchio and the $110 million it owed Blair and thus avoid default.[45]

In 1988, there were more clues that Reliance was overextended. Silverman went on a buying spree. To fulfill his promise of enlarging Telemundo and bringing it to parity with Univision, he spent $50 million to acquire San Francisco's KSTS, Houston's KTMD, and San Antonio's KVDA. He paid incentives to station owners in Dallas, Denver, Philadelphia, San Diego, and Tucson so they would sign on as affiliates. More money went to low-power satelator transmitters in Phoenix and other cities where the network awaited full-power stations.[46]

Then, in a signal move, he purchased the facility in Hialeah where Godoy had launched *Noticiero Telemundo* and Goyco's show was broadcast. Telemundo's spending appeared to have greatly exceeded Reliance's $300 million investment. Analysts discussed the possibility that Telemundo might be bankrupt.

They were surprised when they learned that Univision might be in similar straits. It seemed impossible that Hallmark, a beacon of corporate health, might be facing Chapter 11. Speculation arose when new information cleared up the mystery of why Televisa had sold the Univision network operation in 1987. According to first reports, Hallmark had acquired the network for $50 million, but Hockaday later confirmed a report that, in fact, Azcárraga had sold when Hockaday had agreed to pay him $275 million.[47]

In August 1988, writers Steve McClellan and John Lippman assembled several months of news releases and disclosures. They reported that Univision and Telemundo were pursuing "expensive gambles" with revenue "so disappointing" that "neither is expected to be in black for many years." Despite a growing Latino population, Univision was not increasing sales. Its 1988 sales were projected to be $120 million, barely above SIN's $100

Figure 9. Soon after its launch in 1987, Telemundo acquired and outfitted Spanish-language television's first U.S. network studios at a converted shoe warehouse in the Miami suburb of Hialeah. Inside, Telemundo staged the first Spanish-language entertainment programs produced in the United States. The Hialeah facility was Telemundo's broadcast headquarters for thirty years. Photo courtesy of Craig Allen.

million in 1986. Telemundo's $85 million was "far below expectations." The two networks' long-term obligations were the biggest concern. Telemundo's totaled $244 million. Compared to its rival, Telemundo was in clover. Because of Hallmark's still-unpaid $301 million purchase of SICC and now the $275 million it owed Azcárraga, Univision was at least $514 million in debt.[48]

Eager to capture a booming Latino market, two trusted corporations had abandoned prudence. By 1989, neither could hide their financial distress. Wall Street learned that Hallmark had resorted to issuing junk bonds.[49] At Telemundo, Silverman closed the news division. To save money, he negotiated with Ted Turner, whose Cable News Network fed Telemundo a Spanish-language newscast from Atlanta. At the end of 1989, the two networks reported cumulative earnings of $250 million, but each acknowledged eight-figure losses. After three years, neither had turned a profit.[50]

* * *

Four weeks into the 1990s, both networks flipped upside-down. On January 30, 1990, Silverman resigned from his post as CEO of Telemundo and from his multimillion-dollar post as the president of Reliance. The star financier's fall forced Steinberg, the chair, to the network's helm. Reports that Steinberg had met with nervous creditors, proposed a reorganization, and sought Swiss money touched off speculation that Telemundo was close to collapse.[51]

Two days after Silverman's exit, Hallmark, the darling of the Fortune 500, revealed that it, too, could not pay its bills. It defaulted on the payment on the junk bonds it had issued to cover Univision's $500 million debt. While default was tantamount to bankruptcy, Hallmark denied that it intended to file for Chapter 11 reorganization.[52]

However, by mid-1990, both networks had reversed their financial slides. At Telemundo, Barba laid off scores of Telemundo personnel. Steinberg found cash and bought time through a second issue of Telemundo stock.[53] At Univision, Grimes and Chief Financial Officer George Blank pulled off an improbable feat: they revived Univision by coaxing creditors to accept payment on the junk bonds at fifty cents on the dollar.[54]

Bankruptcies still loomed. However, Univision and Telemundo had prevented crisis at a most auspicious time. The 1990 census recorded 30 million Hispanics. The Hispanic population had tripled in size since 1970. In 1980, in a special edition, *Time* magazine had reported a "Hispanic boom." In 1990 in another special edition, it reported the same discovery.[55]

Yet this time the boom mattered. Word spread of a breakthrough: Nielsen was about to install its meters and paraphernalia in a national sample of Spanish-speaking homes. Those in Spanish-language television could hardly believe the reports. For two decades they had begged for Nielsen ratings. From their perspective, a growing population was meaningless without them. Nielsen ratings would mean new advertising revenue for Spanish-language television, and because of the boom, that revenue promised to be enormous.

The news about the Nielsen plan broke in July 1989. At first, no one cheered. Nielsen was not a public service. Sampling a national audience of 250 million, wiring hundreds of homes, and processing volumes of data were costly, and TV networks always bore the cost. Nielsen executive vice president John Dimling informed Univision and Telemundo that together they had to pay $50 million. Both balked. But in January 1990, Dimling dropped the fee to $38 million and Steinberg and Grimes paid.[56]

In public, Steinberg and Grimes welcomed a watershed development. In private, they faced a moment of truth. While Arbitron's local ratings and SRC's national survey had provided some knowledge, the time had come to discover which network—and which network's programs—truly were number one. Being on top was crucial. Advertisers were certain to race to the network that Nielsen said had the most viewers. Later, spending would spread out. But both Univision and Telemundo were facing bankruptcy and needed cash right away. Only one could be first.

An internal battle at Univision underscored the heightened stakes. Upon learning of the Nielsen ratings, almost every Univision management executive and virtually all of those in the network's sales department rebelled. They demanded that Grimes withdraw from Nielsen and keep using SRC ratings. Grimes told them that advertisers did not believe the SRC ratings. Yet to Univision executives, it was more important to keep the 70 and 80 percent shares from SRC. Despite heated confrontations, calls for his resignation, and his own apprehension about losing the high SRC numbers, Grimes did not consider withdrawing from participating in the Nielsen ratings.[57]

A long wait fed anxieties. Dimling appointed Ceril Shagrin, a Nielsen vice president and an expert on sample selection and methodology, as the director of the National Hispanic Television Index (NHTI). She urged patience. "Doing it right is not easy," she said.[58]

The project was ambitious. Nielsen could not report accurate data merely from the proportion of Latinos in its regular national survey. While the proportion of Latinos in the U.S. population was growing—it had reached around 12 percent—it was too small to extrapolate data from a national survey. Nielsen had conceded that its national sample was not representative. It included only a small proportion of the 12 percent of Latinos. Shagrin's task was to create a separate survey. Like the main Nielsen survey, the NHTI required national sampling and the wiring of 800 new homes.

The separate survey appealed to Univision and Telemundo. It placated those who were angry with Grimes. Without the computations that Arbitron's data required, Nielsen's reports would automatically isolate and emphasize the Spanish-language audience. Moreover, part of the NHTI report was designed to separate out the 50 percent of Latino viewing that went to English-language channels. This meant further isolation of and emphasis on the Spanish-language channels. Because only Univision and Telemundo would be studied, the winners and losers would be easy to see.

Shagrin insisted on at least one test before the new survey went national. Her plan called for a "rehearsal" in Los Angeles that would coincide with Nielsen's next monthly ratings sweep. By late 1990, technicians had installed meters in fifty Los Angeles homes. Shagrin assured the networks that the national survey was next.[59]

She conducted the test in February 1991. It did not go as planned. At Nielsen's data center in Dunedin Beach, Florida, analysts encountered technical problems. Because Nielsen conducted its February sweep at the same time, some of the Hispanic data were missing. Moreover, there were anomalous results. Surprisingly, Telemundo's KVEA was first. Univision's ratings seemed impossibly low; its KMEX finished in third place. Adding to the mystery, a new Spanish-language station called KWHY had not only surpassed KMEX, it had almost finished in first place. KVEA had captured 40 percent of Spanish-speaking viewers, KWHY 35 percent, and KMEX 25 percent.[60]

Shagrin quashed the networks' hopes that national ratings would come soon. She announced that Nielsen needed more time to develop the system. In addition, because Los Angeles was the largest Hispanic market and thus vital to the NHTI, she would not proceed without another test there.

Shagrin finally informed the networks that the next trial in Los Angeles, a statistically reliable survey, would not happen for some time. She moved to the NHTI's most protracted stage: identifying the 800 homes across the United States that would constitute the national sample. Not until the national sample was created could she conduct a retest in Los Angeles, a "sweep" of 200 homes in the Los Angeles area.

Nielsen guarded the information in the first findings. KVEA's first-place and KWHY's second-place finishes did seem anomalous, and Shagrin feared the consequences of making the data public. All past ratings had shown KMEX as the uncontested leader. When she was obliged to share some of the results, Shagrin portrayed them as invalid. "We wanted no reaction until we'd done a second survey," she later explained.[61]

However, Shagrin actually believed that the test results were accurate. So did some others, among them two new Univision board members. They had no doubt that the test numbers were correct.

A curious development emerged in 1990. When Univision began broadcasting programs generated in the United States, the Televisa programs it canceled did not disappear for all viewers. Although Univision was presumed to hold exclusive rights, its contract with Televisa had a loophole that meant that exclusive rights in reality were first rights. Should Univision cancel a Televisa program, Televisa could place the program with a different U.S. provider. Azcárraga acted; he moved the novelas, dramas, and *espectáculos* (spectaculars) that Univision dropped to Galavisión, the U.S. cable channel Televisa still operated.[62] Univision did not seem to care; few Latinos paid to subscribe to cable TV.

However, Azcárraga did more. After Hallmark's takeover of SICC, Azcárraga had continued his 25-year association with Emilio Nicolás. Seeking a return to U.S. broadcasting, Azcárraga had partnered with Nicolás to make agreements with a group of stations in California. By late 1990, the stations were broadcasting the Galavisión cable channel free to air, which viewers elsewhere received by paying cable TV subscriptions. Commercial messages were inserted into the broadcast version of the Galavisión feed, and although Azcárraga shared ad revenues with the stations, his objective was to form an over-the-air television network and once again broadcast into the United States. One of the stations was KWHY.[63] When Nielsen conducted the test in February 1991, KWHY was carrying the Televisa programs that Univision had canceled and that had previously been seen on KMEX.

By that time, Univision president Joaquín Blaya and program director Rosita Perú had further enlarged their schedule of domestically produced programs, and more Televisa programming was appearing on Galavisión. Two newly hired executives raised red flags. Blaya had enlisted 39-year-old Ray Rodríguez, the former manager of singer Julio Iglesias, as talent director. When Rosita Perú left the network, Blaya promoted Ray Rodríguez to program director. Blaya then had named 29-year-old Mario Rodríguez, a graduate of Cornell Law School, as director of promotions. Ray Rodríguez told Blaya that KWHY's 35 percent share reflected viewers' preference for the programs Univision had dropped; it was not a mistake.[64]

Mario Rodríguez went to Dunedin Beach. He examined the data and found little amiss. He then warned Blaya that "the problem is not just the chance we will be beaten in Los Angeles by [KWHY's use of] our own programs." Galavisión soon would be broadcast on stations Nicolás had acquired in San Antonio, Austin, and Corpus Christi. Because Galavisión was broadcast only in California at the time of the Nielsen test, Rodríguez subtracted KWHY's ratings in order to project national competition between Univision and Telemundo. "The problem," he deduced, "is the chance we will lose to Telemundo nationwide."⁶⁵

The time was not right for dire predictions. Both networks' sales departments had begun calculating the increased ad revenue that their Nielsen ratings would generate. Most expected that by 1993 the winning network would be $200 million richer, the loser by one-quarter to one-half that amount. Although Steinberg was battling a debt that was reported to be $300 million, Telemundo's success in the test pointed to its turnaround. Univision's debt lingered at around $250 million. Confident about Univision's "unbroken ratings dominance," Hockaday assured the press of future success.⁶⁶

On March 9, 1991, Blaya inaugurated his long-foreseen "television city." Dignitaries toured the Doral facility, and technicians reenacted the hand-off from Laguna Niguel. The visitors saw a master control synchronized to multiple time zones, a state-of-the-art news center, and three studios. Blaya had outfitted the largest studio, the new home of *Sábado gigante*, with 200 seats.⁶⁷ Broadcasting from Laguna Niguel, Ramos had anchored studio coverage when the war began on January 15. The next day he flew to Kuwait. After two months of reporting the war, Ramos returned to a new home in Miami.⁶⁸

Univision was located only ten minutes away from Telemundo; the two Spanish networks broadcast to all fifty states from studios four miles apart. Yet while Telemundo had kept the converted warehouse between railroad tracks in Hialeah, Univision's "television city" overlooked the famed Doral Country Club. At the ceremony, Blaya celebrated the fact that the network had taken the first steps toward building a "Hispanic Hollywood." Univision, he said, will "be a U.S. network in Spanish, not the other way around."⁶⁹

Immediately, Blaya filled the new facilities. Energies poured into programs for the 1991–1992 season. Working closely with Blaya, Perú had instituted a Hollywood-style chain of command before she left the network. While Blaya and Rodríguez conferred with agents and planned season schedules, executive producers proposed concepts, generated scripts, and directed writers, crews, and talent. Doral buzzed with 300 personnel. In September 1991, Blaya unveiled the latest new programs. As he had promised three years earlier, half of Univision's network programs, around twenty altogether, were produced by Univision.⁷⁰

Figure 10. Hallmark capped its six years as Univision's owner with the first state-of-the-art Spanish-language TV studios in the United States. Univision's 120,000-square foot broadcast center in the Miami suburb of Doral was completed in March 1991. Although Joaquín Blaya envisioned a "Hispanic Hollywood," his U.S.-produced programs failed. Exactly one year after the building opened, Hallmark sold Univision to Jerry Perenchio. Photo courtesy of Craig Allen.

Equally energetic was activity in the nearby Florida city of Dunedin Beach. By the end of 1991, satisfied with the selection and wiring of the 800-home national sample, Shagrin informed the networks that the Los Angeles retest was scheduled for the following February. Next would come a brief test of the national sample during summer sweeps that July. The first formal national ratings would happen in November 1992.[71]

On January 29, 1992, Univision's afternoon lineup showcased three new Univision-produced programs: its children's show, *Platavisión;* a magazine program, *Noticias y más* (News and More); and a game-and-comedy show, *Hola América.* At night, Univision carried one Televisa novela. Lead prime-time programs included Univision's sitcoms *Corte tropical* (Tropical Cut) and *Fama y fortuna* (Fame and Fortune). On Fridays, viewers saw the variety show *Charytín internacional* (Blaya had hired Charytín Goyco from Telemundo). On other nights, Univision broadcast *Desde Hollywood;* Paul Rodríguez's comedy show, *Portada;* and its Miami dating-game show, *Cita con el amor* (Date with Love).[72]

That day, Nielsen lit up the Los Angeles sample. For four weeks that February, data streamed into Dunedin Beach. Around March 1, Hockaday saw the advances, picked up the phone, and, as he would recall, "finally relaxed."[73] He knew he would not be dealing with Univision's ordeals much longer. The Los Angeles survey was disaster for Univision and the end of the road for Hallmark.

Telemundo's KVEA finished in first place. Of the 50 percent of Los Angeles viewers tuned to Spanish-language channels, the Telemundo station scored a 42 share. Much of Telemundo's prime time featured foreign programs, many of which were telenovelas arranged through WKAQ. Again, the Galavisión station, KWHY, claimed second place with a score of 31. Univision's KMEX finished last with a 27. The most viewed programs were two Televisa novelas on KWHY and *Sábado gigante* on Univision. Without *Sábado gigante*'s rating of 60, Univision's rating would have been lower; many of its shows scored in the teens.[74]

The Los Angeles survey staved off bankruptcy for Telemundo, but the network needed to fare as well in the November national survey. It had defaulted on its $307 million debt, but after the victory in Los Angeles, creditors had agreed to avert foreclosure pending the November results.[75] However, Barba had fled. Gustavo and Ricardo Cisneros, the owners of the Venezuelan media conglomerate that owned and controlled the Venevisión TV network, had hired him to mediate a partnership with Televisa for joint sales of programs in the United States. Saul Steinberg needed to locate a new Telemundo network president.

At Hallmark, Hockaday telephoned Jerry Perenchio to ask if he would like to buy the network. During the conversation, Perenchio agreed to purchase Univision for $550 million. Five weeks later, on April 8, 1992, Hallmark held a press conference to announce Perenchio's acquisition. Perenchio declined to appear. Grimes already had resigned.[76]

Hockaday later explained his decision. For months, Hallmark's chief financial officer, Henry Frigon, had warned of a "dangerous situation." Univision needed the highest possible ratings for revenue, and not just so it could pay creditors. The U.S. programs compounded the network's expenses; Univision was paying many salaries. "We needed to prove convincingly that we had the dominant share of the market. As soon as it became clear that we were not going to able to do it, I felt it was time to move on," Hockaday later related.[77]

* * *

The press treated the sale as if it were the happy ending to one of Perenchio's 1970s sitcom plots. Referring to "Mr. Perenchio's Dream Deal," the *New York Times* reported on "a rich prize" for the "60-year-old" billionaire who had "made his big score [with] Norman Lear" and the hit shows *All in the Family* and *The Jeffersons*.[78] The transfer was already being vetted at the FCC, and Perenchio expected to take charge that June.[79] "There should be no problems in completing the deal," the *Times* said.[80]

In Kansas City, Hallmark spokesperson Steven Doyal made the announcement on April 8. Like Perenchio, Hockaday did not appear. When he was later interviewed by the *Kansas City Star,* Hockaday was magnanimous. He confessed to two failures, that he "didn't understand that the Hispanic market was made up of so many nationalities" and that "Hallmark didn't learn to work effectively with our content provider in Mexico." Even so, he maintained, "We developed a concept for the future of Spanish television."[81]

The report of "no problems in completing the deal" in the *New York Times* was not accurate. Blaya was livid. He claimed to have had no notice of Hockaday's dealings with Perenchio. Blaya found out on April 6, when a telephone call from Kansas City interrupted a meeting Blaya was conducting. Hockaday came on the line. While listening Blaya paled, then wrote one word on a piece of paper: "Perenchio."[82] Hockaday informed him that he and Perenchio were headed to Miami. A melodrama began the next day. On April 7, Blaya confronted them at the Doral Hotel. Blaya insisted that the U.S. shows continue. When Perenchio hedged, then revealed additional partners, Blaya was dumbfounded. Perenchio had invited Azcárraga and the Venevisión moguls, the Cisneroses, to join him as owners. He gave them a legal 20 percent share; 6 percent for the Cisneroses and 14 percent for Azcárraga. This meant that Carlos Barba, who had left Telemundo to spearhead Venevisión's negotiations for an alliance with Azcárraga, and who had brought Perenchio, the Cisneroses, and Azcárraga together, was destined for a high Univision post.

More consequentially, it also meant that Azcárraga and his programs were back. Only to obtain them would Perenchio have partnered with someone the FCC had banished six years before. Still, it seemed unthinkable that Perenchio would consent to sharing ownership. "My heart sunk [sic]," Blaya later recalled. He was certain that Azcárraga had enticed Perenchio with a programming deal so favorable that no U.S. programs would remain.[83]

On April 11, the *Miami Herald* reported Blaya's version of his encounter with the new owners four days earlier. "They have shown a complete lack of respect for the group of professionals at Univision who have worked tirelessly to change the face of Spanish television," Blaya said.[84] The next day, controversy engulfed Univision. Employees rallied around Blaya. They lambasted Hallmark and denounced Perenchio and Azcárraga.[85]

By May, Blaya and the employees who had allied with him sensed an incipient victory. Responding to the protest, the FCC stopped the transfer and ordered an indefinite "pendency period." Persuaded that they needed time to evaluate conflicting claims, the commissioners instructed Perenchio not to engage with Univision's management and staff until it had decided whether his takeover was legal. Backed by the Hispanic Media Coalition, Blaya had petitioned for a delay to enable a group of investors he had assembled to make a competing bid. "It's very clear that they are going to cancel all of the U.S.-produced shows," the coalition contended.[86] Some expected Perenchio to withdraw.

* * *

That April, Hockaday was confident that his deal with Perenchio had closed the book on Hallmark's travails with Univision. Yet the next month, the Hallmark president was reeling once again. The pendency period meant that Hallmark's lame-duck ownership of Univision would continue for an indefinite period. Because of circumstances and timing, Hallmark's escape would not be easy. Hockaday had to contend with a network president who was maneuvering to oust the intended new owner and with the first national Nielsen ratings of Spanish-language television. The sale to Perenchio was contingent on Hockaday's ability to hand him a trophy television network. After finishing third in two trials, Hockaday needed to prove that he was not selling damaged goods. Before Hallmark passed the company to Perenchio, it needed to backtrack on its commitment to domestic production and change Univision's programming.

Hockaday needed advice about how to proceed, but Blaya was busy with his petition to the FCC. Hockaday broke the chain of command. In early May, he initiated his first sustained communication with program director Ray Rodríguez, Blaya's subordinate. Hockaday learned much that he had known not before. Rodríguez told him that, contrary to Blaya's portrayal of unanimity, not everyone was comfortable with Blaya's concentration on domestic production. Rodríguez revealed that he himself would welcome

Azcárraga's programs and in fact he had advised Blaya to reinstate Televisa programs after the test ratings failure the year before. Rodríguez also said that he was not alone. Many sales personnel and local station managers had voiced the same opinion, that Univision was impeding its own success and would quickly become the undisputed first in the ratings if it brought back Televisa programs.

Within days, Hockaday asked Rodríguez to change Univision's program schedule. Hockaday was pushing for a revised schedule heavy in Televisa programs that could be implemented in time for the July test ratings, but Rodríguez was not sure he could make that happen. Rodríguez finally agreed to put together a semblance of a new schedule. Univision's agreement with Televisa called for Televisa to ship program recordings to Miami. Complete recordings of several Televisa series had collected in Univision's warehouse. They could be aired immediately.

Nevertheless, Rodríguez was unsure about how the process would unfold; "the thing was a mess," he later said. Not all of the low-rated domestic programs could be replaced. The worst part of the mess was contemplating a conversation with Blaya about the new schedule. Neither Hockaday nor Rodríguez savored the task of telling him of their plans to reschedule (if not cancel) many of the programs he had conceived and developed. However, a surprise development removed their anxieties.[87]

On May 23, 1992, approximately 2,500 people worked somewhere in Spanish-language television. That day, a Saturday, most of them were on the telephone. There was riveting news. Blaya had walked out at Univision and was now the president of Telemundo. There was more. As he left Univision, Blaya posted a notice that promised any Univision employee a job at Telemundo.[88] "I was so close to the people at Univision" that "I wanted them to come with me," Blaya later said.[89]

It was the first day of a Memorial Day weekend. Ray Rodríguez was on a boat in the Florida Keys. Hockaday reached him by telephone. When he learned of Blaya's departure, Rodríguez also learned that his career had taken a pivotal turn. Hockaday had decided that Rodríguez would be Blaya's successor as Univision president and CEO. Rodríguez formally accepted the following day. While he was pleased about his promotion, Rodríguez understood that the job would not be easy. In just a few months, he would be responsible for Univision's performance in the first Nielsen ratings.

He rushed back to Miami. He spent the rest of the weekend contacting shaken Univision management and staff. Over the span of three days, he successfully renegotiated the contracts of twenty front-office personnel, raising their salaries but also assuring each member that he or she was essential to his planned cause of bettering the Spanish-language network. "We must cut Blaya off at the pass," he told them.[90] When business resumed on Tuesday, only four had quit.

Soon, more were inclined to follow. Perenchio had not complied to the letter with the FCC's "hands off" order. All along, he had stayed in contact with Hockaday. He beseeched Hockaday to avoid delay in reinstating the Televisa programming. Adding Rodríguez to his communication, Perenchio reminded the new president that Nielsen's July test ratings were only weeks away.

As Rodríguez later related, Perenchio was appalled by Blaya's "cowardly" exit to Telemundo. He made clear that he wanted Blaya and Telemundo thrashed in the ratings. In further telephone conversations with Rodríguez, Perenchio said that "we will not lose sleep" over Blaya and his betrayal. Rodríguez recalled that Perenchio was so concerned about "the morale of Univision" and "what we could do to have employees be a team" that, again ignoring the FCC'S order, the new owner, who had not yet been approved, agreed to meet the employees.[91]

On June 15, Perenchio traveled to Miami. He met with Univision's 300 employees in the large *Sábado gigante* studio, where he was greeted with catcalls and shouts denouncing him as a traitor for allowing Azcárraga to return. When Perenchio dodged questions from producers and performers about whether their programs and jobs would remain, many walked out of the session. After Perenchio left, several employees told Blaya about the confrontation in the studio. Blaya reaffirmed that Telemundo would find jobs for any who chose to leave.

By that time, the other Rodríguez, Mario, who had joined Univision with Ray Rodríguez two years before and who had implored Blaya to reinstate the shelved Televisa programs, had risen from his post as promotions director. His encyclopedic and analytical knowledge of the Nielsen ratings made him extremely valuable to Univision, and Ray Rodríguez wasted no time in promoting him to program director.

With Blaya no longer an impediment, Mario Rodríguez gave his full attention to the project that had brought Hockaday and Ray Rodríguez together: devising a Univision program schedule that featured Televisa programs. He had met Perenchio at the June 15 session. Reacting to Perenchio's desire to wound Blaya in the July Nielsen trial, he began by placing six Univision-produced series on summer hiatus and replacing them with six Televisa programs. Their complete recordings were sitting in the Miami warehouse.

Employees were distressed by the changes. On July 22, tensions reached a breaking point. Mario Rodríguez held another meeting to tell staff that the test ratings were in. Univision had prevailed, but barely; it had a 45 percent share of the Spanish-speaking audience and Telemundo had 42 percent. While employees expected to see charts showing the ratings, Rodríguez opened with a different display: a revised schedule for fall. Many were stunned to see Televisa programs, mostly novelas, arrayed all over prime time. While some Univision programs remained in prime time, most had been shuffled to other time slots. "Our goal," Rodríguez said, "is fully using the Protele [Televisa] library." He explained that without the Televisa programs he had rushed onto the schedule, Telemundo would have won the July test. Univision's margin of victory was so slim that the "probability of success in Nielsen [is] a main issue."[92] Rodríguez had canceled only one program, *Hola América,* but he left no doubt that more shows would go.

An exodus ensued. In August, dozens of employees resigned, even though the FCC still had not ruled on whether Perenchio's takeover was legal. Then that September, earlier than most had expected, the FCC announced that it had concluded its review. It had unanimously approved Perenchio's acquisition of Univision. The transfer would become official on December 17.

Hearing this news, dozens more people left Univision.[93] Word spread that Perenchio would retain Ray Rodríguez as network president and Mario Rodríguez as program director. Because neither Rodríguez had defended domestic production at Univision, both looked like instruments in Perenchio's alleged plan of deferring to Azcárraga, canceling remaining Univision-produced programs, and eliminating their jobs. Some were skeptical about reports that Perenchio would name Carlos Barba, the new owner's longtime professional associate, as Univision's CEO. "Univision was in upheaval," Ray Rodríguez recalled."[94]

By the end of October, nearly 100 personnel had fled. Most moved to Telemundo. While all but four of Univision's front-line staff and all of its on-air personalities remained, Spanish-language television seemed to have turned inside out. The first president of Univision was running Telemundo. The architect of Telemundo was set to run Univision. Azcárraga, who had been banished six years earlier, had returned. Pranksters who hacked the Univision intercom announced: "The bus for Telemundo leaves in five minutes."[95]

* * *

The National Hispanic Television Index commenced on October 26, 1992. Four weeks later, on November 22, the survey was over. "Following three years of development and an extensive pilot study in Los Angeles, the NHTI is the first nationwide service fully dedicated to monitoring the viewing habits of the diverse Hispanic community," Nielsen announced.[96] Univision and Telemundo braced for the outcome.

Univision won. As had been the case in the Los Angeles ratings trials, Latinos' national viewing was evenly divided between English and Spanish channels. Across all channels, including English-language ones, Univision was first with a rating of 17 and Telemundo was second with a rating of 9. Among Spanish-language channels, Univision had a rating of 52 and Telemundo a rating of 38. By that time, U.S. viewers had access to five Spanish-language TV channels. In addition to Galavisión, HBO Olé and ESPN Deportes were available to the small number of homes with cable TV. The three cable channels and scattered independent local stations divided the remaining 10 percent.[97]

Telemundo's rating of 38 ensured that it was headed to bankruptcy court. Steinberg confirmed reports that only with a decisive victory in the first ratings could Telemundo avert Chapter 11.[98] It was only a matter of time before creditors would decide the network's fate.

Most in the United States knew of Nielsen for rankings that resembled baseball and football standings. From its main survey, the NTI, Nielsen identified and published the nation's most popular TV program followed by the next nineteen. Nielsen used the same metrics for the NHTI; it listed the top twenty programs for Spanish-language TV. Univision programs appeared sixteen times in the November 1992 ratings. *Sábado gigante* ranked fourth, *Cristina* fifth, *Noticiero Univision* eighth, and a second news program twelfth. Every other program on the list of the top twenty, including the four on Telemundo, had come from somewhere other than the United States. The three highest-rated programs were Televisa novelas seen on Univision. Both scoring in the sixties, *Baila comigo* (Dance with Me) ranked third and *Cara sucia* (Dirty Face) second.

The number one program was so far and away the most viewed that Nielsen noted that it could not reliably measure competing shows. Its title was *María Mercedes,* a novela that marked the debut of 20-year-old actress Thalía Sodi, who in the role of María enacted the rags-to-riches trials of a young peasant girl. It was broadcast in more than 100 countries. It was a sensation in Eastern Europe, where it cleared a path for Western TV after the fall of Communism. That November, *María* earned a 70 percent share on each of the twenty nights it was seen.[99]

The day the ratings ended, Mario Rodríguez obtained the advances and flew to Los Angeles. At his June meeting with Perenchio in Miami, he had dazzled him with his ratings acuity. Perenchio invited Rodríguez to his Bel Air residence, a location familiar to virtually every person in the United States: it was the mansion used in the TV series *The Beverly Hillbillies.*

When he arrived, Rodríguez had an inkling of "something in the works." He spotted Azcárraga. According to Rodríguez, "They were whooping it up." As Rodríguez presented the ratings, the two TV giants yelled, slapped furniture, and threw their fists in the air. They were "cheering the bad ratings of [Blaya's] shows." Azcárraga "could not contain his excitement." Raving that "Hockaday and Blaya destroyed the network he built," Azcárraga said "he'd do anything to bring Univision back to its glory."[100]

After meeting with Mario Rodríguez, Perenchio summoned Ray Rodríguez and other members of Univision's new executive team to the mansion for a retreat. The executives expected Perenchio to sign the transfer papers from Hallmark. On December 17, 1992, Perenchio did sign the transfer papers. He also introduced a contract between Televisa and Univision known as the program licensing agreement. It was the most one-sided contract two television executives ever came up with. Azcárraga gave Univision not just exclusive but ironclad rights to all Televisa programs. He dropped fees from 40 percent to almost nothing, 9 percent. He agreed to pay for promoting Univision's programs. Finally, Azcárraga committed to the terms of the program licensing agreement for twenty-five years, until 2017.[101] It now was apparent why Perenchio had permitted Azcárraga to return and had been willing to endure a summer and fall of unrest among the Univision personnel. As Blaya had guessed, Azcárraga had "sold the farm" to Univision's new owner.

The executives were more stunned than jubilant. Barba questioned whether Perenchio "really could enforce that kind of contract for twenty-five years." "I've got his signature," Perenchio snapped.[102] According to Ray Rodríguez, "everyone reacted" not to the contract terms but "what they implied," that Perenchio had proved that "he was not going to repeat the mistakes of Hallmark and knew what he was doing."[103]

Barba recalled that after beginning dramatically, the retreat ended ambiguously. Confident that the executives would make the correct decisions, Perenchio did not give them instructions. He advised them that "if you work as a team and play to win, you will not make mistakes."[104]

Perenchio's finale later became a signature anecdote. The attendees wanted Perenchio to talk about his friendships with Hollywood actors. Instead, he talked about his early career as a U.S. Air Force officer and flight commander. He finished with a prediction for 1993: "What I see for Univision is CAVU—clear air, visibility unlimited."[105]

8

THE PERENCHIO ERA

As they left the retreat on December 17, 1992, attendees puzzled over their new leader's closing words. But Jerry Perenchio had said a great deal when he used pilots' terminology to mark his acquisition of Univision. He had observed the demise of Rene Anselmo and SICC, the breakdown of Hallmark, his own departure from WNJU, and the financial tailspin of Telemundo. He had a mission: to prove that a promising endeavor that too often crashed could fly right.

His metaphor of "clear air" referred to two auspicious shifts in Univision's winds. First, Spanish-language Nielsen ratings promised to carry the endeavor into a new era of flush financial resources. The second big change was that Univision had ended its subservience to its Mexican mother firm. The new program licensing agreement, or PLA, with Televisa had terms that were unprecedentedly favorable to Univision.

Angry that Hallmark's control of Univision had demolished Televisa's foundation in the United States, Azcárraga had been quick to offer his programming to Univision's new owner. But in order to ensure that his programs flourished on U.S. airwaves, he had bargained away Televisa's share of the cash. Perenchio had extracted an agreement by which Univision would pay a token amount, 9 percent of revenue, to fill its schedule with Televisa programs. Perenchio had won exclusive rights, meaning that Televisa could not sell programs to Telemundo or any other U.S. provider. In addition, the 25-year length of the agreement meant that Perenchio could move forward with Univision's future secured.[1] Not surprisingly, jaws dropped when Perenchio disclosed the details of the PLA on December 17.

Yet just as quickly, anxiety set in. The second Nielsen ratings were a month away. Perenchio still sought to soundly defeat Telemundo and its president Joaquín Blaya, the former Univision president who had fled to Telemundo and had enticed away many of Univision's management and staff. Univision viewers were seeing a hodgepodge of a few U.S.-developed programs and the Televisa programs Ray and Mario Rodríguez had rushed onto the schedule. Many decisions needed to be made.

On December 31, Perenchio received the year-end financial report of the network he had owned for two weeks. He was expecting to inherit a windfall from Univision's November Nielsen victory, but instead Hallmark left him a company that finished 1992 with $38 million in losses.

Many managers expected him to name his longtime lieutenant Carlos Barba as Univision's CEO. Instead, Perenchio issued a short statement announcing that he would be corporate CEO and that Azcárraga's deputy, Jaime Dávila, would be Univision's network CEO and second in command.[2] While 46-year-old Dávila was respected and affable, he was tough. Under Azcárraga, Dávila had muscled past rivals at Televisa. It was Dávila who in 1986 had ousted Rene Anselmo as head of the SIN network. And later that year, it was Dávila who had fired Gustavo Godoy during the fracas over Jacobo Zabludovsky. It was unclear whether Dávila's primary loyalty was to Univision or to Azcárraga, but he was certain to reinstate the firm style of leadership Azcárraga had used at Televisa and that had weighed heavily on Anselmo during the years before 1986 when Televisa controlled Univision's predecessor, the Spanish International Network.

Perenchio sent his managers a one-page document listing twenty rules by which Univision would operate. The first rule: "Stay clear of the press. No interviews, no panels, no speeches, no comments. Stay out of the spotlight. It fades your suit." The second: "Never hire politicians, academicians or [others] unless they have successfully worked in the private sector." The third prohibited "re-hiring anyone." The fourth required the managers to delegate work to "people smarter and better than you." Other rules mandated "teamwork," "homework," and "no surprises."[3]

Perenchio titled the document "The Rules of the Road." The managers had not anticipated its odd and arcane orders. But "the rules of the road" were not new. They traced back physician-turned-entertainment entrepreneur Jules Stein, who had risen through the ranks by booking musicians at speakeasies owned by Al Capone in Prohibition Era Chicago. Stein and his associates had formed a firm called the Music Corporation of America. Perenchio owed his career to MCA, and he brought its rules to Univision.

Perenchio retained Ray Rodríguez as network president and chief operating officer. Rodríguez particularly noticed rule twelve: "Think Big. When you suit up each day, it's to play in Yankee Stadium or Dodger Stadium." Rodríguez grasped Perenchio's message: "Jerry made the point that he didn't spend a fortune to play in the minor leagues."[4]

* * *

Perenchio's large résumé also made the point. Born in 1930 into an Italian immigrant family that settled in Fresno, he had worked his way through UCLA. He joined the air force as an officer candidate out of UCLA and won a commission as a jet fighter pilot and flight instructor. The air force was a springboard to his eventual career in entertainment; by 1958, he had found success in a sideline, booking bands at officers' clubs. He was among the first to promote the rock-and-roll music craze. Feted in magazines such as *Billboard*, he took to the spotlight.[5] By 1960, his venture had impressed famed Hollywood producer and agent Lew Wasserman, the head of MCA. Wasserman became his mentor. When he was hired at MCA, Perenchio adopted Wasserman's dictum of avoiding publicity. Wasserman was renowned for encouraging clients to bask in the glow of public adulation while he himself shrank from the spotlight. By lying low, Wasserman won the loyalty of Hollywood's best-known stars. "If you're going to be a mover and shaker, the best way to retain power is through silence," Wasserman said.[6]

After MCA closed its talent agency in 1963 in order to comply with antitrust laws, Perenchio formed his own agency. Clients who included Elizabeth Taylor, Marlon Brando, Richard Burton, Johnny Mathis, and Andy Williams followed Perenchio to his new firm, which he called Chartwell. Perenchio embarked on a career as the "most important person in Hollywood you never heard of."[7]

Perenchio rose as a force in media and popular culture in 1971. After other agents and promoters had failed, he negotiated a blockbuster televised sports event: he brought together Joe Frazier and Muhammad Ali, both of whom claimed the heavyweight boxing title. Frazier won the so-called fight of the century. Perenchio followed two years later by staging the decade's second most widely televised sports event, the tennis match between Billie Jean King, the eventual victor, and Bobby Riggs in a battle of the sexes.

By then, Perenchio had discovered and driven the career of Elton John, the decade's most widely sold solo recording artist. Partnering with Norman Lear to form Embassy/Tandem Productions, he was the executive producer of the 1970s TV series *All in the Family, The Jeffersons, Maude, Diff'rent Strokes, Mary Hartman, Mary Hartman,* and *Fernwood 2 Night.* He went on to produce the 1982 motion picture *Blade Runner* and the 1989 Oscar winner *Driving Miss Daisy.* He refused to allow his name to appear on record labels or in TV or movie credits.

By the late 1970s, Perenchio was one of several who was toying with starting a television network. Another was one of his closest friends, future Fox network founder Barry Diller. Aware that Diller and others thought only of forming English-language networks, Perenchio plunged into Spanish-language TV. While he was not Latino, did not speak Spanish, and was a contributor to Republican politicians who advocated restrictions on immigration, Perenchio foresaw a business opportunity. In 1979, he purchased WNJU. He planned to rekindle Columbia Pictures' dormant network, the venture he had named Network Spanish, or NetSpan.

By 1984, Perenchio needed cash to pay for NetSpan's transmission system. To raise it, he sold out of his partnership with Lear. With $485 million in his pocket, he appeared to be committed to completing NetSpan.[8] He was not. Magnetized by the impending dissolution of the already-established Spanish International Network, Perenchio used the money to secretly bid on SIN. Rene Anselmo's exposure of the bid carried Perenchio out of Spanish-language television. He was forced to sell the NetSpan properties to Saul Steinberg's Reliance corporation. From the sidelines, he witnessed both Reliance's founding of NetSpan as Telemundo and Hallmark's rebirth of SIN as Univision. But he was confident that with Hallmark running Univision, he would have a second try.

Perenchio refused to pursue Univision without Televisa. Years before, in the NetSpan project, Barba had been Perenchio's right-hand man. After Perenchio left NetSpan, Barba had remained and had led the founding of Telemundo. They were reunited when Barba left Telemundo and joined the Venezuelan TV network Venevisión.[9] Owners Gustavo and Ricardo Cisneros sent Barba to Azcárraga to propose that Televisa join Venevisión in an arrangement by which the two companies would work together to increase the international sales and distribution of the two companies' programming. The Cisneroses chose Barba to head the initiative, knowing that Barba was a U.S. citizen who was widely connected in U.S television and likely could stimulate Venevisión's U.S. distribution. Barba was also a key to the Cisneroses' plan of formalizing an association with Azcárraga. Indeed, Azcárraga, whose U.S. dealings with Univision had been stymied and confounded by Hallmark, welcomed Barba as an emissary who promised to reestablish Televisa as a programming force in the United States. Barba then sent Azcárraga and the Cisneroses to his former boss. Open to a partnership by which the others would share 20 percent ownership, Perenchio said that he would not purchase Univision unless Azcárraga provided programs at very low cost.

Azcárraga agreed. By the time Hallmark offered Univision to Perenchio, Azcárraga had agreed to a program licensing agreement that gave Univision exclusive rights to every Televisa program and cheap 9 percent fees for twenty-five years.

The Perenchio era commenced with his opening of Univision's corporate headquarters—his Los Angeles office complex in Century City—and Dávila's move there on January 4, 1993. He began by modeling rule one of his "Rules of the Road." Refusing to appear in public, he had his office issue a brief statement: "Hallmark has done an excellent job.... Now, with the investor group, we have an even broader range of capabilities."[10]

But Hallmark had passed him a financial albatross. It had bled $38 million in 1992 on annual sales of $200 million. Sales had never accelerated during Hallmark's five years, and few wanted to contemplate the hundreds of millions of dollars Univision had hemorrhaged during the Hallmark years.

* * *

The moment Perenchio hired him, Dávila recognized he needed to induce a fever to get to the cure. On his first day as network CEO that January, Dávila conferred with Ray Rodríguez, Univision's new network president and chief operating officer. Rodríguez proposed a bold step, that Univision engage in Spanish-language television's first campaign to pressure advertisers to pay amounts that were commensurate with those they paid the English-language networks. He insisted that the $200 million Hallmark had earned in 1992 should have been double that amount, that Hallmark had been soft in its dealings with ad agencies. He complained that ad agencies had gotten away with sponsoring programs on Univision at rates that were 20 percent of the amounts the programs would have generated had they been seen on ABC, CBS, NBC, or Fox.

Rodríguez proposed a doubling and tripling of the rates advertisers would pay to sponsor programs that were essential to reaching Latinos, such as *Sábado gigante* and *Cristina*. He admitted that the move was risky, that the agencies were certain to resist and might shift their spending to Telemundo. Yet he vowed to persist until Univision received fair payment.[11]

However, advertising was not the first issue that required resolution. Dávila and Rodríguez agreed that stabilizing Univision depended on reinstating programming from Televisa almost around the clock. This move was tricky. It meant canceling all remaining Univision-produced programs and firing scores of personnel. A third executive, Mario Rodríguez, joined Perenchio and Ray Rodríguez in weighing the options. Perenchio had retained Mario Rodríguez as program director and was about to promote him to vice president of programming.

One approach was to gradually phase out Univision's programs. The second Nielsen ratings were four weeks away. Because new programs disrupted viewing, broadcasters rarely changed content while approaching a ratings sweep. Univision needed to come first in the February sweep; its chances of turning a profit rode on projections of extra sales from having won the first ratings. Particularly when they were confronted with Univision's increased rates, advertisers might balk if Univision stumbled in the second round.

The alternative was to act at once. Even if it were rushed onto the schedule, a lineup of Televisa programs might enable Univision to get first place. The major advantage of this strategy was cost savings. The sooner Univision introduced Televisa programming, the sooner it could offset costs with the 91 percent of revenue on every Televisa program that Perenchio had negotiated in the PLA.

There was no debate. The best way to ensure Univision's future was to activate the PLA without delay. Perenchio and the two Rodríguezes opted for fast and decisive change.

On January 15, 1993, Ray Rodríguez informed Univision's 300 Miami employees that three prime-time programs, the newsmagazines *Portada* and *Al mediodia* and the variety show *Charytín internacional*, were canceled. That meant that seventy-five producers and talent had lost their jobs. He told his employees eighteen more Univision-produced programs would cease. Only three Univision programs, *Sábado gigante, Cristina,* and the news, would be spared.

By the end of the day, Univision was rocked by the beginning of what became perhaps the most painful spectacle in the annals of network television. Up to that point, Spanish-language television had not followed the practice of its English-language counterpart of canceling programs. Producers, creators, and talent worked in troupes. When a network chose to terminate a continuing program or when a fixed-duration program had lapsed, managers typically did not terminate the program's group of personnel. Instead, managers reassigned the personnel to new programs. Rodríguez intended to, and eventually did, initiate new programs. Many of those who were fired that day were to return. But as of January 15, Spanish-language television at Univision had new rules, and programs and personnel could be terminated.

Days later, the Doral facility still was reeling. Employees banded together and boycotted work assignments. There were bomb threats and hints of violence. Ray Rodríguez called in two armed guards. Inside the facility, the guards sealed off studios and the master control room; outside, police surrounded the complex. Deputies escorted executives to their offices. As this went on, the firings continued.[12] Univision also confronted a frenzy in local and national news media. "The press ravaged us for killing Univision" and did not report that in fact, "we were saving Univision," Rodríguez recalled.[13]

When the second Nielsen ratings commenced on January 27, calm had returned. The Doral facility had vacant studios and empty desks. Although they regretted the firings, Ray Rodríguez, and more directly Mario Rodríguez, had accomplished a feat. As eighteen Univision programs had vanished, eighteen from Televisa had premiered.[14]

The February 1993 Nielsen ratings arrived. At Univision, pain resumed. They had tied with Telemundo for a 50 percent share of the Spanish-speaking viewership.[15] Univision's rating had slid.

Perenchio was not happy. He blamed Ray Rodríguez for the anger that employees had directed toward him during the firings and for not containing the swell of local and then national publicity. Ray reminded Perenchio that they had agreed that the firings were necessary. But Perenchio was unrelenting; he grilled Mario Rodríguez about the rapid program changes that had brought a lower rating. Rodríguez did not enjoy being lectured by an owner who did not watch Spanish-language television and was unaware of what viewers were seeing. He tried to explain that Univision's viewers were confused and that Telemundo was rising in the ratings because Blaya's programs had improved.[16]

Perenchio's restlessness was illustrated in his willingness to include Barba as a target of his discontent. Years before, at WNJU, Barba had acquainted Perenchio with Spanish-language television. Perenchio trusted and relied on Barba and had rarely questioned his decisions. Only a year before, Perenchio had credited Barba for his initiative at Venevisión that had joined Perenchio, the Cisneroses, and Azcárraga and that had paved the way for Perenchio to acquire Azcárraga's prized programs. While Perenchio had named Davila, not Barba, as CEO, he had installed Barba in the important post of head of the division that managed the local stations Univision owned and operated. Sales generated by the owned stations accounted for more than half of Univision's profits. Yet Barba barely had begun as head of the owned stations when he realized that Perenchio was no longer inclined to preserve their long-standing and friendly relationship.

A signal development occurred when Barba succeeded in fulfilling one of Univision's most pressing needs: establishing an owned-and-operated station in Chicago, the third-largest U.S. market. Univision had long faced a problem in Chicago. When its first Chicago affiliate, WCIU, had joined in 1964, it had continued to air English-language programs. Its classic program *Soul Train* reached a national audience. The current affiliate, WSNS, which had joined in 1989, had switched back and forth between affiliating with Telemundo and affiliating with Univision. Barba was shaken by Perenchio's cold reaction when the situation finally was resolved. When Barba informed Perenchio that another Chicago station, WGBO-TV, was bankrupt, Perenchio instructed Barba to buy it. Barba did so. Yet rather than applauding Barba's acquisition of a long-needed owned station in Chicago, Perenchio berated him for paying too much; Barba had agreed to a price of $35 million. Barba answered that he had had no choice, that competing bids had pushed up the price. He was taken aback when Perenchio appeared to accept his explanation but then lectured him on his past "extravagances."[17]

After five months, tensions brought Univision to a crossroads. Perenchio, who despised Blaya for fleeing Univision for Telemundo and hiring Univision employees, did not heed warnings about Blaya's successes. And then word came of an initiative Blaya had orchestrated that demanded his attention. Both Mario Kreutzberger and Cristina Saralegui had told multiple parties that they, too, planned to leave; they were loyal to Blaya. They were moving the programs Blaya had birthed while at Univision, *Sábado gigante* and *Cristina,* to Telemundo. Kreutzberger and Saralegui had talked to Azcárraga, and it was known that Azcárraga had offered them opportunities to move to Televisa. Yet for weeks, Perenchio did not contact either star with a plan to ensure that they stayed at Univision.

But he did respond when he learned that Blaya had ordered Telemundo to resurrect production of its own network news. Since 1989, Telemundo's news program had been a Spanish-language newscast fed by Ted Turner's CNN. Turner's low-cost news had helped Telemundo avert bankruptcy. When he learned that Turner's news service was available, Perenchio contacted him. Turner's service would be much cheaper than the $20 million Univision was spending each year to produce its own news.

That May, Perenchio and Turner signed a contract to move CNN's Spanish-language newscasts to Univision. The agreement called for Univision to cancel the news programming it was producing, which meant closing its Miami newsroom and firing 100 employees. Turner would hire Univision news anchors Jorge Ramos and María Elena Salinas and move them to Atlanta. Perenchio told Dávila that the changes would happen immediately. Blaya's first Telemundo newscast was scheduled for June 3, and Perenchio wanted *CNN noticiero Univision* on the air that day.

Dávila instructed Ray Rodríguez to execute another round of firings immediately. This time, Rodríguez stalled. He was not sure that Perenchio knew about the order to close Univision's news division. "I was surprised," Rodríguez recalled, "because Perenchio did not consult me." When he told Mario Rodríguez what he had been ordered to do, Mario was furious. He resolved to resign.[18]

Insisting that the plan be reconsidered, Ray Rodríguez faxed Dávila six appeals.[19] Days passed and Dávila did not reply. Mario Rodríguez then prepared a 28-point indictment of CNN and sent it to Dávila on May 11. It spoke of "irreparable damage" that would include "inferior writing and production"; a location, Atlanta, that "lacks appeal for Hispanic media professionals"; and "stories of little importance to U.S. Hispanics." Rodríguez also pointed out "CNN's inferior ratings." Even "in English, they barely deliver [a] 1.0."[20] Dávila did not answer.

On May 17, Ray Rodríguez flew to Los Angeles. Unannounced, he appeared at Century City and asked for a meeting with Perenchio on a day

Figure 11. Ray Rodríguez (*left*) and Mario Rodríguez (*right*) are greeted by Venevisión owner Gustavo Cisneros during Univision's first visit to Caracas in February 1993. Upon Jerry Perenchio's takeover of Univision, Venevisión became part owner. Recently named president, Ray Rodríguez was the architect of Univision's 1990s rise as a TV power. As vice president, Mario Rodríguez masterminded Univision's numerous programming feats. Photo courtesy of Mario Rodríguez.

when Ricardo Cisneros of Venevisión was visiting. A perturbed Perenchio asked Cisneros to step outside and met with Rodríguez. Referring to notes related to the memo he had sent Dávila, Rodríguez urged Perenchio to disengage with CNN and keep Univision's news program. Then he left.

Returning to Miami, Rodríguez expected he might be fired for arriving unannounced, disrupting a meeting, and challenging Perenchio's decisions. But the next day, Perenchio called to say that he had canceled the CNN contract and that Univision's news would remain.[21]

Mario Rodríguez soon had occasion to talk with Perenchio, who told him what had happened after Ray Rodríguez had left his office. Baffled by the surprise appearance of the Univision president who had traveled from Miami for a momentary meeting in Los Angeles, Cisneros asked Perenchio why he had come. When Perenchio explained that he had canceled Univision's news programming in order to save millions of dollars, Cisneros said he was "foolish" for targeting the news. "Don't you realize Univision will die without its heart?" he asked. He then reminded Perenchio that he and Azcárraga could veto any contract any of the three had signed with a U.S. television provider and told Perenchio that he was using his veto now.[22]

Cisneros had saved Univision's news programming. The episode provoked a turning point. Perenchio admitted his mistake. When he apologized and conceded he needed Univision's help, tensions dissipated. While employees still were unsure about a non-Latino profit-centric owner, they began to trust him. Ramos later recalled that this is the point when employees began to believe that "the things he was doing were in the best interests of Univision's mission." Perenchio "never [again] interfered with the news" and "became the greatest owner a journalist could ever have."[23]

Perenchio greatly needed the help he had requested. The ratings remained at a stalemate. Worse, advertisers, aghast at Univision's increased advertising rates, shifted their spending to Telemundo. Univision ended 1993 with $105 million in revenue, far less than Hallmark's trifling $200 million the year before, and its greatest loss to date: $40 million.[24]

* * *

Like SIN in the 1970s, Telemundo had its equivalent of a "golden age." But it was much briefer; it lasted only for the first five months of 1993. Telemundo had entered the year on the upswing of a delicate yet favorable turn of events when owner Saul Steinberg had persuaded creditors not to foreclose. The creditors could not bring themselves to walk away from the gold that everyone said Spanish-language television could generate. Impressed by Blaya's determination, they continued to wait.

After bolting from Perenchio and joining Telemundo in May 1992, Blaya pushed for the same commitment to domestic production that had defined his tenure at Univision. When Telemundo lost the November 1992 Nielsen ratings, Blaya blamed program changes that were still in progress. He was confronting a factor that was to prove a serious constraint:

Figure 12. Telemundo founder Saul Steinberg (*right*) welcomes former Univision president Joaquín Blaya as Telemundo's president in 1992. Blaya had brief success in 1993. He nearly succeeded in moving Univision's two hit U.S. programs, *Sábado gigante* and *Cristina,* to Telemundo. Telemundo's bankruptcy in 1993 and Univision's soaring Nielsen ratings led to Blaya's dismissal in 1995. Photo courtesy of Joaquín Blaya.

Telemundo still broadcast from the converted warehouse in Hialeah. It was not the "Hispanic Hollywood" that Blaya had begun at Doral.

By January, Blaya had replaced Telemundo's preponderance of foreign films and telenovelas with a schedule heavy in Hialeah-produced reality shows. One of them, *Ocurrió así* (It Happened Like This), the first "tabloid" newsmagazine any network had carried in prime time, broke out as Telemundo's first hit show. It reassembled many former Univision staff who had joined Telemundo. Its host, former Univision news anchor Enrique Gratas, emerged as Telemundo's first celebrity.

The program proved that Telemundo was willing to push limits to get attention. It attracted the attention of national media, and in forums on declining mass media ethics, participants discussed its broadcast of a video of a domestic disturbance at a cemetery that ended with a shooting and homicide that viewers saw up close. Observers complained that *Ocurrió así*'s showcase of the killing was a ploy that Telemundo was using to increase its ratings. And the ratings did go up.[25]

Blaya opened other new territory, this time without controversy: Telemundo began producing the first U.S.-made telenovelas. After *Marielena*, Blaya debuted *Guadalupe, El peñón del amaranto,* and *Tres destinos*. Telemundo's novelas lacked the stars and polish of their foreign counterparts, but they demonstrated the genre's prospects for production in the United States.

Fifteen original programs rolled from the Hialeah studios. They contributed to Telemundo's 50 percent share in the February 1993 Nielsen ratings. While Univision was reeling, Telemundo was bounding with high morale. Blaya promoted the programs with ads and videos that conveyed the message ¡Arriba, Telemundo, Arriba!²⁶

The programs Blaya really wanted were *Sábado gigante* and *Cristina*. That May, Blaya was stunned to discover that Perenchio had finally listened to the appeals of his executives and had reached out to Saralegui. While Saralegui was still under contract to Univision and the network owned her program, provisions of the arrangement permitted her to leave Univision and launch a new program at a different network when her contract expired. Although the contract was not due to expire for several months, Perenchio invited Saralegui and her agents to join him in renegotiating the contract's terms. When Blaya heard this, he contacted Saralegui and promised to exceed Perenchio's latest terms. Yet as the process unfolded, it became clear that Blaya was no match for one of the most seasoned negotiators in the United States. Saralegui told Blaya that she had decided not to move. Although Saralegui was indebted to Blaya, Perenchio had "showed [that] he cared in a special way." Although he had not offered her a substantially larger salary, he "knew how to say [in a personal way] he wanted me to stay at Univision," she later said.²⁷

Yet for many more months, *Sábado gigante* appeared certain to become a Telemundo program. Kreutzberger's loyalty to Blaya overpowered even Perenchio's overtures. However, another factor was more salient. Kreutzberger could not perform *Sábado gigante* in Telemundo's cramped facilities. Blaya went to Steinberg and requested funds for expansion. Steinberg's refusal hinted at trouble. Explaining to Blaya that "Telemundo didn't have a big enough studio," Kreutzberger remained at Univision. "It hurt me that our show's success hurt Joaquín," he said.²⁸

Blaya countered the setback. On June 3, 1993, he canceled CNN's newscast and premiered *Noticiero Telemundo* again with the "dream team" that he had assembled at Univision in 1981 and that had ushered in the

Telemundo network in 1987. That day, he also announced a partnership with Reuters for a 24-hour news channel called TeleNoticias.

Five days later on June 8, 1993, Telemundo's golden age ended. Without notice, its creditors went to U.S. Bankruptcy Court in New York and sued for recovery of the $300 million Reliance owed them. When the day ended, Steinberg owned the first bankrupt television network in the United States.[29] The court ordered Steinberg to initiate Chapter 11 proceedings.

Blaya was shattered. He later recalled that "I looked at all this and said to myself, 'Telemundo is not going to survive this thing.'"[30] The reason the creditors had moved traced back to Harry Silverman's sale of stock back in 1987. Most of the cash came from stock Leon Black of Drexel Burnham Lambert had purchased. The lucrative dealings of Black and his associate Michael Milken had rocketed Drexel Burnham Lambert to immense financial success. In the late 1980s, many regarded Drexel to be a household name. However, in 1990, Black resigned just before his company crashed, and Milken was convicted on ninety-eight counts of security fraud.

Because Black and his Apollo Group were Telemundo's largest creditor, Blaya worried about Black's practice of buying distressed firms like Telemundo, dismembering their holdings, and selling the separate holdings at a price that was high enough to fund the original buy. This practice, known as leveraged buyout, had damaged Black's reputation and sent Milken to prison.

Black recommended favorable bankruptcy terms. Returning to court on July 30, he and the creditors agreed to extinguish the debt by acquiring 25 percent of Telemundo's shares, then returning the shares when Telemundo's stock had risen in value, enabling Reliance to pay for and redeem them. The "win-win" plan required that the price of the stock increase. Much of Telemundo's stock remained on the open market. Because raising the price of the stock required increasing revenue, the plan presumed that Telemundo's Nielsen ratings would increase. "The network is worth saving. It just needs to restructure itself and get on with its future," Wilbur Ross of the Apollo Group proclaimed.[31]

Yet by the end of the year, Telemundo's stock price had not increased. An unforeseen development had pushed investors away: Telemundo's Nielsen share had fallen. In November 1993, Univision attracted 48 percent of the total Spanish-language audience and Telemundo had attracted 42 percent. As 1994 began, Blaya pledged that Telemundo would quickly return to first place.[32]

Instead, Telemundo's ratings continued to decline. A revised bankruptcy plan was imminent when in February 1994 Univision finished with a 60 percent share and Telemundo with 40 percent. When Telemundo's stock price dropped, Steinberg averted foreclosure by giving more shares to creditors. After the next ratings in May 1994, the bankruptcy plan began to unravel. Univision again claimed a 60:40 advantage. More shares went to the creditors. By summer, they owned half of Telemundo.[33]

It was apparent that something had happened that had driven viewers to Univision. The network's nightly news program proved popular, and its newscasting team of Jorge Ramos and María Elena Salinas had gelled. *Noticiero Univision* had become a fixture in millions of Latino homes. Univision's other U.S. programs, *Sábado gigante* and *Cristina,* consistently ranked near the top of the Nielsen ratings. In 1993, Univision began broadcasting *Sábado gigante* throughout Mexico on Televisa. The program was seen in thirty other countries.

In addition, Univision had enlarged its reach by investing in stronger stations and affiliates. Although the $35 million purchase price for Chicago's WGBO had rankled Perenchio, Univision's ownership of it had proved to be a boon; it became one of television's most viewed and most profitable local stations. Yet most of Univision's increasing success was accomplished with the combination of the PLA Perenchio had negotiated and Univision's use of Televisa's programming.

Univision's ratings rose when it resumed scheduling telenovelas throughout prime time. First, Univision ordered a lineup of basic novelas that would sustain viewers for hours each night. Univision also worked with Televisa with the idea of selecting blockbuster novelas for ratings periods. As programmer Carlos Flys later related, the idea centered on "using Mexico as one giant focus group." From the "ratings in Mexico, we knew which novelas would be hits in the U.S., and those were the ones we took."[34]

That fall, Dávila arranged for Univision to broadcast a novela that had set ratings records in Mexico. *Marimar* was the second installment of the *María* anthology that starred Thalia Sodi. Two years before, the first installment had secured Univision's victory in the first Nielsen ratings. Univision announced that *Marimar* would debut in October 1994 and headline the opening of its 1994–1995 season.[35]

Broadcast throughout the ratings sweep that November, *Marimar* scored some of the highest ratings Nielsen had ever reported. On some nights, the novela captured 80 percent of the Spanish-language viewing audience. Univision's audience was twice the size of Telemundo's.[36]

For the second time, *María* altered events in Spanish-language television. That December at Telemundo, in an effort to appease the network's creditors, Steinberg announced a reorganization. However, reacting to the high ratings *María* and Univision had amassed, they forced Steinberg to yield all of the shares that were left. On January 3, 1995, almost exactly eight years after it launched Telemundo, Reliance bade it farewell. Telemundo emerged from Chapter 11 with Black as its owner.[37]

Black issued statements affirming that he would continue the network, but the other creditors confronted him and demanded that he dismantle and sell it. Outraged, he told the press "it's not [their] job to peddle Telemundo" and that the "company's not for sale."[38] Black turned to his associate, Roland Hernández, an investor who owned KFWD, Telemundo's Dallas affiliate. Hernández told Black of partnership opportunities with Hollywood studios and a new Mexican network called TV Azteca. Huddling with Hernández, Black did not confer with Blaya.

When Black took over, Blaya's twenty-five years in Spanish-language television came to an end. On March 1, Black asked Blaya to resign. Hernández became both the head of Telemundo and its CEO.[39] Furious with Black, Blaya wound up indirectly praising Perenchio, the person he had been furious with three years earlier. "At the risk of oversimplification," he said, Telemundo's failing "is directly attributable to our lack of access to Mexican telenovelas."[40]

* * *

Blaya was not the only pioneer figure Spanish-language television lost around this time. On April 10, 1994, Barba violated rule one of Perenchio's "Rules of the Road" when he gave an interview to the *New York Times*.[41] Perenchio fired him, saying "I cannot accept what you have done."[42] Perenchio also nearly fired Ray Rodríguez for appearing on the cover of *Broadcasting* but instead fined him $25,000.

On September 20, 1995, at the age of sixty-nine, Rene Anselmo died of heart complications. His funeral was a reminder of the rancor that Spanish-language television had never overcome. Anselmo's longtime associates from Spanish International, Emilio Nicolás and Danny Villanueva, stayed away. Both had become wealthy from the sale of Spanish International nine years earlier, but both believed that Anselmo's self-interest had led to the demise of a venture they had cherished and that they had dedicated their professional lives to for twenty-five years.

Blaya did attend, but he was reluctant, knowing that Perenchio would be there. Dávila viewed Anselmo's passing as "one of [his] most heartbreaking experiences" and contacted the producers of *Noticiero Univision* to offer to assist with their on-air tribute to Anselmo. Not only had they planned no tribute, "they didn't even know who he was," Dávila lamented.[43]

While Perenchio had hired him, Dávila remained an employee and protégé of Emilio Azcárraga. When Azcárraga could not attend Anselmo's funeral because of illness, Dávila had an inkling he might soon be attending another funeral. However, Dávila was absorbed in a different concern. Trouble in Mexico that was draining Azcárraga was testing Dávila's loyalty to Perenchio and Univision in the United States. New difficulties surrounded Televisa; it needed revenue. Knowing where it might come from, Dávila had decided that he needed to broach a difficult subject with Perenchio: renegotiating the PLA.

Televisa's turmoil stemmed from the collapse of the one-party rule of the Partido Revolucionario Institucional (PRI). For sixty years, it had protected the Azcárragas' monopoly. In 1994, Mexico's economy had faltered and the Mexican central bank had floated the peso. This was a mistake; the peso immediately lost half its value. Mexicans repudiated the PRI. En masse, they elected leaders from the rival Partido Acción Nacional (PAN). Determined to open Mexican television to other networks, the PAN instituted a rival network called TV Azteca. For the first time Azcárraga faced competition. Meanwhile, Televisa's revenue, which was tied to the peso, plummeted. Azcárraga fired 5,000 employees.[44]

When Dávila and Perenchio met, the relationship between Televisa and Univision was chilly. Dávila hoped that Perenchio would recognize that because Univision was paying only 9 percent of its revenue to Televisa, it was feasting unfairly on programs that were setting ratings records. Perenchio flatly refused to negotiate a new contract that would pay Televisa more. As Perenchio's second-in-command, Dávila was not in a position to press the issue. From 1994 to early 1996, Azcárraga sent others to Century City to push for a new agreement, but they too failed. Perenchio sent them away, saying "a contract is a contract." Although Azcárraga backed down and Televisa's finances eventually improved, Perenchio's intransigence bothered Televisa executives.

Perenchio was not ready to reveal the reason he would not let go of the PLA. He had embarked on his signal initiative as Univision owner and needed every dollar he could get: he was arranging the first public sale of Univision stock. Since 1961, the company had been held by private owners. All along, Perenchio had planned to put Univision on the open market. It was a risky move, yet only by allowing investors to purchase stock could Univision's fortune be unlocked.

Perenchio's move was motivated by the fact that in 1994 and 1995, Ray Rodríguez had succeeded in convincing ad agencies to pay more to advertise on Univision. For the first time in Spanish-language television, national advertisers paid amounts commensurate with those they paid the English-language networks. As Rodríguez told Perenchio, it was "100 percent on the dollar."[45] After plummeting to annual revenue of $105 million in 1993, Univision's revenue was more than $300 million by the end of 1995. The current year, 1996, had barely begun when Rodríguez informed Perenchio that year-end revenue would approach $450 million and that the network would report its first-ever profit.

In early 1996, Perenchio secretly reorganized Univision as a public firm. He went to New York and enlisted Donaldson, Lufkin & Jenrette; Goldman Sachs; and Morgan Stanley. They wrote Univision's initial purchase offer, or IPO.[46] Ray Rodríguez and Chief Financial Officer Andrew Hobson made stops in numerous cities during the IPO's "roadshow." They met with brokers to pitch a company with soaring revenue, a goldmine program contract, and a 70 percent share of a booming Latino market.

On September 26, 1996, Univision executives unfurled a Univision banner on the speaker's platform above the trading floor of the New York Stock Exchange and rang the opening bell. With an IPO of nine million shares at $23 and the symbol UVN, Univision became the newest member of the exchange.[47] That morning Perenchio eagerly watched TV's financial channels. He remarked, "We are in the major leagues."[48]

Wall Street still knew little about Spanish-language television, and Univision's only hard assets were UHF TV stations. The $23 price seemed high. Perenchio was the most exposed; he owned the equivalent of ten million shares. He would lose $10 million for every point the stock dropped.

Perenchio's risky move paid off. By the end of the day, all nine million shares had sold and the price of Univision stock had jumped to $30. On November 30, Univision closed at $40. Perenchio was $250 million richer.

On December 31, the stock closed at $50. That day, Univision posted its first profit. It finished 1996 with $13 million in profits on record revenue of $460 million. When trading resumed after the New Year's holiday, investors were still buying.

Perenchio's conquest had involved Univision's programming division. Mario Rodríguez later recalled that before the IPO, Perenchio had told him, "It would be great if we could have good ratings when our stock starts to sell."[49] Rodríguez did not let him down. The IPO went out September 26. Four days later, on September 30, Univision premiered *María la del barrio*. Thalia Sodi had returned for the final installment of the *María* trilogy.[50] The first installment in 1992 had decided the first Nielsen ratings; the second in 1994 had forced Reliance to sell Telemundo.

María la del barrio earned the highest Nielsen rating ever for Spanish-language television. Its 75 percent share in the Hispanic survey was second only to the 80 percent share Milton Berle's *Texaco Star Theatre* had earned in the very first Nielsen ratings in 1948.[51] The six-month novela dominated the next ratings in February 1997.

Throughout those six months, Univision published large display ads in trade magazines and newspapers, including the *Wall Street Journal*. In each new ad, tallies of the novela's ratings accompanied bar charts showing Univision's advantage over Telemundo: 80 percent versus 20 percent in the Nielsen ratings. The publicity contributed to investors' scramble for Univision stock during the six months. When the stock reached $100 per share that spring, Perenchio's 10 million shares were worth $1 billion. He had become the first billionaire in Spanish-language television.[52] For the third time, *María* had changed the direction of the industry.

But as *María la del barrio* completed its historic U.S. run, an off-screen soap opera commenced. Doctors had diagnosed Azcárraga with terminal cancer. Dávila resigned as Univision's network CEO and rushed to Mexico City. There, he entered a crisis. Azcárraga had refused to pass the reins to his 29-year-old son, Emilio Azcárraga Jean. Azcárraga argued that his son was too weak to run the mammoth firm. Elbowing for control, executives vied for Azcárraga's imprimatur. However, in March, weak and failing, Azcárraga came to terms with his son's inheritance. He named Azcárraga Jean his successor. He died on April 18.

Televisa interrupted programming for an announcement that was simulcast on all four of its TV networks. Jacobo Zabludovsky choked up on camera. Amazingly, Televisa reporters had to track down the story.

Azcárraga had fled Mexico and escaped to the city he had once hated, Miami. It was on a boat moored at Miami Beach that The Tiger passed away.

* * *

Around the time of Azcárraga's passing, Perenchio convened another retreat, this time to introduce Henry Cisneros as Univision's corporate chief operating officer. Since acquiring Univision in 1992, Perenchio had reserved the title of corporate chief executive officer for himself. Yet much as it had at the retreat five years earlier, the PLA dominated his discussion. This time, though, Perenchio did not forecast clear air.

He began with an ominous report on the change in leadership at Televisa. Mario Rodríguez later recalled that Perenchio was concerned about moves that might force him to give up the PLA. He recounted Azcárraga's deathbed approval of Azcárraga Jean as his successor. Perenchio predicted a power struggle that would elevate whoever rolled the most heads. The victor was certain to strong-arm Perenchio to the bargaining table.

There was another reason that Perenchio was expecting a renewed dispute. Univision's projected revenue for 1998 was $600 million. Perenchio could no longer claim that he could not pay higher fees. The giant Televisa network had annual revenue of $1.3 billion. Univision was approaching half that amount.

Another issue ensured that Televisa would demand fair pay. Perenchio had convinced the late Azcárraga to sign the PLA by signing warrants, documents that give a recipient the first right to purchase a company's stock in the future. Perenchio had stipulated that Azcárraga could eventually purchase Univision at an agreed-upon price—that is, if the FCC eliminated the rule against foreign ownership.[53] Azcárraga had coveted the warrants because in 1992, the FCC, which was headlong into deregulation, had proposed revoking the rule.[54] But in 1996, Congress approved a rewritten Telecommunications Act and the rule remained.

Perenchio issued a surprising directive. After eliminating domestic production in 1993, he wanted Univision to resume making its own programs. He affirmed that under no circumstances would Univision limit Univision's access to Televisa's vast storehouse of programs or renegotiate the PLA. Yet according to Mario Rodríguez, "he was uncomfortable that we were so dependent on their programs." He feared that the new regime at Televisa "would wave the PLA in our face" and "cause us a lot of trouble."[55] Immediately, Perenchio assigned network president Ray Rodríguez the tasks of developing new Univision-produced content and informing Televisa of that change.

Perenchio was aware that Univision's renewed domestic production and displacement of Televisa programs would infuriate Televisa's new leader, Azcárraga Jean, who was fighting for control. Perenchio did not authorize many new shows; he allowed only daytime talk shows and reality programs. In April 1997, with the premiere of *Despierta América* (Wake Up America), a two-hour morning talk show similar to NBC's *Today* show, the Doral facilities came back to life.

Perenchio excited observers and Univision's 1,500 employees when he named Cisneros to the post of corporate chief operating officer.[56] He had recently stepped down as President Bill Clinton's secretary of housing and urban development. He had been the first Latino cabinet member. Previously, he had won acclaim and popularity as the mayor of San Antonio.

On May 14, 1997, Cisneros hosted Univision's maiden appearance at television's premier annual spectacular called the upfronts, gatherings of television industry personnel to sell air time to advertisers. In New York, Univision joined ABC, CBS, NBC, and Fox in courting advertisers during lavish fall previews. Attendees crowded to witness a former presidential cabinet member serving as emcee. According to *Electronic Media*, Univision "stole the show." Advertisers placed orders with Univision totaling $155 million.[57]

Analysts, though, were perplexed about why Cisneros had downplayed the Televisa programs on Univision's schedule. His presentation showcased Univision's new breakfast show. He also touted a forthcoming prime-time Monday night broadcast of *Cristina* and another Univision daytime program, a news magazine series called *Primer impacto*, which also would be seen one night a week in prime time. In *Broadcasting & Cable*, David Tobenkin surmised that "disagreements" over "a deal that locks in [Perenchio's] right to Televisa [content] through 2017" may "cloud the panorama of good news for Univision." Because it was relying on "more than [Televisa's] telenovelas," he wrote, Univision seemed to need to prove that it could "deal from a position of strength."[58]

Another mystery swirled at the 1997 upfronts: Leon Black canceled Telemundo's presentation. By the summer of that year, curiosity had swelled. Several broadcasters told different sources that they had offered to purchase the network. Finally, that August, Black confirmed that the network was for sale. During his two years as Telemundo's owner, Black had done

Figure 13. A key moment in the Perenchio era was his decision to reduce Univision's dependence on Televisa programming beginning with its own morning broadcast, *Despierta América,* seen during its first broadcast on April 14, 1997. Perenchio agreed to revive domestic production because of fears that new Televisa leaders would fight to revoke the one-sided programming contract he and Azcárraga Milmo had signed in 1992. Azcárraga Milmo died two days after *Despierta América* premiered. Photo courtesy of Mario Rodríguez.

all he could. He brought in Danny Villanueva, now a multimillionaire banker from investments of his $10 million share of the sale of Spanish International in 1986. Villanueva provided an infusion of cash. Supporting Black's ownership and direction, Villanueva became a minority owner and board member of Telemundo when his Bastion Capital corporation invested $75 million in Black's Telemundo Division. Under Telemundo's president Roland Hernandez, who also had invested funds and obtained a minority ownership, the network had formed a consortium of Hollywood studios, and his partnership with TV Azteca had given the network access to Mexican novelas.

But against Univision's Nielsen share of 80 percent, Telemundo's 20 percent had repelled advertisers. It was losing the equivalent of $2 million every month. For the second time in three years, its future as a Spanish-language network, even as a network at all, was in doubt. All of the reported potential buyers were English-language broadcasters who were interested in forming new networks and who were prospecting for the local stations Telemundo owned. Fox TV founder Barry Diller was prominent among that group. *Variety* reported "a change of identity at Telemundo—a switch to English-language broadcasting."[59]

Yet Telemundo went on to become one of the world's twenty largest corporations. On November 24, 1997, Black sold Telemundo to Sony for $540 million. Sony's entry marked the arrival of numerous names that were familiar in the TV industry but that were new to Spanish-language television. Instantly, those who had joined Telemundo trumpeted the network as Sony's new engine of global mass communication. The fact that plans called for its union with Sony's formidable subsidiary, Columbia Pictures, brought a historical touch; Columbia Pictures had conceived Telemundo twenty-seven years earlier.

Incoming Telemundo CEO Jon Feltheimer proclaimed that the network was the "centerpiece of [Sony's] worldwide programming strategy." Sony president Jeff Sagansky emphasized the huge firm's "ability [to] make Telemundo extremely competitive."[60]

Press accounts began offering a new story line about Telemundo. *Electronic Media* and *Broadcasting & Cable* both reported a "transformation" at Telemundo and an impending network "showdown." The latter observed that "a potent mix of new Telemundo shows" would challenge Univision's "tiring array" of imported content.[61]

Experts noted that Sony's rival media giants were dabbling only with cable channels. The largest, Time Warner, reached only a few Latinos with HBO Olé, CNN en Español, and the Spanish Cartoon Network. Disney, the owner of ABC, sputtered with ESPN Deportes. Viacom, the owner of CBS, had twice relaunched MTV Latino. It purchased and then shut down Blaya's news channel TeleNoticias. English-language cable channels flourished because their audiences could pay cable subscriptions of almost $100 every month. Only Sony recognized that most Latino families could not afford such fees and that free-to-air channels attracted large Latino audiences.

No one was more impressed than Perenchio. That December, he had Univision's attorneys file a suit to block Sony's acquisition of Telemundo. Univision alleged that Sony's takeover violated the foreign ownership rule. Although the FCC agreed to study the complaint, Telemundo's direct Japanese ownership was within the 25 percent legal limit. (The FCC had recently increased the proportion of a U.S. broadcast property that non-U.S.

companies and individuals could own from 20 to 25 percent.) "It is obvious that Univision is a competitor that sees the end of its dominance coming. And they are obviously concerned and want to delay the inevitable as long as they can," Donald Tringall, Telemundo's new executive vice president, said.[62]

* * *

As observers awaited the showdown, there was little notice of an issue that was unfolding at Univision. At its Fresno station, KFTV, employees confronted management with claims that Univision's compensation was inferior to what their colleagues in English-language TV were paid and attempted to form a union. When Univision refused a union contract, several staged a wildcat strike. One journalist reported that "station workers have likened the situation to the historic exploitation of Hispanic workers."[63]

Cisneros went to Fresno and resolved the issue. Although that was the only such episode, the Fresno flare-up was symptomatic of a discontent that had grown inside Univision. While Perenchio had secured the network, many employees felt disrespected by the person one staff member later would term "the head gringo in charge."[64]

No one publicly accused Perenchio of being a racist, but many Univision employees suspected that he was. His role in the 1996 election had disturbed them. Perenchio had contributed $500,000 to the campaign of California Republican governor Pete Wilson, a leading opponent of immigration reform. Employees had applauded Perenchio's appointment of Cisneros as Univision's chief operating officer, yet in the reorganization that accompanied the IPO, Perenchio had appointed Anglo executives to newly created posts. The term "cloroxification" again was heard.

Ray Rodríguez was aware of the complaints and believed that "they were wrong." He insisted that not having any Anglo representation inside Univision would risk the well-being of the network and thus employees' jobs. "The fact was you were selling to English advertisers," he said. There were few Spanish-language advertisers and "that was our struggle." To survive, "you had to have Anglos who were connected to English-language advertisers."[65]

What most bothered employees was Perenchio's refusal to acknowledge Spanish-language television. When visitors entered Univision facilities, they did not see portraits of Univision's programs and stars. Perenchio displayed paintings and artwork. Nothing was more crushing than reading Univision's annual reports. They were beautifully published coffee-table works, but they never pictured Univision. They featured color photographs of works by Rembrandt and Matisse. One employee later said that Perenchio made the "doing [of] Spanish-language television [seem] like selling crack cocaine."[66]

Perenchio soon dissolved much of the stigma. Cisneros quickly had excelled in his post. When he became Univision's chief operating officer, Cisneros had moved to Los Angeles, where he worked near Perenchio at the Century City complex. Respected and charismatic, Cisneros bolstered Univision's profile among regulators in Washington, advertisers in New York, and the general public. He was more than a figurehead; he had spurred Univision's soaring sales initiatives.

But in December 1997, a grand jury indicted Cisneros on eighteen counts of lying to the FBI about an extramarital affair. Because Cisneros was expected to return to politics and was a likely vice presidential candidate in the 2000 general election, the press subjected him to a crucifixion. At Univision, many understood that Cisneros had to step down.

They were won over when Perenchio came to his defense, not once but twice. He silenced the press with a statement that Cisneros would remain Univision's chief operating officer. Then, when Cisneros entered a guilty plea, Perenchio put out another statement saying that Cisneros could stay for as long as he wanted.[67] The moves were stunning and signaled sincerity, for to have hired and twice defended Cisneros, a politician, Perenchio had disobeyed his "Rules of the Road."

At Telemundo, Feltheimer moved rapidly on what he termed the "repositioning" of the network. In January 1998, he announced a "massive rollout" of new programs for the 1998–1999 season.[68] By spring, the press had noticed two young, charismatic rising executives. They were the faces of the "new" Telemundo. Feltheimer had hired former CBS Entertainment president Peter Tortorici as Telemundo's new network president. He also named 34-year-old Nely Galán as president of Telemundo's programming division. In 1986, Galán had succeeded Barba as the head of WNJU. She was twenty-three at the time; she was the youngest person ever to manage a major market television station. *Broadcasting & Cable* profiled Tortorici and Galán in its November 9, 1998, edition. Headlined as "Telemundo's Turnaround Tandem," they appeared on the cover.[69]

As Telemundo rolled out its fall 1998 schedule, Tortorici promised a "sea change in Spanish television" that would make Univision's foreign fare seem outmoded. "We're going to create programming unique to the experience of Hispanics in the United States," he stated. Galán explained that "Latinos are not a race. We're a culture with many races inside, and nobody ever gets that." She added, "This mission we're on is very important, not just from a business sense but also socially. It's rare to get a job ... where you get to do the right thing too."[70]

Then came the unveiling. Viewers saw Spanish-language versions of shows that resembled *Laverne and Shirley, Hart to Hart, Vegas,* and *Happy Days.* "If I had to describe the ideal model, it would be ABC in [the] '70s," Tortorici said.[71] *Ángeles* was a down-to-the-logo remake of the 1970s version of *Charlie's Angels. Solo en América,* a remake of *One Day at a Time,* portrayed the comedic travails of two middle-class teenage sisters. In *Reyes y Rey,* a remake of *Starsky and Hutch,* two young immigration detectives cruised the border in speeding sports cars.

The result was one of the greatest ratings disasters in the history of network television. Telemundo entered the November 1998 Nielsen ratings with a 20 percent share that later decreased to 15 percent.[72] *Media Week* reported that Sony and Telemundo "appear to have failed," *Electronic Media* that they had "bombed." *Hispanic Market Weekly* conducted a forum. Experts savaged Telemundo's ineffective reading of the Latino community, misleading publicity, and failure to acknowledge the success of its competitor. One complained that "our focus groups tell us that the acculturalization trend is stopping. Second generation Hispanics are making sure their children learn Spanish. So why doesn't Telemundo look for the next great novela?"[73]

For Perenchio, Telemundo's experience provided a lesson on the merits of his "Rules of the Road." Basking in press adulation, Tortorici and Galán had tipped off Univision to every part of their strategy. Alerted to Telemundo's slant toward young viewers, Univision introduced the first prime-time schedule geared toward particular demographics. There was a teen novela at 7:00 P.M., a family novela at 8:00, and an adult novela at 9:00.[74] Also alerted to Telemundo's lack of a fallback plan, Univision tested and premiered more of its own shows. One of them, *El gordo y la flaca* (The Fat and the Skinny), became a hit.

Univision's audience share rose to 85 percent. Ramon Piñeda of Caballero Spanish Media cautioned that "after an 85 share, the only way they can go is down."[75] He was wrong. In the next ratings in February 1999,

Figure 14. Cristina Saralegui poses during a commemorative Univision photo shoot in 1999 occasioned by the network's succession of awards and ratings triumphs as the millennium approached. Then in its twelfth year, Saralegui's afternoon broadcast *Cristina* was one of the most viewed U.S. television programs in any language. Photo courtesy of Mario Rodríguez.

Univision scored 92 percent and Telemundo 8 percent.[76] Weeks later, Sony fired Tortorici and Galán. Before he, too, was fired, Feltheimer rushed a return of Telemundo's foreign programs.

Nineteen-ninety-eight was to Univision what 1927 had been to the New York Yankees. The Radio Television News Directors Association named KMEX's *Noticias 34* as the nation's best television newscast. It honored *Primer impacto* with the Edward R. Murrow Award.[77] The Academy of Television Arts and Sciences awarded Emmys to *Noticiero Univision*, *Sábado gigante*, and *Cristina*. In June, President Clinton praised Univision's telecast of the U.S.-Iran World Cup soccer game as a diplomatic gesture aimed at "ending the estrangement between our nations."[78]

The year also witnessed landmarks in the Nielsen ratings. Univision not only averaged 80 percent of all viewers in Nielsen's Hispanic survey, but

Figure 15. Mario Kreutzberger joins the cast of *Sábado gigante* in Univision's 1999 commemorative photo shoot. To Kreutzberger's left is the black-hooded "El Chacal de la Trompeta," who played the role of nemesis to "Don Francisco" in one of the program's most popular skits. Photo courtesy of Mario Rodríguez.

its huge audiences also began to affect and transform Nielsen's English-language ratings. In 1998, its KMEX was far and away number one in Los Angeles. Its WLTV was number one in Miami. In both cities, Univision's Spanish-language stations had more viewers than any of the English-language stations.

Univision's daily average cumulative audience of 17 million soon broke into Nielsen's main rankings. With a 3 percent share of the entire national audience, Univision trailed ABC, CBS, NBC, and Fox, but not by much. Univision publicized its new status as the "fifth-largest network in any language."[79]

That year, Univision reported $80 million in profits on $700 million in sales. On Wall Street, Univision split $60 shares at two for one. But within months, the value of the stock zoomed back up to $60. Stockholders doubled their money.[80]

* * *

It was not a banner year for Televisa. In the months that followed the passing of Emilio Azcárraga, Televisa's executive headquarters was the site of the battle royal that Perenchio had foreseen. The hierarchy preyed on the young, shy, and pampered Emilio Azcárraga Jean. A faction of Televisa executives and Mexican business leaders joined forces to overthrow him. His cousin briefly seized control.[81]

But Azcárraga Jean prevailed. Rising against dozens of Televisa vice presidents and officials, he fired them one by one. An inside report in *Business Week* affirmed that Azcárraga Jean was not shy about using strong-arm measures to purge rivals and assert command. The magazine reported that Azcárraga Jean had abandoned a lifestyle of "starlets" and "racy cars." He now traveled in armored vehicles flanked by bodyguards.[82]

Observers were surprised not only by his backstage resolve but also by a candid public persona. The public's first glimpse of Azcárraga Jean was from interviews in which he criticized his father. He confirmed reports that his father had left Televisa with $1.8 billion in debts. Soon after that, he hinted that Televisa's finances were constrained because of his father's "1992 programming agreement with Univision." Azcárraga Jean argued that the agreement was outdated and in need of revision, and he expressed confidence that "Univision will see our common interests."[83]

Although he could not remember the date and the setting, Perenchio later testified that he first met the 31-year-old Azcárraga Jean in early 1999. As Perenchio feared, Azcárraga Jean asked that they renegotiate the PLA. Perenchio refused, saying that Univision had nothing to gain and that his decision was final. For the first time, someone confronted him: Azcárraga Jean told Perenchio to dispense with the fiction that he, not Televisa, accounted for Univision's success. When Perenchio finished by repeating that "a contract is a contract," Azcárraga Jean advised him to reread the agreement.[84]

But the Televisa leader did not want a fight. He believed that he could convince Perenchio to agree to draw up a new PLA. Azcárraga Jean was advancing a venture as a solution to another of his father's gaffes. Shortly before he died, Emilio Azcárraga had sold the cable channel Galavisión to Perenchio. That channel had been Televisa's only way of directly transmitting programs into the United States. Azcárraga Jean's solution was the Internet. The 1992 agreement did not restrict Televisa's entry into the United States on the digital platform that had been introduced only the year before. He proposed to partner with Univision if Perenchio was willing to negotiate Internet rights and thus a new PLA.[85] Well into 1999, he waited for Perenchio's reply.

By that time, Perenchio had promoted Mario Rodríguez to president of Univision Entertainment, a subsidiary of the Univision corporation that directed the Univision network's program acquisition and scheduling. In March 1999, Nielsen threw Rodríguez a curve. Anticipating a rare moment to survey the public, the arrival of the millennium, Nielsen announced that it would have a unique one-day ratings sweep on December 31. Rodríguez recognized that this gave Telemundo an opportunity to bite into Univision's 92 percent share. Without regular programs, both networks would go head to head with their coverage of Y2K, a popular acronym for the year 2000. When Rodríguez informed Century City about the unusual survey, Perenchio told him to begin planning a special broadcast that would "run Sony off the map."[86]

Fortuitously, a wildly successful Televisa television season helped Rodríguez. Each spring brought his most difficult duty, choosing Univision's fall programs. However, a Televisa novela called *El privilegio de amar* (The Privilege of Loving) had just recorded the highest ratings a Mexican broadcast ever had achieved. Although the novela finished in Mexico in January 1999, and, technically, Univision had to wait twelve months to initiate its U.S. run, Rodríguez scheduled its U.S. premiere for October 1999. Televisa had ignored the waiting period dozens of the times, and it shipped the recorded episodes to Univision.

Rodríguez's plans for Y2K advanced. So did Univision's promotion of the upcoming fall season. At its annual upfront presentation, Rodríguez spoke of the "superstar cast" and "riveting storyline" of *El privilegio de amar*. It "is a powerhouse . . . novela which assembles one of the most impressive rosters ever, including viewer favorite Adela Noriega," Rodríguez told advertisers. By August, they had placed a record $425 million in orders.[87] That September, publicity and anticipation swelled. Internet postings suggested that viewers awaiting the novela were counting the days. "It will premiere on Univision, Monday October 11!" one wrote. After another said that he had marked "October 11 on [his] calendar," someone else posted, "Wow, sounds good, I'll be there."[88]

Then, on September 11, Mario Rodríguez received a letter from Mexico City. Televisa ordered Univision to cancel *El privilegio de amar*. The communiqué cited Univision's breach of the clause in the PLA about the twelve-month window, and it ordered Univision to return the recordings.

Rodríguez was dumbfounded. Because Mexican TV introduced programs in the winter, Televisa had always permitted Univision to debut its Televisa programs at the beginning of the U.S. season in the fall. That Televisa had invoked the twelve-month rule out of the blue after vast promotion and just a month before the debut smacked of sabotage.[89]

Perenchio immediately telephoned Azcárraga Jean. "A contract is a contract," he said. Azcárraga Jean had meant it when he had advised Perenchio to reread the PLA. When Perenchio hung up, it was apparent that the novela would not appear. Perenchio's attorneys made it clear that if Univision kept the recordings and aired the novela, Azcárraga Jean could terminate the PLA.

Rodríguez scrambled to revise Univision's schedule. Embarrassed, he broadcast announcements that said "due to circumstances beyond our control, *El privilegio de amar* will not be seen." Viewers and sponsors protested. Perenchio cut off communication with Azcárraga Jean. Network president Ray Rodríguez declared, "We are heading for World War III."[90]

The story behind the cancelation of *El privilegio de amar* was one of Univision's most closely guarded secrets. Mario Rodríguez resorted to scheduling two episodes each night of *Tres mujeres,* another of Televisa's blockbusters. But the disruption brought Univision's first ratings decline since 1993. In the November 1999 survey, it fell to an 85 percent share. Telemundo's doubling of its share from 8 to 15 percent suggested that its long-awaited turnaround had begun. And ahead was the duel on New Year's Eve.

Expecting Telemundo's largest-ever broadcast, Rodríguez labored on Univision's version. He formed a Y2K task force. Its concept statement proposed "a marathon" that would involve all Miami employees.[91] Rodríguez feared the expense. Caught off guard by Televisa's broadside and anxious over the ratings decline, Perenchio agreed to pay whatever it cost. While Univision announced what it called *Feliz milenio,* Telemundo did not disclose its plans.

Beginning that December, Univision broadcast a series of specials called "Countdown to 2000!!" that previewed the show. Rodríguez assigned the employees who would be working on these programs. He then hired star entertainers Gloria Estefan, Placido Domingo, Celia Cruz, and Juan Gabriel and boxer Oscar de la Hoya for the broadcast. Univision secured live satellite links around the world from Televisa.[92]

As the broadcast neared, Univision's on-air talent conducted rehearsals. Rodríguez named Mario Kreutzberger as host and Cristina Saralegui as co-host. Every other Univision personality was set to appear, including Jorge Ramos and María Elena Salinas from *Noticiero Univision;* María Celeste Arrarás and Myrka Dellanos from *Primer impacto;* Fernando Arau, Ana María Canseco, Rafael José, Neida Sandoval, and Giselle Blondet from *Despierta América;* and Raúl de Molina and Lili Estefan, the hosts of Univision's two-year-old hit afternoon program *Gordo y la flaca*.[93]

Telemundo finally released its schedule for December 31. It astonished Univision. Telemundo had planned only a two-hour *Fiesta del nuevo milenio*. It scheduled its regular low-rated Friday night programs until 10:30 P.M.

Univision's *Feliz milenio* began at 6:00 A.M. on December 31. U.S. viewers woke to the millennium's arrival in Sydney. Throughout the day, live cameras handed off from Hong Kong to Moscow to Cairo to London to Madrid. That evening, Univision's stage shows commenced from Miami. At one-hour intervals, the performers switched to new cities—Río de Janeiro, Buenos Aires, Caracas, and San Juan—where crowds greeted the millennium. Viewers inundated Univision with calls and emails. Around 10:00 P.M. in Miami, Kreutzberger remarked, "It seems we have a big audience."[94]

At the climactic moment, midnight on the U.S. East Coast, viewers witnessed a collage of fireworks, flashing graphics, hugs, kisses, and tears. The broadcast continued until dawn. Univision unveiled the Year 2000 in each remaining time zone.[95] But for the network, the big moment still was to come.

On Saturday, Nielsen released the ratings. *Feliz milenio* not only averaged a 92 share in the Hispanic survey, but it also scored a 98 share from 11:00 P.M. to 1:00 A.M. Univision quickly prepared a news release that announced its 98 percent. Spanish-language viewers had given *Feliz milenio* the highest rating of any program ever seen on U.S. television.[96]

The elation lasted for a weekend. Univision marked a millennium on Friday and made history on Saturday. When business resumed on Monday, World War III began.

9

FINAL FIGHT

Jerry Perenchio was livid in the fall of 1999 because Televisa's new owner, Emilio Azcárraga Jean, had wasted little time in forcing him to consider revising the programing licensing agreement he had signed with his late father, Emilio Azcárraga Milmo, in 1992. At the last minute, Azcárraga Jean had used a technicality in the agreement to force Univision to cancel the entire six-month run of Televisa's blockbuster novela *El privilegio de amar.*

That fall, Perenchio could not contest Azcárraga Jean's action. Univision's worldwide millennium spectacular required Televisa's satellite links. But on January 3, 2000, after the New Year's Day broadcast was over, Perenchio ordered Televisa personnel off the Univision premises. Azcárraga Jean countered, ordering Univision personnel off Televisa premises. Perenchio sent word that he would sue if Televisa proceeded with plans to feed programs into the United States on the Internet. They would meet in court, Azcárraga Jean replied.

The first skirmish of Spanish-language television's World War III was a draw. Neither leader was prepared for a showdown over the PLA; they rattled their swords and backed away. Univision eventually showed *El privilegio de amar* two years later. The expulsions in 2000 displaced only a few staff. At best, the claims to Internet rights both parties insisted they had existed only on paper. In 2000, the Internet had neither the speed nor the capacity to deliver TV programming.

However, newspaper gossip columns warned of an incipient conflagration. Three years earlier, senior Televisa executives had nearly ousted

Azcárraga Jean, then twenty-nine. To replace his reputation as a carefree playboy with a new narrative, he had married. In early 2000, rumors spread that Azcárraga Jean had separated from his wife and found a new companion who hailed from Mexico City but lived in San Diego.

While Azcárraga Jean dismissed the gossip, Perenchio did not. If he married the companion who was reported to be a U.S. citizen, Azcárraga Jean could expedite his application for U.S. citizenship, and that would entitle him to own broadcast properties in the United States. Azcárraga Jean had hinted that Televisa could take over Univision through the purchase warrants Perenchio had given Emilio Azcárraga in the 1992 PLA accord. He spoke of Televisa's rightful ownership of a U.S. network it founded. For eight years, Perenchio believed the foreign ownership rule would render the warrants moot and that Televisa would have no realistic claim as Univision's future owner. But in 2000, he wasn't so sure.

There was much gossip but few details about the Univision-Televisa tiff. Azcárraga Jean still labored to craft an image of himself as a mature adult. The trick he had used to scuttle Univision's airing of *El privilegio de amar* suggested immaturity, and he kept the ploy from the press. Perenchio, enjoying adulation volunteered by a press he still shunned (in April, *Business Week* honored him as one of the three greatest "overachievers" in the United States), lowered Univision's cone of silence once again.[1] He did not want reporters prying into the dispute, and he certainly did not want the details of the PLA made public. If that happened, Azcárraga Jean could easily allege that if Perenchio was an "overachiever," it was because of the lopsided agreement he had made with Emilio Azcárraga.

As 2000 progressed, Perenchio shifted his attention from Azcárraga Jean to Wall Street, which was reeling from an assault on its communication sector. Univision's stock was in free fall. In addition, since late 1999, Perenchio had been avoiding Barry Diller, one of his close friends. Diller was begging Perenchio to purchase and thus rescue USA Broadcasting, a network of major-market UHF stations that broadcast Diller's Home Shopping Network. Perenchio saw little to gain from that deal. He evaded his friend with a ready excuse: under FCC rules, no one could own two stations in the same market, meaning he could not own two national networks in the same market. But Diller continued to press Perenchio. Perenchio's strategy of dodging Diller—and his excuse—were not to last long.

* * *

Perenchio was not the only one who was worried about his fortune. Frenzy over new media—Internet ventures and new networks like Univision— had inflated the price of many stocks. A chain reaction to cash calls and bankruptcies had caused the dot-com bubble to burst. To make matters worse, announcements about two new networks had caused Univision's stock value to plummet.

Marco Camacho, a wealthy Fort Worth entrepreneur, began the assault. In June 2000, the 45-year-old Camacho introduced plans for the Hispanic Television Network (HTVN). Just weeks later, 54-year-old Harry Pappas, the owner of a group of stations based in Fresno, unveiled Azteca América. Both claimed that they had vast capitalization. Both targeted Univision and its rival, Telemundo. Both planned to launch in May 2001.

Their announcements seemed to fit a narrative that the turn of the millennium had ushered in a new era of Spanish-language television. Univision's time, it seemed, had passed. *Multichannel News* forecast a new century that would be full of "changing choices" and "alternative networks, programs, and packages."[2] *Hispanic Market Weekly* foresaw a panorama of Latino channels that would "grow by leaps and bounds."[3] Predicting an "influx of new channels," Wall Street's Donnelley & Sons urged investors to back "a new environment of Spanish-language television [that will] reduce Univision's position."[4]

The 2000 census reinforced such forecasts. The number of Latinos living in the United States had again increased over the past decade, from 30 to 45 million. Latinos continued their spread into all fifty states. Their collective disposable income had doubled to $300 billion. Notably, the 2000 census was the first to report that immigration was not the primary reason for the latest expansion of the Latino population; the source of growth was a boom in the domestic birth rate. Demographers forecast that by 2010, 60 percent of Latinos would be below the age of thirty-five, the demographic advertisers prized the most.

Camacho's venture rode a first wave of publicity. By mid-2000, trade magazines were reporting that HTVN had $1 billion in capital and had signed twenty-five affiliates. At a news conference that summer, Camacho told the press of a plan that was new to Spanish-language television. The trade publication *Starcom* noted that "HTVN aims at providing an alternative [for] Hispanic adults 18–34, or Generation ñ," a strategy that could "stymie Univision and Telemundo" because of the preponderance of young Latinos.[5]

Gradually, the spotlight swung to Pappas's venture. Because of its structure, observers wondered if Azteca América was positioning itself to topple Univision. The new network traced its origins to the political transformation that had happened in Mexico a decade earlier, when the Partido de Acción Nacional instituted TV Azteca as a counter to the rival Partido Revolucionario Institucional, which had long backed Televisa. By 2000, owner Ricardo Salinas Pliego had built a formidable Mexican TV system. Using the same strategy Televisa had used to form Univision and enter the United States, Pliego laid plans and advanced arrangements for Azteca América. Just as the Azcárragas had needed a U.S. agent, Pliego needed Pappas.[6]

In the fall of 2000, the press was anticipating Azteca América's rollout the following May. Writers marveled over Pappas's reported $1.5 billion capitalization. They reported that he had listed thirty affiliates, including KWHY in Los Angeles. They touted the competitive advantage Pappas foresaw: while Televisa could not control Univision's scheduling, TV Azteca's Mexican programs would beam "straight through" on Pappas's stations. Reports noted that because of TV Azteca's "unimpeded" reach into the United States, Pappas and his team "think they can bump [off] the weaker Telemundo and then go after Univision."[7]

Neither Univision nor Telemundo responded. Azteca América seriously threatened Telemundo. Since 1995, Telemundo and TV Azteca had been partners, but now TV Azteca's programs would go to Pappas.

In August, Univision was back in the news with reports that Henry Cisneros had resigned as Univision's corporate chief operating officer. Cisneros returned to San Antonio and formed Cityview, a real estate venture that built affordable housing in vacated urban areas. Perenchio had lost a nationally known figure whom both Latinos and Anglos respected. He also had lost an important person in Univision's quest for billion-dollar revenue. Cisneros had courted and attracted deep-pocketed advertisers including Ford, Sears, and AT&T. During his three and a half years at Univision, the network's annual revenue had increased from $600 million to $750 million.

Cisneros's exit compounded Perenchio's primary concern, that fearful investors were abandoning Univision on Wall Street. That August, while HTVN and Azteca América were basking in the glow of a bright future, the price of Univision stock fell from $124 to $80. *Hispanic Business* speculated that "Univision's stock tumble [of] 22 percent [in one] week" was related to impending competition from HTVN and Azteca América and to Cisneros's departure.[8]

Advisors at Century City, Perenchio's headquarters in Los Angeles, reassured the owner that Univision merely was caught in the dot-com crash. Univision was not an Internet venture, they said, and its stock still had value. Yet it was evident that investors who had rushed to buy Univision stock in 1996 now believed the predictions that it would fall.

That October, heads turned when Univision's shares fell to $26.[9] Univision still was mum. There was no word on who would replace Cisneros. Analysts waited for Univision's response to HTVN's and Azteca América's publicity. They believed that a statement welcoming the rivals but reminding investors of Univision's command of the Latino market would restore confidence.[10]

One key figure was aware that Perenchio was not oblivious to the shadows the new rivals had cast. Since the exit of Jaime Dávila four years before, Univision's hierarchy had been vague. Dávila, the network CEO, had been Univision's known number two figure. Perenchio had not appointed a successor. Many expected him to elevate Ray Rodríguez as second in command. Rodríguez's star had risen since he had become president of Univision in 1992. He had led the fight for increased advertising rates. Perenchio had begun summoning Rodríguez from Miami to the headquarters in Los Angeles more often. In Los Angeles, Rodríguez had been privy to a great deal.

Rodríguez knew that Perenchio was fully aware of the press's glowing coverage of Univision's new competitors. Perenchio insisted that Rodríguez and others remain mute about HTVN and Azteca América; at a moment that Perenchio would choose, he would be the one to acknowledge them.[11] Perenchio discovered that *Broadcasting & Cable* planned to showcase Pappas and Azteca América in a forthcoming edition. The December 4, 2000, edition, featured a portrait of a gleeful Pappas on the cover.[12]

It arrived in the offices of television industry analysts and executives three days later. However, the story about Pappas was overshadowed. That morning, Barry Diller gathered reporters to reveal that his broadcast career was over: he had sold USA Broadcasting to Perenchio. Minutes later, Univision sent word of an 11:00 A.M. webcast. At that hour, Rodríguez appeared and announced that USA would convert to Spanish and become a sister network to Univision.[13] The news was so sudden that Rodríguez could not disclose the network's launch date, the programs it would carry, or even its name. Reports referred to the mystery network as "Univision 2." Diller added to the intrigue; he said that Perenchio had written him a check for $1.1 billion.[14]

The first reaction in the press was not to the deal but to a transformation of television it portended. Only months before, as Perenchio had reminded Diller, ownership of two networks had been impossible. But in 2000, the FCC had changed its policy, and now companies were permitted to own two stations in every locale. Perenchio was the first broadcaster to capitalize on the so-called duopoly rule. For the first time since 1943, one company owned two networks.[15]

It did not take long before analysts had realized what Perenchio had done. He now had multiple stations in New York, Los Angeles, Chicago, and Miami. Neither HTVN nor Azteca América had a single station in all of these essential locales. Perenchio had "significantly increase[d] the hurdles that Azteca ha[d] to jump to attract advertisers," and he had "remove[d] stations that Azteca could have used," the *Wall Street Journal* explained.[16]

Three weeks later, Univision's stock price increased to $37. It finished 2000 with revenue of more than $1 billion.[17] It was the first time a Spanish-language television network had ten-figure earnings.

* * *

Perenchio's second network meant treasure for Azcárraga Jean. The programming was certain to come from Televisa. Azcárraga Jean fancied Univision 2 as a second flank of Televisa's extension into the United States. Perenchio's move played into his hands in another way: the terms of the 1992 PLA did not cover a second Univision network. To program the new network, Perenchio would have to agree to pay huge fees to Azcárraga Jean. Delighting in Perenchio's predicament, Azcárraga Jean proposed a solution.

In front-page articles on February 21 and 22, 2001, David Luhnow, the Mexico City correspondent for the *Wall Street Journal*, reported that Azcárraga Jean had asked for a merger with Univision. Azcárraga Jean told Luhnow that stock tenders totaling $7.6 billion sat on Perenchio's desk. He also disclosed the two "were at odds" over an "unfair programing agreement." He argued that Televisa's future ownership of Univision derived from a "long history [dating to] 1961" and that the merger would be "natural for us" because it would end the dispute. Azcárraga Jean expected Perenchio to accept his offer.[18]

In an interview for *World Screen News*, Azcárraga Jean noted that Televisa's "opportunities in the United States" were "worth $1.2 to $1.3 billion" and that he had a "historic" right "to succeed [Perenchio] as the owner of Univision." Televisa was "constantly aware" that "we built Univision," and that "our programming has played a fundamental role in their success."[19]

The disclosures and remarks rankled Perenchio. He was irate that Azcárraga Jean had spoken in public about their dispute and that Jean, who had brutalized Univision by canceling *El privilegio de amar,* was casting himself as a gentleman. Perenchio most resented Azcárraga Jean's insinuation he was too old to continue.[20] He debunked the report of a merger. "It is categorically untrue," one of his rare public statements read.[21]

However, without programs for Univision 2, Perenchio had no choice but to comply with Azcárraga Jean's demands. In the spring of 2001, Perenchio agreed to begin renegotiating the PLA. Both sides acknowledged steps toward reconciliation. Forced to communicate, Perenchio and Azcárraga Jean struck a semblance of a friendship. Ray Rodríguez, Univision's president, and Andrew Hobson, its chief financial officer, were the network's negotiators. Across the bargaining table were Televisa vice president Alfonso de Angoitia and others who represented Azcárraga Jean.

Despite the initial camaraderie, Rodríguez bargained hard and refused to yield on major points. Confident that he and Televisa would reach an agreement, Rodríguez anticipated his next assignment: enlarged duties as head of the new network. Mario Rodríguez, the president of Univision Entertainment, also awaited a primary role. Soliciting sponsors for a network with no programs and no name, Mario Rodríguez used humor at Univision's May 16, 2001, upfront meeting for advertisers. He stood on stage before a giant TV screen that said "Please Stand By: New Network in 2002."[22]

Univision did not doubt that its advertisers would stand by. The launches of HTVN and Azteca América were to have occurred that same month. HTVN did launch, but leery of Univision 2, investors had fled and creditors had ousted Camacho. Under James Ryffel, HTVN premiered with four stations.[23] Pappas postponed the start of Azteca América. Rumors circulated that summer and fall that its Mexican mother, TV Azteca, was temporarily or permanently suspending its partnership.[24]

On December 20, 2001—Perenchio's seventy-first birthday—Univision and Televisa announced a new program licensing agreement. In a joint statement, Azcárraga Jean said he was "thrilled" and Perenchio said that he "look[ed] forward to working closely with our partners."[25] However, bargaining from different concepts of the future, they had signed a puzzling contract.

Azcárraga Jean claimed victory because Perenchio had made concessions that Jean felt would lead to his ultimate prize, Televisa's ownership of Univision. Perenchio named him to the Univision board, and he had given Azcárraga Jean the newly created post of corporate vice chair. He agreed to the original 1992 ownership arrangement in which Perenchio held 80 percent of shares, Televisa 14–15 percent, and Venevisión 5–6 percent. Televisa, though, had won two significant new provisions. It now would have voting authority on the board and thus a voice in Univision's future decisions. In addition, Azcárraga Jean was to have the authority to help direct the day-to-day decisions of Univision, Galavisión, and the new network.

But Perenchio had won another lopsided PLA. Azcárraga Jean had agreed to a fee of 13 percent of the new network's income for using Televisa's and Univision's programs. He had also agreed to the term of twenty-five years from the original version of the PLA. Univision still would maintain exclusive rights to Televisa's programs until 2017.[26]

Later, Perenchio related his triumph in preserving virtually the same contract that he had extracted from Emilio Azcárraga in 1992. "There would be no [future] without it," he would explain, for "one of our greatest fears is if we lose the noose [the low-fee, long-duration contract], Televisa will enter the U.S. market . . . and destroy or severely wound Univision."[27]

Now that it was guaranteed access to Televisa's programs for a low fee, Univision hastened to launch the new network. Hobson, Univision's finance chief and its executive vice president, formally announced the venture at the annual UBS Warburg global finance conference on December 6, 2001, where he finally revealed the new network's name: Telefutura. He promised "new Latin television" and pointed out that "never before in the history of this country has a full-fledged television network been launched from scratch on a single day. That's what will happen on January 14."[28]

* * *

By that time, Telemundo had accomplished something of a turnaround. In Nielsen's Hispanic ratings, close to 95 percent of viewing still was divided between Univision and Telemundo. In 1998, when Telemundo had introduced Spanish-language remakes of ABC shows from the 1970s, its audience share had dropped to 8 percent. Its comeback began in July 1999, when Sony fired Jon Feltheimer, Peter Tortorici, and Nely Galán and named James McNamara as president and CEO.

Forty-year-old McNamara had been born in Panama and had been raised in a U.S. family that lived in the Canal Zone. He was a former CEO of Ron Perelman's New World Communications. There he had groomed Feltheimer, another rising executive. In 1994, the two were principals in the re-affiliation of New World's twelve television stations with Rupert Murdoch's Fox network. Their move triggered affiliation switches among stations in cities across the country.

After New World sold its holdings to Murdoch in 1996, Feltheimer had joined Sony, where he became Telemundo's CEO. McNamara moved to Spain and prospered as a consultant. After firing Tortorici and Galán, Feltheimer coaxed McNamara to return to the United States and advise Telemundo. When Sony fired Feltheimer, McNamara became the network's head.

Immediately, McNamara canceled most of the programs that had led to the drop in Telemundo's 1998–1999 ratings. For the fall premiere of the 1999–2000 season, McNamara reinstated as many of the Mexican novelas as were available in the wake of Telemundo's partnership with TV Azteca. He purchased additional novelas from TV networks in Colombia, Perú, and Brazil. Viewers saw a crazy quilt of international programming. Each hour, content shifted from one country's plots and dialects to those of another. Still, in the November 1999 Nielsen sweep, Telemundo doubled its audience share from 8 to 15 percent.[29]

To reduce Univision's 85 percent market share and instill a genuine turnaround, McNamara drew on his experience as a consultant: he studied the competition. Using a video cassette recorder, he recorded Univision's programming. "I earned a Ph.D. in telenovelas," he later said. The task was daunting. Telemundo had nothing to match the Televisa productions Univision broadcast. McNamara later explained that "the best way to understand the impact of their novelas is to imagine the audience you would get if you put on the hottest Hollywood movie every night of the week. That was Televisa."[30]

Although he was resigned to the fact that Univision had a tremendous advantage, McNamara felt that Telemundo still could achieve a sizable audience. Armed with his "Ph.D. in novelas," he traveled to Mexico. In late 1999, he made a shrewd deal; he obtained U.S. rights to the productions of Argos Comunicación. The move ensured that Telemundo would have a supply of Mexican programs. More was at stake in Telemundo's deal with Argos. Argos produced the programs telecast in Mexico on Pliego's TV Azteca, the programs TV Azteca had provided Telemundo beginning with their partnership in 1995. These were the programs that in 2000 Pliego expected to remove from Telemundo and broadcast in the United States on the Azteca América network he and Pappas were developing. But because Telemundo had dealt directly with Argos for the programs and won their U.S. rights, Pappas and Azteca América were cut off from their expected Mexican programming source. Thus, owing to McNamara's move, Telemundo had lost its partnership with TV Azteca but had kept the shows TV Azteca had provided.

Telemundo's rebound began to materialize in January 2000. McNamara went to New Orleans for the trade fair put on by the National Association of Television Program Executives. There he met executives from the Colombian TV network RCN. He was intrigued by an RCN novela. Unlike all others, it did not feature beautiful men and women. The star was a teenage girl with braces, eyeglasses, and greasy hair. McNamara bought the novela even though, at a test screening, "the audience just sat there. It was a zero on the Richter scale."[31]

The Colombian production was titled *Yo soy Betty la fea* (I Am Ugly Betty). Cautiously, McNamara introduced the novela as a summer replacement in August 2000. Kept for the 2000–2001 season, it started slowly but gradually soared in the Nielsen ratings. In the February 2001 ratings, *Betty la fea* registered a 60 percent audience share. It was the highest rating Telemundo had ever achieved. Propelled by *Betty la fea*, Telemundo's overall Latino audience share grew from 15 to 25 percent.[32]

Seeing the success of *Betty la fea*, advertisers began taking a second look at the network that still broadcast from the warehouse-and-railroad district of Hialeah. In January 2001, McNamara released Telemundo's 2000 financial report. For the first time since its inception in 1987, the network finished with a profit: $20 million on record revenue of $400 million. In April, he posted an even more sparkling report for the first quarter of 2001.[33]

In June 2001, Sony president Howard Stringer told McNamara that Sony was debating whether to sell Telemundo. The issue had come up when the dominant figure in Spanish-language radio, McHenry Tichenor, the owner of the 70-station Hispanic Broadcasting Corporation (HBC), offered to purchase Telemundo for $1.8 billion, four times the amount Sony had paid Leon Black four years earlier. Sony was torn. Now that Telemundo was making money, Sony would do well to keep it. On the other hand, Tichenor's $1.8 billion bid made Sony executives curious. They wanted to know how high the price might go.[34]

Stringer decided to hold off on accepting Tichenor's offer. That summer, he took secret bids. By August, Disney, Time Warner, and Viacom had submitted offers. Rumors of the bidding increased Sony's stock price. McNamara later recalled that as of September 10, 2001, Sony had not made up its mind whether to sell and, if so, which offer to accept. "It was the same question.... How much could we get?"[35]

The next day, September 11, terrorists hijacked aircraft and flew them into New York's World Trade Center. More than 3,000 died when both towers of the trade center collapsed. The spectacle and the tragedy shocked and confused America. Many expected more attacks. But access to information was cut off. New York's main radio and television stations transmitted from the World Trade Center. When the structures fell, all of New York's television channels turned to dead air—except for one.

Univision's WXTV continued to broadcast. Twenty-one years before, Rene Anselmo had conducted a hunger strike that had convinced the Port Authority to allow WXTV a transmitter on the World Trade Center. But after discovering that pockets of viewers could not receive WXTV and after authorities consented to boost WXTV's signal power, Anselmo had kept the transmitter at the Empire State Building.

WXTV canceled regular programming. Until WCBS returned with a backup transmitter, Univision provided New York's only broadcast television. Its news anchors, Rafael Piñeda and Denisse Oller, and its reporters spoke in English during the first hours of WXTV's continuous live coverage. WXTV's role in 9/11 was part of the news coverage out of New York that captivated the nation and the world. Viewers inundated WXTV with emails and calls to praise the staff's work. New York mayor Rudolph Giuliani commended Univision.[36]

Exactly one month later, Telemundo achieved a different distinction when it became part of the largest and oldest TV institution in the United

States. On October 11, 2001, Sony sold Telemundo to NBC. The price, $2.7 billion, was almost $1 billion more than Tichenor had offered. NBC chair Robert Wright welcomed Spanish-language television to the most revered address in U.S. television, 30 Rockefeller Center in New York. At a press reception there, he noted "NBC's clout" and "Telemundo's enormous potential." He spoke of a "synergy" that is "completely complementary with the business we are in."[37] However, when NBC president Andrew Lack spoke, he did not mention telenovelas. "NBC wants to create Spanish-language versions of shows like 'Access Hollywood' and 'Weakest Link,'" Lack said.[38]

* * *

On January 14, 2002, Univision launched Telefutura. For opening night, Mario Rodríguez arranged black tie galas in five cities where mayors had proclaimed Telefutura Day. He reunited most of the team that had staged the millennium extravaganza. The broadcast originated at Miami's Biltmore Hotel. Mario Kreutzberger and Charytín Goyco hosted stars and dignitaries who strolled down red carpets. Cameras cut to the different cities. It looked like the Academy Awards.[39]

Telefutura became the first TV entity to attract younger Latinos. Its manager, Valeria Palazio, had scheduled programs similar to those seen on Latino cable channels: music videos, sports talk shows, and Spanish-translated Hollywood action movies. Yet certain that teenage and young adult Latinos would flock to the same high-quality international programs that brought older viewers to Univision—and aware of Televisa's young adult content—Palazio awaited the new PLA. "We got the Televisa programming" and "used it day and night," she later said.[40]

The new network dominated reports of the ratings of May 2003. Although it came third behind Univision's 50 percent and Telemundo's 20 percent shares, Telefutura leapt from its opening 5 percent to 15 percent.[41]

It was evident that Perenchio had triumphed again. Looking ahead to finishing his career, he embarked on two new initiatives. First, he bought out Tichenor. For $3.5 billion, Perenchio purchased the Hispanic Broadcasting Company and its seventy radio stations. It was the largest of his hundreds of business deals. Pending FCC approval, Perenchio was primed to become the undisputed king of Spanish-language broadcasting.

With his second initiative, Perenchio returned to the domain he loved the most. Back in the studio, he sought to prove that he could succeed in the one endeavor that Spanish-language television in the United States had failed to master. He began filming Univision's first original telenovela.

Perenchio and his wife Margaret Perenchio, a fan of the performing arts who had taken up painting as a hobby, had opened a Hollywood studio called Paloma Productions. While at the studio where his wife was engaged in scripting, developing, and appearing in the 2002 Academy Award–winning motion picture *Frida,* Perenchio used the facility and a $6 million investment to produce *Te amaré en silencio* (I Will Love You in Silence). The novela told the story of a deaf-mute woman in opulent Los Angeles who falls in love with the man who killed her parents. "It is packed with scenes of Hollywood, South Bay beaches, and glamorous Rodeo Drive," the *Los Angeles Times* previewed.[42]

Univision president Ray Rodríguez was "not a fan of the novela" but complied with Perenchio's instructions that he schedule and promote it. In mid-2003, Rodríguez announced that the novela's nightly six-month run would commence that December and would be a prime-time attraction. He scheduled *Te amaré en silencio* in Univision's most viewed time slot, 9:00 P.M. He began publicity for "Univision's prime-time blockbuster novela."[43]

Beyond Univision, few cheered. Whether because of Perenchio's prowess or the unreal bombast of HTVN and Azteca América, only one new network, Telefutura, had debuted. Concerns that Perenchio, who was not Latino, owned ever-greater control of Spanish-language media nearly derailed his radio deal.[44] For years, it had been customary for those in Spanish-language broadcasting to speak of separate "Spanish" and "general" broadcast markets. Perenchio's radio deal forced the FCC to consider whether Spanish-language broadcasting was a special domain that was independent of English-language broadcasting. To block Perenchio's takeover of HBC, opponents insisted that his ownership of Univision, Telefutura, Galavisión, and seventy radio stations would monopolize the Spanish-language sector.

The commission's debate was pivotal, for if it denied the deal on grounds that Perenchio monopolized a separate Spanish-language sector, that would mean that the FCC agreed that a separate Spanish-language sector did exist. And if that were the case, the FCC would need to regulate Spanish-language broadcasting using rules that were different from those for English-language broadcasting. Instead, the commission rejected the arguments against Perenchio's application and approved the deal. In effect, the ruling said that there were no separate "Spanish" and "general" markets and thus that there was no Spanish-language sector that one person could monopolize. However, the commissioners were divided; the vote was 3:2.[45]

Perenchio's domination of Spanish-language broadcasting disenchanted other broadcasters who sought the opportunities that had been promised at the turn of the millennium. In 2005, a special report by *Broadcasting & Cable* still spoke of "incredible momentum." Yet although it listed "75 networks targeting the U.S. Hispanic marketplace," the report showed that only Univision, Telemundo, Telefutura, and Galavisión had more than 100,000 daily viewers. Of seventy-two Spanish-language cable channels, only seven were available on most major cable systems.[46]

Azcárraga Jean was also not happy. No one was listening to his concepts and plans. He had yet to complain to Perenchio, but he harbored suspicions that Perenchio had taken advantage of him when they renegotiated their PLA. In addition, Univision's managers were not returning his calls.

Azcárraga Jean despised Univision president Ray Rodríguez. Their feud had begun when Emilio Azcárraga died in 1997. His son, who was battling to keep control of Televisa, had needed Rodríguez's support then. Instead, Rodríguez had used the moment to launch *Despierta América* and revive domestic production at Univision. The antagonism between them grew when Cisneros departed in 2000 and Rodríguez assumed larger duties. Those duties included his role as Perenchio's surrogate in the 2001 PLA negotiations, when he had been very firm. "To them, I was always the bad guy," Rodríguez complained. Suspecting that Rodríguez was undermining the authority Perenchio said he would have and that he had negotiated in the 2001 PLA revision, Azcárraga Jean accused Rodríguez of grabbing control of decision making. Azcárraga Jean sensed that Perenchio actually liked him but that Rodríguez was infecting their relationship.

In late 2003, tensions erupted. Through Rodríguez, Azcárraga Jean had learned of and seen previews of Perenchio's *Te amaré en silencio*. He was aghast and felt that Perenchio's casting of the story around a deaf lead character would repel viewers. While Rodríguez agreed with Azcárraga Jean that the novela would be unsuccessful, he later said that "Jerry wanted to prove to Televisa we could do novelas, [so] I had to push the publicity in front of (Azcárraga Jean and other Televisa executives]."[47] Rodríguez decided to schedule the novela in Univision's key time slot of 9:00 P.M. When Azcárraga Jean ordered Rodríguez to move it out of prime time, Rodríguez refused. Azcárraga Jean sent one statement to Perenchio condemning

Rodríguez for "act[ing] as he sees fit and not always in the best interests of Univision."[48]

As the December 15 debut of the novela approached, the November 2003 ratings arrived. Univision's victory momentarily eased tensions. By that time, NBC had completed its takeover of Telemundo. Replacing some of McNamara's foreign novelas with Spanish-language remakes of sitcoms and dramas taken from NBC, the new owners touted "original shows produced in this country." The promos "raise[d] red flags because of Telemundo's failed attempt in the late 1990s . . . to create shows like Starsky and Hutch," *Broadcasting & Cable* noted. *Variety* puzzled over why there was a "blind spot" in NBC's "rearview mirror."[49]

The concerns were well founded. Telemundo's share of Latino viewers fell to 15 percent, Telefutura's share rose to 20 percent, and Univision's share increased to 55 percent. With a combined 75 percent, Univision's two networks claimed first and second place.[50] Certain *Te amaré en silencio* would generate a large audience, Perenchio awaited its premiere.

* * *

Azcárraga Jean and Perenchio maintained a cordial relationship. The Televisa leader did not seek to disrupt the harmony that followed the 2001 PLA renegotiation. Entering 2004, he told the press that he was planning two initiatives. First, because Internet rights still were unresolved, he wanted to invite Perenchio to revise the PLA again. Second, he wanted one-on-one discussions with Perenchio about the arrangements by which Televisa would acquire Univision when Perenchio retired.[51] Azcárraga Jean hoped that he and Perenchio would come to terms. While Ray Rodríguez remained an irritant, Televisa was doing well. He went so far as to tell the press that he was "get[ting] to know Jerry on a personal level."[52]

That February, Azcárraga Jean married Sharon Fastlicht. Born and raised in the upscale Polanco district of Mexico City, the bride had recently obtained dual Mexican-U.S. citizenship, a factor that boded well for Azcárraga Jean's own pursuit of U.S. citizenship. His marriage to a U.S. citizen had reduced the time for his possible U.S. citizenship to be approved from five years to three. They purchased a $4.8 million mansion in Miami. In an interview, the groom reiterated that his U.S. citizenship would pave the way for Televisa to acquire Univision.[53]

Azcárraga Jean soon had more than a legal reason to hope he could buy the U.S. network. Perenchio had made his first stumble as Univision owner: *Te amaré en silencio* had failed. The novela's ratings were so low that Ray Rodríguez had removed it from prime time; it finished its run in daytime hours. The fallout was serious. Perenchio had not merely shown incompetence; his personal project had put Univision in jeopardy.

After months of amicable dealings, Azcárraga Jean felt that the time had come for the 74-year-old Perenchio to step down. On February 4, 2005, he wrote Perenchio to request that he clarify the "succession process."[54] Four days later—the day before a Univision board meeting—Perenchio replied that he had decided to "make Ray the President and CEO."[55] Azcárraga Jean was dumbfounded.

Azcárraga Jean later recalled that he never was more incensed. He rushed to the meeting to protest Rodríguez's appointment. He alleged that Perenchio had violated policies by neither conducting a search nor consulting Televisa. Nevertheless, in a 7:3 vote, the board approved the decision. Rodríguez became CEO and Perenchio's presumed successor as Univision's chief executive.[56]

Informing the board that he would not tolerate Perenchio's "stiff-arm[ing] of Televisa" and "rubber stamp[ing]" of Rodríguez, Azcárraga Jean returned to Mexico City. He sent messages warning of a confrontation at Univision's stockholders' meeting on May 11. To force Perenchio to overturn his appointment of Rodríguez, he vowed to publicize the fact that the novela had been such a fiasco. In addition, Azcárraga Jean planned to announce that he was investigating whether Univision had failed to pay $118 million in royalties and had edited Televisa programs. Both issues would constitute a breach of their contract. If either were true, Televisa could terminate the one-sided PLA.[57]

Perenchio turned to Univision's attorneys to find out if Azcárraga Jean's accusations were true. They sought explanation from Mario Rodríguez, who had resigned but remained an advisor. He scoffed at the claim about not paying royalties, saying it was trumped up. He seethed at the other allegation. Again and again, Televisa had delivered programs that were either too short or too long to fit one-hour and half-hour time slots, and Univision had had to edit them. Because he had documented voluminous complaints to Televisa that the programs Univision received could not be aired without changes, Mario Rodríguez assured Perenchio that Univision could defend the PLA should Televisa sue for its revocation.[58] Satisfied that Azcárraga Jean had no case, Perenchio affirmed that he would install Ray Rodríguez as CEO at the stockholders' meeting.

On May 9, 2005, Azcárraga Jean and Televisa vice president Alfonso de Angoitia resigned from the Univision board. Another director, Fernando Aguirre, also resigned. That same day, Televisa attorneys filed suit against Univision in Los Angeles federal court. Claiming that Univision had breached their contract with Televisa, they asked for a revocation of the PLA.[59]

The resignations and the lawsuit wounded Perenchio. Two days later, Perenchio convened the stockholders' meeting at the Hotel Bel-Air. Concerned investors demanded an explanation for the *Te amaré en silencio* debacle. The purpose of the meeting was to have stockholders approve a proxy to renew Perenchio's authority in making decisions and acting on stockholders' behalf. To encourage approval, he had circulated a statement extolling his role in securing "exclusive rights to air . . . programs produced by Televisa." Now Perenchio was forced to admit the possible loss of those rights. His evasive answers to their questions angered the attendees. He survived a vote on a resolution that proposed new leaders for Univision and referred to him as a "significant danger." But the vote was close.[60]

Perenchio fought back. On August 15, 2005, Univision countersued Televisa. Attorneys alleged that Televisa had acted in "bad faith," had disrupted programs, and had inflicted harm on sponsors. But stockholders fled. Univision's shares, which had been worth $40 that May, tumbled to $20 in September. According to *Barron's*, Univision had changed "from a hot tamale to a hot potato."[61]

On his seventy-fifth birthday, December 20, 2005, Perenchio told Ray Rodríguez that he had decided to retire and sell Univision. Rodríguez later recalled that "it was bittersweet"; Perenchio was "exhausted by the controversy" and admitted he needed to "move on." He also recalled that Perenchio's retirement "was a big deal at Univision," for "everyone thought he was a great and brilliant leader. He was universally loved at Univision [and] people hated to see him go."[62]

It became more bittersweet when scores of Univision employees lost their jobs. Perenchio had no intention of selling Univision with its stock at an all-time low. Univision's largest-ever layoff returned the price to $35.

When Univision announced that it was up for sale on February 8, 2006, Azcárraga Jean submitted the first bid. He offered $13 billion, twenty-five times more than the amount Perenchio had paid Hallmark to acquire Univision in 1992 and almost double the $7.6 million Azcárraga Jean had offered in 2001.[63] Except for NBC, the owner of Telemundo, every major media corporation reportedly also placed a bid.[64] However, Televisa remained the highest bidder. According to Rodríguez, "Even though we were always fighting, [Perenchio] was not necessarily against Televisa taking over. He wanted the most money."[65]

Yet that spring, rumors circulated that Perenchio was conferring with the head of an investor group the press later dubbed "Team Power Rangers." It consisted of five partners headed by 62-year-old Haim Saban. For years, Saban had been interested in acquiring Univision. He had approached Perenchio numerous times. When Perenchio announced that the network was for sale, Saban assembled his investor group.

Saban had been born into a Jewish family living in Egypt and was raised in Israel during the Suez Crisis and the Yom Kippur War. He was an aspiring musician. In Paris, he excelled as a composer of music for children's cartoons. Settling in Hollywood in 1983, he introduced a kids' TV series called *Power Rangers*. It became the most popular children's TV series of the 1980s and earned Saban billions. He had invested in European television; he owned two of Germany's first private networks, Sat.1 and Pro Sieben.[66]

On June 30, 2006, Perenchio sold Univision to Saban and his associates for $13.7 billion. He "express[ed] my deep gratitude to all of Univision's employees for their many contributions. . . . I am enormously proud of all that Univision has accomplished since 1992." Saban said, "We are extremely pleased to have achieved a successful and timely closing of our acquisition of Univision, a terrific company with a unique position in the U.S. media landscape."[67]

Three weeks later, on July 20, Televisa sued Univision again.[68]

* * *

At Telemundo, President James McNamara was correct in anticipating difficulties in acquainting the network's new owner, NBC, with Spanish-language television. When NBC had taken over in April 2002, McNamara had tangled with NBC executives when they had compelled him to install Spanish-language versions of NBC shows.

Pleading that Latinos preferred foreign programing, McNamara finally won NBC's approval to preserve most of Telemundo's array of telenovelas from Colombia, Perú, and Brazil and from its new Mexican partner Argos Comunicación. But when he tried to explain "we didn't have a powerhouse partner like Televisa," the executives did not take into account Telemundo's impediments to high ratings. "The only thing they understood was the ratings," he recalled.[69]

NBC had paid $2.7 billion to purchase a network that despite the *Betty la fea* ratings spike in 2000 still attracted only 20 percent of the Latino audience. Never before had a Telemundo president been under greater pressure to increase the network's numbers.[70] During their first meetings in 2002, NBC executives, including president and CEO Andrew Lack, had asked McNamara to explain why, fifteen years after its inception, Telemundo had done little more than flounder. McNamara answered by telling them about three conclusions he had reached.

He began by observing that central to Telemundo's problem was the situation exposed when viewers rebuked his predecessor's dive into domestic production, leaving him no option other than to acquire foreign programs, extensively novelas, from any available TV producer. Dominated by the themes and dialects of the countries where they originated, foreign programs were driving U.S. viewers away. Accordingly, he told NBC, Telemundo needed to eliminate imported content and produce its own programs that were genuinely committed to attracting Latino viewers.

Second, measures to "Americanize" programming had competitive advantages. He reiterated that Telemundo was suffering in the competition against the "powerhouse" partnership of Televisa and Univision. Televisa was the only foreign entity that could dependably produce Spanish-language programs of universal appeal across the United States. However, the Latino population was tilting toward younger Latinos, and that made the Televisa-Univision juggernaut vulnerable. Growing numbers of younger Latinos, most of whom had been born in the United States, had little affection for Televisa's traditional "story book" novelas. He insisted that opportunity beckoned, that U.S. Latinos would be "content with American appeal that relates to their lives in the United States" if it was sophisticated and well produced.

McNamara's third point was that the core of Telemundo's problem was finance. If Telemundo was to free itself from imported programming and proceed on its own, NBC would need to spend hundreds of millions of dollars. Having just spent $2.7 billion to acquire Telemundo, Lack and his NBC colleagues listened to but refused to take action on McNamara's appeals for additional expenditures.[71]

However, McNamara, inspired by Telemundo's success with *Betty la fea* and determined to provide more nontraditional contemporary novelas that he knew would draw younger U.S. Latinos, conceived an arrangement that could lead the network toward large-scale domestic production at a relatively low cost. His concept—co-production—centered on NBC's willingness to finance novela projects that Telemundo would originate and steer. Telemundo's ownership and direction would ensure that the novelas featured themes that would appeal to U.S. viewers. NBC would need to invest in only one novela at a time. However, McNamara understood that skill in sophisticated serialized programming and high production values was not available at Telemundo or elsewhere in the United States. Accordingly, his plan called for foreign partners that would provide producers, creators, writers, talent, and, initially, studios in exchange for a share of each program's revenue.

The result was hybrid novelas that were both domestic and international. Viewers saw programs that combined U.S. settings and scripts that appeared to have been written for U.S. audiences with expertise from abroad and, notably, international actors and actresses. To McNamara, a chief benefit of hybridization was the ties foreign studios had to the world's best-known Spanish-language stars. The fact that co-production could be a way for Telemundo to claim that it produced all of its own programming was another key benefit that McNamara foresaw.

Spanish-language television's first co-production agreement was a brief venture in 2001 between Telemundo and Argos Comunicación studios in Mexico. The following year, the concept gelled when Telemundo and Colombia's Radio Televisión Interamericana (RTI) co-produced *Amor descarado,* which became the first top-rated alternative novela since *Betty la fea.* Over its six-month run, which ended in March 2004, the novela averaged a 30 percent share among Latino viewers.[72] Telemundo's ratings topped those of Univision on many of the nights it was shown.

For the first time, NBC began to listen to McNamara's strategy for ending Telemundo's dark ages. When he advocated for filming co-produced programs in the United States, NBC backed him. In mid-2004, NBC financed the first enlargement of Telemundo's Miami studios since its facility in Hialeah opened in 1987; McNamara named it Telemundo Studios. At the end of the year McNamara went public with his bold objective—eliminating all imported programs. From its Hialeah studios and those of its partners abroad, Telemundo would produce all of its own shows.

Telemundo Studios was to prove the final initiative of the network's inventive president and CEO. In 2004, NBC purchased Universal Studios for $6 billion. Despite McNamara's bold predictions about Telemundo's future, the network's ratings had not improved. In April 2005, NBC fired McNamara and named Don Browne as his successor.

At the time, Browne was Telemundo's chief operating officer. He agreed with McNamara's vision for Telemundo's future, including the part that required heavy financing from NBC. Browne had pull with NBC executives that McNamara lacked; he had worked at NBC for twenty-four years and was widely known as a correspondent for *NBC Nightly News*.

When NBC reorganized following its recent acquisition, Browne was thrilled to learn that Telemundo would have access to Universal Studios in Hollywood. Browne's first major public appearance highlighted Telemundo's May 2006 upfront meeting with advertisers. "We are designing our content and programming specifically to speak to and be relevant to a new [U.S. Latino] audience," he told attendees. "It takes time to do that but the audience is speaking back to us and saying that they like it."[73]

* * *

At Univision, things had changed. It no longer was governed by a recluse. The showy Haim Saban was known for cruising the streets of Beverly Hills in a Rolls Royce with a license plate that read "1 RSK TKR."

Saban and his investment group had wagered $13.7 billion on the outcome of a trial. Sixty percent of Univision's revenue came from the PLA that Televisa was in court to revoke. Should the jury side with Televisa, Saban could expect to become liable for huge programming fees—if he was lucky. If Televisa won, it was more likely that it would stop sending any of its programs to Univision. Azcárraga Jean renegotiated the PLA on his understanding that Perenchio had promised him that he would succeed as Univision owner. Instead, Perenchio had sold to Saban. Azcárraga Jean was certain to offer his programs to Telemundo in retaliation and bring Univision to its knees.

Azcárraga Jean was indeed furious. He filed a second lawsuit to sever every remaining contractual agreement with Univision. "Notwithstanding our repeated offers to discuss all aspects of our [purchase] proposal including price, Univision and its advisors refused to enter into any discussions with us after we submitted our initial bid. . . . Given this action by Univision's board, Televisa has a number of alternatives it is considering," Azcárraga Jean said.[74] Univision answered on October 26, 2006. It countersued Televisa's second lawsuit.

While the litigation proceeded in Los Angeles federal court, the FCC approved Saban's purchase of Univision. It was a huge leveraged buyout. Of the $13.7 billion they had bid, Saban and his partners had paid Perenchio only $3.9 billion. Saban had paid the least, only $300 million. His four other partners had each paid $900 million. All of the remaining $9.8 billion was leveraged among creditors. Univision left the New York Stock Exchange and became a privately owned firm again. Analysts expected that Saban would finance the remaining $9.8 billion by paying creditors part of the firm's $2 billion in annual revenue, then profiting from a public sale of Univision stock, as Perenchio had.

In April 2007, Saban's management team took control. They kept the well-liked and well-respected Ray Rodríguez as Univision's president and chief operating officer. Rodríguez told Saban's lieutenants that Azcárraga Jean was still intent on owning Univision and that Televisa was the entity the network should be wary of. He urged them to show resolve.

Rodríguez now answered to 51-year-old Joe Uva, an advertising veteran and former head of OMG Worldwide, whom Saban had named as CEO and second in command. Uva appointed 33-year-old Cesar Conde as chief strategic officer. Six years earlier, President George W. Bush had named Conde as a White House Fellow. In that capacity, he served as an aide to Secretary of State Colin Powell in 2002. In 2005, he joined Univision and moved to Miami, where Rodríguez appointed him as special assistant. On Rodríguez's recommendation, in 2008, Uva brought Conde to New York where he became Uva's top-ranking executive.

In New York, Conde took steps to end the secrecy of the Perenchio era. He told *Broadcasting & Cable* that "Univision is more than a media company... [it is] a social, cultural and political force." Yet after fifteen years of Perenchio's "Rules of the Road," "the biggest challenge is translating [our] success story."[75]

One of Conde's projects was to prepare for Univision's fiftieth anniversary in 2011. "I came to Univision with a sense of its history," he later recalled.[76] He proposed that Univision build toward the anniversary with broadcasting programs to recognize two milestones in Latino affairs in 2010: a new census that was likely to report a further-enlarged and more influential Latino population and Univision's eighth consecutive broadcast of the quadrennial World Cup soccer matches. That would be followed by programs that commemorated Univision's first fifty years.[77]

In late 2007, Uva announced huge plans for domestic production that included a doubling of the Doral facilities, co-production agreements with foreign producers similar to those of Telemundo, and, ultimately, hundreds of hours of programs. Uva spoke of a "transformation" in which Univision no longer would rely on imported content. Uva proposed to implode the "Univision model" of relying on imported foreign fare.

Although the costly project, which Uva named Univision Studios, was years away, by announcing it right away, Uva sent Azcárraga Jean a message: drop the lawsuit, cooperate with Univision, and keep the PLA. If Univision Studios succeeded, it might win in court and break Televisa's lock on the U.S. market.[78]

Televisa did not flinch. It signed a small contract with Telemundo by which Televisa's Pay TV channel in Mexico would carry a few Telemundo productions.[79] For the moment, Televisa's move did not threaten Univision, but the message was clear: Univision could either revise the PLA or confront a future Televisa-Telemundo colossus.

An auspicious development in 2006 and a landmark in 2007 intensified the stakes. First, in November 2006, anticipating a count of 70 million Latinos in the 2010 census, Nielsen shut down its Hispanic ratings. It moved the Spanish-language networks to its main survey, the NTI. Now rated against the scores of English-language networks and channels, Univision and Telemundo no longer registered share percents in the 50s and 20s; instead, they dropped to 1.5 and 0.6.

The change helped both networks. Univision was clearly the number five network in the United States. The combined NTI clearly showed that Univision, averaging 2.5 million daily viewers, trailed only ABC, CBS, NBC, and Fox. Although Telemundo had fewer viewers, around 600,000, it appeared more formidable. It ranked in Nielsen's top ten at number eight.

Nielsen's unified English-Spanish ratings led to the 2007 landmark. On June 29, buoyed by the finale of *La fea mas bella,* Univision reached 7.4 million viewers.[80] That night, more U.S. residents watched a Spanish-language network than any other source of television. Although Univision had topped the English-language networks on previous occasions, its victory that June, during a Nielsen ratings sweep, was the first that was widely acknowledged and reported in the press. Yet Univision knew that it owed the feat to Azcárraga Jean. *La fea mas bella* was a novela Televisa had produced.

* * *

When Don Browne became Telemundo president in April 2005, he reached the same conclusions as his predecessor, James McNamara, had. First, Telemundo's ratings were low because it imported novelas from multiple countries that had too much indigenous content. Second, Telemundo had no prospect for a source of foreign programs that was comparable to Televisa. Third, the only solution was to reinvent Telemundo as its own content provider. Finally and most crucially, to achieve program self-sufficiency, massive finance would be needed.

In April 2006, Browne announced that NBC had agreed to approve expenditures of $100 million. NBC was now known as NBC Universal. The NBC companies, which since 1986 had been a division of General Electric, constituted the world's fifth-largest media conglomerate. The financing sped up new program production at Telemundo's Hialeah studios. On September 28, 2006, Browne traveled to Mexico City to inaugurate a $25 million NBC-Telemundo studio division. It was the first time a U.S. network had opened a studio abroad.[81]

Browne said, "We have planted our flag in Mexico." It had not seemed likely that Telemundo would have the fortitude, let alone the resources, to take this step. Still reaching only 20 percent of a U.S. Latino audience that was 60 percent of Mexican descent, the network's most dependable ratings came from the novelas it continued to import from Mexico's Argos Comunicación. Observers questioned whether Telemundo could compete with Argos, Televisa, and TV Azteca for Mexico's novela producers and actors. Browne conceded there was "no silver bullet" and that Telemundo's first Mexican productions were one to two years away.[82]

Yet momentum gathered after a second and more historic development four months later. On January 1, 2007, when Telemundo marked its twentieth anniversary, it was the first enterprise in Spanish-language television to generate all of its own programming. Everything on Telemundo's schedule was content that it had produced or co-produced. However, the feat was overshadowed by a dispute. As insiders had anticipated, Argos and TV Azteca were not delighted by Telemundo's presence in Mexico City. Neither was the Mexican government. After tangling with all three, Browne agreed to terminate its partnership with Argos.[83] On December 31, 2006, when the contracts on the remaining Argos programs expired, U.S. viewers saw the last of the imported programs on Telemundo. But Browne was prepared; six programs that had been produced in Hialeah were ready for air on January 1.

A different initiative enabled Browne to finally say that Telemundo was the first Spanish-language network "to fly on its own wing." Telemundo's co-production agreement with Colombia's RTI had blossomed. Since teaming in 2002, the two networks had heeded calls for a new type of novela that appealed to youth and could counter the traditional rags-to-riches romantic melodramas that were a staple of Televisa and dominated Univision's schedule.

By 2007, after trial and error, and frequent cancelations of low-rated novelas, Telemundo and RTI had begun to mesh on the type of productions that could draw younger viewers away from Univision. Studios in Bogotá and Hialeah had produced dramas steeped in ironic elements and timely, provocative, and often taboo themes. The work was driven by NBC Universal's infusion of cash. For the first time, viewers of Telemundo saw elaborate settings, acclaimed actors, and high-quality production values. Around twenty promising novelas were in co-production at the end of the year.

The following year, 2008, brought the turning point in the direction Browne had set. *Doña Bárbara,* which RTI co-produced, was about a flawed anti-heroine in 1920s Venezuela, but it stretched to include twenty-first-century U.S. music, cars, and laptop computers. It was among the ten highest-rated novelas Telemundo ever had broadcast. Its ratings were equaled by another cutting-edge program that RTI co-produced, *Sin senos no hay paraíso* (Without Breasts, There Is No Paradise), the story of a young woman who becomes a prostitute and seeks money for breast implants in order to attract a rich cocaine smuggler.

Telemundo also debuted its first Mexican-filmed novela in 2008. *El juramento* (Secret Lies) injected contemporary themes into an adaptation of Caridad Bravo Adams's 1952 novel about a man's revenge on a woman he believes is responsible for his brother's suicide. In addition, from Telemundo Studios, the network broadcast the first highly rated novela it alone had produced. Filmed in Miami, *El rostro de Analía* (Analía's Face) told the story of a female airline executive torn by dual commitments to her family and her career.

On April 2, 2009, a Telemundo news release feted its first ratings achievement since Joaquín Blaya's brief success in 1993. After six months of gains, Telemundo, averaging 1.2 million viewers, had risen from the number 8 to the number 6 U.S. network. There was more good news at the end of the year; Telemundo posted revenue of $1 billion.[84]

Univision still had the upper hand—two million viewers and $2.5 billion in revenue. When he appeared on national television on the C-SPAN network in September 2010, Browne looked ahead to the final "reinvention" of Telemundo. "Seven years ago, we were [close to] going out of business. And we opened the door to the most talented people in the world who happened to be Hispanic and began to transform Telemundo into a content company. . . . That's the opportunity," Browne told the C-SPAN audience.[85]

* * *

At the time of Univision's triumph with *La fea mas bella* in 2007, the drama of *Televisa, S.A. de C.V. v. Univision Communications, Inc.* was in its second year. It played out in U.S. District Court in Los Angeles, the same court where, two decades earlier, Judge Mariana Pfaelzer had presided over *Fouce Amusement Enterprises and Metropolitan Theaters Corp. vs. Spanish International Communications Corp.* A ten-phase litigation that was to span four years passed from two judges to a special master and, finally, to Judge Phillip Gutiérrez. The judge ordered a separate bench trial for Phase Ten, the Internet dispute. That December, Gutiérrez set a trial date in March 2008.[86]

After seventeen preliminary hearings and 249 docket filings, the firms' corporate counsels stepped aside. To try the case, the litigants hired star attorneys known for their combativeness and theatrics. Televisa enlisted Marshall Grossman, Univision John Keker.

During twenty-six more preliminary hearings, the two lead attorneys set the tone for what the jury would see. Grossman rebuked Keker for filing motions to postpone the trial. When the judge did grant a continuance, Keker blasted Grossman for using the delay to subpoena more Univision witnesses. The judge rescheduled the trial for October 2008. Fearing a spectacle in the courtroom, Gutiérrez ruled "that no further trial continuances shall be permitted, and that trial time limits will be set for each side."[87]

But there was an unresolved issue. By that October, the judge still had not ruled on Keker's motions to subpoena Azcárraga Jean and to admit a video deposition by Perenchio. Over Grossman's strenuous objections, Keker won. The judge ruled that the jury would hear from both Azcárraga Jean and Perenchio.[88] Gutiérrez reset the trial date for January 2009.[89]

News organizations previewed the showdown. Univision introduced its own coverage with graphics accompanied by the text "*Guerra de titanes*" (War of Titans). Interviewed in newspapers and on the Fox News Channel, Latino media consultant Julio Rumbaut, explaining that Unvision depended on Televisa for programs and Televisa depended on Univision's delivery of a large U.S. audience, noted that "it comes down to who needs who more." Laura Martínez told listeners of National Public Radio that the trial "is much like a *novella* [sic] itself [with] Emilio Azcárraga Jean pretty much coming out in defense of his dad, the late Emilio Azcárraga Milmo, whom he felt was tricked somehow by [Univision's] owners."[90]

Commentators refrained from predicting what the verdict would be. Univision had irrefutable evidence that Televisa had twice signed the PLA. Televisa's evidence that the contract had become unfair—that Univision had achieved profitability on revenue it generated from its broadcast of Televisa's programs but had held to agreements that permitted Televisa only 9 percent of the revenue as Univision's profits and revenue multiplied—was equally compelling. But observers agreed with José Cancela, owner of the Miami-based market communications firm Hispanic USA who, under Joaquín Blaya, had previously been an executive at both Univision and Telemundo, that "if Televisa wins, this changes overnight the landscape of Spanish television as we know it. If they [Univision] were to lose [Televisa's programming], it has tremendous implications."[91]

On Tuesday, January 6, 2009, spectators, the press, and legions of both companies' executives packed a Los Angeles courtroom. After the attorneys agreed on a seven-man, two-woman jury, Gutiérrez instructed the attorneys on the time limits he had imposed. He told the jury that the trial would be complex but would conclude on schedule in three weeks.

In his opening statement, Grossman asked the jury to think of Televisa as an abused spouse trying to escape a bad marriage. Battered by Univision, "Televisa is saying no more, no more. We hope to put an end to this relationship." When it was his turn, Keker asked jurors to think of Azcárraga Jean as a "crybaby." He lost to Saban, "miscalculated, [and] now wants to bust the contract," Univision's attorney said.[92] Meg James of the *Los Angeles Times* reported that a captivated jury had heard of "heavy-handed tactics," "financial shenanigans," "material breach," and "scare tactics"—all on the first day.[93]

The tone changed the following day. The attorneys' dramatic personal attacks gave way to exhaustive, line-by-line testimony about the details of the PLA. By the end of the first week, Grossman had called two dozen auditors, accountants, lawyers, and bookkeepers. Larry Dam gave persuasive testimony. Dam was the attorney who had defended Spanish International in Frank Fouce's lawsuit. He had subsequently joined Televisa and had teamed up with Emilio Diez Barroso to negotiate the PLA on Televisa's behalf. Prior to Azcárraga Jean's ascension in 1997, Barroso, the great-grandson of Emilio Azcárraga Vidaurreta, was the presumed heir apparent to Emilio Azcárraga Milmo and had expected to succeed him as Televisa's owner. Citing provisions of the PLA he personally had negotiated, Dam told the jurors that merely by failing to pay one royalty, Univision had broken the contract.

Keker then began his case. Also citing language from the contract, his first witness for Univision maintained that Televisa's claim that royalty payments had not been made was supported only by a generalized assertion and that a detailed demand was needed for the claim to be legitimate. Other witnesses testified that Televisa's claims were false and concocted.[94]

In the third week of the trial, Keker called the star witnesses. Ray Rodríguez was questioned for two days. To give the attorneys time to prepare for the final witness, Gutiérrez ordered that the trial resume two days later, on January 22. That day, Keker would begin his examination of Azcárraga Jean.[95]

* * *

On January 22, anticipating Keker's bludgeoning of Azcárraga Jean, spectators and the press arrived early. But the courtroom was empty. *Los Angeles Times* reporter Meg James later recounted that at "8:50 A.M. . . . lawyers representing both sides indicated the trial's start would be delayed by about an hour. Then, about 45 minutes later, one of Univision's attorneys stepped out of the courtroom and hollered, 'It's done.'"[96]

It appeared that the parties had settled the lawsuit. Minutes later, reporters spotted Azcárraga Jean. He confirmed the settlement. "This is good, good for everyone," he said as he left the courthouse. All smiles as they, too, departed, the firms' executives told of an all-night session, then an agreement signed half an hour earlier. Saban also expressed delight.[97]

The jubilation was short lived. The agreement was two pages long.[98] The fact that the attorneys continued to argue suggested that the settlement had settled very little. Appearing on Fox News, where he reported that Univision had agreed to pay Televisa $600 million, Grossman claimed that he and Televisa had vanquished their opponent. "Univision should be glad to dodge a bullet," Grossman said. Keker was angry. Televisa "tried to terminate the [PLA], and didn't" and then "dismissed its case," he said. He said that Televisa had agreed to the 9:30 A.M. settlement because their attorneys knew that minutes later Azcárraga Jean would be forced to take the witness stand.[99]

Rodríguez believed that neither attorney correctly characterized the outcome. Televisa settled, he said, not to avoid Azcárraga Jean's appearance but because appeals certain to prolong the proceeding would have drained Televisa's finances. Since filing the lawsuit in 2005, Televisa had spent an exorbitant amount, $90 million, to ensure victory in the case. Univision had agreed to pay Televisa not $600 million but $45 million. Meanwhile, according to Rodríguez, both sides were saying that "the settlement was huge." "Very little was settled about changing the PLA, but keeping the PLA was big," he maintained.[100]

In *American Law Daily*, Brian Baxter analyzed a "barbarous" settlement in which both firms' futures were still "on the hook." Neither party had addressed the paramount issue with the PLA: it was due to expire in 2017. In addition, Televisa was no closer to owning Univision, and Univision kept the rights to Televisa's programs for eight more years. According to Baxter, "the history of bad blood between the two Spanish-language media companies has . . . spilled into the relationship," their "wars apparently just getting going." Calling attention to an agreement that was good only "through 2017," another analyst, Eriq Gardner, maintained that either "Univision and Televisa [would] kiss and make up" or they would "clash swords" again en route to divorce."[101]

At Univision, CEO Joe Uva and Chief Strategic Officer Cesar Conde were relieved and elated to hear that Univision was assured the rights to air Televisa's programs for seven more years. They were less anxious about what might happen in 2017. Watching the trial, they had had a bellyful of Televisa. Because of fortuitous events in Miami, they were confident that they would need to concern themselves with the Mexican firm no longer.

After nearly two years of planning, Univision Studios had become a reality. This was the enterprise through which Univision would combine foreign and domestic talent, produce world-class Spanish-language programs, and bid Televisa adieu. It had stalled in 2008 during a national recession. The timing for such an expensive project was bad; Saban was still leveraged and in debt from the buyout. At the time he was hoping that Univision's access to Televisa's programs might still be saved.

But in June 2009, Univision defeated Televisa in the bench trial on who had the right to broadcast Televisa's programs on the Internet. The victory rallied Saban and his creditors, and Saban approved $1 billion in expenditures over several years for the studio project. To the press, Conde vowed that Univision Studios will herald "our independence [and] set our future direction."[102]

In 2009, on the occasion of Ray Rodríguez's retirement, Miami mayor Carlos Alvárez proclaimed November 19th Ray Rodríguez Day. Uva joined dignitaries in naming the soon-to-be-massive Doral facility the Ray Rodríguez Broadcast Center. That night, star entertainers Enrique Iglesias and Gloria Estefan toasted Rodríguez and the plans for his namesake facility at a gala celebration at the Fontainebleau Hotel.[103]

Two weeks later, on December 7, dignitaries and the press gathered at the Rodríguez Center. Next to a plaque honoring Rodríguez, Uva and Conde dedicated Univision Studios. The moment was crowned by their introduction of a stellar figure from world television. Luis Fernández, the president of Spain's Radio Televisión Española, had come to the United States to head the project.

Conde also announced a partnership with Venevisión through which Univision would produce and film its first star-studded telenovela. According to Conde, the production, *Eva Luna,* which was scheduled to premiere in December 2011, would set the stage for broadcasts that would commemorate Univision's fiftieth anniversary. Uva, noting Saban's $1 billion investment, said that Univision Studios would produce 4,000 hours of programs.[104]

Uva continued to speak of Univision's "independence" and "new direction." On February 25, 2010, he told the press about Fernández's plans for Univision Studios. He vowed that "the 4,000 hours of programs" would easily sustain Univision by the time the PLA expired in 2017. When asked whether Televisa approved, Uva replied, "We can do whatever we want."[105]

Or so it seemed.

* * *

For both sides, Univision Studios was a bone to be chewed on. Azcárraga Jean faced the reality that in seven years, Televisa was likely to be cast out from the U.S. house it had built. But the onus was on Saban. Years ahead of the expiration date of the PLA, Saban had already faced what it meant for Univision. He could bankroll an infant project and assert Univision's

Figure 16. Mario Kreutzberger hosts Emilio Azcárraga Jean at the annual dinner of the Organización Internacional de Teletones in 2012. As founder and chair of Oritel, an international charity organization, Kreutzberger presented Azcárraga Jean with the group's Grand Order of Solidarity Award. Photo courtesy of Craig Allen.

independence, or he could continue the network's fifty years of prosperity at the hip of its mother firm. That summer, he tested the climate. He invited Azcárraga Jean and his lieutenants to engage in a "fight to end all the fighting."

On October 5, 2010, those at Univision were stunned when Saban announced that history had been made. Following deep and secretive negotiations, he and Televisa's Alfonso de Angoitia had signed a "joint operating agreement." It was the first definitive partnership agreement between the firms since Telesistema Méxicano founded Spanish International in 1961.

This time, the firms struck a genuine agreement. Univision won extension of the PLA and exclusive rights to Televisa's programs until 2025. Televisa won 35 percent ownership of Univision, three seats on the Univision board, and co-governance of Univision's U.S. operations. Televisa reclaimed governing ownership by paying Saban $1.2 billion. Statements extolled the agreement's historical significance. "We are extremely pleased to have . . . finally align[ed] for the long-term," Saban declared.[106] "A relationship started by Don Emilio Azcárraga in 1961 has been fulfilled," de Angoitia announced.[107]

The final fight was not without casualties. While he was planning a broadcast to commemorate Univision's founding, Conde halted the Univision Studios project. Five weeks after the signing, the new regime canceled the program *Cristina,* a Univision fixture for nearly twenty-five years, and dismissed Cristina Saralegui.

Then, in March 2011, when the FCC altered its rules and approved Televisa's 35 percent co-ownership, Univision lost more. Televisa executives removed the plaque and trappings that honored Ray Rodríguez. The plaque was shuffled to a lobby where it could barely be seen. Just as quickly, Univision Studios was mothballed. Uva resigned from Univision, and Conde and Fernández were not far behind. Although Fernández's *Eva Luna* achieved the highest ratings of any U.S.-produced novela, Univision no longer needed Univision Studios.

On December 15, 2011, the official anniversary of the network, San Antonio's KWEX did broadcast a tribute. Station personnel and local dignitaries staged a dinner to honor Emilio Nicolás, the last surviving member of the group that had gathered in San Antonio and incorporated the Spanish International Network in 1961. The 81-year-old Nicolás recalled the news release announcing the launch of SIN and the dismay of Emilio Azcárraga, Rene Anselmo, and Frank Fouce when only the local media reported it.[108]

A half-century of Spanish-language television ended the way it began. At its inception, only San Antonio knew. Fifty years later, only San Antonio remembered.

* * *

Front office uncertainties dashed another observance. Telemundo was due to mark its twenty-fifth anniversary in January 2012, yet the network had been in limbo since January 2011, when telecommunications giant Comcast had acquired Telemundo's parent firm, NBC Universal, and announced a reorganization. Six months later, Don Browne, Telemundo's CEO and president, was gone. Uva and Conde headed Telemundo's next management team.

Browne departed as the most accomplished of the nine presidents who had directed Telemundo during the network's twenty-five years. His tenure of six years was the longest. He had established Telemundo both as a billion-dollar enterprise and the preeminent U.S. producer of Spanish-language programs. In 2010, two novelas produced in Hialeah, *Alguien te mira* and *¿Dónde está Elisa?*, bested Univision in the Nielsen ratings. Two months before June 2011, when Browne left, Telemundo premiered *La reina del sur* (The Queen of the South), which had three to four million viewers each night. The novela amassed the highest ratings Telemundo had ever generated.

Yet Browne's reinvention of Telemundo did not end the way it was intended, in the dethroning of Univision. Browne reduced the rival's audience advantage from three to one to two to one, but Univision remained number one.

The reorganization of Comcast in 2011 concluded with pledges of financial support greater than those NBC had provided. Listing Telemundo as the giant firm's sixth-highest priority, Comcast chair and CEO Brian Roberts vowed to "expand the availability of over-the-air programming to the Hispanic community [and] enhance the current programming of Telemundo."[109]

By mid-2011, Telemundo was headlong into a $100 million project to bolster its stations' local news. Plans for a $250 million broadcast complex in south Miami were announced. That October, Telemundo won the rights to televise the 2018 World Cup. The move meant that Univision's 2014 broadcasts of the World Cup, its ninth run over thirty-six years, would be its last.[110]

Univision did not concede defeat; it did not need to. It had remained the number one source of Spanish-language television for fifty consecutive years. In August 2011, a company statement boasted of Univision's ranking as the number three network among young adults; only Fox and ABC surpassed it. Collectively, Univision, Telefutura, and Galavisión reached nearly 75 percent of the U.S. Latino audience.[111]

In May 2012, Univision loosely acknowledged its fifty-year milestone. When its new managers needed a theme for their upfront meeting with advertisers, they chose "Fifty Years of the Heart." Attendees packed New York's New Amsterdam Theatre. The event began with a pyrotechnic display and a stage show by singer Shakira. "As Univision celebrates its 50th anniversary," new president Randy Falco opined, "the time is now to connect with the Hispanic consumer." Falco and his colleagues spoke of "a "booming Hispanic population," Univision's "powerhouse foreign partnerships," and "international programs and stars." They trumpeted Univision's "73 market share." Looking back, Falco observed "that over 50 years one thing has remained the same—Latinos live here at Univision."[112]

CONCLUSION

Univision did televise a golden anniversary spectacular. On October 27, 2012, a special broadcast of *Sábado gigante* celebrated Univision's fiftieth year as a network and Mario Kreutzberger's fiftieth year as emcee. Kreutzberger did more than host the commemorative show; he *was* the show.

That night, in character as "Don Francisco," Kreutzberger greeted a red-carpet parade of celebrities, reenacted the show's classic skits and spoofs, and was certified as a "special member" of *Guinness Book of World Records*. No one had been on TV longer, had been viewed by more people, or had hosted a program with as many prime-time episodes, approximately 2,000.[1] "After all these years, I had only had two employers," he later reminisced. One was the Catholic Church, the owner of Chile's Canal Trece where *Sábado gigante* began, and the other was Univision. "I worked for the angels" in both jobs, he said.[2]

When Univision marked its fiftieth anniversary in 2012, most of the living pioneers were still active. Nearing their sixtieth anniversary, Emilio and Irma Cortez Nicolás were civic leaders in San Antonio. Danny Villanueva was president of the Pasadena investment bank R. C. Fontis and a leader of efforts to return pro football to Los Angeles. Joaquín Blaya was a director of the Voice of America. During the Iraq War, he had launched the State Department's Middle East TV channel Al-Hurrah. Irvine Hockaday had retired from Hallmark and had become a lifetime trustee of the Aspen Institute in recognition of his contributions to corporate America. At age eighty, Carlos Barba had launched a TV network called Caribevisión. Gustavo Godoy was publisher of *Vista* magazine in Miami, and Jaime Dávila was a media consultant in New York. After Cristina Saralegui's longtime Univision program was canceled in 2010, she had finished her on-air career at Telemundo.

When the National Association of Broadcasters honored Emilio Nicolás and Raoul Cortez with lifetime achievement awards at a ceremony in Las Vegas 2006, Cortez's daughter Irma Nicolás accepted the award for her father, who had died, and Fouce's son was a surprise attendee. Nicolás and Fouce had not spoken to one another since 1976, when Fouce had filed the lawsuit that doomed the Spanish International Network. That Fouce had sent his son to Nicolás's ceremony in 2006 indicated a semblance of a reconciliation. Beset with medical problems and stricken with cancer in 2012, Fouce passed away the following year.

Telemundo founder Saul Steinberg died in December 2012. He remained one of Wall Street's most iconic corporate raiders, although after he sold Telemundo in 1995, financial difficulties plagued the rest of his career. He liquidated the 150-year-old Reliance Insurance Corporation, the firm from which Telemundo had sprung in 1986, and donated his remaining estate to the University of Pennsylvania's Wharton School.

Seventeen years had passed since the death of Rene Anselmo. While he was never honored by the National Association of Broadcasters or any organization, Anselmo was remembered for the fortune he amassed from his PanAmSat venture. When it was sold to Hughes Aircraft in 2004, proceeds of $1.1 billion passed to his wife, Mary Anselmo. *Forbes* magazine listed her as one of the 400 richest individuals in the United States.[3]

With a net worth of $2.6 billion, Jerry Perenchio joined Mrs. Anselmo on that list. For forty years "the most important person in Hollywood no one ever knew," Perenchio finished his career a changed media mogul. In 2012, he abandoned his guarded lifestyle and his "Rules of the Road." He held court with the press and onlookers during a public event celebrating his donation of artwork valued at $500 million to the Los Angeles County Museum of Art. He radiated his new self when he returned to his boyhood home to accept an honorary doctoral degree from Fresno State University. Crowds he had once shunned cheered when Perenchio proclaimed, "This is my hometown and I'm damned proud!"[4]

Although many still recalled Kreutzberger's golden anniversary spectacular of October 2012, a different spectacle again brought the past to life in September 2013. That was when the protest in San Antonio began and the so-called Univision 8 were jailed for their failed effort to prevent the

Figure 17. Lili Estefan, Mario Rodríguez (*center*), and Raúl De Molina gather for a reunion during Univision's fiftieth-anniversary festivities in 2012. Estefan and De Molina hosted the network's popular afternoon program *El gordo y la flaca* for fourteen years. Rodríguez was Univision's longtime program chief. Photo courtesy of Mario Rodríguez.

demolition of the KWEX building. Less than a year after "Don Francisco" in Miami had celebrated Univision's fifty years in television on *Sábado gigante*, the network's birthplace in San Antonio was in ruins.

As condominiums rose at the San Antonio site, citizens joined with the city of San Antonio and the University of Texas-San Antonio in placing a plaque on the walkway of the city's Riverwalk near the original site. The San Antonio Library and the nearby University of Texas-Austin spearheaded projects to ensure that the history of Spanish-language television—not the parts "Don Francisco" spoofed but those that identified the contributions of Cortez, Nicolás, the Azcárragas, and others—was not forgotten. The opinion of Victor Landa, a 2013 protestor who said that the pioneers had succeeded by "beating the odds," continued to resonate among many.[5]

* * *

By the 2010s, interest in Spanish-language television had enlarged beyond remembrances of the founders. Univision was a billion-dollar corporation and Telemundo was an arm of the Comcast-NBC group, and it was difficult to imagine either as enterprises that had "beaten the odds."

Despite the public's move to digital and online media, broadcast networks still attracted the largest media audiences. In 2013, Univision swept the summer Nielsen ratings; the network's average audience of 3.6 million was greater than that of ABC, CBS, NBC, Fox, and all other providers of English-language TV. Blogs, websites, and newspapers noted the novel turn in network television.[6]

Only ten years before, most of the nation's 250 million non-Latinos had had only a vague awareness of Univision. By the 2010s, many non-Latinos were bothered that a network that communicated in a language they did not understand was vying to become the country's largest source of mass communication. Each mention of the success of Univision and Telemundo fed fears that the United States they knew was changing amid a Latino boom at a time that was largely defined by resistance to immigration and xenophobic tendencies. Many politicians and opinion leaders who believed the fabric of U.S. society was tearing apart blamed Spanish-language television.

In 2007, the governor of the nation's largest state publicly castigated Spanish-language television as divisive and dangerous. California governor Arnold Schwarzenegger stirred nationwide controversy when he urged Latino journalists to tell their Latino audiences to "turn off the Spanish-language television set." The Republican governor, a famed Hollywood actor who was also an immigrant from Austria, related his struggle to learn English upon arriving in the United States. He insisted that fluency in English was essential for anyone living in the United States who aspired to succeed there. He maintained that Spanish-language television acted as a narcotic that lulled Spanish-speaking individuals into withdrawing from mainstream U.S. culture. When Latinos stopped watching Spanish-language television, "you're just forced to speak English, and that just makes you learn the language faster," the governor said.[7]

Brent Wilkes, head of the League of United Latin American Citizens, replied that Schwarzenegger was "ignorant on immigration issues [by] once again perpetuating the myth that immigrants have to reject their old culture and language in order to learn English and assimilate." Univision stated, "Spanish-language media plays the essential roles of providing the Hispanic community with the news and information they need and care about, and keeping them connected to their cultural heritage."[8] Schwarzenegger did not note that, in fact, the vast majority of younger Latinos were fluent in English, including the journalists he had addressed in English.

Conservative groups focused on the large audiences that tuned to the networks' daily and nightly news. Ninety percent of Latinos said they regularly viewed *Noticiero Univision*. Univision's daily news audiences of three million exceeded those of the Fox News Channel. Its reach was many times greater than that of CNN. Led by the Washington-based Media Research Center, conservative watchdog groups suggested that Spanish-language television news was biased and was misinforming a large proportion of the U.S. population. They commissioned content analyses that compared Spanish-language and English-language newscasts.

In 2014, a Media Research Center report was widely disseminated on the Internet and seized upon by conservative publications including the *National Review*. The study showed that the Spanish-language networks interviewed "Democratic, left-leaning sources" six times more often than Republican and conservative sources. Democrats appeared 287 times in reports on immigration reform on Spanish-language television; Republicans appeared 135 times in the period November 1, 2013, to February 28, 2014. The study concluded that "bias . . . in the news coverage of the top Spanish-language television networks is a real problem. Just like the rest of America's news consumers, viewers of U.S. Spanish-language networks deserve news coverage that is comprehensive, fair and accurate."[9]

Conservative radio and TV talk show hosts alleged that the news on Spanish-language programs was one-sided and biased. Laura Ingraham said that Univision and Telemundo were "toxic Hispanic-centric outlets that revile the American Experience."[10] Her colleagues Rush Limbaugh, Sean Hannity, and Bill O'Reilly also disparaged Spanish-language television. O'Reilly accused Univision of persisting "in demonizing conservative politicians as racist" and said that the network itself was "dedicated to racism."[11]

Two conservative politicians also stepped forward. Republican senator Marco Rubio of Florida said he was the victim of what the *New Yorker* termed a "war with Univision."[12] After refusing an interview appearance at Univision, Rubio accused the network of measures that sought to destroy his political career because his opposition to immigration did not conform to Univision's "liberal line."[13] In August 2015, after announcing that he would run for president in the 2016 general election, Donald Trump appeared before reporters. While Trump was calling on different reporters, Univision news anchor Jorge Ramos stood up and pressed Trump to explain his proposals to limit immigration. Trump asked Ramos to wait his turn three times. When Ramos persisted, Trump told Ramos to "go back to Univision." Before live cameras, Trump then ordered security guards to remove Ramos from the room. Veteran media observer Howard Kurtz said that Trump's "performance" brought Spanish-language television an unprecedented "avalanche of publicity."[14]

Trump's confrontation with Ramos, which was recounted in the news media and replayed on television, may have been the turning point when Trump connected with "silent majority" voters who were dissatisfied with politicians' and the news media's neglect of traditional U.S. values; he went on to win the 2016 Republican nomination. Opinion polls showed that Trump's approval rating among GOP voters was 15 percent in July 2015. In the two weeks after his exchange with Ramos in August, it increased from 22 percent to 33 percent. Trump remained unchallenged as the Republican front-runner. Observers suggested that Trump's willingness to confront the alleged "grandstanding" of a leader of the Latino community created a "Ramos effect" that solidified his "silent majority" base.[15]

Univision CEO Randy Falco blasted Trump and defended Ramos. Falco termed Trump's behavior "beyond contempt." Ramos remained at odds with Trump, maintaining that the U.S. president was racist. He insisted that when Trump told him to "go back to Univision," he "really meant to go back to Mexico. And I think hate is contagious."[16]

* * *

Yet it was not in the political ring but in the arena of study and analysis that complaints about Spanish-language television were most trenchantly expressed. In critiques that reflected their awareness of Univision's multibillion dollar operating agreement with Televisa in 2010 and Comcast's acquisition of Telemundo the following year, some of the closest observers of Spanish-language television, most Latino, voiced concern that the endeavor's push into big business exposed a long-standing retreat from the interests and needs of its Latino constituency.

Much of the concern was aroused by new and more critical perspectives on the international pursuits of Spanish-language television. Although newer observers still honored its role in globalizing the medium as a distinguishing feature of its contribution to U.S. television, gone was sentiment that Spanish-language television's opening of domestic television to foreign content and perspectives also had opened international communication, understanding, and good feeling. Many believed that the fact that Spanish-language networks offered content from abroad was a function of their proprietors' capitalism and self-interest.

Some dismissed the once-lauded flow of media from South to North. Years before, the south-to-north flow was considered historic because it brought TV content from Mexico and Latin America to the United States, reversing a one-way flow of U.S. content to those locales and elsewhere around the world. But in a 2003 article, Raúl de Mora Jiménez argued that the south-to-north media flow was a myth, that it was a corporate scheme of Mexico's Televisa, which all along had been the only genuine source of south-to-north media flow.[17]

But it was not reconsideration of media flow that most inspired critics' reassessment of Spanish-language television's international imprint. More unsettling was the south-of-the-border programming that appeared on U.S. TV screens. Although those programs had long been treated as benign, newer observers laid bare three problems such programming had always posed. First, it was profuse. Second, it typically was banal; it appealed to a "lowest common denominator" audience as a means of earning high ratings and high revenue. Finally, a few proprietors' reliance on foreign programming for profit detached tens of millions of U.S. Latinos from their lives in the United States.

There were never exact estimates of the total proportion of Univision and Telemundo content that was imported. At Univision, it probably consisted of around 90 percent of total content during its SIN period, 1961–1986. Starting with Univision's domestic production initiatives in 1997 and the premieres of *Despierta América, Primer impacto,* and *El gordo y la flaca,* the proportion likely settled at around 50 percent. Telemundo's proportion over time was likely less than 50 percent because of that network's commitment to domestic production.

It was certain, though, that close to 100 percent of the programming Univision and Telemundo provided Latinos during peak prime-time viewing periods was either imported or produced through foreign coproduction agreements. The preponderance of prime-time programming consisted one genre of programs, the soap opera–like foreign telenovela.

Many observers reviled the networks' willingness to show mainly these programs at hours when the largest numbers of Latinos tuned in.

Few doubted the banality of telenovelas. Danny Villanueva had anticipated that novelas would turn Spanish-language television into a "fantasyland" fifty years earlier. Now, author Marietta Morrissey argued that broadcasting foreign "Cinderella" stories harmed U.S. Latinos by reinforcing the "class, racial, and gender stereotypes" of other countries.[18]

The novelas' detachment of U.S. Latinos from the nation and their communities was felt acutely. Observers who had taken closer looks at Spanish-language television in the 2000s and, increasingly, in the 2010s often vehemently accused Univision and Telemundo of shirking a duty and a responsibility to help U.S. Latinos by exposing them to and, in the case of immigrant Latinos, helping them adjust to lifestyles in the United States. This was the same issue Schwarzenegger had raised. Media studies scholar Hector Amaya argued that the networks' relentless provision of programming showing life in Mexico, Venezuela, and elsewhere illustrated Spanish-language television's fundamental failure. He maintained that although Univision's and Telemundo's public statements often spoke of their concern for the welfare of Latinos, the preponderance of what they put on the air showed little regard or care for them. Their "lack of interest in servicing the ... cultural and political needs of [U.S.] Latinas/os [and their] hypercommodified practices even included the importation of [Mexican] news programming," Amaya said. Spanish-language television "behaved as if the Spanish-speaking Latina/os it served did not have national or local interests."[19]

Dolores Inés Casillas concurred. She argued that the founders' push to create a nationwide Latino audience by offering foreign programming left Spanish-language television structurally unable to acclimate Latinos to U.S. lifestyles. In her 2014 book ¡Sounds of Belonging!, Casillas insisted that only Spanish-language radio had the means of connecting U.S. Latinos to their local communities. Television does not have "the same intimate capability as radio," she said, and it does not help Latinos navigate "the often hostile terrain of the United States" the way radio does.[20]

* * *

The issue that most concerned newer critics of Spanish-language television was the homogenization of Latino societies into a "Pan Latinidad" in the United States. There was no dispute that "Latinidad" prevailed in the United States or that Spanish-language television had played the definitive role in creating it. In the United States, diverse Latino populations identified by nationality and lived in different regions and locales. National Spanish-language television in the United States needed to construct and maintain an undifferentiated U.S. Latino audience, and through messaging, advertising, and programming that appealed to Latinos of all nationalities, Univision and Telemundo persuaded Latinos that they now belonged to a single, homogeneous U.S. Spanish-speaking group.

Newer observers presented the idea of Latinidad as a powerful audience effect that distinguished Spanish-language television's role in the development of U.S. television. Yet for some observers, Latinidad had troubling implications, most conspicuously that network proprietors had perpetrated a form of subjugation that submerged Latinos' natural identities.

When América Rodríguez first proposed the idea of Latinidad in 1999, it was conjecture derived from historical analysis. Rodríguez showed that early Spanish-language radio station owners and a few who had produced and distributed Spanish-language motion pictures through the 1920s and 1930s were impeded because Latinos of differing nationalities populated different parts of the country. That obstacle was removed when the Spanish International Network began broadcasting from coast to coast. However, Rodríguez provided little evidence that Mexicans, Cubans, and Spanish speakers from other nations perceived SIN's homogenization measures or that Latinos realized they were sharing a viewing experience with Latinos from other nations and cultures who lived elsewhere in the United States.[21]

In 2001, Arlene Dávila's book-length examination of Spanish-language advertising, marketing, and television, *Latinos, Inc.*, showed how Latinos' constant exposure to culturally generic advertising and programming devoid of national themes and dialects had removed Latinos' sense of their native/ancestral nationalities and made them "Americans." Spanish-language television needed to reduce diverse Latinos into a lucrative U.S. Latino market, and Dávila argued that it had done just that.

Her work was a foundation for many of the critical writings that followed. Subsequent authors were drawn to her chapter "The Focus (or Fuck Us) Group," which provided the first empirical evidence that Latinidad existed. After examining data from collections of focus groups of Latinos of different nationalities, Dávila wrote that "separately and collectively, participants' responses suggest that, despite their criticism of the category or representation in the media, they have in fact internalized, or made theirs, particular dynamics and conventions of commercial Latinidad."[22]

Dávila conceded that Latinidad was complex, emphasizing that by the 2000s, Latinos' U.S. citizenship, or their quest for it, and an increasing political and social consciousness contributed to their sense they were members of a U.S. Latino "whole." "For many U.S. Latinos, a common identity is far from based on ... media-generated notions of Hispanic authenticity," she wrote.

Nevertheless, the "homogenization of heterogeneous populations into a single 'Latino market'" raised questions. "This industry first advanced the idea of a common 'Hispanic market,'" she wrote. She illustrated the problem with homogenization by describing a TV advertisement Latinos had seen multiple times on both Univision and Telemundo. In it, a "middle-aged [Latina] woman who holds dear her traditional values nonetheless likes hamburgers and can afford a luxury Ford car." Dávila argued that "it is naïve to ignore the embedded inequalities that are forged by this common Latino market."[23]

Latinidad became the dimension of Spanish-language television that newer observers reacted to with the most vehemence. Subjugation was a theme in Viviana Rojas's 2010 study of Spanish-speaking women. The people she studied described "ambivalent and conflicted relationship[s] with [culturally generic] television programs." Some "Latinas felt attacked, insulted, offended and embarrassed by women's portrayals in certain entertainment and humor shows," Rojas found.[24]

The newer critique of Spanish-language television was most clearly spelled out in 2015 in media studies scholar Christopher Chávez's *Reinventing the Latino Television Viewer*. Chávez proposed that "Hispanic television may be seen as a site of domination.... Latino audiences are coerced by more powerful media institutions that are competing with one another for economic capital. In doing so, [the institutions] are exploiting" both Latinos and "the politics of difference that occur when two languages come in contact with one another."[25]

In 2019, *The Nation* magazine hosted a forum of Latino leaders and journalists. Participant Miguel Salazar conceded that "Latinidad provides an opportunity to educate Americans about a growing demographic that ... over the past half-century has worn many hats—'Latin American,' 'Hispanic,' 'Latino,' and most recently, 'Latinx.'" Yet while ethnic identity has been "useful for raising awareness of migrant family separations,

Washington's insistence on militarizing borders in Mexico and Central America, and mass shooters warning of a 'Hispanic invasion' of the United States," its "most vocal critics... have not minced words in their critique of what they see as an exclusionary identity fabricated by—and for the benefit of—white and mestizo elites," including those who control the media.

Participant Daniel Alvarenga added, "Latinidad in general doesn't make room to talk about US imperialism, either. It doesn't make room to talk about conflict. [As a Salvadoran,] I might have a stronger bond with people from countries that have undergone conflicts, but I can't make those connections so easily because I'm stuck in this Latinx box."[26]

* * *

Thus, in the 2010s, Spanish-language television received its first thorough critique. However, much of what critics said did not square with the past. For example, although proprietors did profit from having diverse Latinos perceive themselves as members of a single U.S. Latino population, every proprietor believed that this was a socially desirable objective. Some risked their own job security and threatened the profitability of their company when they took measures that sought to offer Latinos a U.S. identity.

One of them was Jerry Perenchio, the most profit-minded proprietor of all. In 1993, when CNN's offer to supply a Spanish-language national newscast presented Perenchio with an opportunity to eliminate hundreds of millions of dollars of losses, he chose to keep Univision's costly news division, understanding that it served a larger purpose than profits. The Univision news anchor, Jorge Ramos, applauded Perenchio as the "best owner a journalist could have," because by backing and eventually bolstering Univision's news, Perenchio ensured that Latinos would have a source of news and information as a basis for discussion of events and issues.

In 1987, Joaquín Blaya risked his post as Univision president when he replaced Televisa programs with Univision-produced content aimed at uniting U.S. Latinos. The programs, which employed producers and actors of all U.S. Latino nationalities, were extremely costly. At a "moment when Hispanics are taking their place in American society," television will reflect "their American experience," Blaya said at the time. In the period 1987 to 1992, Hallmark lost hundreds of millions of dollars, defaulted, and sold Univision—all because it supported Blaya's call for "Latinidad."

Throughout his twenty-five years as head of the Spanish International Network, Rene Anselmo preached that U.S. Latino unity was necessary and that only Spanish-language television could create it. Anselmo was motivated as much by his contempt for a U.S. government that he was convinced was doing nothing to recognize and assist U.S. Latinos as he was by a search for profits. He plunged SIN into financial chaos in the 1970s by acquiring Televisa's universally appealing programs and purchasing East Coast stations, all along refusing the Azcárragas' claim that SIN would succeed only as a "Mexican" network that spread Mexican identity across the United States. Further, Anselmo was not thinking of "Latinidad" when SIN entered New York and prepared to reach Caribbean-descended audiences with the Azcárragas' Mexican shows. He discovered through trial and error that foreign novelas appealed to Latinos regardless of nationality.

Network proprietors were not solely responsible for the popularity of Spanish-language programming. If anything was clear in Spanish-language television, it was Latinos' extreme preference for banal novelas. Critics of Spanish-language television found that the programs they most disdained were ones audiences most preferred. This was not a new dynamic. In the 1960s, critics had made the same observations about consumers of English-language television. By the 1980s, assaults on the English-language networks had faded; critics had grasped that commercial television is not in hands of owners and managers who come and go; it is organized around a permanent task of giving viewers what they want.

Other aspects of the newer critiques do not ring true. Spanish-language television was not a TV machine without intimacy that was incapable of connecting Latinos to their local communities, as some critics said it was. Even the largest of the networks' local stations excelled in community broadcasting. Spanish-language television enabled each Latino to see and perceive his or her community. On daily and weekly public affairs programs, Latinos saw leaders of local agencies, schools, churches, and groups and local on-air personalities whom they often regarded as personal friends. The stations conducted uncounted telethons. Thousands of South Florida Latinos pledged money and assistance during WLTV's 1980 telethon for the Mariel boatlift refugees. When Emilio Nicolás Jr. organized a grassroots campaign in 1980 called Destino '80, he launched Univision's longest-running public affairs initiative. Every two years, the stations and their local personalities reached into Spanish-speaking communities to encourage voters to register.

Nor was it accurate to portray Televisa solely as a corporate octopus in Mexico whose control of SIN reduced the prospects for international understanding with its exclusive Mexican-based programming. From 1977 to 1986, Televisa's global Univision network enabled U.S. viewers to watch programs from all over the world.

Strangely, most critiques of Spanish-language television omitted or ignored its news programs. Amaya, one of the few to mention news, scorned Spanish-language television for a "lack of interest in servicing the ... needs of Latinas/os [and its] hypercommodified practices." But Amaya also said that "Spanish-language media ... is significantly better than English-language media at addressing the particular needs of Latinas/os. [Spanish-language] news broadcasts do not go unnoticed. ... Eighty-four percent of bilingual Latinas/os use Spanish-language news, a percentage that speaks to the importance viewers place on language and ethnic perspectives."[27]

Spanish-language television news is evidence of the importance the proprietors placed on not merely entertaining but also, in fact, servicing the needs of Latinos. As late as the early 1960s, news on Spanish-language stations consisted of fifteen-minute, single-newscaster broadcasts. The first proprietors did not foresee the evolution of Spanish-language television news into a function that matched English-language television news. They conceived SIN as an entertainment service and regarded news programs as too expensive. Yet at numerous moments when a network's future was in doubt, the owner made sure that Latinos had access to Spanish-language television news.

One such turning point was Perenchio's decision in 1993 to preserve and bolster Univision's network news program. And Blaya hastened to reinstate *Noticiero Telemundo* after demands by Telemundo's creditors had forced the network to suspend it. Before that, Anselmo had initiated TV's first half-hour newscast at KMEX in 1963, then the first Spanish-language national newscast in 1981. Both times, Anselmo not only took on sizable costs but risked his position to defy the Azcárragas and their rule against U.S.-produced programs. Ultimately, the priority owners and managers gave to Spanish-language television news was proof that their networks did attend to the needs and interests of Latinos.

One of the most noteworthy and radical projects of Spanish-language television was its articulation of and practice of advocacy journalism. During his tenure as news director of KMEX in 1968, Danny Villanueva realized that no news is objective and that all news is slanted in some way. He saw that mainstream journalists who believed they were paragons of objectivity worked for news organizations that set news agendas that diminished or ignored Latinos. Mainstream news organizations were promotional billboards for the establishment.

Villanueva knew that Latinos had a perspective and were capable of practicing a definition of news objectivity that was no less legitimate than that of the *New York Times* or CBS News. Villanueva became the founding father of advocacy journalism. "What helps our people—that's our journalism," Villanueva said.[28]

Villanueva's KMEX protégé Rubén Salazar is regarded as a saint for reporting news from a Latino perspective in 1970. He departed from the establishment agenda when he exposed discriminatory housing, underfunded public schools, insufficient public services, and the indifference of government officials. His successors continued to push for reform and for appropriate citizen action such as voter registration. They identified and concentrated on politicians and leaders who were attentive to Latino concerns—and those who were not.

In the 2010s, when conservative watchdog groups discovered that Spanish-language television news informed large numbers of Americans, they assailed news prepared by Latinos that sought to present Latino perspectives as illegitimate. During the furor stirred by detractors of Spanish-language television and in the aftermath of his 2015 confrontation with Donald Trump, Jorge Ramos joined with his Univision co-anchor María Elena Salinas to publicly affirm their "long-practiced pursuit of advocacy journalism."[29] There is little doubt that Spanish-language television connected with Latinos and cared about their interests and needs.

* * *

While political and academic arguments about whether Spanish-language television is beneficial or dangerous increased public interest in the medium, it was apparent that the crucial issues were the practical ones owners wrestled with. After fifty years, owners had not resolved a central question: could the large providers of Spanish-language television develop a coherent entertainment philosophy that was relevant to Latinos and at the same time satisfied the profit motives of owners and stockholders? It was a question that English-language television had rarely confronted.

Over the decades, Spanish-language television had engaged in a back-and-forth dance over programming that had confused its Latino audiences. Most of its history could be reduced to separate pursuits of two conflicting models of program production, one foreign, the other domestic, that left

Latino viewers unsure about what Spanish-language television really was. The findings of the earliest audience ratings that half of Latinos' TV viewing was devoted to English-language television illustrated that uncertainty.

Latinos easily recognized a Univision model. Foreign content had defined Univision since 1961, when the Azcárragas founded the Spanish International Network. Their purpose was to broadcast programs from their Mexican studios into the United States. That model was affirmed at two major junctures: in 1992, when Jerry Perenchio extracted from Azcárraga Milmo the programming licensing agreement that locked in Univision's access to Televisa's programming for twenty-five years; and in 2010, when Haim Saban and Azcárraga Jean signed the Univision-Televisa joint operating agreement that ensured Univision's access to Televisa's programming for another twenty-five years.

Latinos could also discern a Telemundo model that featured domestic production. This model became a trait of Telemundo under Carlos Barba. Barba initiated the first sequence of U.S.-produced Spanish-language programs in the early 1970s at New York station WNJU. Barba's domestic ventures formed the backbone of the Telemundo network's first programming when it commenced network broadcasting in 1987 from WNJU. Although Telemundo went on to import much foreign content, it affirmed its association with domestic production several times. In 1992, Joaquín Blaya accelerated domestic output from Telemundo's Hialeah studios, and in 1997, Peter Tortorici and Nely Galán unveiled a fully domestic prime-time schedule. In the 2000s, owner NBC financed Spanish-language television's first large-scale domestic production initiatives.

Neither concept, though, was certain to lead to success. While Univision's foreign programming attracted the largest audiences, the network never escaped the clutches of Televisa. Azcárraga Milmo confronted Anselmo in 1975 over unpaid programming fees. In 1986, he insisted that new owner Irvine Hockaday pay the exorbitant programming fees of 40 percent. In 2005, the lawsuits Azcárraga Jean filed in order to break a PLA with low programming fees threatened Univision's survival. While Telemundo's alternative strategy avoided foreign entanglements, domestic productions had low ratings and earned low revenue. Telemundo perennially suffered from audiences that were a fraction of the size of those of Univision.

The fact that neither network strictly adhered to its model contributed to viewers' confusion. Both Univision and Telemundo offered a mix of foreign and domestic programs, and at times viewers were hard pressed to distinguish between them. For example, after extracting the PLA from Azcárraga Jean in 1992, Perenchio appeared to be wedded to Univision's commitment to foreign programing. Yet in 1997, anticipating troubles with Azcárraga Jean over the PLA, Perenchio revived domestic production.

Viewers' perceptions of Telemundo were the most muddled. In order to chase Univision's huge ratings, Telemundo, too, acquired foreign programming. In 1995 it developed a partnership with Mexico's then-fledgling TV Azteca. Telemundo's quest for foreign novelas led to dealings with networks in multiple Latin American countries that produced second-tier novelas. Telemundo's pursuit of both domestic and foreign programming puzzled Latino viewers. In addition, they perceived Telemundo as inferior. Telemundo's domestic programs typically were low-budget talk and reality shows. Its foreign programs from second-tier providers consisted of scripted novelas with plots and dialects that were indigenous to the countries where they were produced. They did not compare to the expansive and universally appealing Televisa productions Latinos witnessed on Univision.

While the separate models of foreign and domestic programming continued to inhibit the identity of Spanish-language television, a late-arriving third concept—co-production—suggested that its programming might finally settle into a coherent mode of production. Univision dipped its toes in the water of the third model with its multinational Univision Studios project, a response to concerns that it would lose the rights to Televisa's programs. But the concept was a hallmark of Telemundo, which began co-production in 2002 when NBC approved financing for telenovelas that Telemundo would control. Telemundo's ownership and direction ensured the production of novelas with U.S. settings or that offered themes that would appeal to a U.S. Latino audience.

The concept showed promise in the 2010s when viewers, particularly younger Latinos, responded positively to co-produced novelas with plots about contemporary issues and themes. Telemundo's ratings increased, and for the first time Latinos saw programs that were as sophisticated as those they saw on Univision. Telemundo's co-productions were the conceptual centerpiece that U.S. Spanish-language programming had always lacked.

Still, like the other models, co-production brought uncertainties. It was expensive; it required investments in studio facilities, infrastructure, and large numbers of domestic and foreign personnel. Telemundo could not have introduced co-production had it not been for NBC Universal's huge infusion of cash. At Univision, co-production ventures were slowed because of financial constraints. Meanwhile, both networks remained aware of what had always been true: they could import a foreign provider's video recordings at relatively little expense.

One constraint remained. Telemundo's first co-produced programs were filmed in Colombia, Venezuela, and other non-U.S. locales. That they showcased foreign talent reinforced one of the issues that long had aroused criticism of Spanish-language television, that the U.S. networks did not actively groom and hire U.S. Latino producers, creators, and performers.

* * *

Those who celebrated the golden anniversary of Spanish-language television were disquieted by an inescapable question: would the endeavor continue for another fifty years? Both networks faced two huge problems. First, the U.S. public was no longer loyal to broadcast television. ABC, CBS, NBC, Fox, Univision, and Telemundo had been hurt first by the advent of cable and satellite channels and then by the infinite video and interactive alternatives that cellphone technology made possible. While few were willing to acknowledge the truth, the epoch of big television was over.

The end of the big-TV era began in 1995, when cable systems enlarged to 500 channels and the combined reach of the English-language broadcast networks dropped below 25 percent for the first time. Ironically, that was the time when Spanish-language television expanded to become big television. Its numbers increased because the Spanish-speaking population grew by 50 percent in the 1990s.

Although Univision and Telemundo grew in the 2000s, it was apparent that audience fragmentation was shrinking their viewing audiences, just as it had at ABC, CBS, NBC, and Fox. The total audiences of both networks decreased by 2 to 5 percent with each TV season. Although Univision was the number one network in the summer of 2013, its audience of 3.6 million that year was one-third the number it had drawn in the 1990s. As late as 2000, Univision regularly reached 80 percent of Latino TV viewers, but by the mid-2010s, only 40 percent of Latinos regularly viewed the network. In addition, the combined reach of all broadcast networks among all U.S. viewers had shrunk to around 10 percent.[30]

The decline of broadcast television was irreversible. Occasional broadcasts, such as the live airing of the Super Bowl, still drew mass audiences, but none of the broadcast networks typically averaged more than 2 percent in Nielsen's national ratings. Univision and Telemundo were resigned to a situation with no solution. The problem was not that viewers liked Univision and Telemundo less; it was that they liked the digital universe more.

The second problem was potentially far more serious. Evidence was unmistakable that Spanish speaking in the United States was declining. Although the trend was not fully evident until the 2020s approached, close readers of the 2000 census, which predicted that by 2010, 60 percent of the U.S. Latino population would be under thirty-five, knew it was coming. Evidence in 2000 of a Latino generation gap foretold what would happen twenty years later—that the majority of U.S. Latinos would routinely use English in their everyday lives.

Those in Spanish-language television grasped what this meant. Because six of ten U.S. Latinos would have no upbringing or roots in Spanish-speaking countries, they would attend U.S. schools where English was taught and would interact with other Latinos who had no foreign background and with non-Latino friends and associates. The Latino population was certain to swell with individuals whose natural first language would be English.

Such conclusions emerged from analysis of the history of the composition of the U.S. Latino population. The first influx of immigrants, who had arrived in the period 1945 and 1970, constituted a "first" generation of U.S. Latinos. Their sons and daughters and a second influx of immigrants who arrived between 1970 and 1995 populated a "second" generation. After 1995, immigration slowed and domestic birth rates accelerated. Demographers referred to the Latinos born after 1995 as the "third" generation.

Although Univision and Telemundo expected that the "third" generation would reshape their audiences, the initial problem they anticipated was not language. Younger Latinos were more affluent than their predecessors. They had access to the Internet, mobile devices, and social media. The networks' initial concern was reaching an audience that used traditional television sparingly if at all.

Concern broadened when more and more experts spoke of the Latino generation shift. Their revised thinking led to a shift in how the future of Spanish speaking in the United States was understood. In no small measure because of Spanish-language television, Spanish had become a recognized second language in the United States over a short span of two or three decades. There were at least 60 million fluent Spanish speakers. Many experts predicted the number would double to 130 million by 2050, making the United States the world's largest Spanish-speaking country.[31]

However, study after study emphasized that younger Latinos embraced and naturally used English. As the 2010s ended, some believed that the future of Spanish speaking in the United States was in danger. In 2018, Professor Phillip M. Carter published an article titled "How the 'Three Generation Pattern' Could Wipe Out Spanish in the US."[32] The pattern Carter suggested was reflected in surveys, in a 2017 Census Bureau population update, and in studies Simmons Research conducted in 2018. Simmons reported that while 95 percent of "first"-generation and 75 percent of "second"-generation Latinos communicated in Spanish, only 29 percent of "third"-generation Latinos did so. Sixty-four percent of "third"-generation Latinos communicated "only in English."[33]

There was plentiful evidence that the Spanish language was still vital. Univision actively sought to quash growing perceptions to the contrary. In April 2016, Univision News posted an article that emphasized that 60 percent of U.S.-born Latinos spoke Spanish at home. Two months later, it posted an article that reiterated findings from a Pew Research Center study that replicated the findings of the survey done for *Spanish USA* in 1980. Virtually all Latinos reported that they were exposed to Spanish communication, and most younger Latinos continued to identify themselves as bilingual. Further, "95% believe it's important for future generations to speak Spanish."[34]

At Univision and Telemundo, what really mattered was whether Latinos were watching Spanish-language television. A 2012 Pew Research Center study presented startling data that many were not. It reported that "among third-generation Hispanics, more than eight-in-ten (83%) say they use English when watching television. Only 11% say they use both languages. And just 5% of third-generation Hispanics say they watch television mainly in Spanish."[35] In response, Univision began offering Spanish-language programs with English-language subtitles. Using a similar system, Telemundo transmitted Spanish-language programs with English-language voice tracks. In 2013, Univision introduced Fusion, an English-language news and news satire channel.

It was unlikely that the main Univision and Telemundo networks would evolve as channels of news and entertainment that was partially or predominantly provided in English. That would alienate Spanish-language proponents, invite intervention by Latino groups and regulators, and, most prohibitively, risk losing advertisers still enamored with the Latino market. Nevertheless, needing to reach an audience among whom 83 percent used English-language television, the networks were certain to consider broadcasting some English-language programs.

* * *

It also was certain that, despite modern broadcast television's disconnection to the heyday of its past, the age of television would continue to attract interest and exploration. Because its past was meaningful, television was not dead on arrival in the digital age. It was integral to the American experience from around the end of World War II until at least the end of the twentieth century. And Spanish-language television was part of the television age. More significant is that fact that it was the largest part of the TV age that scholars and authors have overlooked. The account here reveals that TV's past is not a closed book but instead beckons with new avenues that can rejuvenate study of the history of television. At nearly the dawn of the television age, Spanish-language television diversified the medium. It is the best explanation for the rise of the Spanish language as a factor in issues ranging from electing presidents to shaping the direction of U.S. social and cultural affairs. It globalized U.S. television and created a "Latinidad" that united a Latino population that had grown from fewer than 5 million in 1945 to 70 million in 2010. It gave Latinos an identifying and anchoring institution

Yet in the last analysis, Spanish-language television was a very improbable achievement. It did not rise because governments, universities, or public foundations felt that Latinos should be served. There was no Spanish-language PBS. What the endeavor had instead was an unlikely partnership of U.S. and Mexican founders that was succeeded by a progression of visionaries, innovators, problem-solvers, and architects who frequently were also egoists, autocrats, moneygrubbers, and backbiters. The least-known and most distinctive of that group, Rene Anselmo, was considered both a crackpot and a genius. For these men, success was a function of balancing strides with conflicts and finishing with one more of the former than the latter.

APPENDIX I

UNIVISION TIMELINE

1895	Azcárraga Vidaurreta born
1905	Raoul Cortez born
1955	Azcárraga Vidaurreta founds XEW
1955	June: Telesistema Méxicano forms under Azcárraga Vidaurreta
1955	June: Cortez launches KCOR in San Antonio
1955	September: Vidaurreta forms Teleprogramas de México and names Rene Anselmo director
1958	Azcárraga Vidaurreta partners with Frank Fouce Sr. to plan a Spanish-language network in the United States
1961	December: Azcárraga Vidaurreta acquires KCOR
1961	December: Spanish International Network (SIN) begins in San Antonio under Emilio Nicolás
1962	January: Fouce Sr. dies; Anselmo is appointed as new president of SIN; heir Frank Fouce Jr. protests Anselmo's appointment
1962	September: Anselmo launches KMEX (Los Angeles); *Sábado gigante* premieres in Chile
1968	August: Anselmo launches WXTV (New York)
1968	First continuous telenovelas on WXTV defeat rival WNJU, deter Columbia Pictures' plan for a network to compete against SIN
1971	Anselmo launches WLTV-Miami
1972	September: Azcárraga Vidaurreta dies; Azcárraga Milmo succeeds as owner of Telesistema Méxicano

1972	December: Azcárraga Milmo confronts Anselmo about the program fees SIN owes Telesistema Méxicano
1973	Telesistema Méxicano reorganized as Televisa
1974	Spring: Anselmo forms a pay-TV venture, MagnaVerde, to televise World Cup and generate revenue to pay SIN's debt to Televisa
1974	April: Launch of first commercial satellite, Westar 1; Televisa initiates satellite TV delivery
1974	July: MagnaVerde fails; Azcárraga Milmo agrees to Anselmo's revised repayment plan
1975	Debt finally repaid; Fouce Jr. confronts Anselmo about irregularities of the repayment; Anselmo ousts Fouce as chair of SIN board
1976	September: Through Televisa, SIN initiates first satellite delivery of broadcast TV in U.S.
1976	November: Fouce Jr. sues SIN, claiming that Anselmo has mismanaged the network
1976	December: Anselmo reports SIN's first profits
1977	SIN's participation in Azcárraga Milmo's global satellite network, Univisión, begins a ten-year "golden age" in U.S. Spanish-language television
1980	Judge Mariana Pfaelzer takes over Fouce's lawsuit; because she suspects Televisa's ownership of SIN is illegal, she orders the FCC to investigate
1981	First Spanish-language network newscast, *Noticiero SIN*, begins; Gustavo Godoy manages
1983	FCC judge John Conlin conducts hearing to consider revoking SIN's licenses
1986	January: FCC revokes SIN licenses
1986	Winter: FCC names Pfaelzer as master to preside over SIN's dissolution
1986	April: SIN's board ousts Anselmo, names Emilio Nicolás as head

1986	June: Pfaelzer opens bidding on SIN properties; Hallmark Cards submits high bid of $301 million
1986	July: Pfaelzer awards ownership of SIN to Hallmark, which agrees to keep network intact
1986	September: Televisa asserts control of SIN network properties, including network news, which it legally owned
1986	October: Godoy protests Televisa's takeover SIN news and the presence of Jacobo Zabludovsky; protest by SIN staff forces Televisa to withdraw
1986	October: Rival network Telemundo announced
1986	November: Hallmark head Irvine Hockaday agrees to pay high fees to retain Televisa's programs
1986	December: Hallmark concludes reorganization; SIN's ends the year with profits
1987	January: SIN is renamed Univision
1987	January: Univision begins broadcasting *Sábado gigante* from coast to coast
1987	November: Hallmark pays $275 million to acquire Televisa's U.S. properties
1987	December: Univision's first year ends in losses
1988	August: Joaquín Blaya named Univision president
1988	September: Blaya premieres domestic programs and cancels Televisa's foreign programming
1989	Hallmark defaults on $500 million Univision debt
1991	Univision loses Nielsen's first test ratings. It trails the Galavisión channel, which initiates over-the-air broadcasts of programs Univision had canceled.
1992	February: Univision loses second test ratings
1992	March: Hallmark sells Univision to Jerry Perenchio for $550 million
1992	March: Perenchio reinstates Azcárraga Milmo as part owner in exchange for Milmo's concessions in a program licensing agreement (PLA)

1992	April: Blaya protests the sale to Perenchio and Azcárraga Milmo's return as part owner
1992	May: Blaya resigns, becomes president of Telemundo
1992	July: New Univision president Ray Rodríguez reinstates many canceled Televisa programs
1992	Summer: Factions unsuccessfully petition FCC to invalidate Perenchio's takeover
1992	November: Univision wins first official Nielsen ratings
1992	December: Perenchio signs PLA, Azcárraga Milmo agrees to provide Televisa programs to Univision until 2017 at a very low cost
1993	Rodríguez reinstates full schedule of Televisa programs, terminates Univision personnel
1994	October premiere of Televisa novela *Marimar* begins Univision's dominance of Latino audience
1994	Advertisers pay rates equal to English-language networks for first time; Univision nears first profits since forming in 1987
1995	Spring: Televisa executives complain that Univision profits unfairly because of the PLA; Perenchio refuses requests to renegotiate
1996	September: Perenchio triumphs with public stock offering, Univision's value multiplies
1996	September: Premiere of Televisa novela *María la del barrio* sets ratings records; Univision reaches 80 percent of Latino audience
1997	April: Azcárraga Milmo dies; Perenchio fears successors will force termination of PLA
1997	Spring: Heir Emilio Azcárraga Jean takes control of Televisa, says PLA is unfair
1998	Univision reaches 93 percent of Latino audience and wins awards; revenue exceeds $500 million
1999	Spring: Perenchio refuses to renegotiate the PLA with Azcárraga Jean

1999	September: Azcárraga Jean cancels Univision's access to the telenovela *El privilegio de amar;* Univision alleges sabotage
1999	December: Univision's *Feliz milenio* achieves 98 percent share in Hispanic ratings
2000	Univision forms sister network, needs Televisa programs not covered in 1992 PLA
2001	January: Azcárraga Jean forces Univision to renegotiate the PLA, asserts that Televisa has the right to succeed Perenchio as Univision owner
2001	December: Univision and Televisa negotiate a new PLA; Azcárraga Jean becomes vice chair but retains original terms of the PLA that favor Univision
2001	December: Univision's revenue reaches $1 billion
2002	Univision launches sister network Telefutura
2003	September: FCC approves Perenchio's acquisition of HBC radio group
2003	December: Failure of Perenchio's novela *Te amaré en silencio* heats up battle between Azcárraga Jean and Rodríguez
2005	Perenchio names Rodríguez as chief, which angers Azcárraga Jean; Televisa sues Univision to terminate PLA
2006	July: Televisa files second lawsuit
2007	Ratings for *La fea mas bella* top ratings on all English-language networks, is most viewed program on all U.S. television
2009	January: *Televisa v. Univision* ends with surprise in-court settlement, but PLA issues are not resolved
2009	December: Saban launches Univision Studios, anticipating loss of Televisa programs when the PLA expires in 2017
2010	Summer: Univision Studios begins production of *Eva Luna*
2010	Autumn: Saban and Azcárraga Jean agree to negotiate remaining PLA issues
2010	October: Univision and Televisa sign first definitive agreement since Televisa's predecessor, Telesistema Méxicano, formed the Spanish International Network, Univision's predecessor, in 1961

2011   Televisa renews direct control of Univision; Univision is assured access to future Televisa programming, closes Univision Studios

2012   Telecast of *Sábado gigante* commemorates the fiftieth anniversary of both the program and SIN/Univision

APPENDIX 2

TELEMUNDO TIMELINE

1960s	Columbia Pictures/Screen Gems expands Spanish-translated program distribution
1965	WNJU (New York) launched; first Spanish-language TV station on East Coast
1968	Columbia Pictures acquires WNJU, which shares programs with sister station WAPA (San Juan, Puerto Rico)
1970	Carlos Barba heads WNJU and initiates Columbia Pictures' plan for second Spanish-language network to compete with SIN
1972	Second network advances; WNJU and WAPA programs syndicated to WSNS (Chicago), WSCV (Miami), and KVEA (Los Angeles)
1974	Columbia Pictures suspends second network
1976	Jerry Perenchio acquires KVEA
1979	Columbia Pictures sells WNJU to Perenchio; Barba revives second network project
1983	Barba forms NetSpan and syndicates Spanish-language programs to twenty non-SIN stations
1984	Saul Steinberg and Harry Silverman of Reliance Insurance acquire share of KVEA
1985	Reliance acquires John Blair TV stations, including WSCV and WKAQ (San Juan)
1986	Perenchio sells WNJU and NetSpan holdings to Reliance; Silverman announces a new network named Telemundo and names Barba head

1987	January: Telemundo premieres; first program, *Noticiero Telemundo*, scores ratings victory over Univision (new name of SIN)
1987	August: Silverman issues cash call
1990	Financial difficulties continue and intensify; Steinberg ousts Silverman; Barba departs
1991	Telemundo defeats Univision in first test of Nielsen ratings; unexpected victory calms creditors
1992	May: Joaquín Blaya becomes Telemundo president after leaving Univision
1992	November: Telemundo loses first official Nielsen ratings; creditors uneasy
1993	Spring: Blaya's domestic production boosts audience; Telemundo ties Univision in ratings
1993	June: Telemundo declares bankruptcy
1995	March: Chapter 11 reorganization fails; Steinberg yields ownership to Leon Black; Roland Hernández replaces Blaya as head
1995	Summer: Ratings tumble; Hernandez partners with Mexico's TV Azteca
1996	Telemundo's share of Latino audience falls to 20 percent; rival Univision reaches 80 percent
1997	Black sells Telemundo to Sony
1998	Spring: Sony reorganizes Telemundo, plans turnaround with major rollout of domestic shows
1998	November: New programs fail; Telemundo at 7 percent and Univision at 93 percent in ratings
1999	Sony again reorganizes; new head James McNamara replaces failed programs with foreign telenovelas
2000	McNamara premieres the Colombian novela *Betty la fea*, Telemundo's first hit show
2001	Spring: Telemundo's share of Latino audience increases to 30 percent

2001	Summer: Telemundo's first profits entice buyers who make billion-dollar offers to Sony
2001	October: NBC acquires Telemundo from Sony for $2.7 billion
2002	McNamara initiates first co-production agreements with Mexican and South American studios
2004	NBC acquires Universal Studios, pledges finance for co-production and other ventures to increase Telemundo's program production
2006	NBC finances Browne's initiatives for enlarged program production and ownership of programs
2007	Telemundo eliminates imported programs and becomes first network to self-produce or co-produce all shows
2008	*Doña Bárbara* leads a succession of modern novelas that outperform Univision in ratings
2011	January: Comcast acquires NBC Universal, lists Telemundo as a company priority
2011	Summer: Backed by Comcast, Telemundo outbids Univision for 2018 World Cup; breaks ground on first expansive U.S. Spanish-language television studios
2012	Telemundo's 25th anniversary

NOTES

Introduction

1. Elaine Ayala, "Only Memories Remain at TV Site," *San Antonio Express-News*, November 14, 2013, https://www.expressnews.com/news/local/article/Only-memories-remain-at-TV-site-4981880.php.
2. Victor Landa, "First U.S. Spanish-Language TV Station, Demolished," News Taco, November 7, 2013, https://newstaco.com/2013/11/07/first-u-s-spanish-language-tv-station-demolished/.
3. Landa, "First U.S. Spanish-Language TV Station, Demolished."
4. Jim Forsyth, "Protesters: Univision Demolition Shows Lack of Respect for Latino Heritage," woai.iheart.com, November 13, 2013; Victor Landa, "First U.S. Spanish-Language TV Station, Demolished," News Taco, November 7, 2013, https://newstaco.com/2013/11/07/first-u-s-spanish-language-tv-station-demolished/; Joey Palacios, "Eight Arrested Trying to Halt KWEX Univision Building Demolition," Texas Public Radio, November 13, 2013, https://www.tpr.org/post/eight-arrested-trying-halt-kwex-univision-building-demolition; Elaine Ayala, "Only Memories Remain at TV Site," *San Antonio Express-News*, November 14, 2013, https://www.expressnews.com/news/local/article/Only-memories-remain-at-TV-site-4981880.php.
5. América Rodríguez, "Creating an Audience and Remapping a Nation: A Brief History of Spanish Language Broadcasting 1930–1980," *Quarterly Review of Film and Video* 16 (1999): 357–374.
6. Arlene Dávila, *Latinos, Inc.: The Marketing and Making of a People* (Berkeley: University of California Press, 2001), 181–215; Arlene Dávila, "Mapping Latinidad: Language and Culture in the Spanish TV Battlefront," *Television & New Media* 1 (2003): 75–94; Viviana Rojas, "The Gender of Latinidad: Latinas Speak about Hispanic Television," *Communication Review* 7 (2010): 125–152; Christopher Chavez, *Reinventing the Latino Television Viewer: Language, Ideology, and Practice* (Lanham, MD: Lexington, 2015), 9; Miguel Salazar, "The Problem with Latinidad," *The Nation*, September 16, 2019, https://www.thenation.com/article/archive/hispanic-heritage-month-latinidad.
7. Rodríguez, "Creating an Audience and Remapping a Nation," 370.
8. Rodríguez, "Creating an Audience and Remapping a Nation."

9. Félix F. Gutiérrez, "México's Television Network in the United States: The Case of Spanish International Network," in *Proceedings of the Sixth Annual Telecommunications Policy Research Conference,* edited by H. S. Dordick (Lexington, MA: Lexington Books), 135–159.

10. Rick Wartzman and Lisa Bannon, "A Media Mogul Who Steers Clear of Media," *Wall Street Journal,* August 14, 1999, 1, 6.

11. Rodríguez, "Creating an Audience and Remapping a Nation," 366–370.

12. Gutiérrez, "Mexico's Television Network in the United States," 135–159; see also Nicholas Alfred Valenzuela, "Organizational Evolution of a Spanish Language Television Network" (PhD diss., Stanford University, 1985), 196–205.

13. Federico Subervi-Vélez, "Mass Communication and Hispanics," in *Handbook of Hispanic Cultures in the United States: Sociology,* edited by Félix Padilla (Houston: Arte Público Press, 1994), 304–351; John Sinclair, *Latin American Television: A Global View* (New York: Oxford University Press, 1999), 92–120.

14. Philip J. Auter and Douglas A. Boyd, "DuMont: The Original Fourth Television Network," *Journal of Popular Culture* 29 (2005): 63–83; Clarke Ingram, Clarke Ingram's DuMont Television Network Historical Website, http://www.dumontnetwork.com/index.html.

15. In *The Gutenberg Galaxy: The Making of Typographic Man* (1962), McLuhan proposed that radio and television created an electronic culture that removed individualism and instilled a "tribal base" from which individuals would organize into a "global village." McLuhan's subsequent works, including *Understanding Media: The Extensions of Man* (1964), proposed theories about peoples' adoption and viewing of television, including his concept that "the medium is the message." He maintained that, like the invention of the light bulb, the invention of television altered society not by its content but by immersing individuals in a collective and instantaneous audiovisual experience. Although his theories were considered anecdotal, McLuhan rose as a major figure in 1960s popular culture. His ideas inspired and influenced subsequent empirical study and discourse on television's effects.

Chapter 1. Lone Star Dawn, Mexican Light

1. Gene Fowler and Bill Crawford, *Border Radio: Quacks, Yodelers, Pitchmen, Psychics, and Other Amazing Broadcasters of the American Airwaves* (Austin: University of Texas Press, 2002), 202–203.

2. "Importers Organize in Mexican Capital," *Automotive Industries,* March 24, 1921, 674, 678.

3. Alexandro Olmos, "La huella de los Azcárraga I y II," *Revista Méxicana de Comunicación* 58 (Spring 1998): 49–54.

4. Barry Mazor, *Ralph Peer and the Making of Popular Roots Music* (Chicago: Chicago Review Press, 2015), 160–161.

5. Maria del Carmen Olivares Arriagas, *Emilio Azcárraga Vidaurreta: En empresario ejemplar* (Victoria, México: Universidad Autónoma de Tamaulipas, 2002), 119–127.

6. Joy Elizabeth Hayes, *Radio Nation: Communication, Popular Culture, and Nationalism in Mexico, 1920–1950* (Tucson: University of Arizona Press, 2000), 25.

7. Donald Andrew Henriques, "Performing Nationalism: Mariachi, Media and Transformation of a Tradition (1920–1942)" (PhD diss., University of Texas at Austin, 2006), 114–117.

8. Donald Lee Smith, *Pre-PRI: The Mexican Government Party, 1929–1946* (Fort Worth: Texas Christian University, 1974), 24–33.

9. Mary Williams Walsh, "Mexican TV Empire a Near Monopoly," *New York Times*, May 30, 1986, 1, 14.

10. Olmos, "La huella de los Azcárraga I y II."

11. Leah Brenner, "Memo from South of the Border," *New York Times*, January 17, 1943, X12; "Radio King of Mexico," *Los Angeles Times*, July 16, 1944, A22.

12. Seth Fein, "Transcultured Hollywood," in *Visible Nations: Latin American Cinema and Video*, edited by Chon A. Noriega (Minneapolis: University of Minnesota Press, 2000), 84–86.

13. Claudia Fernández and Andrew Paxman, *El Tigre: Emilio Azcárraga y su imperio televisa* (México City: Raya en el Agua-Grijalbo, 2000), 5.

14. Edward Helmore, "Emilio Azcárraga," *The Independent*, June 2, 1997, 17–18.

15. "Azcárraga Walks Out on Mestre's 'Free Radio' Push in B.A. Bombshell," *Variety*, July 14, 1948, 24.

16. Olmos, "La huella de los Azcárraga I y II"; Lois Benjamin, "South of the Border: Rapidly Growing Television Industry Is Now as Mexican as Hot Tamales," *New York Times*, November 18, 1956, X13. The Televicentro facility housed five radio and television networks and ten television studios.

17. Joseph Skinner, "Octopus of the Airwaves," *Monthly Review*, September 1987, 44–46.

18. Stanley Lebar, "The Color War Goes to the Moon," *Invention and Technology* (Summer 1997): 53–54, https://www.hq.nasa.gov/alsj/Invent-Tech1997.pdf.

19. John Sinclair, *Latin American Television: A Global View* (New York: Oxford University Press, 1999), 35–36.

20. [Liliam Flores O. Rodriguez], "Desarrollo Social" [Social Development], Mexican Congress—Chamber of Deputies, October 7, 2009, http://archivos.diputados.gob.mx/Centros_Estudio/Cesop/Eje_tematico/2_dsocial.htm.

21. "Azcárraga States Channel 2," *Novidades*, March 22, 1951, 6.

22. Emilio Azcárraga Vidaurreta, "Televicentro: Una gran estacion at servicio de Mexico," *Revista de Revistas*, December 31, 1950, 59.

23. María Francisca Morales, "Vernacular Spanish and Chicano Culture Content in the Language Arts Curriculum for Bilingual Education" (PhD diss., Stanford University, 1982); Emilio Azcárraga, "Mexican TV Developments Act as School for Latin America," in *The Radio Annual and Television Year Book* (New York: Radio Daily Corporation, 1955), 72.

24. Reynold Anselmo, deposition, New York, New York, February 2–4, 1977, 26, in Depositions, *Fouce Amusement Enterprises v. Spanish International Communications Corp.*, case no. CV 76-4345, Civil Case Files, 1938–2994, Record Group 21, Records of the U.S. Circuit Court for the Central District of California, National Archives at Riverside, Perris, CA (hereafter Depositions, *Fouce v. Spanish International*); "Rene Anselmo:

Proving in an Outspoken Way that You Don't Need to Be Spanish to Run SIN," *Broadcasting*, May 6, 1974, 65; Hon. Bill Richardson, "Rene Anselmo," in the House of Representatives, Sept. 29, 1995, *Congressional Record* 145: 1895–1897.

25. "Monterrey to Get TV," *Washington Post*, March 17, 1953, 10.

26. "Telesistema Méxicano, S.A," Mexican Television 1962 Report, *Variety*, January 9, 1963, 135.

27. Olmos, "La huella de los Azcárraga I y II."

28. Anselmo deposition, 26.

29. Todd Vogel, "Rene Anselmo Can Sure Dish It Out," *Business Week*, May 26, 1991, https://www.bloomberg.com/news/articles/1991-05-26/rene-anselmo-can-sure-dish-it-out.

30. Anselmo deposition, 36; Emilio Nicolás Sr., interview with the author, San Antonio, TX, March 30, 2007.

31. Thomas B. Rosensteil, "Azcárraga Owns Huge Secretive Empire," *Los Angeles Times*, June 3, 1989, 4, 12.

32. "Telesistema Méxicano, S.A.," *Variety*, January 9, 1963, 135.

33. Douglas W. Webbink, "The Impact of UHF Promotion: The All-Channel Television Receiver Law," *Law and Contemporary Problems 34* (Summer 1969): 535–561.

34. Francisco Hernández Lomelí, "Racionalidad limitada y efectos perversos: Ensayo sobre el origen de la television en México," in *IX Anuario de Investigación de la Communicación* (Guadalajara, México: National Council for Education and Research of Communication Sciences, 2007), 338–339.

35. Richardson, "Rene Anselmo," E1895–E1896.

36. Emilio Azcárraga, affidavit, November 5, 1979, box 2, volume 9, Proceedings, *Fouce Amusement Enterprises v. Spanish International Communications Corp.*, case no. CV 76-4345, Civil Case Files, 1938–2004, Record Group 21, Records of the U.S. Circuit Court for the Central District of California, National Archives at Riverside, Perris, CA (hereafter Proceedings, *Fouce v. Spanish International*).

37. Frank Fouce, deposition, March 2–3, 1977, 18–23, Depositions, *Fouce v. Spanish International*.

38. Erik A. Stilling, "The History of Spanish-Language Television in the United States and the Rise of Mexican International Syndication Strategies in the Americas," *Howard Journal of Communications* 6, no. 4 (1995): 231–249.

39. "License Ownership Restrictions," Code of Federal Regulations, 47 U.S.C. No. 310 (1934).

40. Department of Communication, "Ley Federal de Radio Y Televisión," Mexico City, D.F., January 20, 1960, http://www.sct.gob.mx/fileadmin/_migrated/content_uploads/Ley_Federal_de_Radio_y_Television.pdf.

41. "Azcárraga on Spending Spree for Facilities," *Variety*, January 18, 1961, 29, 51.

42. Olmos, "La huella de los Azcárraga I y II."

43. Skinner, "Octopus of the Airwaves," 45.

44. "Azcárraga Plans to Produce Own Vidfilm Entries," *Variety*, January 4, 1961, 94.

45. Thomas Y. Buckley, "Television in Mexico," *New York Times*, May 18, 1958, X11.

46. "FCC Clears ABC in San Diego," *Broadcasting*, January 28, 1957, 60; "In Booming San Diego: XETV," *Broadcasting*, November 10, 1958, 11.

47. Fouce deposition, 24–25.

48. Anselmo deposition, 52–58.

49. Emilio Nicolás interview, July 27, 2007.

50. "Azcárraga on Spending Spree for Facilities," 29, 51.

51. "Mex TV Spreads Wings, Invading U.S. with Shows," *Variety*, February 22, 1961, 32–33.

52. Olmos, "La huella de los Azcárraga I y II."

53. "Azcárraga Scans Future Horizons of Television and Radio in Mexico," *Variety*, March 8, 1961, 8.

54. "El diez años de XEW," *El Imparcial*, March 27, 1961, 1.

55. Fouce deposition, 22–28.

56. Fouce deposition, 25.

57. Rene Anselmo, affidavit, November 19, 1979, box 2, volume 10, Proceedings, *Fouce v. Spanish International*.

58. Anselmo deposition, 52–58, 68.

59. Emilio Azcárraga, affidavit, November 5, 1979, box 2, volume 9, Proceedings, *Fouce v. Spanish International*.

60. "Dice adiós Don Francisco Cortés," *El Mañana Nuevo Laredo*, December 27, 2015, http://elmanana.com.mx/noticia/88897/Dice-adios-Don-Francisco-Cortes.html.

61. "Raoul A. Cortez," family biography, private collection of Guillermo Nicolás, San Antonio, TX.

62. Irma Nicolás, interview with the author, July 28, 2007, San Antonio, TX.

63. Jorge Reina Schement-Flores and Ricardo Flores, "The Origins of Spanish-Language Radio: The Case of San Antonio, Texas," *Journalism History* 4 (1977): 57.

64. Irma Nicolás interview.

65. "Saludos Amigos Welcome KCOR," *San Antonio Light*, February 14, 1946, 8G.

66. "On the Air: KCOR 1350," KCOR ad, February 1946, 1946 file, Guillermo Nicolás Collection.

67. "KCOR Daily Program Schedule," *San Antonio Express*, February 15, 1946, 9.

68. "KCOR Regular Advertisers," *San Antonio Light*, February 14, 1946, 8-B.

69. KCOR list of sponsors, February 1946, Guillermo Nicolás Collection.

70. Schement-Flores and Flores, "The Origins of Spanish-Language Radio," 57.

71. "KCOR-TV Test Pattern Starts," *San Antonio Express*, June 3, 1955, 1C.

72. Emilio Nicolás Sr., deposition, 6–8, June 1, 1978, San Antonio, TX, Depositions, *Fouce v. Spanish International*.

73. "Emilio Nicolás, Sr.," family biography, Guillermo Nicolás Collection.

74. Eve Alden, "Spanish TV Opens Here," *San Antonio Express*, June 12, 1955, 1M.

75. "Four Prominent San Antonians Congratulate Another," *San Antonio Express*, June 11, 1955, 2A.

76. Gerald Ashford, "Show Marks KCOR-TV Opening," *San Antonio Express*, June 11, 1955, 2C.

77. "La estacion KCOR-TV inicio sus programas regulares," *La Prensa San Antonio*, June 12, 1955, 2.

78. "KCOR-TV, Spanish Television," *San Antonio News*, June 12, 1955, 2M.

79. "UHF Headquarters," Hopps TV Service ad, *San Antonio Express*, June 28, 1955, 5B; "TV Converter," Sears Roebuck and Co. ad, *San Antonio Express*, June 20, 1955, 5A.

80. Emilio Nicolás interview, August 14, 2006.

81. "KCOR-TV," *San Antonio Express*, December 14–18, 1959, 7B–9B.

82. "KCOR-TV," *San Antonio Express*, June 11–15, 1960, 5B–8B.

83. "KCOR-TV," *San Antonio Express*, January 6–12, 6B–8B.

84. Elizabeth C. Ramírez, "Astol, Leonardo García [Lalo]," Handbook of the Texas State Historical Association online, https://tshaonline.org/handbook/online/articles/faso8.

85. Emilio Nicolás interview, August 14, 2006.

86. "KCOR-TV," *San Antonio Express*, June 16, 1958, 3B.

87. Irma Nicolás interview.

88. "KUAL-TV Channel 41," *San Antonio Express and News*, December 17, 1961, 3. Government agencies and companies produce handout films and send them to TV stations and networks to broadcast free of charge. They were abundant in the 1950s and 1960s because agencies and companies knew that stations and networks needed content and likely would broadcast material they could get for free.

89. Red McCombs, interview with the author, July 25, 2007, Miami, FL.

90. Irma Nicolás interview.

91. Ibid.

92. Emilio Nicolás interview, February 10, 2007.

93. Emilio Nicolás interview, August 14, 2006.

94. Fouce deposition, 25–26.

95. Emilio Nicolás interview, August 14, 2006.

96. Ibid.

97. "Changing Hands: KUAL-TV," *Broadcasting*, December 11, 1961, 68–69; Emilio Nicolás interview, August 14, 2006.

98. "Spanish TV Station Sold," *San Antonio Light*, December 16, 1961, 3.

99. "Station KUAL Sale Announced," *San Antonio Express and News*, December 16, 1961, 8D.

Chapter 2. MEX, UHF, and NFL

1. "Frank Fouce, Theatre Owner, Dies," *Los Angeles Times*, January 13, 1962, 3.

2. Emilio Nicolás interview with the author, San Antonio, TX, November 10, 2016.

3. "KWEX-TV, Channel 41," *San Antonio Express and News*, February 3, 1962, 5B.

4. "Deaths: Frank Fouce," *Broadcasting*, January 22, 1962, 86; "Heart Attack Claims Frank Fouce," *Variety*, January 18, 1962, 17; "For the Record," *Broadcasting*, January 1, 1962, 62.

5. Reynold Anselmo, deposition, New York, New York, February 2–4, 1977, 52–58, 68, Depositions, *Fouce Amusement Enterprises and Metropolitan Theaters Corp. v. Spanish International Communications Corp.*, case no. CV 76-4345, Record Group 21.6.8, Records

of the U.S. Circuit Court for the Central District of California, National Archives at Riverside, Perris, CA (hereafter Depositions, *Fouce v. Spanish International*).

6. Anselmo deposition, 60–63.

7. The major component of Fouce's inheritance was a theater chain that included an auditorium in Hollywood called the Million Dollar Theatre, a venue where people in Los Angeles came to watch his father's Spanish-language stage acts and Azcárraga's first-run Mexican movies.

8. Frank Fouce, deposition, February 2, 1977, 1–3, Depositions, *Fouce v. Spanish International*.

9. Spanish International Network Sales to Clients, September 1, 1962, box 2, volume 10, Proceedings, *Fouce Amusement Enterprises and Metropolitan Theaters Corp. v. Spanish International Communications Corp.*, case no. CV 76-4345, Record Group 21.6.8, Records of the U.S. Circuit Court for the Central District of California, National Archives at Riverside, Perris, CA (hereafter Proceedings, *Fouce v. Spanish International*).

10. Fouce deposition, 25–27.

11. Anselmo deposition, 58–59; Emilio Azcárraga, affidavit, November 5, 1979, box 2, volume 9, 2–3, Proceedings, *Fouce v. Spanish International*.

12. Anselmo deposition, 60–69; Azcárraga affidavit, 2–3.

13. Azcárraga affidavit, 3–4.

14. Fouce deposition, 46.

15. Anselmo deposition, 498–500.

16. Emilio Nicolás interview, August 14, 2006.

17. Fouce deposition, 25–27.

18. "Spanish-Language TV Opens L.A. Office," *Los Angeles Times*, June 26, 1962, B9.

19. "Kaufman's Rundown on All-Spanish UHF Network, Lots of Mex Programs," *Variety*, June 6, 1962, 22.

20. Rene Anselmo affidavit, November 19, 1979, 5–10, box 2, volume 10, Proceedings, *Fouce v. Spanish International*; "Mex TV's Azcárraga Stepping Up U.S. Vistas," *Variety*, April 18, 1962, 34.

21. Nicolás deposition, 27–31.

22. "KWEX Channel 41," *San Antonio Express and News*, February 3, 1962, 5B.

23. *Elena* and *Estafa de amar* (telenovela profiles), Alma Latina, accessed August 10, 2015, http://www.alma-latina.net.

24. Emilio Nicolás interview, November 10, 2016.

25. "UHF-VHF Set Bill Whizzes by Senate," *Broadcasting*, June 18, 1962, 42–43.

26. Federal Communications Commission Public Notice 28141, 47 U.S.C. § 303(s) All Channel Receiver Act of 1962, Pub. L. No. 87-529, 76 Stat. 150, Legal Information Institute, Cornell Law School, https://www.law.cornell.edu/uscode/text/47/303.

27. "Kaufman's Rundown on All-Spanish UHF Network," 22.

28. Emilio Nicolás interview, November 10, 2016.

29. Cecil Smith, "Ultra-High TV on the Horizon," *Los Angeles Times*, July 17, 1962, C8.

30. Anselmo deposition, 84.

31. Anselmo affidavit, 3.

32. "Success Is Writing 'How to Do It' Article at Right Time," *Broadcasting*, February 11, 1963, 81.

33. "New! Coming to L.A. Sept. 15," Thrifty Drug Stores ad, *Los Angeles Times*, September 3, 1962, 6.

34. "Spanish-Language TV Transmitter Rising," *Los Angeles Times*, August 8, 1962, C15.

35. "KMEX-TV, Drug Chain Join in UHF Promotion," *Broadcasting*, August 27, 1962, 70. Bus cards were cards inserted in holders on the sides and backs of buses.

36. "Spanish TV Station Sues KALI for Libel," *Los Angeles Times*, January 21, 1963, 20.

37. Daniel Villanueva Sr., interview with the author, Camarillo, CA, May 23, 2006; Cecil Smith, "Mexico Station's UHF Bow Delayed," *Los Angeles Times*, September 14, 1962, 14.

38. Smith, "Ultra-High TV on the Horizon," C8.

39. "Channel 34 Turns Switch," *Los Angeles Times: TV Times*, September 30, 1962, 39.

40. Pepe Arciga, "Mexican UHF Debut Here Stars Kennedy," *Los Angeles Times*, October 2, 1962, 11.

41. Pepe Arciga, "The Image of KMEX: Good, Bad," *Los Angeles Times*, October 18, 1962, 20.

42. Cecil Smith, "Bullfight Action from Mexico," *Los Angeles Times*, October 16, 1962, 11.

43. "Don Emilio on Bullfighting," *Variety*, October 24, 1962, 48.

44. "Success Is Writing 'How to Do It' Article at Right Time," 81.

45. "Spanish-Speaking Now Number Five Million: NTS Study Shows Centers in Fla, N.Y., Southwest," *Broadcasting*, September 24, 1962, 40. This article is a summary of a Pulse national time sales report.

46. "Rene Anselmo," *Broadcasting*, May 6, 1974, 65.

47. Azcárraga affidavit, 3.

48. "Spanish TV Station Sues KALI for Libel."

49. Cecil Smith, "Negro Station Sets All-Live Programs," *Los Angeles Times*, March 13, 1963, C12.

50. Cecil Smith, "He Found Chink in VHF Armor," *Los Angeles Times*, September 30, 1963, D14.

51. "Top 10 Clients in the Spanish-Language Field," *Sponsor*, October 19, 1964, 48.

52. "KMEX-TV Slates Live Newscast," *Los Angeles Times*, April 11, 1963, C13.

53. "KWEX Plans JFK Programs," *San Antonio Express and News*, November 21, 1963, 16A.

54. "SICC Stations" (ten-year cost and revenue summary), March 21, 1978, box 2, volume 7, Proceedings, *Fouce v. Spanish International*.

55. Anselmo affidavit, 5.

56. "Air Media: U.S. Spanish-Speaking Market," *Sponsor*, October 19, 1964, 41–61; "Spanish-Voiced TV: New Boost for UHF," *Sponsor*, October 18, 1965, 56–67.

57. "Yan Qui," *Television*, May 1967, 30–31, 57–60.

58. "Big Advertising Turnout for KMEX's 'Latino Fest,'" *Variety*, November 29, 1967, 34.

59. "Profile: Rene Anselmo," *Broadcasting,* May 6, 1974, 65.
60. "Yan Qui," 60.
61. Red McCombs, interview with the author, San Antonio, TX, July 25, 2007.
62. "Warning to KMEX-TV and KWEX-TV," Spanish International Network ad, *Sponsor,* Oct. 18, 1965, back cover.
63. "Channel 34 Manager Resigns," *Los Angeles Times,* November 23, 1964, C11.
64. Villanueva deposition, 1–11, Daniel Dario Villanueva, Box 7, Depositions, *Fouce v. Spanish International.*
65. John Hall, "The Promoter," *Los Angeles Times,* October 26, 1977, 63.
66. "Profile: Daniel Villanueva," *Broadcasting,* September 22, 1975, 81.
67. Hall, "The Promoter," 63.
68. Villanueva interview, May 23, 2006.
69. Al Wolf, "Danny Boy's Now a Cowboy," *Los Angeles Times,* July 31, 1965, A2.
70. Villanueva interview, May 23, 2006.
71. "Villanueva Wants to Return to Rams," *Los Angeles Times,* July 17, 1966, H7.
72. Mal Florence, "Gamble Puts Ice-ing on Packers' Cake," *Los Angeles Times,* January 1, 1968, B1, B4.
73. Villanueva interview, May 23, 2006.
74. Villanueva deposition, 10–13.
75. Villanueva interview, May 23, 2006.
76. "SICC Stations," March 21, 1978
77. Azcárraga affidavit, 6.
78. Anselmo deposition, 175–176.
79. Azcárraga affidavit, 5.
80. Anselmo affidavit, 5.
81. Andrew S. Zimbalist and John Weeks, *Panama at the Crossroads: Economic Development and Political Change in the Twentieth Century* (Berkeley: University of California Press, 1991), 22–30.
82. Azcárraga affidavit, 4–5.
83. "En el testamento, partes iguales a Paula Cussi, Adriana Abascal, las hermanas Azcárraga Surmont y los hermanos Azcárraga Jean," *Proceso,* July 19, 1997.
84. Report of the Special Master, July 15, 1983, box 4, volume 18, Proceedings, *Fouce v. Spanish International;* Anselmo deposition, 151–160.
85. "Spanish, CATV Owners, Buy into UHF Station," *Broadcasting,* July 3, 1967, 41.
86. Anselmo affidavit, 7.
87. "Spanish U's Move into the Black," *Variety,* July 20, 1966, 35.
88. Julia Preston, "Emilio Azcárraga Milmo, Billionaire Who Ruled Mexican Broadcasting, Is Dead at 66," *New York Times,* April 18, 1997, 7.

Chapter 3. Breakout of Spanish International

1. "Teléfonos de Mexico S.A. de C.V. History," Funding Universe, http://www.fundinguniverse.com/company-histories/telefonos-de-mexico-s-a-de-c-v-history/.
2. "Canal 2, Cadena nacional de costa a costa en vigor partir del 1 de enero de 1969," *Boletín Mensual de Telesistema Mexicano SA,* November–December 1968, 3.

3. "Global Report: Latin America," *Television Age*, January 1, 1968, 58–59.

4. "Something New Is Born in Old Mexico," Televisión Independiente de Mexico ad, *Broadcasting*, May 5, 1969, 45; "Don Eugenio Garza Sada," Instituto Tecnológico de Monterrey, https://tec.mx/en/about-us/our-history/eugenio-garza-sada.

5. "Screen Gems Buys Hygo, United, Sets Up TV Ownership Division," *Broadcasting*, December 10, 1956, 60; "Columbia, SG Complete $24.5 Million Merger," *Broadcasting*, December 23, 1968, 53.

6. Rene Anselmo affidavit, November 19, 1979, box 2, volume 10, 420–421, Proceedings, *Fouce Amusement Enterprises and Metropolitan Theaters Corp. v. Spanish International Communications Corp.*, case no. CV 76-4345, Record Group 21.6.8, Records of the U.S. District Court Southern Division, National Archives at Riverside, Perris, CA (hereafter Proceedings, *Fouce v. Spanish International*).

7. "New Image in WCIU-TV's Future," *Chicago Defender*, May 7, 1967, 9; "KPAZ-TV, Channel 21, Begins," *Arizona Republic*, September 16, 1967, D1.

8. "Television," *New York Times*, May 17, 1965, 71.

9. "N.Y.'s First Commercial UHFer Bows," *Variety*, May 19, 1965, 62.

10. Bernard Weinraub, "Channel 47: Station with an Ethnic Look," *New York Times*, May 16, 1965, X11.

11. Charles G. Bennett, "Trade Center Action Put Off as Hearings End," *New York Times*, June 17, 1967, S26.

12. "TV Showcase for Latin World," *Billboard*, October 8, 1966, 22.

13. "Now It's Our Turn," WNJU ad, *New York Times*, September 18, 1967, 94.

14. Fred Ferretti, "Soap Opera: Winner for Spanish TV Here," *New York Times*, September 5, 1969, 75.

15. WNJU Program Schedule, January 1968, History of WNJU website, accessed November 1, 2016, wnjutv47.com/schedules/1968.

16. "Spanish-Language Broadcasting Grows: First Spanish Network," *Television/Radio Age*, October 2, 1972, 23.

17. "Columbia Pictures and Screen Gems," *New York Times*, September 19, 1968, 75.

18. "Profile: Rene Anselmo," *Broadcasting*, May 6, 1974, 64.

19. "A Dozen Good Reasons Why WXTV Is the Amazingest Success in TV History," WXTV ad, *New York Times*, August 20, 1968, 62.

20. "WXTV, Ultra-High Station Starts Operating July 1," *New York Times*, February 7, 1968, 67.

21. Daniel Villanueva Jr., interview with the author, Camarillo, CA, May 23, 2006.

22. Carole Bird, interview with the author, Miami, FL, July 21, 2008.

23. Villanueva interview, May 23, 2006.

24. "WNJU-TV's Founder Resigns in Dispute," *New York Times*, February 3, 1969, 71.

25. Robert E. Dallos, "WXTV Telecasts to Start Sunday," *New York Times*, July 30, 1968, 79.

26. "Telecasts Begin on Station WXTV," *New York Times*, August 5, 1968, 79.

27. Author's interview with Carole Bird, Miami, FL, July 21, 2008.

28. Lorraine Ramer, interview with the author, Miami, FL, July 21, 2008.

29. R. K. Doan, "Ole: Say Millions of Fans," *TV Guide*, May 10, 1969, 28–30.

30. Ferretti, "Soap Opera," 75.
31. *La leona* (Telenova profile), Alma Latina, accessed August 1, 2012, alma-latina.net.
32. Valeria Palazio, interview with the author, Miami, FL, July 22, 2008.
33. Mario Rodríguez, interview with the author, Miami, FL, August 1, 2007.
34. Kathleen Murray, "Banging the Drums as Spanish TV Comes of Age," *New York Times,* April 10, 1994, https://www.nytimes.com/1994/04/10/business/profile-banging-the-drums-as-spanish-tv-comes-of-age.html; "Biografia: 50 años al servicio de las telecomunicaciones," January 2011, Carlos Barba personal website, accessed August 1, 2016, carlosbarba.com.
35. "El Gato de Wapa" (Screen Gems station identification, 1971), YouTube video, https://www.youtube.com/watch?v=dukG29x7_2U.
36. U.S. Department of Commerce, "Coverage of the Hispanic Population of the United States in the 1970 Census: A Methodological Analysis," Special Studies P-23, no. 84, [November 1979], 6–40, https://www2.census.gov/library/publications/1979/demographics/p23-082.pdf.
37. Al Stump, "They Call Him the Cyclone," *TV Guide,* June 23, 1973, 4–7.
38. Maury Green, "Villanueva—From Dream to Reality," *Los Angeles Times,* August 4, 1972, F18.
39. Villanueva interview, May 23, 2006.
40. "Ruben Salazar: Man in the Middle," City Projects LLC, 2013, YouTube video, https://www.youtube.com/watch?v=6iOPTHIsRQo, at 25:50.
41. Rubén Salazar, "Best Kept Secret in L.A. Television," *Los Angeles Times,* May 8, 1970, G33.
42. Arturo González, "Case Study of KMEX-TV" (MA thesis, California State University-Northridge, 1978), 114–115.
43. Alicia Escalante letter in "The Anniversary of Rubén Salazar's Death," *Los Angeles Times,* September 14, 1985, A3.
44. Frank del Olmo, "Rubén Salazar: Los Angeles' Misunderstood Martyr," *Los Angeles Times,* August 24, 1980, F1.
45. Video recording, KMEX News Coverage of Chicano Moratorium, August 29, 1970, Ruben Salazar Project, Annenberg School for Communication and Journalism, University of Southern California, Los Angeles.
46. "Peace . . . On Our Time"; Los Angeles County Office of Independent Review, "Review of the Los Angeles County Sheriff's Department's Investigation of the Homicide of Rubén Salazar," February 2011, http://digitallibrary.usc.edu/cdm/singleitem/collection/p15799coll78/id/65.
47. Paul Houston, "Jury Splits 4–3 on Salazar Death," *Los Angeles Times,* October 6, 1970, 1.
48. Los Angeles County Office of Independent Review, "Review of the Los Angeles County Sheriff's Department's Investigation into the Homicide of Ruben Salazar."
49. Frank del Olmo, "A Memory, a Legacy," *Los Angeles Times,* August 29, 1985, C5; Del Olmo, "Rubén Salazar: Los Angeles' Misunderstood Martyr," *Los Angeles Times,* August 24, 1980, F1.

50. Rosa Martinez letter in "The Anniversary of Ruben Salazar's Death," *Los Angeles Times*, September 14, 1985, A3.
51. Dan Rustin, "The Spanish Market: Its Size, Income and Loyalties Make It a Rich Marketing Game," *Television/Radio Age*, October 2, 1972, 22, 50.
52. "Profile: Rene Anselmo," *Broadcasting*, May 6, 1974, 64.
53. Villanueva interview, February 17, 2011.
54. Celeste González de Bustamante, "1968 Olympic Dreams and Tlatelolco Nightmares: Imagining and Imaging Modernity on Television," *Mexican Studies/Estudios Mexicanos* 26 (Winter 2010): 1–30.
55. Fernando Mejía Barquero, "Zabludovsky y los Tres Azcárraga," Milenio 2020, September 7, 2015, https://www.milenio.com/opinion/fernando-mejia-barquera/cambio-de-frecuencia/zabludovsky-y-los-tres-azcarraga.
56. Celeste González de Bustamante, *Muy buenas noches: México, Television, and the Cold War* (Lincoln: University of Nebraska Press, 2013), 189–195.
57. Robina Bustos, "The Hemispheric Village: The Case of Televisa," *Méxican Journal of Communication* 2 (1995): 107–120.
58. Emilio Azcárraga affidavit, November 5, 1979, box 2, volume 9, pages 3–4, Proceedings, *Fouce v. Spanish International*.
59. Rene Anselmo affidavit, November 19, 1979, box 2, volume 10, page 3, Proceedings, *Fouce v. Spanish International*.
60. Azcárraga affidavit.
61. Mario Rodríguez interview, February 13, 2007.
62. Azcárraga affidavit, November 5, 1979, page 3.
63. J. Harvey, Blackburn Associates, to R. Anselmo, November 29, 1972, box 2, volume 8, Proceedings, *Fouce v. Spanish International*.
64. Emilio Nicolás interview, July 27, 2007.
65. Azcárraga affidavit, page 3.
66. "Channel 23 to Stress Programs in Spanish," *Miami Herald*, March 6, 1971, 22A.
67. Joaquín Blaya, interview with the author, Basalt, CO, December 18, 2009.
68. "Today's Television: Reporter 23," *Miami Herald*, March 20, 1971, 2G.
69. J. Harvey to R. Anselmo, November 29, 1972.
70. Ibid.
71. Joaquín Blaya, "Network Television Makes Miami Its Home," 2006, 18–19, unpublished memoir in author's possession.
72. "Mexico's Emilio Azcárraga, 77, Dies; Powerful B'caster and Film Pioneer," *Variety*, October 4, 1972, 72.
73. Marine Midland Bank Loan Agreement, December 29, 1972, box 6, volume 1, Exhibits, *Fouce Amusement Enterprises and Metropolitan Theaters Corp. v. Spanish International Communications Corp.*, case no. CV 76-4345, Record Group 21.6.8, Records of the U.S. District Court Southern Division, Records of the U.S. District Court Southern Division, National Archives at Riverside, Perris, CA (hereafter Exhibits, *Fouce v. Spanish International*).
74. "SICC Stations," March 21, 1978, box 2, volume 7, Proceedings, *Fouce v. Spanish International*.

75. Emilio Nicolás interview, August 14, 2006; Villanueva interview, May 23, 2006.
76. Villanueva interview, May 23, 2006.
77. Emilio Nicolás interview, August 14, 2006.
78. James Jacobson affidavit, November 24, 1976, box 2, volume 8, pages 2–3, Proceedings, *Fouce v. Spanish International*.
79. Spanish International Communications Corporation & Trans-Tel Merger Agreement, December 12, 1972, box 5, volume 1, Exhibits, *Fouce v. Spanish International*.
80. "Edition 14—Unveiling the 'Tele-Guía' magazine. Chapter 2, 1973: Roberto Gómez Bolaños (Chespirito): Charla con Tele-Guía," *La Chicharra*, June 26, 2011, http://lachicharrabrasil.blogspot.com/2011/06/edicao-14-desvendando-revista-tele-guia.html.
81. Alan Riding, "Monterrey Group: A Family of Wealth and Symbol of Economic Independence," *New York Times*, October 21, 1974, 53.
82. "Historia: El inicio de una gran empresa" [History: The start of a great company], Televisa, https://www.televisa.com/corporativo/historia.

Chapter 4. The Wages of SIN

1. Emilio Nicolás, interview with the author, San Antonio, TX, November 10, 2016.
2. Rene Anselmo deposition, 151–160, box 7, Depositions, *Fouce Amusement Enterprises and Metropolitan Theaters Corp. v. Spanish International Communications Corp.*, case no. CV 76-4345, Record Group 21.6.8, Records of the U.S. Circuit Court for the Central District of California, National Archives at Riverside, Perris, CA (hereafter Depositions, *Fouce v. Spanish International*).
3. Rene Anselmo affidavit, November 19, 1979, box 2, volume 10, Proceedings, *Fouce Amusement Enterprises and Metropolitan Theaters Corp. v. Spanish International Communications Corp.*, case no. CV 76-4345, Record Group 21.6.8, Records of the U.S. Circuit Court for the Central District of California, National Archives at Riverside, Perris, CA (hereafter Proceedings, *Fouce v. Spanish International*).
4. Anselmo deposition, 151–160.
5. Arturo García Hernández, "Hoy llegan los restos Emilio Azcárraga," *Jornada*, April 17, 1997.
6. SICC Combined Balance Sheet 1972, box 6, Exhibits, *Fouce Amusement Enterprises and Metropolitan Theaters Corp. v. Spanish International Communications Corp.*, case no. CV 76-4345, Record Group 21.6.8, Records of the U.S. Circuit Court for the Central District of California, National Archives at Riverside, Perris, CA (hereafter Exhibits, *Fouce v. Spanish International*).
7. Frank Fouce deposition, 46–48, 159–160, Depositions, *Fouce v. Spanish International*.
8. Emilio Nicolás interview, August 14, 2006.
9. Daniel Villanueva Sr., interview with the author, Camarillo, CA, February 17, 2011.
10. "Lee Deplores Excessive Reliance on Ratings," *Broadcasting*, November 20, 1972, 64.
11. "Are Minorities Undermeasured in TV Ratings?" *Broadcasting*, December 18, 1972, 33–34; "Profile: Rene Anselmo," *Broadcasting*, May 6, 1974, 64; "Radio Rating System Assailed as Unfair by Minority Groups," *New York Times*, April 30, 1977, 36.

12. "What R. E. Lee Told the FCC about Ratings: Government Should Leave Them to the Pros," *Television/Radio Age,* February 19, 1973, 26–27, 71–79.

13. "Station Rankings to Shift in Ethnic Ratings Storm?" *Television/Radio Age,* February 19, 1973, 23–25, 68–71.

14. Rene Anselmo, "Well Done Article," *Television/Radio Age,* April 16, 1973, 19.

15. "Cross-Tabulations of Markets Will Be Possible with ARB's Arbitron System," *Television/Radio Age,* April 16, 1973, 39.

16. SICC Combined Balance Sheet 1973, box 6, exhibits volume, Exhibits, *Fouce v. Spanish International.*

17. Declaration of William Stiles, November 4, 1979, box 2, volume 8, Proceedings, *Fouce v. Spanish International.*

18. Emilio Azcárraga affidavit, November 5, 1979, box 2, volume 9, Proceedings, *Fouce v. Spanish International.*

19. There was no satellite over the Atlantic that could accommodate continuous relay of soccer matches from Europe to Mexico. The Mexicans had many satellite dishes in the United States, at home, and in Latin America that could receive transmissions from Westar 2 (which was positioned above Ecuador), but an over-the-Atlantic satellite with a full-time relay wasn't available.

20. Anselmo deposition, 440–449.

21. Villanueva remained a director of the company that became MagnaVerde Promotions, which pioneered televised closed-circuit events at auditoriums across the United States. In the late 1970s, Villanueva was a prominent boxing promoter; he staged boxing matches at The Forum sports arena in Inglewood, CA, and Sunnyside Garden in Queens, NY, before it closed in 1977. Joe Jares, "A Welter of Welters: Cuevas Is the WBA Champ, Palomino is the WBC Champ. They Want Each Other," *Sports Illustrated,* July 31, 1978, https://vault.si.com/vault/1978/07/31/a-welter-of-welters-cuevas-is-the-wba-champ-palomino-is-the-wbc-champ-they-want-each-other.

22. "LA UHF Goes All News in Daytime," *Broadcasting,* June 18, 1973, 72.

23. Jerry Buck, "Villanueva Not Kicking about Collapse of News Channel," *Long Beach Independent and Press Telegram,* November 14, 1973; Greg Crister, "The Feud that Toppled a TV Empire," *Channels,* January 1987, 28; Villanueva interview, February 17, 2011.

24. Anselmo deposition, 418–421.

25. "The Dominant Selling Medium in the Super-Growth Spanish Market," SIN ad, *Television/Radio Age,* October 2, 1973, 45.

26. Villanueva interview, May 23, 2006.

27. United Nations Educational, Scientific and Cultural Organization, "Declaration of Guiding Principles on the Use of Satellite Broadcasting for the Free Flow of Information, the Spread of Education and Greater Cultural Exchange," November 15, 1972, http://portal.unesco.org/en/ev.php-URL_ID=17518&URL_DO=DO_TOPIC&URL_SECTION=201.html.

28. In re Applications of Riverside Cable TV, Inc., United Cablevision, Inc., Loma Linda and Riverside, FCC 75-172, in Federal Communications Commission, *Federal Communications Commission Reports: Decisions, Reports, and Orders of the Federal*

Communications Commission of the United States, February 21, 1975 to April 11, 1975 (Washington, DC: Federal Communications Commission, 1976), 551–555.

29. "Spanish-Language Television," *Television/Radio Age*, October 23, 1978, A26.
30. Villanueva interview, May 23, 2006.
31. Daniel Villanueva Sr. deposition, 28, 145, box 7, Depositions, *Fouce v. Spanish International*.
32. Dave Anderson, "Role Thinks United States Can Dominate Soccer," *Chicago Tribune*, July 6, 1974, Section 2, 3.
33. Anselmo deposition, 444–449.
34. William Leggett, "Theatre Soccer Sort of Socko," *Sports Illustrated*, July 8, 1974.
35. "MagnaVerde Productions," MagnaVerde report, January 1, 1977, box 1, volume 3, Proceedings, *Fouce v. Spanish International*.
36. Notes to Financial Statement, MagnaVerde Corporation, January 31, 1976, box 1, volume 3, Proceedings, *Fouce v. Spanish International*.
37. Rene Anselmo affidavit, box 7.
38. Emilio Nicolás interview, November 10, 2016.
39. SICC Combined Balance Sheet 1974, box 6, Exhibits, *Fouce v. Spanish International*.
40. Report As Is, December 31, 1974, box 6, Exhibits, *Fouce v. Spanish International*.
41. Board meeting minutes, January 14, 1975, box 5, Exhibits, *Fouce v. Spanish International*.
42. Fouce deposition, 170–182.
43. Rene Anselmo affidavit, 21.
44. Fouce deposition, 170–185.
45. Emilio Nicolás interview, May 23, 2006.
46. Emilio Azcárraga affidavit, November 5, 1979, box 2, volume 9, 7, Proceedings, *Fouce v. Spanish International*.
47. Fouce deposition, 104–105.
48. Federal Communications Commission, Construction Permit to Build San Francisco Station; Bahia de San Francisco Articles of Incorporation, July 1973, both box 2, volume 11, Proceedings, *Fouce v. Spanish International*.
49. "Spanish-Language Outlets Have Hookup for Live Programming," *Broadcasting*, August 11, 1975, 33.
50. "SICC Stations," March 21, 1978, box 2, volume 7, Proceedings, *Fouce v. Spanish International*.
51. Legends of Cibola Articles of Incorporation, box 6, Exhibits, *Fouce v. Spanish International*.
52. SICC Report on Examination, December 31, 1975, box 2, volume 8, Proceedings, *Fouce v. Spanish International*.
53. Joaquín Blaya affidavit, November 19, 1979, box 2, volume 10, Proceedings, *Fouce v. Spanish International*.
54. Board meeting minutes, December 15, 1975, box 5, Exhibits, *Fouce v. Spanish International*.
55. Photos and materials on SIN satellite telecasts, September 1976, private collection of Guillermo Nicolás, San Antonio, TX.

56. Les Brown, "Seven U.S. Stations to Broadcast TV Shows Directly from Mexico," *New York Times*, September 9, 1976, 78.

57. Edmond M. Rosenthal, "Indicators of Growth Abound in Spanish Media Community," *Television/Radio Age*, October 23, 1978, A19.

58. Villanueva interview, May 23, 2006.

59. SICC Combined Balance Sheet 1976, box 6, Exhibits, *Fouce v. Spanish International*.

60. Fouce deposition, 212–232.

61. J. Harvey to R. Anselmo, September 9, 1976, box 1, volume 2, Proceedings, *Fouce v. Spanish International*.

62. Anselmo deposition, 503–510; Fouce deposition, 212–232.

63. Board meeting minutes, August 20, 1976, box 5, Exhibits, *Fouce v. Spanish International*.

64. Villanueva interview, May 23, 2006.

65. Greg Crister, "The Feud that Toppled a TV Empire," *Channels*, January 1987, 28.

66. First complaint, November 4, 1976, box 1, volume 1, Proceedings, *Fouce v. Spanish International*.

67. Transcript of Proceedings on Order, filed December 6, 1976, box 1, volume 2, Proceedings, *Fouce v. Spanish International*.

68. Joaquín Blaya, interview with the author, Basalt, CO, December 18, 2009.

Chapter 5. The Golden Age

1. Rene Anselmo's remarks recalled in Daniel Villanueva Sr., interview with the author, Camarillo, CA, July 27, 2007; and Emilio Nicolás, interview with the author, San Antonio, TX, February 17, 2011. Also see "Spanish USA Sees a World on SIN," SIN anniversary ad display, December 1976, private collection of Guillermo Nicolás.

2. Carole Bird, interview with the author, Miami, FL, July 21, 2008.

3. Emilio Nicolás interview, March 30, 2007.

4. Network Television Program Schedule February 6, 1977, SIN Network Television Sales Office, private collection of Guillermo Nicolás.

5. Sam Quinones, "Mexico and the Monopoly of Power," *Los Angeles Times*, December 28, 1997, 17.

6. "SIN Raises the Volume of Satellite Feeds," *Broadcasting*, January 23, 1978, 52.

7. Soledad Robina Bustos, "Hemispheric Village: The Case of Televisa," *Méxican Journal of Communication* 2 (1995): 113.

8. "On October 11, 1981, UNIVISION," SIN ad, *New York Times*, August 20, 1981, D17.

9. "Spanish-Language TV Network Formed," *Los Angeles Times*, October 6, 1981, G8.

10. Laurie Johnson, "Hispanic Parade Honors Columbus Early," *New York Times*, October 12, 1981, B1.

11. Savannah Waring Walker, "In the Grip of SIN," *Channels*, July–August, 1983, 46–49.

12. "Bullfight," SIN ad, *New York Times*, November 21, 1981, 52.

13. "Spanish Spending Power Growing Dramatically," *Television/Radio Age*, December 10, 1984, A41.

14. Andrew Martinez, interview with the author, San Antonio, TX, July 24, 2007.

15. Anne Arrante Moncreiff, "And Galavisión Makes Three," *Advertising Age,* February 12, 1990, 52.

16. Because internal components wore out and devices gradually shifted to an orbit that was not optimal for maintaining their "footprint" on Earth, satellites had an expected life of six to ten years. Westar 2, which launched in 1975, stopped transmitting in 1984.

17. "SIN squabbles with AFTRA," *Broadcasting,* February 26, 1979, 80.

18. Arturo González, "Case Study of KMEX-TV" (MA thesis, California State University-Northridge, 1978), 107–108.

19. R. K. Doane, "Ole: Say Millions of Fans," *TV Guide,* May 10, 1969, 28–30.

20. Rene Anselmo, "To Tally All Who Live in the United States," *New York Times,* January 20, 1980, 20.

21. SICC Statement of Income, December 31, 1980, box 4, volume 20, Exhibits, *Frank Fouce v. Spanish International,* case no. CV 76-4345, Records of the U.S. District Court Southern Division, National Archives at Riverside, Perris, CA.

22. Rick DuBrow, "Spanish-Language Stations Boom in the '80s," *Los Angeles Herald Examiner,* July 30, 1980, 17.

23. Kim Parker, Juliana Menasce Horowitz, Rich Morin, and Mark Hugo Lopez, "Race and Multiracial Americans in the U.S. Census," in *Multiracial in America,* Pew Center, June 11, 2015, https://www.pewsocialtrends.org/2015/06/11/chapter-1-race-and-multiracial-americans-in-the-u-s-census/.

24. Table 1, Selected Characteristics of Households—Number of Households and Median Income in 1980 and 1979 Based on 1980 and 1970 Census Population Controls, in Edward J. Welniak and Mary F. Henson, *Money Income of Households, Families, and Persons in the United States: 1980* (Washington, DC: U.S. Department of Commerce, Bureau of Census, 1982), 10; "It's Your Turn in the Sun," *Time,* October 16, 1978, 48–61.

25. "Hispanics—A World of Third Own: Sensibly Reaching Hispanics," *Madison Avenue,* July 1982.

26. Robert Weiner, "Hispanic Population's Growth Has Big Marketing Implications," *Television/Radio Age,* October 23, 1978, A16.

27. Edmund M. Rosenthal, "Indicators of Growth Abound in Spanish Media Community," *Television/Radio Age,* October 25, 1978, A18–A21.

28. "Hispanic Market Study," *Television/Radio Age,* December 19, 1984, A3.

29. Villanueva interview, May 23, 2006.

30. Emilio Nicolás interview, July 27, 2007.

31. "Yankelovich Answers Questions on Spanish USA," *Broadcasting,* July 20, 1981, 20.

32. Yankelovich, Skelly and White, *Spanish USA* (New York: Yankelovich, Skelly and White, 1981), 7, 15–28.

33. "Advertisers Turning Their Attention to Hispanics," *Broadcasting,* April 3, 1989, 48.

34. John Naisbitt, *Megatrends: Ten New Directions Transforming Our Lives* (New York: Warner, 1982), 76.

35. Nicholas Alfred Valenzuela, "Organizational Evolution of a Spanish Language Television Network" (PhD diss., Stanford University, 1985), 187–204.

36. "WNJU-TV Sold by Columbia Pictures to Jerry Perenchio," *Broadcasting*, January 14, 1980, 50.

37. "Tall Problem," *Broadcasting*, March 3, 1980, 50.

38. "Anselmo Would Rather Go Hungry," *Broadcasting*, May 19, 1980, 86.

39. "Top of the Week," *Broadcasting*, May 12, 1980, 27.

40. "Trade Center May Permit WXTV to Transmit June 8," *New York Times*, May 18, 1980, 55.

41. Tony Schwartz, "President of Channel 41 Finally Makes His Point," *New York Times*, May 29, 1980, C22.

42. RCA-SATCOM 3, National Aeronautics and Space Administration, n.d., https://nssdc.gsfc.nasa.gov/nmc/spacecraft/display.action?id=1979-101A.

43. "Programmers Up Heat on RCA over T'sponders," *Broadcasting*, April 7, 1980, 30.

44. "Anselmo Angry over Satellite Allocations," *Broadcasting*, May 14, 1979, 53.

45. "FCC Extracts RCA from Tangle of Satcom Claims," *Broadcasting*, June 30, 1980, 70–71.

46. Savannah Waring Walker, "In the Grip of SIN," *Channels*, July–August, 1983, 46–49.

47. "SIN Gets Its Transponders After All," *Broadcasting*, February 15, 1982, 78.

48. At the time, Anselmo was conferring with Reagan's White House advisors to arrange the president's christening of the first SIN national newscast in June 1981. According to Joaquín Blaya, Anselmo's confidant who was the manager of SIN's Miami station, Anselmo had told him he sent the 1982 and 1983 mailings to Reagan and that the president's advisors were familiar with SIN and aware of Anselmo's satellite initiatives. However, there is no evidence that Reagan contacted Hughes and arranged for SIN to receive the satellite relays.

49. "Narrowcasting Momentum Paves the Way for SIN's Expansion," *Television/Radio Age*, September 21, 1981, 57.

50. Villanueva interview, February 17, 2011.

51. "47 CFR § 74.733—UHF Translator Signal Boosters," Cornell Law School Legal Information Institute, n.d., https://www.law.cornell.edu/cfr/text/47/74.733.

52. Villanueva interview, February 17, 2011.

53. In Re: The Seven Hills Television Company, 2 FCC Red Volume 23, in *FCC Record: A Comprehensive Compilation of Decisions, Reports, Public Notices, and Other Documents of the Federal Communications Commission of the United States* (Washington, DC: Federal Communications Commission, 1987), section 20, page 6872.

54. Clark Secrest, "Spanish Talk Program to Kick Off Channel 31's Sunday Show," *Denver Post*, February 18, 1980, 8.

55. "How SIN Television Network Reaches Spanish USA," SIN ad, private collection of Guillermo Nicolás.

56. Frederick Cusick, "New Network Debuts Tomorrow; Area Reception Is Scant," *Philadelphia Inquirer*, May 31, 1980, 25C.

57. C. L. Smith Muniz, "State Spanish TV Station to Start Operating," *Hartford Courant*, June 21, 1980, 22.

58. Joaquín Blaya, interview with the author, Basalt, CO, January 12, 2010.

59. Donnel Numes, "TV in Spanish to Start Here Sunday," *Washington Post,* June 28, 1980, B3; "Translator Gala," *Broadcasting,* July 7, 1980, 45.

60. "How SIN Television Network Reaches Spanish USA: RCA F4 83 Transponder 1," Spanish International Network 1980 system plan, private collection of Guillermo Nicolás.

61. Lori Kesler, "Low Power Stations Build Up SIN's Strength," *Advertising Age,* August 11, 1986, 56–58.

62. "47 CFR Subpart G—Low Power TV, TV Translator, and TV Booster Stations," Cornell Law School Legal Information Institute, https://www.law.cornell.edu/cfr/text/47/part-74/subpart-G.

63. Edwin Krasnow and Michael Botein, "Deregulation of Broadcasting in the United States: Quo Vadimus," *Journal of Media Law and Practice* 7 (1986): 56–61.

64. "FCC Investigates Spanish-Language TV Service," *Hartford Courant,* September 5, 1980, 29; "FCC Investigating Ownership of Spanish Network," *Broadcasting,* September 15, 1980, 82; "Latin Network Target of U.S. Antitrust Probe," *Los Angeles Times,* October 21, 1980, E1.

65. Denial of Plaintiff's Motion for Summary Judgment, December 12, 1980, box 2, volume 11, Proceedings, *Fouce Amusement Enterprises and Metropolitan Theaters Corp. v. Spanish International Communications Corp.,* case no. CV 76-4345, Records of the U.S. District Court Southern Division, National Archives at Riverside, Perris, CA.

66. Villanueva interview, February 17, 2011.

67. Joaquín Blaya, "Network Television Makes Miami Its Home," 2006, 18–22, unpublished memoir in author's possession.

68. Declaration of William Stiles, November 4, 1979, box 2, volume 9, Proceedings, *Frank Fouce v. Spanish International,* case no. CV 76-4345, Records of the U.S. District Court Southern Division, National Archives at Riverside, Perris, CA.

69. Blaya interview, December 18, 2009.

70. "Remember Ralph Renick? He Was a Legend on Local TV, and Then He Suddenly Quit on Air," *Miami Herald,* March 17, 2019, https://www.miamiherald.com/entertainment/tv/article227454549.html.

71. Gustavo Godoy, interview with the author, Miami, FL, August 1, 2007.

72. Blaya interview, December 18, 2009.

73. "SIN Crosses Another Frontier in Programming," *Broadcasting,* June 8, 1981, 98–99; "Spanish Network News to Begin on TV on June 1," *New York Times,* April 26, 1981, 58.

74. Godoy interview, August 1, 2007.

75. "Hispanic TV Network Moving Here," *Miami Herald,* May 25, 1982, 1B.

76. George Folksy, "Spanish Network Talks of Gains in Broadcasting from Miami," *New York Times,* January 14, 1982, A14.

77. Blaya, "Network Television Makes Miami Its Home," 33.

78. Bendixen & Law, Inc., "The Political Pulse of Latin America: Voter Attitudes in El Salvador, Colombia, Guatemala, Perú, Honduras," SIN Television Network, 1986, private collection of Mario Rodríguez, Miami, FL.

79. Jeanne Jakle, "KWEX Gives All for Quake Relief," *San Antonio Express-News,*

September 28, 1985, 10; "SIN National News Brings Nicaraguan Crisis to Spanish USA," SIN ad, *Broadcasting,* June 11, 1984, 11; "Hispanic Market Study," *Television/Radio Age,* December 19, 1984, A36.

80. Godoy interview, August 1, 2007.

81. Manuel A. Guerro, *The Emergence of Political Pluralism in Mexican Broadcasting* (Riga, Latvia: VDM Verlag, 2009), 127–129.

82. Godoy interview, August 1, 2007.

83. "Spanish Network to Be Reorganized in U.S.," *Miami Herald,* September 9, 1986, 2B; "SIN Newscast to Be Run by New Agency," *Miami Herald,* September 11, 1986, 1D.

84. Frank del Olmo, "Sour Sweetheart Deal for Spanish-Language TV?" *Los Angeles Times,* September 12, 1986.

85. Godoy interview, August 1, 2007.

86. Lourdes Meluza, "15 Quitting Jobs in Spanish-Language News Show Upheaval," *Miami Herald,* October 31, 1986, 1A; Lourdes Meluza, "Prohiben a dimitentes de SIN entrar," *El Nuevo Herald,* November 1, 1986, 1.

87. Eleanor Randolph, "Reporters Walk Out of Hispanic TV Network," *Washington Post,* November 2, 1986, 5.

88. William Finnegan, "The Man Who Wouldn't Sit Down," *New Yorker,* October 5, 2015, 44.

89. Jon Nordheimer, "Resignations Upset Hispanic TV News Program," *New York Times,* November 4, 1986, C17.

Chapter 6. Armageddon

1. *In re Spanish International Communication Corporation,* FCC 86D-1 (Admin. L.J. rel. January 8, 1986)("Initial Decision"), *Frank Fouce Amusement Enterprises vs. Spanish International Communications Corporation* (76CV3451), Civil Case Files, 1938–2004, U.S. District Court for the Central District of California, Record Group 21, Records of District Courts of the United States. National Archives at Riverside, Perris, California (hereafter Civil Case Files, *In re Spanish International Communication Corporation*).

2. "Mass Media Bureau Settlement Would Allow SICC to Sell Its Stations," *Broadcasting,* June 30, 1986, 45.

3. First complaint, November 4, 1976, box 1, volume 1, Proceedings, *Fouce Amusement Enterprises and Metropolitan Theaters Corp. v. Spanish International Communications Corp.,* case no. CV 76-4345, Records of the U.S. District Court Southern Division, National Archives at Riverside, Perris, CA (hereafter Proceedings, *Fouce v. Spanish International*).

4. Transcript of Proceedings on Order, filed December 6, 1976; Order for Preliminary Injunction, December 22, 1976, both in box 1, volume 2, Proceedings, *Fouce v. Spanish International.*

5. Revised Complaint, January 10, 1977, box 1, volume 2, Proceedings, *Fouce v. Spanish International.*

6. Fouce affidavit, November 30, 1976, box 2, volume 8, Proceedings, *Fouce v. Spanish International.*

7. Answer of Defendants to Complaint, January 31, 1977, box 1, volume 2, Proceedings, *Fouce v. Spanish International*.

8. Stipulation Requesting Continuance of Pre-Trial Hearing on Fouce v. SICC, March 18, 1977, box 1, volume 2, Proceedings, *Fouce v. Spanish International*.

9. Revised Complaint, January 10, 1977.

10. Reynold Anselmo deposition, 52–68, Depositions, *Fouce Amusement Enterprises and Metropolitan Theaters Corp. v. Spanish International Communications Corp.*, case no. CV 76-4345, Records of the U.S. District Court Southern Division, National Archives at Riverside, Perris, CA (hereafter Depositions, *Fouce v. Spanish International*).

11. Anselmo deposition, 151–157.

12. Section 73.658 of the FCC Rules And Regulations—Affiliation Agreements And Network Program Practices; Territorial Exclusivity In Non-Network Program Arrangements, Subsection i, https://www.ecfr.gov/cgi-bin/text-idx?SID=a8146a5d39588c884a0531919c98658e&mc=true&node=se47.4.73_1658&rgn=div8. For the chain broadcasting report, see *Report On Chain Broadcasting*, Federal Communications Commission, Commission Order No. 37, Docket No. 5060, May 1941, Section 8, https://earlyradiohistory.us/1941cb08.htm.

13. "Skimming" came to refer to networks taking the 15 percent commissions on local spot sales above the 100 percent they earned on network ads placed in network programs that local stations had to carry.

14. Frank Fouce deposition, 46–48, 159–165, Depositions, *Fouce v. Spanish International*.

15. R. Rosen to R. Anselmo, December 4, 1975, box 1, volume 6, Exhibits, *Fouce Amusement Enterprises and Metropolitan Theaters Corp. v. Spanish International Communications Corp.*, case no. CV 76-4345, Records of the U.S. District Court Southern Division, Records of the U.S. District Court Southern Division, National Archives at Riverside, Perris, CA (hereafter Exhibits, *Fouce v. Spanish International*).

16. Continued Examination before Trial, June 3, 1977, box 2, volume 11, Proceedings, *Fouce v. Spanish International*.

17. Emilio Azcárraga affidavit, November 5, 1979, box 2, volume 9, Proceedings, *Fouce v. Spanish International*.

18. Notice of Transfer of Civil Action, February 16, 1979, box 4, volume 9, Proceedings, *Fouce v. Spanish International*.

19. Motion for Summary Judgment, August 17, 1979, box 8, Exhibits, *Fouce v. Spanish International*.

20. Opposition of Defendants to Plaintiff's Motions for Summary Adjudication, November 19, 1979, box 2, volume 9, Proceedings, *Fouce v. Spanish International*.

21. Report of the FCC Independent Review Board, September 1987, box 4, volume MRP, Exhibits, *Fouce v. Spanish International*.

22. Denial of Plaintiff's Motion for Summary Judgment, December 12, 1980, box 2, volume 11, Proceedings, *Fouce v. Spanish International*.

23. "Hispanic Convocation," *Broadcasting*, March 26, 1979, 72.

24. SRBA Complaint to the FCC, March 20, 1980, in Report of the Special Master, May 15, 1983, box 4, volume 19, Proceedings, *Fouce v. Spanish International*.

25. "FCC Investigates Spanish-Language TV Service," *Hartford Courant*, September 5, 1980, 29; "FCC Investigating Ownership of Spanish Network," *Broadcasting*, September 15, 1980, 82.

26. An intervenor is a third party that is allowed to participate in a civil proceeding while having no ties to the two litigants. Pfaelzer named the SRBA as an intervenor because of the possibility that her decision in Fouce's lawsuit would both affect the SRBA's petition to the FCC and inspire litigation that the SRBA might (and eventually did) bring.

27. "Latin Network Target of U.S. Antitrust Probe," *Los Angeles Times*, October 21, 1980, E1; Defendant's Joint List of Prospective Exhibits, January 22, 1981, box 3, volume 12, Proceedings, *Fouce v. Spanish International*; Defendant's List of Witnesses, January 22, 1981, box 3, volume 12, Proceedings, *Fouce v. Spanish International*; List of Plaintiff's Exhibits, January 21, 1981, box 3, volume 12, Proceedings, *Fouce v. Spanish International*; SICC and SIN Response to FCC Informational Request, September 13, 1981, box 3, volume 13, Proceedings, *Fouce v. Spanish International*.

28. "Broadcast Bureau Threatens SIN with Hearings," *Broadcasting*, August 23, 1982, 81.

29. Defendant SICC Report on Settlement Discussions, March 14, 1983, box 3, volume 13, Proceeding, *Fouce v. Spanish International*.

30. L. Dam to F. Stern, April 15, 1983, box 3, volume 14, Proceedings, *Fouce v. Spanish International*.

31. F. Stern to L. Dam and L. Petrich, April 14, 1983; and L. Dam to F. Stern, April 15, 1983, both in box 3, volume 13, Proceedings, *Fouce v. Spanish International*.

32. Appointment of Special Master, April 22, 1983, box 3, volume 14, Proceedings, *Fouce v. Spanish International*.

33. Report of the Special Master, July 15, 1983, box 4, volume 19, Proceedings, *Fouce v. Spanish International*.

34. Norman Black, "FCC Orders Full Probe of Spanish TV Network," *Washington Post*, May 27, 1983, D2; "F.C.C. to Investigate Influence of Aliens over 7 T.V. Stations," *New York Times*, May 29, 1983, 26; "SIN Licenses Up for Hearing," *Broadcasting*, June 6, 1983, 79.

35. "Public Probe of TV Network Urged," *Los Angeles Times*, May 24, 1983, E8.

36. Pretrial Conference Order, June 6, 1983, box 3, volume 14, Proceedings, *Fouce v. Spanish International*.

37. Report of the Special Master, July 15, 1983, box 4, volume 19, Proceedings, *Fouce v. Spanish International*.

38. "KROQ License Renewal Denied By FCC Judge," *Billboard*, February 13, 1982, 27.

39. Before the FCC, Denial of SICC Licenses, September 29, 1986, box 4, volume 18, Proceedings, *Fouce v. Spanish International*.

40. Report of the Special Master, July 15, 1983, box 4, volume 19, Proceedings, *Fouce v. Spanish International*.

41. Defendant's Joint List of Prospective Exhibits, January 22, 1981; Defendant's List of Witnesses, January 22, 1981; and List of Plaintiff's Exhibits, January 21, 1981.

42. Notice of Indefinite Postponement, February 19, 1985, box 8, volume 4, Proceedings, *Fouce v. Spanish International*.

43. Report of FCC Review Board in *The Seven Hills Television Company*, 4 FCC Red (General Counsel, 1987), in *FCC Record: A Comprehensive Compilation of Decisions, Records, Public Notices, and Other Documents of the Federal Communications Commission of the United States* (Washington, DC: Federal Communications Commission, 1987), 6867–6895.

44. R. Anselmo to SIN/SICC employees, November 18, 1985, box 3, volume 16, Proceedings, *Fouce v. Spanish International*.

45. Howard Fields, "Fall of the Mexican Empire," *Television/Radio Age*, November 23, 1987, A47.

46. *In re Spanish International Communication Corporation*, FCC 86D-1 (Admin. L.J. rel. January 8, 1986)("Initial Decision"), Civil Case Files, *Frank Fouce Amusement Enterprises vs. Spanish International Communications Corporation*.

47. Joaquín Blaya, interview with the author, Basalt, CO, December 18, 2009.

48. Emilio Nicolás Sr., interview with the author, San Antonio, TX, August 14, 2006.

49. Blaya interview, December 18, 2009.

50. "KWEX-TV's General Manager Is Named New President of SIN," *San Antonio Light*, May 3, 1986, F1.

51. Emilio Nicolás interview, August 14, 2006.

52. "SICC to Sell Stations," SICC news release, May 13, 1986, box 3, volume 17, Depositions, *Fouce v. Spanish International*.

53. Emilio Nicolás interview, November 16, 2011.

54. Motion by Hallmark Group, November 6, 1986, box 4, volume 18, Proceedings, *Fouce v. Spanish International*.

55. "SICC to Sell Stations," *Broadcasting*, April 19, 1986, 79.

56. "Hispanic Bid for 5 TV Stations," *New York Times*, July 4, 1986, D8.

57. Daniel Villanueva Sr., interview with the author, Camarillo, CA, February 17, 2011.

58. Memorandum of TVL Corporation to Intervene, October 6, 1986, box 4, volume 9, Proceedings, *Fouce v. Spanish International*.

59. Nancy Riviera Brooks, "KMEX-TV, Other Stations to Be Sold to Non-Latinos," *Los Angeles Times*, July 22, 1986, 1, 15.

60. Order re Matter Referred to Court for Decision by Sales Committee for SICC, U.S. District Court, July 18, 1986, box 3, volume 17, Proceedings, *Fouce v. Spanish International*.

61. Individual proceeds received by SICC's departing owners were not made public. From the $301 million Hallmark paid to acquire SICC and based on the predecessor SICC's division of individual ownership shares as of 1986, individuals likely received the following amounts: Frank Fouce $77 million (25.5 percent); Rene Anselmo $72 million (23.9 percent); Emilio Azcárraga $60 million (20 percent); James Jacobson $27 million (9.1 percent); Emilio Nicolás $20 million (6.7 percent); and Daniel Villanueva $18 million (6.0 percent). Others, including Stiles and Blaya, likely received around $27 million (9.0 percent). Estimates are derived from details of the Hallmark purchase agreement in Motion of the Hallmark Group for Affirmation of July 18 Order, September 22, 1986, box

4, volume 18, Proceedings, *Fouce v. Spanish International;* and in information on SICC'S preceding owners and their ownership shares in Report of FCC Review Board in *The Seven Hills Television Company,* 4 FCC Red (General Counsel, 1987).

62. Richard W. Stevenson, "Hallmark, Partner Buy TV Outlets," *New York Times,* July 22, 1986, D1, D4.

63. Denial of Appeal to Intervene, U.S. Court of Appeals for Ninth Circuit, June 6, 1987, box 4, volume MRP, Proceedings, *Fouce v. Spanish International; Coalition for the Preservation of Hispanic Broadcasting v. FCC,* 893 F.2d 1349 (1990).

64. Report of FCC Review Board in re Spanish International Communication Corporation, 4 FCC Red (General Counsel, 1987).

65. *Spanish International Communications Corp.,* 2 FCC Red 3336, 3339 (1987), remanded sub nom; *Coalition for the Preservation of Hispanic Broadcasting v. FCC,* No. 87-1285, D.C. Cir. January 12, 1990.

66. Report of FCC Review Board in *The Seven Hills Television Company,* 4 FCC Red (General Counsel, 1987).

67. "A 'Vindication' of Anselmo," *Television/Radio Age,* November 21, 1987, A47.

68. Motion of the Hallmark Group for Affirmation of July 18 Order, September 22, 1986, box 4, volume 18, Proceedings, *Fouce v. Spanish International.*

69. Irvine Hockaday, interview with the author, Kansas City, MO, April 2, 2007; Marilyn Achiron, "Mexican TV Aims North," *Newsweek,* October 13, 1986, 49.

70. "Reliance Subsidiary to Buy WNJU-TV," *New York Times,* October 28, 1986, D5.

71. Steve Beale, "Hallmark Si, Hallmark No," *Hispanic Business,* December 1986, 50–51.

72. Victor Valle, "Competition Heats Up Latino TV," *Los Angeles Times,* December 8, 1986, E1.

73. Hockaday interview.

Chapter 7. Univision and Telemundo

1. Drexel Burnham Lambert, *Prospectus: Telemundo Group,* August 19, 1987, in Definitive Additional Proxy Material as Filed with the Securities and Exchange Commission on February 12, 1998, Schedule 14a, Information Statement Pursuant to Section 14(A) of the Securities Exchange Act of 1934, pages 147–161, https://www.sec.gov/Archives/edgar/data/5272/0000950123-98-001385.txt; Victor Valle, "KVEA To Carry Rose Parade," *Los Angeles Times,* November 26, 1986, D14.

2. "Hispanic Network Power," Telemundo ad, 1987, private collection of Carlos Barba, Miami, FL.

3. "Introducing Univision," Hallmark ad, January 1, 1987, private collection of Guillermo Nicolás.

4. Richard Mahler in Victor Valle, "Competition Heats Up in Latino TV," *Los Angeles Times,* December 8, 1986, E1; José de Córdoba, "Spanish-Language TV Faces Changes with Emergence of a Second Network," *Wall Street Journal,* November 26, 1986, 1.

5. Greg Crister, "The Feud that Toppled a TV Empire" and "New Players," *Channels,* January 1987, 24–31; Steve Beale, "Turmoil and Growth," *Hispanic Business,* December 1986, 48–52.

6. Amy Barrett, "Henry Silverman's Long Road Back," *Business Week*, February 28, 2000.

7. Ana Vecino-Suarez, "Spanish-Language Television," Hispanic Marketing Association report, January 1987, private collection of Mario Rodríguez, Miami, FL.

8. José de Córdoba, "Rivalry Intensifies within Spanish-Language Television," *Wall Street Journal*, March 11, 1987, 1.

9. "Prospectus: Telemundo Group," 153–155.

10. "Prospectus: Telemundo Group," 150.

11. Carlos Barba, interview with the author, Miami, FL, January 8, 2008.

12. "Prospectus: Telemundo Group," 159.

13. "Reliance Steps in to Buy Blair," *Broadcasting*, June 9, 1986, 125.

14. "Hispanic TV Programming a Novela Idea," *Television/Radio Age*, April 3, 1989, 40–49.

15. Stephanie Loudis, "Moving Day for HBC," *Miami Herald*, December 26, 1986, 12C.

16. "Telemundo TV Network to Air Nationally Tonight," *Wall Street Journal*, January 12, 1987, 1.

17. Barba interview, January 8, 2008.

18. Lee Winfrey, "Phila. TV in Spanish and Other Languages," *Philadelphia Inquirer*, May 14, 1990.

19. *Angélica mi vida*, IMDb, https://www.imdb.com/title/tt5270336/companycredits?ref_=tt_dt_co.

20. "The Media Business: Telemundo-MTV Pact," *New York Times*, June 10, 1988, D18.

21. SICC Statement of Income, December 31, 1986, box 4, volume 20, Exhibits, *Fouce Amusement Enterprises and Metropolitan Theaters Corp. v. Spanish International Communications Corp.*, case no. CV 76-4345, Record Group 21.6.8, Records of the U.S. Circuit Court for the Central District of California, National Archives at Riverside, Perris, CA.

22. Irvine Hockaday, interview with the author, Kansas City, MO, April 2, 2007.

23. SIN/Univision Satellite Program Schedule, January 24–31, 1987, Grids 1983–1992, private collection of Mario Rodríguez.

24. "Mario Kreutzberger," in *Sábado gigante* commemorative publication, Santiago, Chile, Editorial American S.A., 1993, private collection of Mario Rodríguez.

25. Mario Kreutzberger, interview with the author, Miami, FL, July 23, 2009.

26. Norma Libman, "Spanish 'King,'" *Chicago Tribune*, June 25, 1995, https://www.chicagotribune.com/news/ct-xpm-1995-06-25-9506250188-story.html; "Guinness Makes It Official: 'Sábado Gigante' Is the World's Longest Running TV Variety Show," Univision news release, Business Wire, December 17, 2003, https://www.businesswire.com/news/home/20031217005366/en/Guinness-Official-Sabado-Gigante-Worlds-Longest-Running.

27. Bert Sobel, "Where's Spanish TV Going?" *Television/Radio Age*, November 23, 1987, A15–A38.

28. Joaquín Blaya, interview with the author, Basalt, CO, December 18, 2009.

29. Univision continued to broadcast from the California location for three more years. Control of the network did not switch from Laguna Niguel to Miami until 1991,

when Hallmark completed a telecasting center there. Soon after Hallmark acquired the "network," Univision president Joaquín Blaya pushed for the relocation of the network to Miami. He facilitated the relocation upon his opening of Univision's "Television City" in the Miami suburb of Doral in March 1991. The Doral facility remained Univision's broadcast headquarters.

30. "Another Spanish Buy for Hallmark," *Broadcasting*, November 30, 1987, 92.

31. "Grimes Leaves ESPN to Join Hispanic Network," *Broadcasting*, August 22, 1988, 26.

32. Daniel F. Cuff, "Univision Names Head of Spanish Network," *New York Times*, August 31, 1988.

33. Laura Landro, "Univision Expansion Plan Is Under Way," *Wall Street Journal*, January 23, 1989, 1.

34. "Univision: The Vision for America," Univision ad, 1989, private collection of Mario Rodríguez.

35. Univision Satellite Program Schedule, April 16, 1989, Grids 1983–1992, private collection of Mario Rodríguez.

36. "Sampling Hispanic Television Shows," *Broadcasting*, December 10, 1990, 80.

37. Cristina Saralegui, interview with the author, Miami, FL, July 24, 2008.

38. Univision Satellite Program Schedules, April 23, May 28, July 2, 1989, Grids 1983–1992, private collection of Mario Rodríguez.

39. "The Coming of Age of Hispanic Broadcasting," *Broadcasting*, April 3, 1989, 38–39.

40. Victor Valle, "Villanueva Quits General Manager Post at KMEX, Channel 34," *Los Angeles Times*, March 2, 1989, 9.

41. Victor Valle, "Ethnic Fight Heats Up at Latino Station," *Los Angeles Times*, May 19, 1989, 1.

42. "Telemundo Stakes Its Future on Hispanic Audience," *Broadcasting*, August 10, 1987, 87.

43. "Prospectus: Telemundo Group," 147.

44. "Prospectus: Telemundo Group," 173.

45. Robert Barker, "Steinberg May Have Trouble Making Money in Spanish," *Business Week*, August 10, 1987, 29–30.

46. "Prospectus: Telemundo Group," 161–163.

47. Steve Weiner, "Do They Speak Spanish in Kansas City?" *Forbes*, January 25, 1988, 46.

48. [Steve McClellan and John Lippman], "Reliance, Hallmark Refinance Spanish TV Network Holdings," *Broadcasting*, August 8, 1988, 33–34.

49. "Hallmark Extends Bid to Buy Junk Bonds of Univision TV Unit," *Wall Street Journal*, March 8, 1990, 83.

50. Joanne Lipman, "Nielsen to Track Hispanic TV Ratings," *Wall Street Journal*, July 20, 1989, 1.

51. "Silverman to Leave Telemundo for Blackstone Group," *Los Angeles Times*, January 30, 1990, A7; "Investor Joins Blackstone," *New York Times*, January 30, 1990, 37; "Swiss Insurer Buys into Reliance," *Los Angeles Times*, A15.

52. Robin Blumenthal, "Univision Fails to Pay Interest to Banks, Holders," *Wall Street Journal,* February 2, 1990, B4.

53. Telemundo Group Annual Report 1990, December 31, 1990, in Definitive Additional Proxy Material as Filed with the Securities and Exchange Commission on February 12, 1998, Schedule 14a, Information Statement Pursuant to Section 14(A) of the Securities Exchange Act of 1934, pages 178–181, https://www.sec.gov/Archives/edgar/data/5272/0000950123-98-001385.txt.

54. "Hallmark Cards Buy-Back Offer Completed for Univision Junk Bonds," *Wall Street Journal,* April 25, 1990, 1.

55. William A. Henry III, "Beyond the Melting Pot," *Time,* April 9, 1990, 28–35.

56. Ceril Shagrin, interview with the author, Miami, FL, July 24, 2009.

57. Mario Rodríguez, interview with the author, Miami, FL, July 23, 2008.

58. "Tracking Nielsen Viewing Is a Three-Way Race," *Broadcasting,* December 10, 1990, 78–79.

59. Ceril Shagrin, interview with the author, Miami, FL, July 24, 2009.

60. Mario Rodríguez notes on 1991 Nielsen test ratings, February 1991, private collection of Mario Rodríguez.

61. Shagrin interview.

62. "Galavisión Proudly Salutes Channel 6 in Palm Springs, California," *Broadcasting,* October 1, 1990, 15; "Galavisión Channel of the Stars," 1990, Galavisión ads, private collection of Mario Rodríguez.

63. "Hispanic Media: Familiarity Breeds Compensation and Competition," *Broadcasting,* December 10, 1990, 68–69.

64. Ray Rodríguez, interview with the author, Miami, FL, July 22, 2009.

65. Mario Rodríguez interview, July 23, 2009.

66. Hockaday interview.

67. Juan Carlos Coto, "War Is Sweeping News Programs Away," *Miami Herald,* January 31, 1991, 5G.

68. Jorge Ramos, interview with the author, Miami, FL, July 24, 2008.

69. Blaya interview, December 18, 2009.

70. "Programs on Univision," Univision fact page, November 1991, private collection of Mario Rodríguez.

71. Mario Rodríguez notes on plans for Nielsen ratings, October 1991, private collection of Mario Rodríguez.

72. Univision Satellite Program Schedules, February 3, 1992, Grids 1983–1992, private collection of Mario Rodríguez.

73. Hockaday interview.

74. Mario Rodríguez notes on 1992 Nielsen test ratings, February 1992, private collection of Mario Rodríguez.

75. Telemundo Group Annual Report 1993, December 31, 1993, in Definitive Additional Proxy Material as Filed with the Securities and Exchange Commission on February 12, 1998, Schedule 14a, Information Statement Pursuant to Section 14(A) of the Securities Exchange Act of 1934, pages 182–184, https://www.sec.gov/Archives/edgar/data/5272/0000950123-98-001385.txt.

76. Multimedia Elects Grimes," *Broadcasting,* April 27, 1992, 10.

77. Hockaday interview.

78. Richard Stevenson, "Mr. Perenchio's Dream Deal," *New York Times,* April 12, 1992, 123.

79. A. Jerrold Perenchio statement, April 8, 1992, private collection of Mario Rodríguez.

80. Richard Stevenson, "Hallmark to Sell Its Univision TV Group," *New York Times,* April 9, 1992, D1-D4.

81. Jennifer Mann, "Outgoing Hallmark CEO reflects on successes, setbacks," *Kansas City Star,* October 9, 2001, B1.

82. Ray Rodríguez interview, July 22, 2009.

83. Blaya interview, December 18, 2009.

84. Beatriz Paiga, "Soplan Vientos de Cambio en TV Hispañia," *El Nuevo Herald,* April 11, 1992, 1.

85. Ramos interview, July 24, 2008; and Jorge Ramos, *No Borders* (New York: Harper Collins, 2002), 98–99.

86. Jon Krampner, "La Novela Grande," *Emmy,* June 1993, 32–35.

87. Ray Rodríguez interview, July 22, 2009.

88. "Blaya Named Telemundo President," Telemundo Group news release, June 1, 1992, private collection of Mario Rodríguez.

89. Blaya interview, December 18, 2009.

90. Ray Rodríguez interview, July 22, 2009.

91. Mario Rodríguez interview, August 6, 2019.

92. Mario Rodríguez, Univision Program Presentation: Responding to Results of Nielsen Hispanic People-Meter Service, July 22, 1992, private collection of Mario Rodríguez.

93. In re applications of Univision Holding, Inc. and Perenchio Television, Inc., for Transfer of Control of Univision Station Group, Inc., Licensee of Television Stations, Federal Communications Commission, 7 FCC Red 6672 (21), September 30, 1992, https://www.fcc.gov/document/re-applications-univision-holding-inc-and-perenchio-television; Carlos Navarro, "U.S. Regulatory Commission Approves Sale of Univision to Televisa Consortium, Notimex," October 7, 1992, https://digitalrepository.unm.edu/cgi/viewcontent.cgi?article=3213&context=sourcemex. For departures of employees, see Mario Rodríguez interview, February 13, 2007; Ray Rodríguez interview, August 6, 2019; Jorge Ramos interview, July 24, 2008; and María Elena Salinas interview, July 24, 2008.

94. Ray Rodríguez interview, July 22, 2009.

95. Mario Rodríguez interview, August 2, 2007.

96. "Nielsen Releases First National Hispanic Report," Nielsen Media Research, December 22, 1992, private collection of Mario Rodríguez.

97. National Hispanic Television Audience, November 1992, Nielsen Media Research, private collection of Mario Rodríguez.

98. Geoffrey Folsie, "Hispanic TV's Top Two Networks Still Growing," *Broadcasting,* October 26, 1992, 60–62.

99. National Hispanic Television Audience, November 1992.

100. Mario Rodríguez interview, August 3, 2007.
101. Program Licensing Agreement, December 17, 1992, Exhibit 545, Exhibits, *Televisa, SA v. Univision Communications*, case no. 05-3444, Record Group 21.6.8, Records of the U.S. Circuit Court for the Central District of California, National Archives at Riverside, Perris, CA.
102. Barba interview, July 20, 2009.
103. Ray Rodríguez interview, July 22, 2009.
104. Barba interview, July 20, 2009.
105. Rick Wartzman and Lisa Bannon, "No Comment: Univision Chief Steers Clear of Media," *Miami Herald*, August 14, 1999, 2-1-2-2.

Chapter 8. The Perenchio Era

1. Program Licensing Agreement, December 17, 1992, Exhibit 545, Exhibits, *Televisa, SA v. Univision Communications*, case no. 05-3444, Record Group 21.6.8, Records of the U.S. Circuit Court for the Central District of California, National Archives at Riverside, Perris, CA.
2. "Official Is Back at Univision," *New York Times*, January 15, 1993, 17.
3. J. Perenchio to Univision managers, "The Rules of the Road," 1993, private collection of Mario Rodríguez, Miami, FL.
4. Ray Rodríguez, interview with the author, Miami, FL, July 22, 2009.
5. Eliot Tiegel, "Rock Is 'Perplexing' the College Booker," *Billboard*, October 22, 1966, 62.
6. Dennis McDougal, *The Last Mogul: Lew Wasserman, MCA, and the Hidden History of Hollywood* (New York: Crown, 1998).
7. Rick Wartzman and Lisa Bannon, "A Media Mogul Who Steers Clear of Media," *Wall Street Journal*, August 14, 1999, 1, 6.
8. "Lear, Perenchio Make $1000 Share Bid for ENA," *Broadcasting*, August 5, 1985, 24–26.
9. Beatriz Parga, "Carlos Barba nombrado presidente de cadena Venevisión Internacional," *El Nuevo Herald*, October 1, 1991, B1.
10. "Perenchio Announces Univision Purchase," news release, April 8, 1992, private collection of Mario Rodríguez.
11. Ray Rodríguez interview, July 22, 2009.
12. Claudia Puig, "Univision Scraps Three U.S.-Made Shows," *Los Angeles Times*, January 22, 1993, E1; Jane Bussey, "Univision: Cesanatias despiertan temor por politicia noticiosa," *El Nuevo Herald*, February 7, 1993, 1B; Mario Rodríguez, interviews with the author, Miami, FL, July 22, 2009, and August 6, 2019.
13. Ray Rodríguez interview, July 22, 2009.
14. "Fifth Estater: Ray Rodriguez," *Broadcasting*, February 14, 1994, 61.
15. National Hispanic Television Audience, February 1993, Nielsen Media Research, private collection of Mario Rodríguez.
16. Mario Rodríguez interview, July 23, 2008.
17. Carlos Barba, interview with the author, Miami, FL, July 20, 2009.
18. Mario Rodríguez interview, July 23, 2009.

19. Ray Rodríguez interview, July 22, 2009.

20. M. Rodríguez to Univision headquarters, "Producing Spanish-Language TV News from Atlanta," May 11, 1993, private collection of Mario Rodríguez.

21. Mario Rodríguez interview, July 23, 2009.

22. Mario Rodríguez interview; M. Rodríguez to R. Rodríguez, "Followup Report on Producing Spanish-language TV News from Atlanta," June 1, 1993, private collection of Mario Rodríguez.

23. Jorge Ramos, interview with the author, Miami, FL, July 24, 2008.

24. "Top 100 Companies," *Broadcasting,* June 27, 1994, 40.

25. "Asesinato en cementerio North Lauderdale Florida Testigo en Video vhs83," excerpt from *Ocurrio asi* broadcast of January 19, 1993, YouTube video, youtube.com/watch?v=NZRgLIXchno; Stephanie Loudis, "Airing Graphic Video a Tough Call," *Miami Herald,* January 22, 1993, 7E.

26. "¡¡Arriba Telemundo, Arriba Caso Cerrado!!" Telemundo, 1993, YouTube video, youtube.com/watch?v=-aJFFi5Cbos.

27. Cristina Saralegui, interview with the author, Miami, FL, July 24, 2008.

28. Mario Kreutzberger, interview with the author, Miami, FL, July 23, 2009.

29. "Group Seeks to Force Firm into Chapter 11 Proceedings," *Wall Street Journal,* June 9, 1993, A4; Telemundo Group Annual Report 1993, December 31, 1993, in Definitive Additional Proxy Material as Filed with the Securities and Exchange Commission on February 12, 1998, Schedule 14a, Information Statement Pursuant to Section 14(A) of the Securities Exchange Act of 1934, pages 182–184, https://www.sec.gov/Archives/edgar/data/5272/0000950123-98-001385.txt.

30. Joaquín Blaya, interview with the author, Basalt, CO, December 18, 2009.

31. "Creditors Push Telemundo into Bankruptcy Court," *New York Times,* June 9, 1993, D1.

32. "Top 100 Companies," *Broadcasting,* June 27, 1994, 40.

33. "Telemundo Plan Backed," *New York Times,* July 21, 1994, C5.

34. Carlos Flys, interview with the author, Phoenix, AZ, February 14, 2010.

35. "Univision Premieres *Marimar,*" Univision news release, October 27, 1994, private collection of Mario Rodríguez.

36. National Hispanic Television Audience, November 1994, Nielsen Media Research, private collection of Mario Rodríguez.

37. Telemundo Group, Inc., Form S-3, Registration Statement under Securities Act of 1933, filed November 27, 1995, pages 46–54, https://sec.report/Document/0000912057-95-010437/.

38. Linda Sandler, "A Showdown between Investors Is in Progress to Determine the Fate of Telemundo Group," *Wall Street Journal,* October 2, 1995, C2.

39. "Company Town: Spanish-Language Network Replaces CEO," *Los Angeles Times,* March 10, 1995, https://www.latimes.com/archives/la-xpm-1995-03-10-fi-41144-story.html.

40. Steve Coe, "Ray Rodríguez: Leading Univision to New Heights," *Broadcasting & Cable,* January 9, 1995, 40–48.

41. Kathleen Murray, "Banging the Drums as Spanish TV Comes of Age," *New York Times*, April 10, 1994, F10.

42. J. Perenchio to C. Barba, April 17, 1994, private collection of Carlos Barba, Miami, FL.

43. Jaime Dávila, interview with the author, New York, NY, August 13, 2009.

44. Debra Johnson, "Televisa, a Multi-Media Leader," *Broadcasting & Cable*, November 18, 1996, 62–63.

45. Ray Rodríguez interview, July 22, 2009.

46. Prospectus: Univision Communications, Inc., Donaldson, Lufkin and Jenrette, September 26, 1996, private collection of Mario Rodríguez.

47. "New Listings: Univision," *Wall Street Journal*, September 28, 1996, C19.

48. J. Perenchio to Univision managers, September 27, 1996, private collection of Mario Rodríguez.

49. Mario Rodríguez interview, February 17, 2015.

50. "Thalia's Back with a New Blockbuster," *What's Up On Univision*, August/September 1996, private collection of Mario Rodríguez.

51. National Hispanic Television Audience, November 1996, Nielsen Media Research, private collection of Mario Rodríguez.

52. "UVN Financials—Wow!/More Good News Going Forward," The Motley Fool, July 21–22, 2000, accessed August 24, 2017, boards.fool.com.

53. Amended and Restated Program License Agreement, December 1, 1996, Exhibit 546, *Televisa, SA v. Univision Communications*, case no. 05-3444, Record Group 21.6.8, Records of the U.S. Circuit Court for the Central District of California, National Archives at Riverside, Perris, CA.

54. Harry A. Tessell, "Televisa Wants Back in TV Station Ownership," *Broadcasting*, December 2, 1991, 52.

55. Mario Rodríguez interview, July 23, 2008.

56. "Univision Communications, Inc., Names Henry Cisneros President & Chief Operating Officer," Univision news release, January 23, 1997, private collection of Mario Rodríguez.

57. "Univision Network Unveils '97–'98 Season at Its Premiere Upfront Presentation," Univision news release May 14, 1997, private collection of Mario Rodríguez; Mike Galetto, "Univision Debuts First Upfront Pitch," *Electronic Media*, May 19, 1997, 8, 36.

58. David Tobenkin, "Univision vs. Telemundo," *Broadcasting & Cable*, October 6, 1997, 34–42.

59. Steve McClelland, "Majors Line Up for Telemundo," *Broadcasting & Cable*, August 3, 1997, 6; Andrew Paxman, "Telemundo on Rebound," *Variety*, May 27, 1996, 63.

60. "Apollo Management, Bastion Capital Fund, Sony Pictures Entertainment, and Liberty Media Make Successful Bid for Telemundo Group, Inc.," Sony and Liberty Media news release, November 24, 1997, businesswire.com, private collection of Mario Rodríguez.

61. Mike Galetto, "Huge Deal to Rescue Telemundo," *Electronic Media*, December 1, 1997, 1; Steve McClellan, "Telemundo: Time for Plan B," *Broadcasting & Cable*, November 9, 1998, 30–34.

62. Rick Mendosa, "Unwelcome Competition," *Hispanic Business*, June 1998, 14.

63. Joel Russel, "Controversy Colors Network Success," *Hispanic Business*, May 2000, 30.

64. "Thomas," "The Head Gringo in Charge," Melting blog, August 3, 2004, accessed September 16, 2016, newamericandimensions.com.

65. Ray Rodríguez interview, July 22, 2009.

66. Mario Rodríguez interview, July 23, 2009.

67. "Statement of Univision Communications Inc. in Response to Indictment of Henry Cisneros," Univision news release, December 11, 1997, private collection of Mario Rodríguez.

68. María Zate, "The Big Picture," *Hispanic Business*, May 1998, 21–30.

69. "Telemundo's Turnaround Tandem: President Peter Tortorici and Entertainment President Nely Galan," *Broadcasting & Cable*, November 9, 1998.

70. Kevin Baxter, "As Telemundo Turns," *Los Angeles Times*, December 20, 1998, C8; Andrew Paxman, "Telemundo Turns Up Heat," *Variety*, November 1, 1998, 7, 72; McClellan, "Time for Plan B," 30–34.

71. McClellan, "Time for Plan B," 34.

72. National Hispanic Television Audience, November 1998, Nielsen Media Research, private collection of Mario Rodríguez.

73. Michael Freeman, "American Programs Failing," *Media Week*, December 7, 1998, 14; Steve Donahue, "Telemundo Stanches Rating Slide," *Electronic Media*, March 6, 2000, 1; "Telemundo," *Hispanic Market Weekly*, December 19, 1998, 1–4.

74. Lawrie Mifflin, "Where the Young Are," *New York Times*, March 31, 1999, 17.

75. Andrew Bowser, "Univision Rules with Telenovelas," *Broadcasting & Cable*, November 9, 1998, 4.

76. National Hispanic Television Audience, February 1999, Nielsen Media Research, private collection of Mario Rodríguez.

77. "Univision Congratulates Primer Impacto" and "Univision Congratulates KMEX," Univision ads, August 1998, private collection of Mario Rodríguez.

78. "Excerpt of Videotaped Remarks on the United States-Iran World Cup Game," June 18, 1998, in *Public Papers of the Presidents of the United States: William J. Clinton, 1998*, Book I, *January 1 to June 30, 1998* (Washington, DC: U.S. Government Printing Office, 2000), 986. See also "Pres. Clinton on the US-Iran World Cup Match," June 21, 1998, YouTube video, https://www.youtube.com/watch?v=2yv3KnX1cOM.

79. "Home of the Stars," Univision and KTVW-TV, 2000, video recording in author's possession.

80. Univision Communications 1998 Annual Report, private collection of Mario Rodríguez.

81. John Watling, "Azcárraga Jean in Full Control of Mexican Net as Cousin Exits," *Hollywood Reporter*, October 1999, 1.

82. Elizabeth Malkin, "Son of El Tigre," *Business Week*, October 17, 1999, 66E4–66E10.

83. "Televisa Coin Bump Not Up to Projection," *Variety*, January 15, 1998, 79.

84. Transcript of A. Jerrold Perenchio video deposition, June 10, 2009, *Televisa, SA v. Univision Communications Depositions*, case no. CV 04-344, Docket 638, Record Group

21.6.8, Records of the U.S. Circuit Court for the Central District of California, National Archives at Riverside, Perris, CA.

85. "Televisa Taps Sky Exec to Oversee Pay-TV Operations," *Advertising Age*, February 11, 1999.

86. Mario Rodríguez interview, July 23, 2009.

87. "Univision Announces Record $425 Million in Upfront Advertising Results for 1999–2000," Univision news release, August 18, 1999, private collection of Mario Rodríguez.

88. "Rinconlatino" at viewer forum, Telenovela World, September 23, 1999, accessed July 16, 2016, telenovela-world.com; and "Luis" and "Zachary" at Network 54, accessed July 16, 2016, September 23, 1999, network54.com.

89. Mario Rodríguez interview, July 23, 2009.

90. Ray Rodríguez interview, July 22, 2009.

91. Mario Rodríguez's notes on YK2 telecast, September 1999, private collection of Mario Rodríguez.

92. "Countdown to 2000: Univision Gears Up for the Biggest Millennium Telecast in the Spanish-Speaking World," Univision news release, December 7, 1999, private collection of Mario Rodríguez.

93. "Feliz Milenio," *What's Up On Univision*, December 1999, private collection of Mario Rodríguez; "Countdown to 2000!!: Univision's Award-Winning News Team Joins the Network's Live Millennium Telecast," Univision news release, December 28, 1999, private collection of Mario Rodríguez.

94. Kreutzberger interview.

95. "Feliz Milenio Retrospective," *What's Up On Univision*, March 2000, private collection of Mario Rodríguez.

96. "Univision's 24-Hour Millennium Show Receives Unprecedented Market Share and Rating," Univision news release, January 6, 2000, private collection of Mario Rodríguez.

Chapter 9. Final Fight

1. Michael Arndt, "Overachievers," *Business Week*, April 17, 2000, 103.

2. "Changing Channel Choices" and "Eight Trends to Watch," *Multichannel News*, October 30, 2000, 30–34.

3. "Television," *Hispanic Market Weekly*, December 11, 2000, 1–9.

4. "Univision Communications, Inc.," R.R. Donnelley and Sons, December 31, 1999, https://pro.edgar-online.com/ipo.aspx?ColLeft=613ecf6a-b2a7-4b42-a0c8-80916 1372aec&ColRight=76baaeb6-2549-44f5-8e1d-cd700701e704&cikid=11906&tabIndex=2 &coname=UNIVISION+COMMUNICATIONS+INC&fnid=21368&ipo=0.

5. Elizabeth A. Rathbun, "Hispanic Network to Fix Itself," *Broadcasting & Cable*, July 17, 2000, 56; "Azteca América," *Starcom Insider's Guide to Latino-Targeted Television 2001–2002*, Starcom, Inc. (Chicago, Illinois: Starcom Worldwide, 2001), 5–6.

6. Daniel J. McCosh, "Salinas sale al encuentro . . . de nuevo" [Salinas Meets . . . Again], Ricardo B. Salinas Pliego, November 2001, https://www.ricardosalinas.com/es/Articulo/171.

7. "Azteca América Independent Channels Still Await Coverage," *Broadcasting & Cable*, September 25, 2000, 5; Steve McClellan, "If You Can't Join 'Em, Beat 'Em," *Broadcasting & Cable*, December 4, 2000, 27.

8. Peter Brennan, "Cisneros Switches Channels," *Hispanic Business*, October 2000, 16.

9. Lee Romney, "Univision Shares Drop over Azteca News," *Los Angeles Times*, September 9, 2000, E1.

10. "Univision Splits Stock Amid Strong Growth in Earnings," *Los Angeles Business Journal*, July 24, 2000, https://labusinessjournal.com/news/2000/jul/24/coporate-focus-univision-splits-stock-amid-strong/; Ray Rodríguez, interview with the author, Miami, FL, August 6, 2019.

11. Rodríguez interview, July 22, 2009.

12. Steve McClelland, "Room for Tres?" *Broadcasting & Cable*, December 4, 2000, 26–32.

13. "Univision to Acquire USA Broadcasting from USA Networks, Inc., for $1.1 Billion in Cash," Univision news release, December 7, 2000; and Notes on Webcast by Ray Rodríguez and Andrew Hobson, December 7, 2000, private collection of Mario Rodríguez, Miami, FL.

14. "Television," *Hispanic Market Weekly*, December 11, 2000, 1–9.

15. The last previous owner of two networks was NBC. Until 1943, NBC owned and operated the NBC "Red" and NBC "Blue" radio networks. That year, the FCC forced NBC to sell the "Blue" network. Under new owners, the "Blue" network became NBC.

16. Eduardo Porter, Joe Flint, and Martin Peers, "Hispanic Giant Agrees to Buy USA Networks for $1.1 Billion," *Wall Street Journal*, December 7, 2000, 1.

17. Univision 2000 Annual Report, private collection of Mario Rodríguez.

18. David Luhnow, "Mexico's Televisa Looks into a Univision Deal," *Wall Street Journal*, February 21, 2001; "Buffeted on Home Turf, Televisa Has Big Plans for Growth in U.S.," *Wall Street Journal*, February 22, 2001.

19. Interview with Emilio Azcárraga Jean, *World Screen News*, October 2001, 58–59.

20. Rodríguez, interview with the author, July 22, 2009.

21. "Univision Response to Statements Made by Televisa," Univision news release, February 21, 2001, private collection of Mario Rodríguez.

22. Photos of Univision-Telefutura Upfront Presentation, New York City, NY, May 16, 2002, private collection of Mario Rodríguez.

23. "Hispanic TV CEO Out; New Capital Expected," *Houston Chronicle*, February 8, 2001, https://www.chron.com/business/article/Briefs-City-and-state-2010718.php.

24. Simeon Tegel and Mary Sutter, "Azteca América Launches Stateside," *Variety*, August 1, 2001.

25. "World's Leading Spanish-Language Media Companies Form Landmark Multi-Faceted Alliance," Grupo Televisa, Univision, and Corporación Venezolana de Televisión news release, December 20, 2001, http://www.televisair.com/~/media/Files/T/Televisa-IR/press-releases/english/12-20-2001/tvuvnvfinaleng.pdf.

26. Amended and Restated Program Licensing Agreement, December 26, 2001, Exhibit 546, Exhibits, *Televisa, SA vs. Univision Communications*, case no. CV 05-3444, Record Group 21.6.8, Records of the U.S. Circuit Court for the Central District of

California, National Archives at Riverside, Perris, CA (hereafter Exhibits, *Televisa, SA vs. Univision Communications*).

27. Transcript, A. Jerrold Perenchio video deposition, June 10, 2009, *Televisa, SA vs. Univision Communications Depositions,* case no. CV 05-3444, Docket 638, Record Group 21.6.8, Records of the U.S. Circuit Court for the Central District of California, National Archives at Riverside, Perris, CA.

28. John Consoli, "Telefutura Talks Tough: Univision Spinoff Projects $100 Million in Advertising Revenue in First Year, *Media Week,* December 10, 2001, 6–7, https://www.americanradiohistory.com/Archive-Mediaweek/2001/Mediaweek-2001-12-10.pdf.

29. National Hispanic Television Audience, November 1999, Nielsen Media Research, private collection of Mario Rodríguez.

30. James McNamara, interview with the author, Miami, FL, January 20, 2010.

31. Ibid.

32. National Hispanic Television Audience, February 2001, Nielsen Media Research, private collection of Mario Rodríguez; Magaly Morales, "New Telemundo Novela Has Modern Feel," *Sun Sentinel,* April 4, 2001, 2.

33. "Hasta La Vista Old Ratings," Telemundo brochure, April 2001, private collection of James McNamara, Miami, FL; "Telemundo Group, Inc. Reports First Quarter Results," Telemundo news release, May 14, 2001, January 5, 2016, prnewswire.com.

34. "AOL in for Telemundo?/CNN Parent Joins Viacom, NBC in Bidding War," CNNMoney, August 30, 2001, https://money.cnn.com/2001/08/30/deals/aol_telemundo/index.htm.

35. McNamara interview.

36. Jerry Barmash, "Iconic WXTV/Channel 41 Anchor Rafael Pineda Says 9/11 Made 'Impact on Me,'" *FishbowlNY,* September 22, 2011.

37. "NBC to Acquire Telemundo Communications Group, Inc.; Network," General Electric and NBC news release, October 11, 2001, https://www.bloomberg.com/press-releases/2001-10-11/nbc-to-acquire-telemundo-communications-group-inc-network.

38. Steve McClellan, "Lo mas grande deal de NBC," *Broadcasting & Cable,* October 15, 2001, 6–7.

39. Photos and materials on Telefutura inaugural telecast, January 14, 2002, private collection of Mario Rodríguez.

40. Valeria Palazio, interview with the author, Miami, FL, July 22, 2008.

41. National Hispanic Television Audience, May 2003, Nielsen Media Research, private collection of Mario Rodríguez.

42. Meg James, "A Telenovela with the Sights, Sounds of L.A.," *Los Angeles Times,* December 1, 2003.

43. "Univision's Primetime Blockbuster Novela 'Te amaré en silencio' Captures the Struggles of Life and Love in Hispanic America," Univision news release, December 12, 2003, private collection of Mario Rodríguez.

44. Daniel Gross, "The Univision Division: A Fight about Spanish-Language Media Jostles Washington," *Slate,* June 27, 2003, https://slate.com/business/2003/06/the-battle-for-univision.html.

45. Federal Communications Commission, "FCC Grants Conditioned Approval of Univision/HBC Merger, Company Must Comply with New Radio Ownership Limit Six Months from Effective Date," September 22, 2003, https://www.fcc.gov/document/fcc-grants-conditioned-approval-univisionhbc-merger; U.S. Department of Justice, Documents pertaining to *United States v. Univision Communications Inc.*, Civ. Action No. 1:03CV00758, May–July 2003, https://www.justice.gov/atr/exhibit-2.

46. Chuck Bolkcom, "Publisher's Note," and George Winslow, "Guide to Hispanic TV Channels," both in *Broadcasting & Cable*, December 6, 2004, 1, E18–E24.

47. Rodríguez interview, July 22, 2009.

48. Answer of Televisa, S.A. de C.V. and Grupo Televisa, S.A. to the Counterclaims of Univision Communications, Inc. and Telefutura Network, Exhibit 99.1, Part C, Section 114, January 30, 2006, Exhibits, *Televisa, SA vs. Univision Communications*.

49. Kevin Downey, "Telemundo Gets Its Share," *Broadcasting & Cable*, September 9, 2003, 30; Meredith Amdur, "Univision in the Lead," *Variety*, May 15, 2003, 1.

50. National Hispanic Television Audience, November 2003, Nielsen Media Research, private collection of Mario Rodríguez.

51. "Program License Agreement Between Televisa and Univision Makes Clear that Univision Does Not Hold Internet Rights to Televisa's Programming," Grupo Televisa statement, June 6, 2006, private collection of Mario Rodríguez; Ken Besinger, "Televisa Topper Has Eyes for Univision," *Variety*, February 1, 2004, 1.

52. Geri Smith, "Emilio Azcárraga on 'Televisa's Advantage,'" Bloomberg Businessweek, October 3, 2004, https://www.bloomberg.com/news/articles/2004-10-03/online-extra-emilio-azc-rraga-on-televisas-advantage.

53. Ken Besinger, "Top Televisa Brass Set for Miami Move," *Variety*, February 25, 2004.

54. E. Azcárraga Jean to J. Perenchio, February 4, 2005, Exhibit 99. 1, Exhibits, *Televisa, SA vs. Univision Communications*.

55. J. Perenchio to E. Azcárraga Jean and G. Cisneros, February 8, 2005, Exhibit 99. 1, Exhibits, *Televisa, SA vs. Univision Communications*.

56. "Ray Rodríguez Named President and Chief Operating Officer, Univision Communications Inc.," Univision news release, February 9, 2005, private collection of Mario Rodríguez.

57. Answer of Televisa, Part C, Sections 105–110, Exhibits, *Televisa, SA vs. Univision Communications*.

58. M. Rodríguez to L. M. Camporrdando, April 9, 2003, July 6 and September 5, 2001, Exhibits 548, 541, 539, *Televisa, SA vs. Univision Communications*.

59. *Televisa S.A. de C.V. v. Univision Communications, Inc.*, case no. CV 05-3444 ABC (MANx), May 9, 2005, Proceedings, *Televisa, SA vs. Univision Communications*, Record Group 21.6.8, Records of the U.S. Circuit Court for the Central District of California, National Archives at Riverside, Perris, CA (hereafter Proceedings, *Televisa, SA vs. Univision Communications*).

60. Univision Communications Definitive Proxy Statement, filed March 15, 2005, for the period ending May 11, 2005, private collection of Mario Rodríguez.

61. Jim McTague, "Univision, Si!," *Barron's Online*, July 18, 2005, 1–4.

62. Ray Rodríguez interview, July 22, 2009.

63. "Grupo Televisa Announces Filing of an Amended Form 13-D with Respect to Univision," *International Entertainment News*, May 12, 2006, http://internationalentertainmentnews.blogspot.com/2006/05/grupo-televisa-announces-filing-of.html.

64. "Let the Bidding Begin," CNNMoney.com, February 28, 2006; John Lyons and Dennis K. Berman, "Televisa Enlists Equity Funds for Univision Bid," *Wall Street Journal*, May 12, 2006.

65. Ray Rodríguez interview, July 22, 2009.

66. Stephanie Mehta, "The Man with the Golden Gut," *Fortune*, May 14, 2007, fortune.com.

67. "Broadcasting Media Partners Completes Acquisition of Univision," news release, Univision press release, March 29, 2007, https://www.sec.gov/Archives/edgar/data/1017008/000119312507074568/dex991.htm; Univision PR Team, "Broadcasting Media Partners Completes Acquisition of Univision," March 29, 2007, https://corporate.univision.com/press/press-releases/2007/03/29/broadcasting-media-partners-completes-acquisition-of-univision/.

68. *Televisa, S.A. de C.V. v. Univision Communications*, United States District Court, C.D. California April 2, 2009, 635 F. Supp. 2d 1106 (C.D. Cal. 2009).

69. McNamara interview.

70. Eduardo Porter and Kathryn Kranhold, "Telemundo Falls Short of GE's Expectations," *Wall Street Journal*, June 2, 2003.

71. McNamara interview.

72. Magaly Morales, "Debut of Broad-Targeted Amor Descarado Pleases Telemundo Execs," *Sun Sentinel*, September 10, 2003.

73. "Don Browne President of Telemundo," *Multichannel News*, May 15, 2006.

74. "Grupo Televisa Issues Statement Regarding Univision Board Action," *International Entertainment News*, June 27, 2006, http://internationalentertainmentnews.blogspot.com/2006/06/grupo-televisa-issues-statement.html.

75. Claire Atkinson, "Conde Committed to Growth at Univision," *Broadcasting & Cable*, September 26, 2009, https://www.broadcastingcable.com/archive/conde-committed-growth-univision-110424.

76. Cesar Conde, interview with the author, New York, NY, July 23, 2009.

77. Mario Rodríguez, interview with the author, Miami, FL, July 23, 2008.

78. Anna Marie de la Fuente, "Univision Prexy to Keep Order Inhouse," *Variety*, September 18, 2009, https://variety.com/2009/tv/news/univision-prexy-to-keep-order-inhouse-1118008849/.

79. "NBC Universal's Telemundo and Grupo Televisa Sign Strategic Alliance Agreement for Mexico," Grupo Televisa and Telemundo NBC Universal news release, March 17, 2008, http://www.televisair.com/~/media/Files/T/Televisa-IR/press-releases/english/03-17-2008/tv-telemundo-eng.pdf.

80. "'La Fea Mas Bella' Big Hit for Spanish-Language Univision in Slow TV Week," *Deseret News*, July 4, 2007, https://www.deseret.com/2007/7/4/20027973/la-fea-mas-bella-big-hit-for-spanish-language-univision-in-slow-tv-week; "Univision #1 among Adults 18–34 and 18–49, with Beautiful Ending of 'La fea mas bella,'" Businesswire, June

26, 2007, https://www.businesswire.com/news/home/20070626006295/en/Univision-1-Adults-18-34-18-49-Beautiful-La.

81. "Telemundo Might Start a Network in Mexico," *Los Angeles Times*, September 29, 2006.

82. Michael O'Boyle, "Telemundo Opens in Mexico City," *Variety*, September 28, 2006; Michael O'Boyle, "Telemundo Produces First Novela," November 18, 2007, *Variety*.

83. Michael O'Boyle, "Telemundo Dreams of Flying South to Mexican Market," *Variety*, October 8, 2006.

84. "Telemundo Delivers Best March and First Quarter Ratings in Network History among Key Demos," TV by the Numbers, April 2, 2009, https://tvbythenumbers.zap2it.com/sdsdskdh279882992z1/telemundo-delivers-best-march-and-first-quarter-rating-in-network-history-among-key-demos/.

85. "Hispanic Issues," video recording of C-SPAN, September 14, 2010, at 1:51:50, https://www.c-span.org/video/?295457-1/hispanic-issues.

86. Order Denying Defendants' Partial Motion for Summary Judgment, December 17, 2007, Dockets 170 and 242, Proceedings, *Televisa, SA vs. Univision Communications*.

87. Minutes, Motion for Continuance of Trial Date, February 5, 2008, Docket 307, Proceedings, *Televisa, SA vs. Univision Communications*.

88. Minutes, Status Conference, March 20, 2008, Docket 431, Proceedings, *Televisa, SA vs. Univision Communications*; Order Granting Defendant's Motion to Compel Trial Testimony of Emilio Azcárraga Jean, November 13, 2008, Docket 550, Proceedings, *Televisa, SA vs. Univision Communications*.

89. Minutes, Status Conference, September 9, 2008, Docket 534, Proceedings, *Televisa, SA vs. Univision Communications*.

90. "Univision VS Televisa," YouTube video, youtube.com/watch?v=68Ye-ZlVEQA; "Televisa, Univision Trial Delayed," *Los Angeles Business Journal*, Wednesday, April 30, 2008, https://labusinessjournal.com/news/2008/apr/30/televisa-univision-trial-delayed/; comments of Laura Martinez in "Programming Battle Lands Univision in Court," National Public Radio, January 12, 2009, https://www.npr.org/templates/story/story.php?storyId=99238616.

91. Comments of Jose Cancela on *Expansion*, CNN, aired January 6, 2009.

92. Transcript, First Day of Jury Trial, January 6, 2009. Docket 618, Proceedings, *Televisa, SA vs. Univision Communications*.

93. Meg James, "Curtain Rises on Televisa-Univision Trial," *Los Angeles Times*, January 7, 2009, C2.

94. Transcript, Fourth Day of Jury Trial, January 13, 2009, Docket 644, Proceedings, *Televisa, SA vs. Univision Communications*.

95. Transcript, Ninth Day of Jury Trial, January 21, 2009, Docket 670, Proceedings, *Televisa, SA vs. Univision Communications*.

96. Meg James, "Univision and Televisa Settle High-Stakes Lawsuit," *Los Angeles Times*, January 23, 2009, 1.

97. "Grupo Televisa and Univision Amend Program License Agreement; Litigation Settled," Univision news release, Businesswire, January 22, 2009, https://www.businesswire.com/news/home/20090122006009/en/Grupo-Televisa-Univision

-Amend-Program-License-Agreement; "Univision Communication Inc. and Subsidiaries 2009 Year-End Reporting Package," February 25, 2010, 29–30, http://s2.q4cdn.com/417187916/files/doc_financials/2009/q4/4q_2009_reporting_package.pdf.

98. Mutual Release and Settlement Agreement, Docket 674, January 22, 2009, Proceedings, *Televisa, SA vs. Univision Communications*.

99. "Televisa Gets $600 Million in Univision Settlement," Fox News, January 22, 2009; https://www.nydailynews.com/latino/televisa-univision-settle-lawsuit-article-1.422806; "Univisión / Televisa amplian su relación en USA" [Univision and Televisa Agree], Radio AM FM, January 23, 2009, https://laradioamfm.blogspot.com/search?q=UNIVISION+TELEVISA.

100. Rodríguez interview, August 6, 2019.

101. Brian Baxter, "Bingham, Keker Trade Barbs over Televisa-Univision Settlement," *The AmLaw Daily*, January 23, 2009, https://amlawdaily.typepad.com/amlawdaily/2009/01/bingham-keker-trade-barbs-over-televisa-univision-settlement.html; Eriq Gardner, "Univision and Televisa Kiss and Makeup [sic] . . . Well, Until the Next Episode," *Hollywood Reporter*, January 26, 2009, https://reporter.blogs.com/thresq/2009/01/univision-and-televisa-regret-that-dealmaking-isnt-more-bloodletting.html.

102. Conde interview.

103. "Univision Communications Inc. Honors Ray Rodríguez by Dedicating Network Building," Univision news release, Businesswire, November 19, 2009, https://www.businesswire.com/news/home/20091119006224/en/Univision-Communications-Honors-Ray-Rodriguez-Dedicating-Network; Jillian Labato, "Univision Celebrates the Work of Ray Rodríguez," *Haute Living*, December 11, 2009, 1.

104. "Univision Announces Launch of Univision Studios," Businesswire, December 7, 2009, https://www.businesswire.com/news/home/20091207005550/en/Univision-Announces-Launch-Univision-Studios.

105. Transcript, Univision conference call, New York, NY, February 25, 2010, accessed September 26, 2006, businesswire.com. See also David Goetzl, "Univision TV Revenues Rise 7%, Optimistic for '10," *MediaDailyNews*, February 25, 2010, https://www.mediapost.com/publications/article/123268/univision-tv-revenues-rise-7-optimistic-for-10.html.

106. "Grupo Televisa and Univision to Expand Strategic Relationship in the U.S.," Televisa and Univision news release, October 5, 2010, http://www.televisair.com/~/media/Files/T/Televisa-IR/press-releases/english/05-10-2010/grupo-televisa-and-univision-to-expand-strategic-relationship-in-the-us.pdf.

107. "Grupo Televisa and Univision to Expand Strategic Relationship in the U.S."

108. Emilio Nicolás, interview with the author, San Antonio, TX, November 10, 2016; video recording, "Emilio Nicolas, Sr. Pioneer of Spanish Language Television," SINTV41, December, 2011, YouTube video, https://www.youtube.com/watch?v=IbPK_joETj8.

109. Brian L. Roberts and Jeff Zucker, Joint Written Statement to the Senate Judiciary Committee, February 4, 2010, https://www.judiciary.senate.gov/imo/media/doc/10-02-04%20Roberts-Zucker%20Testimony.pdf.

110. "NBC Universal's Telemundo Acquires Exclusive Spanish Language U.S. Media Rights to FIFA World Cup Soccer from 2015 through 2022," Comcast NBC Universal

news release, October 21, 2011, Businesswire, https://www.businesswire.com/news/home/20111021006188/en/NBCUniversal%E2%80%99s-Telemundo-Acquires-Exclusive-Spanish-Language-U.S.

111. "Univision Announces 2011 Second Quarter Results," Univision press release, August 4, 2011, http://s2.q4cdn.com/417187916/files/doc_news/2011/08042011-univision_announces_2011_second_quarter_results.pdf.

112. "Univision Delivers Clear Message at 2012 Upfront: Total Market Media Drives Growth," Univision news release, Businesswire, May 15, 2012, https://www.businesswire.com/news/home/20120515005534/en/Univision-Delivers-Clear-Message-2012-Upfront-Total.

Conclusion

1. "Longest Running TV Variety Show," Guinness World Records, https://www.guinnessworldrecords.com/world-records/longest-running-tv-variety-show.

2. "Sábado Gigante 50 años la gala Parte 1," YouTube video, youtube.com/watch?v=9SsnzQFmvA; "*Sábado gigante* 50th Anniversary Telecast Reaches Nearly Seven Million Viewers and Makes Univision the #3 Broadcast Network," Univision news release, October 31, 2012, accessed November 15, 2015, https://corporate.univision.com/press/press-releases/2020/10/31/sabado-gigante-50th-anniversary-telecast-reaches-nearly-seven-million-viewers-and-makes-univision-the-#3-broadcast-network.

3. "The 400 Richest Americans," *Forbes*, September 21, 2006, https://www.forbes.com/lists/2006/54/biz_06rich400_The-400-Richest-Americans_land.html.

4. "Entertainment Icon Perenchio Awarded Honorary Doctorate," *Fresno State News*, May 21, 2011, http://www.fresnostatenews.com/2011/05/21/entertainment-icon-perenchio-awarded-honorary-doctorate/.

5. Victor Landa, "First U.S. Spanish-Language TV Station, Demolished," *News Taco*, November 7, 2013, https://newstaco.com/2013/11/07/first-u-s-spanish-language-tv-station-demolished/.

6. Anna Marie De La Fuente, "Univision to Big Four: We're No. 1 and Rising," *Variety*, July 30, 2013; "Univision Set to Finish July Sweep in First Place in Demos," *Deadline*, July 22, https://deadline.com/2013/07/univision-set-to-finish-july-sweep-in-first-place-in-demos-546768/; Natalie Abrams, "Univision to Finish First in July 2013 Sweep Ratings," July 23, 2013, https://www.tvguide.com/news/univision-ratings-july-1068195/.

7. "Schwarzenegger: Don't Watch Spanish TV," CBS News, June 15, 2007, https://www.cbsnews.com/news/schwarzenegger-dont-watch-spanish-tv/#:~:text=California%20Governor%20Arnold%20Schwarzenegger's%20remarks,Hispanic%20journalists%20shaking%20their%20heads.

8. "Hispanic Leaders Blast Schwarzenegger's Advice to Turn Off Spanish TV," Fox News, June 15, 2007, https://www.foxnews.com/story/hispanic-leaders-blast-schwarzeneggers-advice-to-turn-off-spanish-tv.

9. "Hispanic Media in the Balance," Media Research Center, Reston, VA, April 2014, https://www.mrc.org/special-reports/hispanic-media-balance; Julian Key Melchior, "Liberal Bias on Univision, Telemundo," *National Review*, April 2, 2014, https://www.nationalreview.com/2014/04/liberal-bias-univision-telemundo-jillian-kay-melchior/.

10. *The Laura Ingraham Show,* Westwood One Network, aired November 4, 2018.

11. *The O'Reilly Factor,* Fox News Channel, aired March 17, 2016.

12. Ken Auletta, "War of Choice: Marco Rubio and the G.O.P. Play a Dangerous Game on Immigration," *New Yorker,* January 9, 2012.

13. Spencer Irvine, "Univision vs. Marco Rubio: Hispanic Media Biased," Accuracy in Media, April 19, 2015, https://www.aim.org/on-target-blog/univision-vs-marco-rubio-hispanic-media-biased/.

14. Howard Kurtz, "Why Jorge Ramos Crossed the Line in Confronting Donald Trump," Fox News, August 27, 2015, https://www.foxnews.com/politics/why-jorge-ramos-crossed-the-line-in-confronting-donald-trump.

15. Alberto Nardelli and Cristina Abellan-Matamoros, "Donald Trump's Polling Lead Means Little at This Stage, Past Data Shows," The Guardian, December 9, 2015, https://www.theguardian.com/us-news/datablog/2015/dec/09/donald-trump-polls-past-elections-republican-nomination; "The Doctor Is in as Carson Ties Trump in GOP Race Quinnipiac University National Poll Finds; Carson Tops Clinton by 10 Points in General Election," Quinnipiac University, November 4, 2015, https://poll.qu.edu/national/release-detail?ReleaseID=2299; Ronald Bishop, "An Unimaginable Combination: Journalists React to the Jorge Ramos-Donald Trump Confrontation," *International Journal of Hispanic Media* 8 (2015): 38–49, https://jorgeramos.com/en/wp-content/uploads/2016/02/Volume-8_04-AnUnimaginableCombination.pdf.

16. Jorge Ramos, "We Can't 'Be Neutral' with a President Like Trump," PRI, May 4, 2018, https://www.pri.org/stories/2018-05-04/jorge-ramos-we-cant-be-neutral-president-trump.

17. De Mora Jiménez, "Development of Hispanic TV in the United States," 2–8.

18. Marietta Morrisey, "Tres Mujeres: Reclaiming National Culture in the Post-Colonial Telenovela," *Studies in Latin American Culture* 21 (2002): 222.

19. Hector Amaya, *Citizenship Excess: Latino/as, Media, and the Nation* (New York: New York University Press, 2013), 130.

20. Dolores Inés Casillas, *¡Sounds of Belonging!* (New York: New York University Press, 2014), 10, 152.

21. América Rodríguez, "Creating an Audience and Remapping a Nation: A Brief History of Spanish Language Broadcasting 1930–1980," *Quarterly Review of Film and Video* 16 (1999): 357–374.

22. Arlene Dávila, *Latinos, Inc.: The Marketing and Making of a People* (Berkeley: University of California Press, 2001), 181–215.

23. Ibid., 8, 88, 163; also see Arlene Dávila, "Mapping Latinidad: Language and Culture in the Spanish TV Battlefront," *Television & New Media* 1 (2003): 75–94.

24. Viviana Rojas, "The Gender of Latinidad: Latinas Speak about Hispanic Television," *Communication Review* 7 (2010): 125–152.

25. Christopher Chávez, *Reinventing the Latino Television Viewer: Language, Ideology, and Practice* (Lanham, MD: Lexington, 2015), 9.

26. Miguel Salazar, "The Problem with Latinidad," *The Nation,* September 16, 2019, https://www.thenation.com/article/archive/hispanic-heritage-month-latinidad.

27. Amaya, *Citizenship Excess,* 152–153.

28. Arturo González, "Case Study of KMEX-TV" (MA thesis, California State University-Northridge, 1978), 114–115.

29. Christine Mai-Duc, "Jorge Ramos Is on the Defensive over His Role as Journalist and Immigrant Advocate," September 3, 2015, *Los Angeles Times;* Kevin Allocca, "So What Do You Do, María Elena Salinas, Univision Network News Anchor? Salinas on Gender, Advocacy, and Spanish-Speaking Media," Media Bistro, [2014], https://www.mediabistro.com/interviews/so-what-do-you-do-maria-elena-salinas-univision-network-news-anchor/

30. Rick Porter, "52-Week Broadcast Ratings: NBC, CBS Remain on Top as 2018–19 Wraps," *Hollywood Reporter,* September 19, 2019, https://www.hollywoodreporter.com/live-feed/52-week-broadcast-ratings-nbc-cbs-remain-top-2018-19-1240945.

31. Instituto Cervantes report in Javier Cámara, "Spanish Will Be the Most Spoken Language in the US by 2050," beBee, September 4, 2016, https://www.bebee.com/producer/@javierbebee/spanish-will-be-the-most-spoken-language-in-the-us-by-2050#:~:text=Spanish%20will%20be%20the%20most%20spoken%20language%20in%20the%20US,2050%2C%20according%20to%20Cervantes%20Institute.

32. Phillip M. Carter, "A Linguist Explains How the 'Three Generation Pattern' Could Wipe Out Spanish in the US," Quartz, February 1, 2018, https://qz.com/1195658/spanish-to-english-us-is-increasingly-monolingual-despite-latino-immigration/.

33. Simmons Research, "The State of the Hispanic-American Consumer," Spring 2018, http://hispanicad.com/sites/default/files/simmons_2018_state_of_the_hispanic_american_consumer.pdf.

34. David C. Adams, "English Is on the Rise among Young U.S. Latinos, but Spanish Still Valued," *UnivisionNews,* April 20, 2016, https://www.univision.com/univision-news/united-states/english-is-on-the-rise-among-young-us-latinos-but-spanish-still-valued; Rachel Glickhouse, "Will Hispanic Bilingualism Survive in the United States?" *UnivisionNews,* June 17, 2016, https://www.univision.com/univision-news/united-states/will-hispanic-bilingualism-survive-in-the-united-states.

35. Paul Taylor, Mark Hugo Lopez, Jessica Martínez, and Gabriel Velasco, "Language Use among Latinos," Pew Research Center, April 4, 2012, https://www.pewresearch.org/hispanic/2012/04/04/iv-language-use-among-latinos/#:~:text=Among%20immigrant%20Hispanics%2C%20two%2Dthirds,of%20Spanish%20falls%20to%2018%25.

BIBLIOGRAPHY

Primary Sources

INTERVIEWS

Barba, Carlos. Miami, FL, January 8, 2008; July 20, 2009.
Bird, Carole. Miami, FL, July 21, 2008.
Blaya, Joaquín. Basalt, CO, December 18, 2009; January 12, 2010.
Conde, Cesar. New York, NY, July 23, 2009.
Dávila, Jaime. New York, NY, August 13, 2009.
Flys, Carlos. Phoenix, AZ, February 14, 2010.
Godoy, Gustavo. Miami, FL, August 1, 2007; July 21, 2008; July 20, 2009.
Hockaday, Irvine. Kansas City, MO, April 2, 2007.
Kreutzberger, Mario. Miami, FL, July 23, 2009.
Martinez, Andrew. San Antonio, TX, July 24, 2007.
McCombs, Red. San Antonio, TX, July 25, 2007.
McNamara, James. Miami, FL, January 20, 2010.
Nicolás, Emilio, Sr. San Antonio, TX, August 14, 2006, February 10, 2007; March 30, 2007; July 27, 2007; November 10, 2016.
Nicolás, Irma. San Antonio, TX, July 28, 2007.
Palazio, Valeria. Miami, FL, July 22, 2008.
Ramer, Lorraine. Miami, FL, July 21, 2008.
Ramos, Jorge. Miami, FL, July 24, 2008.
Rodríguez, Mario. Miami, FL, February 13, 2007; February 20, 2007; August 1–3, 2007; July 23, 2008; July 23, 2009; February 17, 2015.
Rodríguez, Ray. Miami, FL, July 22, 2009; August 6, 2019.
Saralegui, Cristina. Miami, FL, July 24, 2008.
Shagrin, Ceril. Miami, FL, July 24, 2009.
Villanueva, Daniel, Sr. Camarillo, CA, May 23, 2006; February 17, 2011.

PRIMARY DOCUMENTS

Annenberg School for Communication and Journalism, Los Angeles, University of Southern California.

Ruben Salazar Project
National Archives at Riverside, Perris, CA
  Record Group 21, Records of the U.S. Circuit Court for the Central District of California
Private collection of Carlos Barba, Miami, FL
Private collection of Guillermo Nicolás, San Antonio, TX
Private collection of James McNamara, Miami, FL
Private collection of Mario Rodríguez, Miami, FL

Secondary Sources

Albarran, Allan B., and Don Umphrey. "An Examination of Television Motivations and Program Preferences by Hispanics, Blacks, and Whites." *Journal of Broadcasting and Electronic Media* 37 (1993): 95–103.

Amaya, Hector. *Citizen Excess: Latino/as, Media, and the Nation.* New York: New York University Press, 2013.

Auter, Philip J., and Douglas A. Boyd, "DuMont: The Original Fourth Television Network," *Journal of Popular Culture* 29 (2005): 63–83.

Azcárraga, Emilio. "Mexican TV Developments Act as School for Latin America." In *The Radio Annual and Television Year Book*. New York: Radio Daily Corporation, 1955.

Blaya, Joaquín. "Network Television Makes Miami Its Home." 2006. Unpublished memoir in author's possession.

Bustamante, Celeste González de. *Muy buenas noches: México, Television, and the Cold War.* Lincoln: University of Nebraska Press, 2013.

———. "1968 Olympic Dreams and Tlatelolco Nightmares: Imagining and Imaging Modernity on Television." *Mexican Studies/Estudios Mexicanos* 26 (Winter 2010): 1–30.

Bustos, Robina. "The Hemispheric Village: The Case of Televisa." *Méxican Journal of Communication* 2 (1995): 107–120.

Bustos, Soledad Robina. "Hemispheric Village: The Case of Televisa," *Méxican Journal of Communication* 2 (1995): 107–120.

Casillas, Dolores Inés. *¡Sounds of Belonging!* New York: New York University Press, 2014.

Chavez, Christopher. *Reinventing the Latino Television Viewer: Language, Ideology, and Practice.* Lanham, MD: Lexington, 2015.

Cox, Dorrit Sue. "Spanish-Language Television in the United States." Master's thesis, University of Illinois, 1969.

Dávila, Arlene. *Latinos, Inc.: The Marketing and Making of a People.* Berkeley: University of California Press, 2001.

———. "Mapping Latinidad: Language and Culture in the Spanish TV Battlefront." *Television & New Media* 1 (2003): 75–94.

De la Garza, Rodolfo O., Robert Brischetto and David Vaughn. *The Mexican American Electorate: Information Sources and Policy Orientations.* Austin: University of Texas Center for Mexican American Studies, 1983.

Del Carmen, María Olivares Arriaga. *Emilio Azcárraga Vidaurreta: En empresario ejemplar.* Victoria, México: Universidad Autónoma de Tamaulipas, 2002.

De Mora Jiménez, Raúl. "Development of Hispanic TV in the United States: Ethnic Television in the Context of Globalization." Paper presented at Universidad Complutense de Madrid, 2004. https://www.yumpu.com/en/document/read/25438365/1development-of-hispanic-tv-in-the-united-states-ethnic-television-.

Fein, Seth. "Transcultured Hollywood." In *Visible Nations: Latin American Cinema and Video*, edited by Chon A. Noriega, 81–99. Minneapolis: University of Minnesota Press, 2000.

Fernández, Claudia, and Andrew Paxman. *El Tigre: Emilio Azcárraga y su imperio televisa*. México City: Raya en el Agua-Grijalbo, 2000.

Fowler, Gene, and Bill Crawford. *Border Radio: Quacks, Yodelers, Pitchmen, Psychics, and Other Amazing Broadcasters of the American Airwaves*. Austin: University of Texas Press, 2002.

Fox, Elizabeth. *Latin American Broadcasting: From Tango to Telenovela*. Bloomington: Indiana University Press, 1997.

González, Arturo. "Case Study of KMEX-TV." MA thesis, California State University-Northridge, 1978.

González de Bustamante, Celeste. *Muy Buenas Noches: México, Television, and the Cold War*. Lincoln: University of Nebraska Press, 2013.

Guerro, Manuel A. *The Emergence of Political Pluralism in Mexican Broadcasting*. Riga, Latvia: VDM Verlag, 2009.

Gutiérrez, Félix F. "México's Television Network in the United States: The Case of Spanish International Network." In *Proceedings of the Sixth Annual Telecommunications Policy Research Conference*, edited by H. S. Dordick, 138–159. Lexington, MA: Lexington Books, 1979.

———. "More than 200 Years of Latino Media in the United States." In *American Latinos and the Making of the United States: A Theme Study*, 99–121. Washington, DC: National Park Service, 2012.

———. "Spanish-Language Media in America." *Journalism History* 4 (1977): 34–41, 65–68.

Hayes, Joy Elizabeth. *Radio Nation: Communication, Popular Culture, and Nationalism in Mexico, 1920–1950*. Tucson: University of Arizona Press, 2000.

Henriques, Donald Andrew. "Performing Nationalism: Mariachi, Media and Transformation of a Tradition (1920–1942)." PhD diss., University of Texas at Austin, 2006.

Krasnow, Edwin, and Michael Botein. "Deregulation of Broadcasting in the United States: Quo Vadimus." *Journal of Media Law and Practice* 7 (1986): 56–61.

Lomelí, Francisco Hernández. "Obstaculous para el Establecimiento de la Televisión Comercial en México (1950–1955)." *Comunicación y Sociedad* (September–December 1996): 147–171.

Mazor, Barry. *Ralph Peer and the Making of Popular Roots Music*. Chicago: Chicago Review Press, 2015.

McDougal, Dennis. *The Last Mogul: Lew Wasserman, MCA, and the Hidden History of Hollywood*. New York: Crown, 1998.

Molina, Gabriel Gonzalez. "The Production of Mexican Television News: The Supremacy of Corporate Rationale." PhD diss., University of Leicester, 1990.

Morales, María Francisca. "Vernacular Spanish and Chicano Culture Content in the Language Arts Curriculum for Bilingual Education." PhD diss., Stanford University, 1982.

Moran, Kristin C. "The Development of Spanish-Language Television in San Diego: A Contemporary History." *The Journal of San Diego History* 50 (2004): 42–54.

Morrisey, Marietta, "Tres Mujeres: Reclaiming National Culture in the Post-Colonial Telenovela." *Studies in Latin American Culture* 21 (2002): 221–232.

Naisbitt, John. *Megatrends: Ten New Directions Transforming Our Lives*. New York: Warner, 1982.

Olmos, Alexandro. "La huella de los Azcárraga I y II." *Revista Méxicana de Comunicación* 58 (Spring 1998): 49–54.

Pew Hispanic Center. "Latinos' Choices in News Media Are Shaping Their Views of Their Communities, the Nation, and the World." Press releases and statements. Pew, April 19, 2004. https://www.pewtrusts.org/en/about/news-room/press-releases-and-statements/2004/04/19/latinos-choices-in-news-media-are-shaping-their-views-of-their-communities-the-nation-and-the-world.

Ramos, Jorge. *No Borders*. New York: Harper Collins, 2002.

Rios, Diana, and Stanley O. Gaines. "Latino Media Use for Cultural Maintenance." *Journalism and Mass Communication Quarterly* 75 (1998): 746–761.

Robina Bustos, Soledad. "The Hemispheric Village: The Case of Televisa." *Méxican Journal of Communication* 2 (1995): 107–120.

Rodríguez, América. "Creating an Audience and Remapping a Nation: A Brief History of Spanish Language Broadcasting 1930–1980." *Quarterly Review of Film and Video* 16 (1999): 357–374.

———. *Making Latino News*. Beverly Hills, CA: Sage, 1999.

Rodríguez-Rodríguez, Aixa. "Spanish Language Television in the United States: Hegemony in the Employees' Views and Perceptions." MA thesis, University of Massachusetts, 1990.

Rojas, Viviana. "The Gender of Latinidad: Latinas Speak about Hispanic Television." *Communication Review* 7 (2010): 125–153.

Salinas, María Elena. *I Am My Father's Daughter*. New York: Harper Collins, 2006.

Salazar, Miguel. "The Problem with Latinidad." *The Nation*, September 16, 2019, https://www.thenation.com/article/archive/hispanic-heritage-month-latinidad/.

Schement, Jorge Reina, and Ricardo Flores. "The Origins of Spanish-Language Radio: The Case of San Antonio, Texas." *Journalism History* 4 (1977): 56–61.

Sinclair, John. *Latin American Television: A Global View*. New York: Oxford University Press, 1999.

———. "Spanish-Language Television in the United States: Televisa Surrenders Its Domain." *Studies in Latin American Popular Culture* 9 (1990): 39–63.

Smith, Donald Lee. *Pre-PRI: The Mexican Government Party, 1929–1946*. Fort Worth: Texas Christian University, 1974.

Stilling, Erik A. "The History of Spanish-Language Television in the United States and the Rise of Mexican International Syndication Strategies in the Americas." *Howard Journal of Communications* 6, no. 4 (1995): 231–249.

Subervi-Vélez, Federico. "Mass Communication and Hispanics." In *Handbook of Hispanic Cultures in the United States: Sociology,* edited by Félix Padilla, 304–351. Houston: Arte Público Press, 1994.
United States Bureau of Census. *1970 Census of the Population.* Vol. 1, *Characteristics of the Population.* Washington, DC: Government Printing Office, 1973.
——. *1980 Census of the Population.* Vol. 1, *Characteristics of the Population.* Washington, DC: U.S. Government Printing Office, 1982.
Valenzuela, Nicholas Alfred. "Organizational Evolution of a Spanish Language Television Network." PhD diss., Stanford University, 1985.
Webbink, Douglas W. "The Impact of UHF Promotion: The All-Channel Television Receiver Law." *Law and Contemporary Problems* 34 (Summer 1969): 535–561.
Wilkinson, Kenton Todd. *Spanish-Language Television in the United States: Fifty Years of Development.* New York: Routledge/Taylor & Francis, 2015.
Yankelovich, Skelly and White. *Spanish USA.* New York: Yankelovich, Skelly and White, 1981.
Zimbalist, Andrew S., and John Weeks. *Panama at the Crossroads: Economic Development and Political Change in the Twentieth Century.* Berkeley: University of California Press, 1991.

INDEX

Page numbers in *italics* refer to illustrations.

ABS network, Philippines, 111
Acculturation, 114–18, 255–56
Actualides y personalidades, 59
Advertising: advertising agencies, 114–15; advertising revenue, 186–87, 199; advertising sales, 202; spot sales, 134; upfront meetings, 202–3, 220
Advocacy journalism, 78–79, 260–61
African American network television, 58
Aguirre, Fernando, 230
Alemán Valdés, Miguel, 18–20
Alguien te mira, 246
Ali, Muhammad, 184
"Alien influence." *See* Foreign ownership rule, Communications Act
All-Channel Receiver Act, 52
All in the Family, 174, 185
Alma de mi alma, 75
Al mediodia, 187
Alvarenga, Daniel, 258
Alvárez, Carlos, 243
Amaya, Hector, 255, 260
América network, Perú, 111
American Federation of Radio and Television Artists (AFTRA), 113
Amor descarado, 233
Ángeles, 207
Ángeles de le calle, 20, 39
Angélica mi vida, 158
Anselmo, Mary, 249
Anselmo, Reverge, 23
Anselmo, Reynold "Rene," *46, 116, 144*; background and formative years, 22–23; death and funeral, 197–98; ethnicity, views on, 91–92, 113–18, 258–59; FCC ruling on SICC, 132, 142, 148–49; financial worth, 249; Fouce, feud with, 45, 46–49, 94, 99, 101, 145; Fouce lawsuit, 102–4, 123–24, 133–34; KMEX, Los Angeles, 49–50, 54–55; MagnaVerde, 97, 101–2; personality, 59–60; and satellite distribution, 52–53, 92–93, 119–23; SIBC, 30–31, 77, 85–86; SICC, 89–91, 143–44, 145–46; SIN, 42, 72–75, 106–7, 125–26; SIN, financial issues, 63–66, 92; Telesistema, 23–24, 27, 38, 57; work with Azcárraga, 21, 23, 82–85, 88–89, 97–99; WXTV, 118–19
Arau, Fernando, 213
ARB (ratings agency), 38, 39, 60, 91–92
Arbitron, 92, 112
Arciga, Pepe, 54–55
Argentina, Canal Siete, 111
Argos Comunicación, 223, 231, 233, 237
Arrarás, María Celeste, 213
Ashford, Gerald, 36
Astol, Lalo, 37
Audience ratings: data from Spanish-language homes, 56, 161, 167–69; and ethnic bias, 60, 91–92, 161; importance of Spanish-language ratings, 33, 37–38, 39, 164–65; Med-Mark, 70; National Hispanic Television Index, 179–80; Telemundo, 157–58, 246; and telenovelas, 196–97, 246; Univision, 3; Univision/Telemundo rivalry, 179–80, 187–88, 195–96, 200, 207–9, 222. *See also* Nielsen ratings
Avedon, Bert, 57, 61

328 · Index

Azcárraga Jean, Emilio, *244*; agreement with Perenchio, 221; courtroom appearance, 241; feud with Ray Rodríguez, 227–28, 229; rivalry with Perenchio, 202, 210, 214–15, 228–30; as successor to father, 200; Univision 2, 219–20

Azcárraga Milmo, Emilio, *64*; and Anselmo, 23, 97–99, 143; background and early years, 8, 18; cancer diagnosis/death, 200; FCC investigation ruling, 142; inception of Univisión, 106–9; merger with Garza Sada, 86–87; Mexican Embassy gathering 1980, 122–23; operations after Hallmark purchase, 150, 153–54; satellite transmission and World Cup, 112; SIN financial issues, 63–66, 88–89; SIN News, 128–29; Televisa deal with Univision, 181, 182–83; testimony concerning SIBC incorporation, 31

Azcárraga Vidaurreta, Don Emilio, *28, 64*; announcement of U.S. plans, 28; background, 7, 15–16; death, 85; delivery system in U.S. for Mexican programs, 38–39; early business experience, 16–18; early years of Mexican television, 18–22; FCC investigation's final ruling, 141–42; foreign ownership and SIN, 134; Fouce's funeral, 44; incorporation of SIBC, 30–31; and KMEX launch, Los Angeles, 51; Olympic Games, 1968, 68; partnership with Fouce, 25–30; plans for U.S. network, 28–29; PRI involvement, 17–18; purchase of KCOR, 40–43; radio stations, 17; rivalry with Anselmo, 45–46, 82–85; SIN financial issues, 63–66; spouse, 16–17; Telesistema as monopoly, 27; Televicentro and telenovelas, 20–21

Azteca América, 216, 217, 220

Baila comigo, 180
Balaban and Berman, 102–4
Barba, Carlos, *151*; archival material, 11; Caribevisión, 248; and formation of Telemundo, 9, 150; NetSpan, 127, 145; on Univision, 181; WNJU, 76, 118; work with Perenchio, 189–90; work with Venevisión and Televisa, 185–86
Barroso, Emilio Diez, 241
Bass, Dick, 61
Bastion Capital, 203

Bauman, Jeffrey, 137–38
Baxter, Brian, 242
Beale, Steve, 154
Beautiful Brazil, 33
Belisario, Hernán Pérez, 109
Berger, Alex, 115
Betty la fea, 13, 223
Beville, Hugh, 91–92
"Bicycle" network distribution system, 4, 50–51, 68, 72, 156
The Big Picture, 38
Bilingualism among Latinos, 265–66
Bird, Carole, 13, 73–74
Black, Leon, 195, 197, 202–3, 204
Blade Runner, 185
Blair, John, 156
Blank, George, 167
Blaya, Joaquín, *144, 193*; Anselmo's resignation, 143; background of, 9; on domestic production, 159–60, 162–63, 170; move from Univision to Telemundo, 176; rivalry with Univision, 189–90; *Sábado gigante*, 161; on sale of Univision, 174–75; SICC, 142, 144; SIN, 124–27; termination by Perenchio, 197; as Univision network president, 149–50, 162, 258; Voice of America, 248; WLTV, 85, 101
Bondet, Giselle, 213
Botifoll, Carlos, 127
Boxeo desde México, 160
Brando, Marlon, 184
Bravo Adams, Caridad, 238
Brazil, Globo, 156
Broadcast Ratings Council (BRC), 91–92
Broadcast television, decline of, 264–65
Brown, Les, 102
Brown, Pat, 54
Brown, Ricardo, 127
Browne, Don, 234, 237–39, 246
Bullfights, televised, 54, 55
Burton, Richard, 184
Bush, President George W., 235

Caballero, Eduardo, 115, 117, 140
Caballero Spanish Media, 207
Cadena Uno, Colombia, 111
Call letters, disputes over, 49
Camacho, Marco, 216
Canal de las Estrellas (Channel of the Stars), 21, 95

Canal Siete, Argentina, 111
Canal Trece, Chile, 160, 248
Cancela, José, 240
Canseco, Ana María, 213
Capó, Bobby, 71
Cara sucia, 180
Caribbean-descended Latinos, 13, 73, 84, 111, 154
Caribevisión, 248
Carita de primavera, 102
Carter, Phillip M., 266
Carter, President Jimmy, 113, 135
Casillas, Dolores Inés, 255
Castañeda, Antonia, 1, 2
Castro, Fidel, 26, 84, 125
Celaya Coronado, Jorge Luis, 122–23
Cernan, Eugene, 137
Cervantes, Miguel de, 112
La Cervecería Perla, 32
Channel of the Stars (Canal de las Estrellas), 21, 95
Charrito, 39
Chartwell, 184
Charytín internacional, 172, 187
Chávez, Christopher, 257
Chile: Canal Trece, 160, 248; TV Chile, 109
Churubusco Studios, 18
Cine millionario, 158
The Cisco Kid, 38
Cisneros, Gustavo, 109, 173, 174, 185–86, 191
Cisneros, Henry, 201, 202, 205–6, 217
Cisneros, Ricardo, 109, 173, 174, 185–86
Cita con el amor, 163, 172
Citizenship, U.S., 113. *See also* Immigration policy
Clinton, President Bill, 202
"Cloroxification" at Univision, 164, 205
CNN (Cable News Network), 94, 190
CNN en Español, 204
CNN noticiero Univision, 190
Colombia: Cadena Uno, 111; RCN, 223; RTI, 238
Color television, 19
Columbia Pictures, 69, 71–72, 76, 118, 204
Comcast, 246–47
Communications Act of 1934, foreign ownership rule, 12, 25–26, 29–30, 47, 131, 137–39, 140
Conde, Cesar, 11, 235, 242, 243, 245, 246

Conlin, Judge John H., 131–32, 139–40, 141–42
Converters, for UHF channels, 37, 53
Cooperstein, Edwin, 70, 71, 72
Co-production of telenovelas, 263–64
Corrida de toros, 54, 55
Corte tropical, 172
Cortez, Genoveva, 39, 40
Cortez, Raoul, 34; archival material, 11; background, 31–32; foundation of KCOR, 7; KCOR (radio station), 32–35; KCOR, sale of, 26, 29, 40–43; KCOR-TV, 24, 35–40; KWEX, 1; lifetime achievement award, 249; purchase of Mexican programming, 38
Crister, Greg, 154
Cristina: advertising rates, 187; cancellation of, 245; and controversial topics, 163; Emmy award, 208; importance to Univision, 188, 190, 194, 196, 202; and ratings, 179
Cronkite, Walter, 14
Cruz, Celia, 212
Cuban refugees, 111

Dam, Lawrence (Larry), 138, 241
Dávila, Arlene, 256–57
Dávila, Jaime: on Anselmo's death, 198; as CEO of Univision, 183, 186–87; as media consultant, 248–49; negotiation with Hallmark, 150; at SIN, 143; at SIN News, 128, 129; at Univisa, 128, 142
De Angoitia, Alfonso, 220, 230, 244–45
"Death penalty" for television networks, 12, 124, 131, 140
DeBakey, Michael, 85
Decker, Blair, 144
De Córdoba, José, 154
De la Hoya, Oscar, 212
Dellanos, Myrka, 213
Del Olmo, Frank, 80
Demographic data: 1970 census, 76–77; 1980 census, 114; 1990 census, 167; 2000 census, 216, 265; Yankelovich survey, 116–17
De Molina, Raúl, 213, *250*
De Mora Jiménez, Raúl, 254
Descalzi, Guillermo, 127
Desde Hollywood, 163, 172
El desfile de la hispanidad, 111
Despierta América, 202, 203, 213, 227

330 · Index

Diaz-Balart, José, 127, 129, 157
Díaz Ordaz, Gustavo, 67–68, 81
Diff'rent Strokes, 185
Diller, Barry, 185, 204, 215, 218–19
Dimling, John, 167, 168
Diversity of Spanish-speaking culture in U.S.: Cuban culture contrasted with Mexican, 84; Cuban culture contrasted with Puerto Rican, 154; and global media distribution, 13; Hallmark's misunderstanding of, 174; and Mexican-American emphasis, 56; Pan Latinidad, 5–6, 255–58, 267; and ratings, 85, 207; use of print media, 80
El dolor de amar, 75
Domestic production of Spanish-language content: Blaya's vision for Hallmark/Univision, 159, 161–62, 162–63; contrasted with imported programming, 254–55, 262–63; at Telemundo, 192–93, 228, 232–33, 246; at Univision, 175–76
Domingo, Plácido, 112, 212
Doña Bárbara, 238
¿Dónde está Elisa?, 246
Down in Argentina, 33
Doyal, Steven, 174
Driving Miss Daisy, 185
DuBrow, Rick, 114
DuMont network, as fourth network, 12
Duopoly rule, 219
Durán y Casahonda, Juan, 27

Echevarría Álvarez, Luis, 82, 85
Elena, 51
Elton John, 185
Embassy/Tandem Productions, 185
Emmy awards, 208
Empire State Building, 73, 74, 118–19, 224
Empresa de Comunicaciones Orbitales (ECO), 112, 128
English language use by younger Latinos, 265–66
Escalante, Alicia, 79
ESPN, 162
ESPN Deportes, 179, 204
Estafa de amor, 51
Estefan, Gloria, 212, 243
Estefan, Lili, 213, 250
Estévez, Humberto, 84–85
Estrella Communications, 155

Ethnic bias, 91–92, 114, 250–51
Ethnic group data. See Demographic data
Ethnic identity, 114–18, 255–56. See also Diversity of Spanish-speaking culture in U.S.
Eva Luna, 243, 245

Falco, Randy, 247, 253
Fama y fortuna, 172
Fastlicht, Sharon, 228
Father Knows Best, 27
FCC (Federal Communications Commission): anti-trust regulations, 48, 134; and deregulation, 4–5; diversity and violation of rules, 136; duopoly rule, 219; and foreign language stations, 32–33; and foreign ownership rules, 4–5; license revocation, 140; Mass Media Bureau investigation, 138–39; review of Anselmo's appeal, 148; ruling on retransmission consent, 95–96; and SIN licensure, 122, 123, 141–42; and station licensing, 24
La fea mas bella, 236, 239
Fears, Tom, 61
Federal Communications Act, citizenship requirement, 25–26, 29–30, 47, 131
Feliz milenio, 212, 213
Feltheimer, Jon, 204, 206, 208, 222
Fernández, Luis, 243, 245
Fernwood 2 Night, 185
Ferris, Charles, 137
Fiesta del nuevo milenio, 213
FIFA (Fédération Internationale de Football Association), 109
Fifteen Minutes in Cuba, 33
Films, Mexican, in U.S. theatres, 25
The Flintstones, 69
The Flying Nun, 69
Flys, Carlos, 196
Foreign ownership rule, Communications Act, 12, 25–26, 29–30, 47, 131, 137–139, 140
Fouce, Frank, Jr.: background, 8; conclusion of lawsuit, 135, 147–48; feud with Anselmo, 46–49, 94, 99, 101, 105, 145; formation of partnership with Azcárraga, 29–30; incorporation of SIBC, 30–31; lawsuit, 102–4, 105, 123–24, 131, 132–34; SICC, sale of, 142–43; SICC board, 27, 86, 90–91, 98–99; and SIN, 42; son's attendance at National Association of Broadcasters, 249

Fouce, Frank, Sr., 7–8, 25–26, 44, 45
Four-part thesis of television history, 14
Fowler, Mark, 123, 139
Fox network, 154
Frazier, Joe, 184–85
Frida, 226
Frigon, Henry, 173
Fuentes, Daisy, 158
Fusion (channel), 266

Gabriel, Juan, 212
Galán, Nely, 206–7, 208, 222
Galavisión, 113, 170, 179
Galaxy satellites, 110, 119–20
Garasa, Ángel, 45
Gardner, Eriq, 242
Garza Sada, Eugenio, 68, 82, 86–87
Gestoso, Jorge, 157
Giuliani, Rudolph, 224
Glaser, Jerry, 58
Globo, Brazil, 156
Godoy, Gustavo, 125–27, 129, 157, 163, 248
Goldman, Andrew, 144
Gómez, Ed, 136–37
Gonzalez, Arturo, 113
González Camarena, Guillermo, 19–20
El gordo y la flaca, 207, 213, 250
Goyco, Charytín, 158, 225
Goytisolo, Josie, 127, 129
Gratas, Enrique, 193
Green, Maury, 78
Grimes, William, 162, 167–68, 173
Grossman, Marshall, 239, 240–42
Guadalupe, 194
Guitarras, 45
Gutiérrez, Félix, 10
Gutiérrez, Judge Phillip, 239–40, 241
Guzmán, Armando, 127

Hall, John, 61
Hallmark and Univision, 146–47, 149–52, 165, 167, 173
Hallmark Channel, 146
Hannity, Sean, 252
HBO Olé, 204
Hechizada, 71
Hernández, Roland, 197, 203
Highway Patrol, 27, 38
La hija de Ángela, 102
Hill, Judge Irving, 105, 133, 134–35

Hirsch, Elroy, 61
"Hispanic," as term on 1970 census, 76–77
Hispanic Broadcasting Company, 225
Hispanic Broadcasting Corporation (HBC), 224
Hispanic identity. *See* Diversity of Spanish-speaking culture in U.S.
Hispanic Television Network (HTVN), 216
Hobson, Andrew, 199, 220, 221
Hockaday, Irvine, 146–47, 149–52, 159–60, 173, 174–76, 248
Hola América, 172, 178
Hombres de Mexico, 55
Home Box Office (HBO), 100
Hooper (ratings agency), 38, 39
Hope, Bob, 34
La Hora de Paco Malgesto, 20, 21
Hora deportes, 36
Hughes Aircraft labs and satellites, 82, 87, 92, 110, 119–20
Humoroso musical, 55

I Dream of Jeannie, 69
Iglesias, Enrique, 243
Iglesias, Julio, 112, 170
Immigration policy, 250–51, 253
Ingraham, Laura, 252
Intelsat, 87, 149

Jackson, Michael, 117
Jacobson, James, 86
James, Meg, 240, 241
The Jeffersons, 174, 185
The Jetsons, 69
Jewish Caravan, 70
José, Rafael, 213
El jue, 163
El juramento, 238

KABC, San Antonio, 32
KABQ, Albuquerque, 136
KALI, Los Angeles, 54, 57–58
Kaufman, Julian, 30, 45, 47, 49–50, 53
KBNO, Denver, 136
KCBA, Salinas, 95
KCOR, San Antonio: audience ratings, 35; distribution of Mexican programs, 24; FCC application process, 32–33; Raoul Cortez, 7
KCOR-TV, 7, 29, 35–40

KDOG, Houston, 102
KDTV, San Francisco, 100
Keker, John, 239, 241, 242
KEM, Mexicali, 50
Kennedy, President John F., 59
Kerouac, Jack, 23
KFTV, Fresno, 69, 95, 205
KFWD, Dallas, 197
KHFA, Nogales, 50
KIIX, Los Angeles, 58
King, Billie Jean, 185
KLOC, Sacramento, 95
KMAC, San Antonio, 32
KMEX, Los Angeles: and advocacy journalism, 260–61; audience ratings, 155–56, 169, 173, 209; disputes over call letters, 49–50; domestic/imported programming, 113; and Hallmark, 164; launch process, 51–55; licensure by Fouce, 7–8; newscasting, 59, 77–79; *Newstelevision*, 94; Peabody Award, 81; Villanueva as sportscaster, 62
KMXN, Albuquerque, 102
KNXT, Los Angeles, 78
Koch, Mayor Ed, 119
KORO, Corpus Christi, 121
KPAZ, Phoenix, 69
KPTV, Portland, 95
Kreutzberger, Mario, 209, 244; *Sábado gigante*, 11, 160–61, 213; Telefutura, 225; and Univision, 190, 194, 248
KRIO, Brownsville, 102
KROQ, Los Angeles, 140
KSCI, Los Angeles, 72
KSTS, San Francisco, 165
KTMD, Houston, 165
KTVW, Phoenix, 100–101, 121–22, 148–49
Kurtz, Howard, 253
Kuykendall, Ed, 36
KVDA, San Antonio, 165
KVEA, Los Angeles, 118, 155–56, 158, 169, 173
KWEX, San Antonio: history of station, 1–2, 102, 245; programming, 50; protest of demolition, 1–3, 249–50
KWHY, Los Angeles, 169, 170, 173, 217
KWKW, Los Angeles, 54

Lack, Andrew, 225, 232
Landa, Victor, 2, 250
Landry, Tom, 62

Language use in U.S.: bilingualism among Latinos, 265–66; English use by younger Latinos, 265–66; Spanish language use, 114–17
Lapin, Al, 83
Latinidad, 5–6, 10, 255–58, 267
Latino community. *See* Diversity of Spanish-speaking culture in U.S.
Latino market, 6, 9–10, 154, 257–58
Latinos, Inc., 256
League of United Latin American Citizens, 251–52
Lear, Norman, 118, 185
Lee, Robert E., 91
Lemela, Esteban, 84
La leona, 75
Leventhal, Norman, 92, 99, 103, 119–20, 122
Lilly, Bob, 62
Limbaugh, Rush, 252
Lippman, John, 165
Lockwood, Gary, 71
López Mateos, Adolfo, 26, 28
López Portillo, José, 125
Los Angeles, TV station launch, 46–47
Los Cantabros, 36
Low Power Television Act, 123
Lucha Libre Chicago, 38
Lucha libre Los Ángeles, 113
Luhnow, David, 219

MagnaVerde, 93–94, 96–97
MagnaVerde 2, 99–100
Maharis, George, 71
Mahler, Richard, 154
Majul, Pedro, 51
Malgesto, Paco, 20, 21
Mapy y Papi, 158
María, 196–97
Mariachi Feminino, 36
María la del barrio, 13, 200
María Mercedes, 180
Mariel boatlift, 111
Marielena, 194
Marimar, 196–97
Market research, 5–6, 56, 115–17
Martinez, Andrew, 112–13
Martínez, Laura, 240
Martinez, Matthew, 147
Martínez, Rosa, 80
Mary Hartman, Mary Hartman, 185

Mateos, Adolfo López, 67–68
Mathis, Johnny, 184
Maude, 185
McClellan, Steve, 165
McCombs, Red, 60
McKenna, James, 92, 99, 103
McNamara, James, 222–23, 231–34
Media Research Center, 252
Med-Mark, 70
Meek, James, 121
Megatrends (Naisbitt), 117
Memories of Mexican Yesterday, 33
Meredith, Don, 62
Mexico: elections 1986, 128; infrastructure, 16–17; Mexican films, 25; Mexican telenovelas, 196–97; modernization under López Mateos, 26–27, 67–68; radio stations, 17; socioeconomic issues, 20; telephone system, 67–68; television, early years, 18–22
Mexico Music, 16
Miami and launch of SIN, 82–85
Microwave transmission systems, 100
Milken, Michael, 195
Milmo, Laura, 17
Milner, Martin, 71
Minow, Newton, 13, 52
Mitchell, John H., 69
The Modesto Ríos Show, 95
Montalbán, Lana, 157
Montgomery, Elizabeth, 71
Moreno, Rita, 54
Morín, Andrés Ricardo, 2, 3
Morrissey, Marietta, 255
Morse, Richard, 121
Morton, Mary, 23
MTV Latino, 204
Mujeres insólitas, 109
Multilingual programming, 70
Murdoch, Rupert, 222
Murrow, Edward R., 14
Music Corporation of America (MCA), 184

Naisbitt, John, 117
Naked City, 69
NASA (Telstar), 52
National Archives, SIN materials, 10–11
National Hispanic Television Index (NHTI), 168–69, 179

Nationality, as basis of Latin American identity, 6
NBC (National Broadcasting Company), formation, 16
NBC Nightly News, 234
Negro Builders of America, 70
NetSpan (Network Spanish), 118–19, 127, 145, 150, 156, 185
Newscasting: advocacy journalism at KMEX, 78–79; bias in, 252; content analyses, 252; electronic newsgathering, 77; local, 125–27; Mexican national news on SIN, 109; Spanish-language, 56, 124, 192; Telemundo's debut, 157
Newstelevision, KMEX, 94
Nicolás, Emilio, *103, 116*; advertising sales at SIN, 60; after Hallmark purchase, 149; Anselmo's resignation, 143–44; archival material, 11; civic leadership, San Antonio, 248; dispute over call letters KMEX, 49; on domestic production, 159; formation of Telesistema Méxicano, 7; funding from Marine Midland National Bank, 85–86; inception of Univisión, 107–8; KCOR-TV management, 35–36, 37–42; launch of KMEX, Los Angeles, 49–51; launch of SIN, 1; recognition of lifetime achievements, 245, 249; sale of SICC, 144; study of Spanish language use, 115–16
Nicolás, Guillermo, and archival material, 11
Nicolás, Irma, 32, 39, 41, 248
Nielsen ratings: after decline of broadcast television, 265; combined English/Spanish ratings, 236; and ethnic bias, 60, 91–92; NHTI, 179–80; Spanish-language household data, 167–70; Telemundo/Univision rivalry, 173, 196, 207–9, 211, 222
9/11, 224
Nixon, Richard, 54
Noble, Ed (nephew of Edward), 30
Noble, Edward, 30, 42, 45, 47
Noriega, Adela, 211
Noticias 34, 77, 208
Noticias Italia, 70
Noticias y más, 172
Noticiero nacional SIN, 125–26
Noticiero SIN, 157
Noticiero Telemundo, 157, 194–95, 260
Noticiero Univision, 157, 179, 196, 198, 208, 213, 252

334 · Index

Obregón, General Alvaro, 17
Ocurrió así, 193
O'Farrill, Rómulo, 19, 21–22, 27–28
Oller, Denisse, 224
Olmos, Alexander, 17–18, 29
Olympic Games, Mexico City, 1968, 68, 81
On the Road (Kerouac), 23
O'Reilly, Bill, 252

Palazio, Valeria, 75, 225
Paley, William, 14, 18
Paloma Productions, 226
Panama, and VT Latin, 65, 134
PanAmSat, 149
Pan Latinidad, 5–6, 10, 255–58, 267
Pappas, Harry, 216, 217, 218, 223
Paramount Pictures, 71–72
Partido Acción Nacional (PAN), 128, 198, 217
Partido Revolucionario Institucional (PRI), 17, 20, 82, 128, 198, 217
Pay-per-view, 93, 96
Peabody Award, KMEX, 81
Peer, Ralph, 16
Pelé, 111
El peñon del amaranto, 194
Pepsi, 117
Perelman, Ron, 222
Perenchio, A. Jerrold "Jerry": agreements with Azcárraga Jean, 210–12, 219–20, 221, 228–30; background, 9, 10–11, 184–85; bid for purchase of SICC, 145–46; later in life, 249; on Latino identity, 258; meeting at Univision after Blaya's departure, 177; ownership of multiple stations, 219; public sale of Univision stock, 199–200; purchase of Univision, 173–74; racist attitudes of, 205; "Rules of the Road," 183–84, 186, 197, 206, 235; secrecy, 11, 118; Televisa program licensing agreement, 198, 214; transfer from Hallmark, 180–81, 182–83; Univision after Azcárraga's death, 201–2; Univision-produced telenovelas, 226; work with Barba, 189–90
Perenchio, Margaret, 226
Pero, John, 159
Perú, América network, 111
Peru, broadcasts from Lima, 112
Perú, Rosita, 160, 162, 170
Petrocino, Osvaldo, 127

Pfaelzer, Judge Mariana, 124, 135–43, 144–45, 146, 147
Philippines, ABS network, 111
Piñeda, Rafael, 224
Piñeda, Ramon, 207
Platavisión, 172
Pope John Paul II, 111
Portada, 163, 172, 187
Porter, Robert, 121, *144*
Powell, Colin, 235
Power Rangers, 231
Presta nombres, 12, 26, 142
PRI (Partido Revolucionario Institucional), 17, 20, 82, 128, 198, 217
Primer impacto, 202, 208, 213
Prío, María Elena, 84
El privilegio de amar, 13, 211–12, 214
Programa Paco Malgesto, 51
Pulse Corporation, 33, 35, 56. *See also* Audience ratings
Pumarejo, Gaspar, 71

Racism. *See* Ethnic bias
Radio Caracas Televisión, 109
Radio Televisión Española, Spain, 243
Radio Televisión Interamericana, Colombia, 233
Raider, Donald, 156, 164–65
Ramer, Loraine, 74
Ramos, Jorge: and Donald Trump, 253, 258, 261; KMEX, 127, 129; Univision, 190, 192, 196, 213; war coverage, 171
Randolph, Eleanor, 129
Rank, Joseph, 62, 77
Ratings, audience. *See* Audience ratings
Ray Rodríguez Broadcast Center, 243
Ray Rodríguez Day, 243
RCA (Radio Corporation of America), 16, 121–22
RCN, Colombia, 223
Reagan, President Ronald, 120, 126
Reality shows, 193
Rebeca Ríos, 36
El regreso de Charytín, 158
La reina del sur, 246
Reinventing the Latino Television Viewer (Chávez), 257
Reliance Capital Corporation, 150, 165, 185
Reliance Insurance, 155, 156, 249
Renfro, Mel, 62

Renick, Ralph, 125
Reportador 23, 84
Restrepo, Guillermo, 77, 126
Retransmission consent, 95–96
Reyes y Rey, 207
Riggs, Bobby, 185
Roberts, Brian, 246
Robot TV stations. *See* Satelators
Rodríguez, América, 5, 6, 9–10, 256
Rodríguez, Mario, *191, 250*; interviews concerning Univision history, 11, 75–76; Telefutura, 225; Univision, Director of Promotions, 170–71; Univision and Televisa, 177–78, 180, 211–12; Univision program licensing agreement, 201–2; Univision programming, 187, 190–92, 200, 220
Rodríguez, Paul, 172
Rodriguez, Ray, *191*; advertising revenue, 199; on ethnic bias, 205; leadership, 186–88, 190–92, 235; promotion at Univision, 176–77; retirement, 243; and telenovelas, 226; Univision, 170, 178, 180–81, 184, 201–2; Univision 2, 218–19, 220
Rojas, Viviana, 257
Romero, Ed, 136
Rosen, Ronald, 134
Roslow, Dr. Sydney, 33
Ross, Wilbur, 195
El rostro de Analía, 238
RTI, Colombia, 238
Rubio, Marco, 252
Ruíz Cortines, Adolfo, 21–22
Rumbaut, Julio, 240
Ruta 66, 71
La ruta del sol, 71
Ryffel, James, 220

Sábado gigante, 209; advertising revenue, 187; Emmy award, 208; format, 160–61; importance to Univision, 188, 190, 194, 248; ratings, 163, 173, 179, 196; TV Chile, 109
Sábados especiales, 109
Saban, Haim, 11, 231, 243–45
Safir, Nathan, 33, 35
Sagansky, Jeff, 204
Salazar, María Elvira, 127, 157
Salazar, Miguel, 257
Salazar, Rubén, 55, 78–80, 261

Salinas, Dr. Peter, 115
Salinas, Maria Elena, 190, 196, 213, 261
Salinas Pliego, Ricardo, 217
San Antonio, Texas, 31–32, 249–50. *See also* KCOR, San Antonio; KWEX, San Antonio
Sánchez, Francisco "Paco," 136
Sandoval, Neida, 213
Saralegui, Cristina, *208*; as celebrity, 11; Countdown to 2000, 213; as *Sábado gigante* guest, 161; talk show debut, 163; Univision/Blaya, 190, 194; Univision cancellation, 245, 249
Sarnoff, David, 14, 16, 18
Satcom, 119–20, 121–22
Satelators, 122, 123, 136–37, 148
Satellite broadcasting: debut by SIN, 4, 119; satellite connections for television, 52; satellite delivery, 87, 89; satellite programming, 102; and satellite translators, 121–22; satellite transmission, 82, 92–93, 95–97, 100, 108–11, 149; Western Union, 92–93, 110, 119–20
Scheftel, Herbert, 66
Schmitt, Harrison, 137
Schneider, Abe, 71
Schwarzenegger, Arnold, 251–52
Screen Gems, Columbia Pictures, 69, 71–72, 76
Secrest, Clark, 122
Section 310 (Communications Act). *See* Communications Act of 1934, foreign ownership rule
Señorita española, 70
Serials. *See* Telenovelas
Shagrin, Ceril, 168–69, 172
Shakira, 247
El Show de Paul Rodríguez, 163
SIBC (Spanish International Broadcasting Corporation): early history of, 6, 7; foreign ownership, 47–48; incorporation process, 30–31; merger with Trans-Tel, 86
SICC (Spanish International Communications Corporation), 86; first board meeting, 89–91; and foreign ownership rule, 131; and Fouce lawsuit, 105, 132–34; and MagnaVerde restructuring, 99–100; Mass Media Bureau investigation, 138–39; ruling in FCC investigation, 141–42; sale of holdings, 142–43

Siempre en domingo, 102, 111
Silverman, Harry, 150, 155–56, 165, 167, 195
SIN (Spanish International Network): after MagnaVerde 2 restructuring, 100, 101–2; "bicycle" distribution network, 50–51; early history of, 1, 6–8, 10, 42-43, 44–45, 48; FCC licensure, 122, 123; financial issues, 59, 88–89, 97–99; foreign ownership rule, 124, 127–28, 134; launch in Miami, 82–85; loss of licensure, 4–5; media coverage of, 59; newscasting, 125–27; and non-U. S. content, 10; satellite transmission, 92–93, 102, 110–11, 119–20, 121; Telesistema program fees, 63–66; and Univisión's official launch, 111–13
SIN Case. *See* Fouce, Frank, Jr.: lawsuit
Sinclair, John, 10
SIN Sales, 57–58, 142
Sin senos no hay paraíso, 238
SIN-WEST, 95, 100
Smith, Cecil, 55, 58
Smith, Chester, 95
Soap operas. *See* Telenovelas
Soccer, televised, 82, 208, 235, 246
Sodi, Thalía, 180, 196, 200
Solo en América, 207
Sony and Telemundo, 204–5, 224
Soul Train, 189
Sounds of Belonging!, 255
Spain, TV Española, 109
Spanish Advertising and Marketing Service, 114
Spanish Cartoon Network, 204
Spanish International, 245
Spanish-language television: advertising revenue, 186–87, 199; attempts to sell Mexican programs in U. S., 24; Caribbean programs contrasted with Mexican, 73; critique of, 258–59; cultural importance of, 2–3, 117; debut of KCOR-TV, 36; and decline of Spanish language use, 265–66; domestic production, 159–60, 161–62; early documents, accessibility of, 11; early newscasts, 38; and FCC, 4–5; formation of SIN, 1961, 42; Hallmark's commitment to Spanish-language content, 147, 149–50; and history of U. S. television, 5–6; impact of news, 80; KMEX, 77–78; negative attitudes toward, 250–52; new networks in 2000, 216; newscasting, 56, 126–27, 252,

260; overview of significant figures, 8–9; reality shows, 193; role in national media history, 3–4; and south-to-north media flow, 253–54; Spanish-language content after SICC sale, 145; Spanish-language programming at Telemundo, 158; stock prices, 215–16; treatment in history texts, 9–10; WNJU, New York, 70–71
Spanish language use in U. S., 114–17
Spanish Media, Inc., 115
Spanish Radio Broadcasters Association (SRBA), 136–37
Spanish USA (Yankelovich), 116–17
Sportscasting: as discussed in Pepe Arciga's *LA Times* column, 55; TV Española, 109; World Cup soccer, 93–94, 96–97, 109–11, 112
Spot sales, 134
Starr, Bart, 62
Stein, Jules, 184
Steinberg, Saul, *193*; death, 249; purchase of WNJU, 150; Reliance Insurance, 155–56, 185; Telemundo, 167, 171, 173, 192; Telemundo financial issues, 194, 195, 196, 197
Stern, Frederick, 103, 105, 132–34, 135, 138
Stiles, William, 94, 100, 122, 143, 144, 149
Strategy Research Corporation (SRC), 161, 168
Stringer, Howard, 224
Suárez, Amancio, 157
Subervi-Vélez, Frederic, 10

Taylor, Elizabeth, 184
Te amaré en silencio, 226, 227–28, 229, 230
Teatro, 39
Teatro fantástico, 44
Teatro KCOR, 37
Teléfonos de Mexico, 67–68
Telefutura, 221, 225
Telemundo: bankruptcy court, 1993, 195–96; under Comcast, 246–47; competition with Univision, 171; Don Browne's leadership, 237–39; financial struggles, 165–67; Golden Age, 192–95; imported content, 254–55; initial programming, 156–58; launch and early history, 150–51, 153–54, 155–58; under NBC, 231–34; offered for sale, 202–4; purchased by Sony, 204–5; ratings rivalry with Univision, 168, 173, 178, 179–80; sale of public stock, 165;

sale to NBC, 225; studio in Mexico, 237; telenovelas, 194
Telemundo centro deportes, 158
Telemundo MTV, 158
Telemundo Studios, 233
TeleNoticias, 195, 204
Telenovelas: filmed by Univision, 226; history of, 2, 7; Latino preference for, 259; Mexican, 20–21, 203, 211, 238; nontraditional, 232–33; and stereotypical content, 255; on Telemundo, 222, 231; Televisa "story book" novelas, 232; universal appeal of, 75; at Univision, 207; and Univision ratings, 196; U.S.-made, 194; U.S.-produced at Telemundo, 158; Venezuelan, 109; on WXTV, 74, 75
Teleprogramas de Mexico, 22–24
Telesistema Méxicano: anti-monopoly actions against, 81–82; delivery of programs to U. S., 44–45; and domestic (Mexican) production, 22–23; formation of, 7; under López Mateos' reforms, 26–27; monopoly in Mexico, 67–69; SIN indebtedness for program fees, 63–66. *See also* Televisa (Television Via Satellite)
Televicentro, 20
Televisa (Television Via Satellite): advertising revenue, 89–90; after SICC's sale, 145; Azcárraga Jean, 210–12; contract after Hallmark purchase, 151–52; formation and early history, 6–7, 8, 87; Miami teleport, 125; negotiations with Univision, 198; programming, 169–70, 176; and satellite transmission, 10, 92–93, 98; SIN and programming fees, 98; Univision lawsuit, 234–35, 239–43; Univision PLA, 221, 262; Zabludovsky incident, 128. *See also* Telesistema Méxicano
Television: broadcast television, decline of, 264–65; color television, 19
Television history: four-part thesis, 14; fourth network, 12–13; literature on, 9–10
Televisión Independiente de México, 68
Telstar, 52
"Third" generation model, 265–66
Tichenor, McHenry, 224
Time-Life satellite broadcasting, 100
Tiovivo, 33
Tirado, Tony, 158
Tobenkin, David, 202

Tortorici, Peter, 206–7, 208, 222
Translators (remote transmitters), 121
Trans-Tel, 66, 86
Tres destinos, 194
Tres mujeres, 212
Tringall, Donald, 205
Trío Gypsy, 36
Trump, Donald, 253, 258, 261
Turner, Ted, 94, 166, 190
TV Azteca, 197, 198, 220, 223
TV Chile, 109
TV Española, 109
TVL (Latino investment consortium), 147–48
24 horas, 82, 109, 125

UHF (ultra-high frequency) channels, 4, 24, 37, 52–54
Under the Spanish Sky, 33
Undocumented residents, U.S., 113–14
UNESCO debates, 5
Universal Studios, 233–34
Univisa, 128, 142
Univision: after Blaya's departure, 177; awards, 208; criticism of, after Hallmark purchase, 164; domestic production, 159–63, 172; *El privilegio de amar*, 211–12; 50th anniversary, 235–36, 243, 245, 247, 248; financial struggles, 165–67; imported content, 254–55; inception of and official launch, 107–8, 111–13; launch, 153–54; as multinational network, 111; negotiations with Televisa, 198; news division, 190–92; Nielsen ratings, 250, 251; program cancellations, 187–88; program licensing agreement with Televisa, 182–83, 221; public sale of stock, 199–200; purchase by Saban, 234–35; rivalry with Telemundo, 168, 171, 173, 178, 179–80; under Saban's leadership, 235–36; sale to Hallmark, 162; sale to Saban, 230–31; satellite transmission, 110; stock prices, 217–18, 219; strike at KFTV, Fresno, 205; Televisa lawsuit, 234–35; Televisa PLA, 244–45, 262; Televisa programming, 169–70, 176, 178, 201–2; "television city" facility in Doral, 171, *172*; use of name after Hallmark purchase, 152; World Cup soccer, 1978, 109–11
Univision 2, 219–20
Univision 8, 3, 14, 249–50

338 · Index

Univision Studios, 236, 242–43, 245
Upfronts, 202–3, 220
La usurpadora, 109
Uva, Joe, 11, 235–36, 242, 243, 245, 246

Valenzuela, Nicholas, 117–18
Van Deerlin, Lionel, 123
Vargas, Pedro, 39
Velasco, Raúl, 111
Venezuela: Radio Caracas Televisión, 109; Venevisión, 109, 112, 156, 173–74, 185–86, 243
VHF (very-high frequency) channels, 4, 24
Victor Corporation, 16
Villanueva, Danny, *116*; on acculturation, 115; and advocacy journalism, 260–61; after Hallmark purchase, 149–50; archival material, 11; background of, 8–9, 61; as bank president, 248; Bastion Capital investment in Telemundo, 203; on domestic production, 159; on Hallmark's purchase of SICC, 146–47; and MagnaVerde, 97; Marine Midland Bank loan, 94–95; Marine Midland National Bank loan, 85–86; news director at KMEX, 77–79; *Newstelevision*, 94; on programming for Caribbean viewers, 73; resignation, 164; sale of SICC, 144; and Satcom relays, 121–22; second vice president, SIBC, 77; SIN and cable systems, 95–96; SIN-WEST, 95; on telenovelas, 255; on WJNU and NetSpan, 118–19; working relationship with Anselmo, 120–21
VT Latin, 65, 134

Wallach, Joe, 155
WAPA, San Juan, Puerto Rico, 72, 76
Wasserman, Lew, 9, 184
WCIU, Chicago, 69, 189
WCIX, Miami, 72
Westar 1 and Westar 2, 92–93, 97, 110, 113
Westar 3, 108, 110, 113
Western Union and satellite transmission, 92–93, 110, 119–20
WGBO, Chicago, 196
WGBO-TV, Chicago, 189
Wilkes, Brent, 251–52
Williams, Andy, 184

Wilson, Governor Pete, 205
WKAQ, San Juan, 156–57, 173
WLTV, Miami, 84–85, 101, 111, 124–25, 160, 209
WNJU, New York: Carlos Barba, 150, 158; competition with WXTV, 75–76, 118–19, 158; Perenchio purchase, 118–19, 145; Puerto Rican programming, 154; Reliance purchase, 156; TV innovation, 70–72
Wollenberg, Judge J. Roger, 139
World Cup soccer, 208, 235, 246
World Trade Center, 119, 224
WPBT, Miami, 126
Wright, Robert, 225
WSCV, Miami, 154
WSNS, Chicago, 72, 189
WTVJ, Miami, 125
WXTV, New York: competition with WNJU, 75–76, 118–19, 158; newscasting, 81; 9/11 coverage, 224; SIN as international network, 111; as SIN station, 72–73

XEBK, Nuevo Laredo, 32
XEFE, Nuevo Laredo, 50
Xenophobia, 250–51
XEQ, Mexican radio network, 18
XETV, Tijuana, 27
XEW, Loma Linda, 95–96
XEW, Mexican radio network and station, 17, 18
XEW, Mexican television station, 19
XEWT, San Diego, 95
XEWT, Tijuana, 50
XHJ, Juarez, 50

Y2K, 211, 212
Yankelovich, Daniel, 116–17
Yankelovich, Skelly & White, 116–17
Yesenia, Super cine, 160
Yorty, Sam, 54
Yo soy Betty la fea, 13, 223
Young, Calvin, 58
Younger, Evelle, 80

Zabludovsky, Jacobo: and Azcárraga Milmo's death, 150, 157, 200; PRI scandal, 128–29; as Telesistema anchor, 82, 85, 109
Ziv, Frederick, 38

Craig Allen is associate professor at the Walter Cronkite School of Journalism and Mass Communication at Arizona State University. He specializes in media history, politics, and analytics. His past books include *Eisenhower and the Mass Media* and *News Is People: The History of Local Television News*.

REFRAMING MEDIA, TECHNOLOGY, AND CULTURE IN LATIN/O AMERICA

Edited by Héctor Fernández L'Hoeste and Juan Carlos Rodríguez

Reframing Media, Technology, and Culture in Latin/o America explores how Latin American and Latino audiovisual (film, television, digital), musical (radio, recordings, live performances, dancing), and graphic (comics, photography, advertising) cultural practices reframe and reconfigure social, economic, and political discourses at a local, national, and global level. In addition, it looks at how information networks reshape public and private policies, and the enactment of new identities in civil society. The series also covers how different technologies have allowed and continue to allow for the construction of new ethnic spaces. It not only contemplates the interaction between new and old technologies but also how the development of brand-new technologies redefines cultural production.

Telling Migrant Stories: Latin American Diaspora in Documentary Film, edited by Esteban E. Loustaunau and Lauren E. Shaw (2018; paperback edition, 2021)

Mestizo Modernity: Race, Technology, and the Body in Postrevolutionary Mexico, by David S. Dalton (2018; first paperback edition, 2021)

The Insubordination of Photography: Documentary Practices under Chile's Dictatorship, by Ángeles Donoso Macaya (2020; first paperback edition, 2023)

Digital Humanities in Latin America, edited by Héctor Fernández L'Hoeste and Juan Carlos Rodríguez (2020; first paperback edition, 2023)

Pablo Escobar and Colombian Narcoculture, by Aldona Bialowas Pobutsky (2020)

The New Brazilian Mediascape: Television Production in the Digital Streaming Age, by Eli Lee Carter (2020)

Univision, Telemundo, and the Rise of Spanish-Language Television in the United States, by Craig Allen (2020; first paperback edition, 2023)

Cuba's Digital Revolution: Citizen Innovation and State Policy, edited by Ted A. Henken and Sara Garcia Santamaria (2021; first paperback edition, 2022)

Afro-Latinx Digital Connections, edited by Eduard Arriaga and Andrés Villar (2021)

The Lost Cinema of Mexico: From Lucha Libre to Cine Familiar and Other Churros, edited by Olivia Cosentino and Brian Price (2022)

Neo-Authoritarian Masculinity in Brazilian Crime Film, by Jeremy Lehnen (2022)

The Rise of Central American Film in the Twenty-First Century, edited by Mauricio Espinoza and Jared List (2023)

www.ingramcontent.com/pod-product-compliance
Lightning Source LLC
Chambersburg PA
CBHW031754220426
43662CB00007B/401